Surveillance and Terror in Post-9/11 British and American Television

Darcie Rives-East

Surveillance and Terror in Post-9/11 British and American Television

palgrave
macmillan

Darcie Rives-East
Augustana University
Sioux Falls, SD, USA

ISBN 978-3-030-16902-2   ISBN 978-3-030-16900-8   (eBook)
https://doi.org/10.1007/978-3-030-16900-8

Cover illustration: eStudio Calamar

This Palgrave Macmillan imprint is published by the registered company Springer Nature Switzerland AG
The registered company address is: Gewerbestrasse 11, 6330 Cham, Switzerland

ACKNOWLEDGMENTS

I owe many thanks for the assistance and support I have received in the several years it took me to develop and write this book project. First, I must thank Augustana University for its generosity in awarding me the Zaloudek Faculty Research Grant and the Augustana Research and Artist Fund (ARAF) Grant that enabled me to travel to conduct research as well as receive financial support for materials and student assistance that helped me complete my manuscript. I also want to acknowledge the wonderful institutions where I did research for my book, including the British Library, the New York Public Library, the Charles Dickens Museum, the New York City Municipal Archive, the U.K. National Archives, the City of London Police Museum, and the British Film Institute (BFI) Reuben Library. Many thanks to all the librarians and archivists at these institutions for kindly assisting me in finding material crucial to writing this manuscript. Of course, I also wish to thank many colleagues, students, and family who helped me in so many ways. I wish to thank especially Dr. Olivia Lima for doing the hard work of developing the book index. Thanks to Dr. Jeffrey Miller for his keen ideas, advice, and critiques during the writing process. I want to thank Dr. Janet Blank-Libra for her generosity in taking over as department chair so that I could finish the book. Thanks very much to Shi Almont, my advisee and student research assistant, for compiling valuable documents and information that informed my work. Thanks also to all my students for their patience while their professor was trying to balance writing with grading their essays and exams. Finally, of course, I thank all my friends and family for their never-ending patience, caring, and support during the writing process. In particular, I owe so much to my mother, Nadine Rives, and my husband, Danny East, who kept me sane and kept me going with their encouragement and love.

CONTENTS

1 Introduction: Surveillance and Terror in Post-9/11 British and American Television   1

2 Captive Viewing: Prisons, Surveillance, and Social Control   55

3 Policing, Surveillance, and Terror—and the Return of Sherlock Holmes   107

4 We Spy: Espionage and the National Intelligence Agency   191

5 Conclusion: Double-Conditioning, Surveillance, and the Future of Television   237

Index   249

Introduction: Surveillance and Terror in Post-9/11 British and American Television

"You are being watched." These ominous words, spoken by computer gen ius Harold Finch (played by Michael Emerson) in voiceover, introduce each episode of the 2011–2016 CBS surveillance drama *Person of Interest*. I begin with this phrase because it represents an important trend in television narratives since 9/11: series that focus on the increased prevalence in state surveillance and techniques of social control, in response to fears of terrorism, since the deadly attack nearly two decades ago. The wealth of critical attention regarding the effect of 9/11 on U.S. and U.K. television and film affirms that British and American television series have increased their focus on surveillance and terror in the past two decades.[1] Further, while these television and film studies do not include the related issue of surveillance per se, academic consideration of how surveillance is narrated and portrayed in film and television has nevertheless also grown since 9/11.[2] These studies focus mainly on U.S. and U.K. film and programming and thus help support my claim that it is primarily, although not exclusively, in British and American television that viewers have seen an increase in themes of surveillance since 9/11.

It is my contention in this book that the two issues, 9/11 and surveillance, are interconnected in terms of the development of British and American television series since the attack on the Twin Towers. As Stephen Lacey and Derek Paget write, "9/11 has become a cultural 'meme'"[3] in television storytelling in the years since, offering what Paget terms "critical and therapeutic unit[s] of understanding" to cope with "epoch-making

© The Author(s) 2019
D. Rives-East, *Surveillance and Terror in Post-9/11 British and American Television*,
https://doi.org/10.1007/978-3-030-16900-8_1

1

events like 9/11."[4] I would extend Paget's use of "meme" to include concerns about government surveillance as a safeguard against terrorism that have arisen since 2001. As Paget contends is the case with 9/11, I maintain that numerous British and American series incorporate the meme of government surveillance as a way of wrangling with and, to borrow John Ellis's term, "witnessing"[5] the significant rise in panopticism because of the subsequent (and ongoing) "war on terror" in both nations. Ellis emphasizes that television functions as a witness to historical events like 9/11, although this does not mean television prompts us as viewers to act on what we see. Rather, television offers "a particular form of representation that brings with it a sense of powerless knowledge and complicity with what we see."[6] It is viewers' paradoxical sense of powerlessness and complicity regarding the growth of state surveillance post-9/11 that British and American programs attempt to imagine and work through narratively.

Important to this argument is that the U.S. and U.K. were the nations most affected by 9/11. After the U.S., the U.K. lost the most citizens in the attack. According to Stephen E. Atkins, "Although the terrorist attacks on September 11, 2001, targeted the United States, many other countries throughout the world were also affected. In addition to the 2,657 Americans killed, 316 foreign nationals from 84 different countries also died in the attacks, including 67 Britons, 28 South Koreans, 26 Japanese, and 25 Canadians. The shock and horror engendered by the attacks were truly international in scope."[7] Because of 9/11, as well as because of the close alliance between the U.S. and U.K., Tony Blair's government chose to join the U.S. in its 2003 invasion of Iraq in the years following the attacks. As Lacey and Paget note, 9/11 and the invasion of Iraq "marked a crucial moment in the relationship between the U.K. and its American allies, wedding the former even more firmly to the foreign policy objectives of the latter."[8] Given the significant effect of 9/11 and the concomitant expansion of state surveillance on the U.S. and U.K. publics, it makes sense that American and British screens have seen a growth in television programming centered in and around the primary government surveillance apparatuses of the prison, the police, and the national intelligence agency—all of which are designed to monitor, control, and protect a nation's population.

Using Ellis's concepts of "witnessing" and "working through," I argue that dramas like *Person of Interest* enable television writers, producers, and viewers alike to acknowledge and wrestle with how these state surveillance apparatuses operate, if they do so ethically and legally, and if their surveillance is worth the price in personal privacy and civil liberties. Ellis concurs that "witnessing" allows us as viewers to "work through" difficult cultural concepts, questions, or situations.[9] This book aims to connect this working through of institutions of surveillance and social control in transnational television since 9/11 with earlier narratives of panopticism and terror prior to the twenty-first century. In the following chapters, I will analyze primary sources, including seventeenth-century captivity narratives and nineteenth-century newspapers and police reports. I will then connect these sources to post-9/11 programs about prisons, policing, and espionage. My goal in doing so is to demonstrate that television's ability to witness and work through the problems of surveillance, terror, and control is not new, although, certainly, these issues have become acute as the result of the war on terror since 9/11. In addition, I consider the inclusion of these older sources and narratives an important means of rectifying the amnesia we have in Britain and America of the history of post-9/11 television narratives we tell about state surveillance apparatuses. The Anglo-American[10] series I address in this book build, consciously or unconsciously, on these older fictional and non-fictional sources that were influential in establishing and priming how British and American television series responded to increased government surveillance and fears of terrorism in the years following 9/11.

My book, then, adopts an interdisciplinary and multivalent approach to this topic. It employs television studies as a critical lens, and it also incorporates textual analysis of the various series as well as literary analysis of the older surveillance narratives which I argue influence today's Anglo-American programs. In addition, I apply critical theory, surveillance studies, and historical archival research in my understanding of the series I cover in these pages. Only this interdisciplinary methodology can allow us to consider what kind of surveillance narratives are being offered in British and American series and why. It is an important question, given, as Ellis argues, that "[t]elevision imbues the present moment with meanings. [...] [I]t enables viewers to work through the major public and private concerns of their society. Television has a key role in the social process of working through because it exists alongside us, holding our hands."[11] In this way, television serves a crucial function in allowing audiences to collectively encounter and grapple with relevant current national issues such as surveillance and terrorism.

Therefore, it is important to link these television series with older narratives which affect them, particularly if those earlier understandings of when surveillance and control should happen and who should be surveilled and monitored carry with them prejudices that continue to harm and affect large segments of the U.S. and U.K. population. This volume seeks to remind the reader of the historical nature of how we in the U.S. and U.K. have long grappled with the tensions created by state apparatuses of surveillance and social control. Particularly, we have always been concerned about balancing our need for these institutions to keep our nations safe with our desire for individual rights, civil liberties, and identity; in other words, we wish for these apparatuses to be restrained so that their power does not become excessive. Outside of academic discourse, many have worked through these problems since the beginning of the modern state using literature and popular culture. We have created, read, watched, and participated in stories that construct how these apparatuses should operate, who they should control, and how we the public should interact with and view these institutions. As I will show in the following chapters, these narratives, then and now, have never been monolithic; that is, they are often contradictory and present many ways of understanding surveillance, social control, and terror. Nevertheless, they have also laid the groundwork for how we currently narrate, through television, our post-9/11 interactions with government apparatuses of surveillance and social control, even if we might not be aware of this narrative history. In this way, there is a continuum of storytelling linking our present-day concerns about these institutions with those of the past. To better understand how we are grappling with our current situation, we need to understand these connections and consider how these older narratives may be shaping our television responses to present concerns.

To frame the purpose and scope of this book, this introductory chapter will explain the choices I make in terms of my focus on British and American post-9/11 television programs about surveillance, social control, and terror and their relationship to earlier literary and popular narratives about these concerns. Although I have somewhat touched on these questions thus far, I will answer more in depth the following: (1) why television? (2) why a historical approach and a focus on 9/11? (3) why limit the study to U.S. and U.K television? and (4) why state apparatuses of surveillance and control—the prison, the police, and the national intelligence agency? Along with explaining these choices, I will also address the theoretical framework I will use in the following chapters in terms of integrating television, surveillance, and textual studies.

WHY TELEVISION?

As noted above, my book takes an interdisciplinary approach that draws on television studies but also incorporates textual and literary analysis to connect current television series to earlier texts and mediums, including print books and journalism. My goal is to encourage us to consider post-9/11 television in a broader context: especially, its connection to historical narratives and how television drama is shaped by earlier mediums and texts. I argue that television programs and how we watch them should not be divorced from understanding and analyzing them as texts that tell a story and that are part of a continuum of narratives originating in print texts. Raymond Williams, for instance, explains the importance of this connection in an interview with *Screen Education*; for instance, he notes that his university class, "Police Fiction," began with an analysis of crime novels and linked that inquiry to television series about the police.[12]

In addition, Lynn Spiegel notes that "television studies in the humanities has always been a hybrid, interdisciplinary venture, drawing on fields of inquiry that are often at odds with one another."[13] Toby Miller also advocates an interdisciplinary approach to television studies but advises that we "never reduce television to TV itself or to the social relations surrounding it."[14] Indeed, to conduct proper television studies, Miller argues that one must look at the medium from the following multiple angles: "To understand a program or genre, we require an amalgam of interviewing people involved in production and circulation, from writers to editors to critics and audiences; content and textual analyses of shows over time, and of especially significant episodes; interpretations of knowledge about social issues touched on; and an account of programs' national and international political economy."[15] My approach certainly does not reduce television to the medium or social relations, but my focus does remain on how television narratives function socially to provide a means of staging or working through major events, like 9/11 and terrorism, and the issues we face as a culture, such as increased state surveillance.

Next, I choose to focus on television versus films and current literary texts in part because scope dictates that a book cannot cover all mediums and narratives. However, more significantly, television is a medium which is enjoyed and shared by a wide spectrum of the public in ways that literary texts often are not. Further, while film, like television, can capture a wide audience, it does not have a serial component that allows for examining the development of a narrative over time, which Miller argues is crucial to television studies.[16] Therefore, my choice of television is one of breadth of audience and time in order to argue that narratives of surveillance and social control are not limited in importance to niche audiences or finite points in time. In the current television landscape, we can witness an interesting pattern that indicates interest on the part of writers and producers of television programming on the one hand, and the audience on the other, regarding crafting and viewing narratives about surveillance and social control since 9/11.

Amanda D. Lotz's and Spiegel's theorizations about modern television programming are key here. Both state that we can no longer discuss television episodes as an event seen by most viewers, as was the case prior to the advent of cable programming.[17] Lotz specifically uses 9/11 as an event to illustrate how we must alter the "cultural forum" model of television developed by Horace Newcomb and Paul Hirsch during the network era.[18] Lotz argues that we can still use the idea of a "cultural forum"—much like Ellis advocates for understanding television as a site for "working through" issues—as long as we acknowledge the realities of a post-network era.[19] This reality entails the plethora of television series available across various viewing platforms that include the multitude of streaming services in addition to cable and satellite channels. Lotz writes that "[t]his seems to make individual series and networks less significant and requires us to search for trends, discourses, and representations that occur across networks and series."[20] Spiegel agrees, using the term "narrowcasting" to describe how networks or streaming platforms today tailor programs to suit specific audiences, versus the "broadcasting" model of network television, which was designed to appeal to as wide an audience as possible.[21] Lotz then uses 9/11 as an example of an event that must be analyzed for patterns that occur across television dramas in order to understand how the medium is functioning as a cultural forum to "work through" the terrorist attack.[22]

Indeed, it is becoming increasing difficult to speak about "television programs" in the traditional sense, since viewers now watch these programs on devices other than television screens, like smart phones, laptops, or tablets. Anecdotally, I have experienced this issue with my students. When I speak about watching television, students claim they do not watch it much. However, if I change the wording to "streaming," then students speak at length about various series of which they are avid fans. To a younger generation, "television" means network or cable programming, while "streaming" is something else. As someone of an older generation,

I think of serial programming as "television" whether I view it on a television set or on an iPhone, or whether I am watching network television or using a streaming service such as Netflix. As Spiegel notes, television is in this way converging with the internet.[23] However, given that much of this episodic programming is still produced by companies that are associated with television networks—either public or cable, in both the U.S. and U.K.—I will continue to use the term "television" in this book.[24] But, the point is, according to both Lotz and Spiegel, if we want to talk about trends in television, we need to show that these developments extend across multiple audiences, programs, delivery systems, and viewing platforms. Otherwise, we cannot truly claim that television is working as a cultural forum on a specific issue.

I argue that such a widespread trend does exist regarding narratives about state apparatuses of surveillance and social control and their responses to terrorism and other security threats post-9/11. While each of the chapters will discuss this claim more in depth, we can see across various and differing audiences, platforms, and programs a heightened interest in creating and viewing programs about prisons, the police, and intelligence agencies. As noted earlier, these series are not all in agreement with each other about how these institutions should be depicted; often, these dramas are contradictory within themselves, which is inevitable in episodic programming over the course of several seasons. Nevertheless, we can perceive a rise in the production and consumption of these narratives. For instance, as I will explore further in Chap. 2, a brief canvassing of programs in the U.S. and U.K. about prisons reveals few prior to 9/11, with notable exceptions such as *Oz* (which continued its run post-9/11). However, after 2001, there is a marked increase in both fictional programs and docuseries about the purpose and ethics of imprisonment on various platforms.

When it comes to police and intelligence agency series (Chaps. 3 and 4), the trend is slightly different, given that there have been a vast number of television shows about both which have been popular with audiences since the inception of television. For example, police procedurals have consistently filled the slate of network programming, and, especially during the Cold War, various series such as, *The Avengers, Mission: Impossible*, or *The Man from U.N.C.L.E*, were prevalent across British and American screens. Here, it is not the presence of these programs that have changed so much as their focus. In the case of the police and spy agencies, the series (1) make connections, either implicitly or explicitly, to earlier narratives about these

institutions, and/or (2) ruminate on the ethics and efficacies of these apparatuses of surveillance and social control. For example, since 2001, some
programs, such as *Ripper Street* and *Copper*, have depicted policing and
forensic science in its infancy in the nineteenth century, and there is a trend
in dramas that have similar nostalgia for the beginnings of American spycraft
during the Revolutionary War (*Turn*) or espionage during the height of the
Cold War (*The Americans*). In looking backward, these programs suggest
some awareness on the part of writers, producers, and viewers that there are
connections to be made between how we understand surveillance and social
control in our post-9/11 world, and how we have understood these issues
in previous eras. Further, this understanding involves questioning the purpose of these apparatuses, and numerous programs about the police and the
intelligence agency, from reality series like *Traffic Cops* to dramas like *Spooks*
or *Berlin Station*, involve thinking *about* the nature of the apparatus itself.
They reflect our culture's doubts about the institutions we want to protect
us from terrorist or criminal threats and our fears that they can take away our
privacy and civil liberties.

Again, in drawing on television studies theory, particularly regarding
the power of the viewer, these trends are significant because such programs are popular enough that they are created, produced, and renewed
by networks and streaming platforms. There even exists enough of an
audience to continue these series from one network or platform to another
if canceled (e.g., *Ripper Street* was dropped by BBC1 but picked up for a
final season by Amazon Studios). As Ellis, Ian Ang, and John Hartley
point out, the power of the viewer is significant,[25] and it has only grown
more so now in an era of greater choice for the viewer in how he or she
decides not only what to watch, but when and how. "Appointment viewing," the traditional model of a set time and place a series would air, has
been superseded by the ability to watch programs on demand through
streaming services, such that a viewer can "binge watch" an entire season
at once. Further, the extensive selection of programs, from traditional
over-the-air networks to streaming services, means that producers must
develop programs that will catch the eye of the viewer, rather than rely on
the viewer to watch whatever might be on at that moment, as was the case
during the broadcast era. That is not to say that networks during the
broadcast era did not have to appeal to audiences. Ang rightly states that
"television [...] does not have the means to coerce people into becoming
members of its audience."[26] She cites the "enormous amount of money
and energy spent to reinforce and update people's desire to watch

television."[27] After all, even during the broadcast era, one had the power either to change the channel, to relegate a program or commercials to the background while doing other activities, or to turn the set off altogether.

However, I agree with Hartley that the power of the audience to influence television production has grown exponentially since the advent of streaming services and social media. If this is the case, then trends like a focus on surveillance, social control, and terror are in part driven by the viewers themselves and their response to programs on social media, which now give producers and network executives an additional understanding of who is watching programs along with the traditional Nielsen-style ratings system. Hartley describes this integrated model of viewers and producers as "participatory" and "productive" (in that viewers participate in the life of a series by producing ancillary media that discuss, celebrate, or critique a program).[28] Hartley observes that "a new model [of television] is emerging, based on social networks, consumer-created content, multiplatform publication, and a semiotic long tail."[29] He cites *Coronation Street* fan websites, such as *Corrie* and *Corrie Blog*, as examples of viewer-produced content that intertwine producers and consumers of a series in a "*social network* of fans and professionals."[30] Similarly, Henry Jenkins terms this change "convergence," which "represents a cultural shift as consumers are encouraged to seek out new information and make connections among dispersed media content."[31]

Social media can also illuminate small but dedicated fan bases that can provide the impetus to continue additional seasons of a program. Jenkins, for instance, discusses the power of fandom, or what he terms "knowledge communities" (in that fans possess and collate vast information about a series).[32] An interesting example of this community knowledge occurred during a *Doctor Who* pub quiz in the U.K. in which the actual star and writers of the revived program's tenth season only managed to place third—*Doctor Who* fans thus demonstrated they possess more knowledge about the program than those who produce it.[33] Further, a recent example of a fan community encouraging producers to continue a program would be the science fiction series *The Expanse*. When the American cable network Syfy canceled the series in 2018 after three seasons, the enormous outcry from fans led to the program being picked up for a fourth season by Amazon Prime shortly thereafter.[34]

Together, these small communities for more obscure series, in conjunction with larger viewership for more traditionally popular programs, can evidence a desire on the part of audience members to grapple with narratives about institutions of surveillance and social control and these institutions' responses to terrorism and other threats. However, both Ellis and Miller caution that we should not overestimate the power of the audience, either. For example, Ellis writes that the television image can produce a kind of "complicity" in the viewer in that he or she passively moves "his or her gaze across the sights in the TV eye" while television does the "look[ing]."[35] Similarly, Miller surmises that "[i]t would be odd to assume that control of audiences has ever been total; and equally odd to assume that the resistance of audiences is either absolute or novel."[36]

Given that other critics have amply theorized the connections between the act of surveillance and the television medium itself,[37] the purpose of this book is not to re-tread that ground but to employ it as a further justification for my focus on television narratives of surveillance, social control, and terror. Although he is not writing about surveillance per se, Ellis observes that the very the act of watching television is panoptic. As cited earlier, Ellis discusses the way in which viewers passively monitor what they see on television. He further elaborates that "[t]he TV-looker is a viewer, casting a lazy eye over proceedings, *keeping an eye on events,* or, as the slightly archaic designation had it, 'looking in'" (emphasis mine).[38] While I disagree with the degree of laziness or passivity Ellis attributes to the viewer, nevertheless, he is correct that the audience is like the prison guard in Michel Foucault's panoptic model of surveillance[39]: the viewer can watch without him or herself being watched in return. However, the difference from Foucault's model is that the audience functions as the many watching the few (the actors). Surveillance scholar Thomas Matiesen terms this a "synopticon," and that through the synopticon, we live in a "viewer society."[40] And yet, I would argue, there is still an element of Foucault's panopticon here; after all, one watches television most often in the privacy of one's home, either alone or in the company of a few people, versus the typical movie-going experience of seeing a film alongside many others. Therefore, watching television becomes a more powerful and intimate experience than viewing a film in a theater.[41] This point is even more true if one is consuming television on a smart phone or tablet, with earbuds blocking out the rest of the world.

Further, this panoptic/synoptic power arises because the viewer is not only watching but also judging and assessing the action without being personally implicated in that process. We can see this passive participation in the rise of reality programs (such as *Survivor* or *Big Brother*) designed specifically for viewers to monitor and critique contestants or participants.

This passive television surveillance works together with social media, which itself is a surveillance space where people monitor, watch, and judge others on Twitter, Facebook, and other platforms. This general surveillance culture gives rise to what scholars like John McGrath note are "psychologies of narcissism and reflection"; in other words, the enormous power and pleasure in seeing as well as being seen.[42] Therefore, it seems apt that an increase in surveillance-themed programming occurred after 9/11, particularly on television, given the panoptic/synoptic nature of the medium. It is not coincidental that here the medium is the narrative (to paraphrase Marshall McLuhan) in a world that has become more aware of surveillance and social control because of the war on terror.

However, this book will argue that while television is certainly panoptic in nature, so is a print text, given that the reader can "view" the text without being judged or monitored in return. I agree with David Rosen and Aaron Santesso's contention that there are important similarities between surveillance and literature, and that they are "kindred practices," that of "discovering the truth about other people."[43] Particularly important for my purposes is their point that "key developments in surveillance theory [were] first […] worked out *in* literature" (emphasis original).[44] Indeed, many of the older narratives of surveillance, social control, and terror addressed in this book specifically interpellate the reader as a panoptic observer and evaluator. Such is the case, for instance, with Puritan captivity narratives or the detective fiction of Sir Arthur Conan Doyle. While an extensive investigation of panopticism and narrative is beyond the scope of this book, these connections suggest a certain surveillance power in consuming stories, whether print or visual, and perhaps therein lies an unexplored facet of the act of reading or viewing a narrative.

In terms of both historical and current narratives of surveillance, social control, and terror, the audience gains a sense of watching and monitoring those institutions that are designed to watch and monitor us, the public. However, the result of this situation can be complex. On the one hand, as I earlier noted, the structure of television does not require the viewer to act based on what they see; in this sense, there is a disturbing passivity to watching a program.[45] However, one could contend the same is true for reading a print text, although, arguably, there might be less passivity in terms of needing to imagine the action of the story; thus, one could maintain that there is more involvement of the reader in the creation of the text. Nevertheless, the viewer or reader can watch and judge without having to do anything about the surveillance apparatus on display.

In other words, there is no impetus on the part of the viewer or reader to change the institution, particularly if the narrative chooses to absolve the institution of any responsibility or wrongdoing.

On the other hand, as Ang, Ellis, and John Fiske point out,[46] we should not be so quick to understand television as a completely passive activity. If viewers can determine what programs are produced by either watching them or not, then viewers can also take these narratives and use them to act. Audiences actively discuss various programs on social media sites such as Reddit to debate and argue about how and why those narratives are constructed. This discussion demonstrates active viewing on the part of the audience, and viewers can and often do disagree with how the writers and producers are developing a series. Indeed, with today's social media, viewers often have much more input in the writing of television, such that programs can respond to viewer demands (sometimes, as some fans and critics grumble, too much so).[47]

Finally, my focus on television arises from the fact that these surveillance narratives are shared by many people on an ongoing basis, and from the ongoing, episodic nature of television drama. Ellis notes that television series comprise "continuity with a difference"; that is, a series "has no end in view. The series always envisages its own return."[48] Internet forums attest to the enormous investment viewers make in watching television by discussing new episodes or reviewing previous episodes or seasons. This shared nature, one that keeps pace with the program itself, means that we should pay attention to television programs about surveillance, social control, and terror, and how they depict these apparatuses. In other words, this shared nature, plus the continual renewal of the drama through additional episodes, means that television programming can tackle real-life issues of surveillance and social control that play out in our culture. Ellis confirms that series "do not reproduce ideology [...]. Instead, they are involved in a process of renewal or refreshment of society's layers of common sense, its basic understandings of the universe."[49] For instance, issues of police brutality or new terror attacks can influence the program and be addressed either directly or indirectly by the storyline(s) of a series. In this way, television texts have the unique ability to interact in real time with issues that concern the audience, and they can engage in dialogue with the audience about those events, just as the audience in turn might discuss the incorporation of those events via social media.

Overall, I want to emphasize that there is a complex interaction between the audience, writers, and producers when it comes to narratives about surveillance, social control, and terror. However, we should keep in mind that this interaction, like surveillance narratives themselves, is not necessarily new. For instance, audience response was key to how Charles Dickens and Arthur Conan Doyle developed their characters and serial stories. Jennifer Keishin Armstrong observes that pressure from rabid Sherlock Holmes fans encouraged Doyle to reluctantly bring back the famous detective after famously killing him off in "The Final Problem."[50] By contrast, E.D.H. Johnson describes Dickens as more amenable to reader response. Dickens indeed enjoyed "the sense of audience participation which he derived from serial publication."[51] Further, "[r]eaders, periodically renewing acquaintance with Dickens' characters over nineteen months, came to think of them as living people; and they did not hesitate to communicate to the author their hopes and fears over what future installments might hold in store."[52] Johnson notes how Nell's death in *The Old Curiosity Shop* resulted in "widespread mourning" by readers, like how Holmes fans in later years openly mourned the death of their favorite detective.[53] As a result, Dickens did alter characters or plots in response to reader input: "The novelist's tenderness for the sensibilities of his readers made him chary of causing gratuitous [...] offense, even when some compromise of artistic purpose was required."[54] Certainly, while this book demonstrates how television texts present or refashion previous narratives of surveillance, social control, and terror, we should be careful not to assume the audience always accepts those narratives. On the one hand, they might do so, and those narratives can shape their views of these issues. However, viewers (and readers) can also reject these narratives. But, above all, it is important to discuss the fact that these narratives exist, and we should explore their implications and influence, including why they have maintained their appeal over time.

Why a Historical Approach to 9/11?

A historical approach to post-9/11 television narratives of surveillance, terror, and social control is important to consider because as viewers, producers, and writers, we together should understand the programs we are creating, consuming, and discussing. For example, is the influence of older narratives on current television series helpful in allowing viewers to grasp the complicated issues of the surveillance state we currently find ourselves in? Or, are these television series, which can replicate older divisions and prejudices, preventing us from considering new ways of interacting with surveillance and its growth since 9/11? As this book will show, these television narratives often do all these things—they complicate, they deepen understanding, yet they replicate older and/or pernicious narratives. Certainly, there is a lack of commentary about how television in general relates to earlier print narratives, and this absence is especially noticeable with narratives of surveillance, social control, and terror.

In British and American post-9/11 society, we often believe we are living in an entirely new age of surveillance and terror, one marked by unprecedented events and circumstances that have never occurred before. This conviction is borne out by the rhetoric that surrounded 9/11, particularly in its immediate aftermath, that there was an America (and a West) before and after 9/11. For example, Paget quotes playwright Mark Ravenhill's phrase, "tear in the fabric," as representative of how many characterized the 9/11 attacks.[55] However, Paget then reminds us that this feeling of anxiety and difference "pre-date[ed] the attacks. At the end of the last millennium there was a distinct darkening of tone on both big and small screens" caused by "the approach of a new millennium; and the absence of, as it were, any designated Enemy Other."[56] In other words, after the collapse of the Soviet Union, there was no clear organizing structure regarding who were "the good guys" and who were not.

In some ways, our sense of an alteration of the U.S. and U.K. following 9/11 is in some ways true, especially in terms of the amount and sophistication of technology we use to monitor and surveil potential terrorists or to screen people at various venues, such as football matches or airports. But we should be aware that the idea of a "before" and "after" 9/11 is itself a narrative, a story we tell ourselves. If we examine fictional and non-fictional texts before 9/11, we find how often this same story has been told before. In other words, we encounter narratives of earlier terrorist attacks or moments that shook society and led to discussions of how society would be forever changed.[57] Then, as now, amid these narratives were ones that focused on the responsibilities of the state apparatuses charged with surveillance and social control; those apparatuses were questioned as either being too lax in preventing violent acts, and/or as overreaching their mandate in response to such acts.

In this way, many of these narratives echo concerns we see today in television narratives grappling with these state apparatuses post 9/11. From this similarity, we can argue that television programs, sometimes consciously, sometimes not, address and adopt these earlier narratives to tell our own story of post-9/11 surveillance and social control. This book does not seek to judge this adaptation, but, rather, I want to explore and illuminate how our current narratives are interacting with ones from the past. Whether producers or consumers of texts, we should all consider how these earlier narratives are shaping our popular as well as political responses to surveillance, social control, and terror. Whether we agree or not with these narratives, we should nevertheless be aware not only of how much we are influenced and formed by them, but also of how long a history they have. If we can understand that telling stories about surveillance and social control is not new, it might offer us a deeper and more complex understanding of our current cultural concerns. What is different about our post-9/11 world is the increase in television storytelling about surveillance, social control, and terror, especially in the U.S. and U.K. markets.

WHY THE U.S.–U.K. FOCUS?

Politically and emotionally, the two nations most affected by 9/11 were the U.S. and U.K. The U.S. and U.K. lost the most citizens in the attack, and it was Tony Blair's government that chose to stand most closely with the Bush administration even if, as the war on terror wore on, much of the British populace did not support him doing so. As Paget and Lacey affirm, Blair's decision to align with the U.S. in the Iraq War was "[h]ugely unpopular in the U.K. (and in Europe as a whole)."[58] In addition, the U.K. was itself the target of a major terrorist attack on London's transport network on 7/7/05, which meant that the U.K., like the U.S., had to face questions of increasing surveillance and social control versus the civil liberties of individuals.

At the same time, in the years following 9/11, the two nations have become ever more connected regarding television production and consumption. As other scholars of transnational television have noted,[59] producing television programs has become increasingly expensive in part because audiences are more discerning and demanding in their tastes; for instance, in response to audience demand, television in recent years has aspired to attain an aesthetic, particularly in terms of special effects, on par with those of Hollywood films. Hence, the U.K. has often imported American television programs as a means of compensating for a lack of resources to produce series with high production values. As Paul Rixon states, "[T]elevision broadcasting is an expensive business, [and] few nations [such as the U.K.] can afford the necessary finance to fill all their hours with expensively made domestic productions."[60] By contrast, the

U.S. television industry has historically possessed more resources to fund television series, especially those with high production values. Rixon adds, "American imports have, for a long time, provided British broadcasters programmes they have occasionally found difficult to finance."[61] He quotes Gerald Beadle, former Director of BBC Television, as saying that American series "provide an element of entertainment and realistic story-telling which it would be difficult, and sometimes impossible, to achieve any other way."[62]

But television has also become more expensive because it is riskier to produce series in an age when the viewer has so much more power and choice with access to a multitude of programs on multiple platforms. Elke Wiessmann observes that "most productions, including increasingly those of the U.S.A., can no longer recoup their production costs in the national markets and hence rely on exports or co-financing deals to secure their funding."[63] This new television model contrasts with television in earlier decades when viewership was more guaranteed because of the limited network selection available (whether commercial or public broadcasting).[64] Therefore, beginning in the late 1990s, increased cooperation took place between U.S. and U.K. production companies and networks.[65] Networks in both nations could pool their money (with the American networks and companies often the ones contributing the most to the budget of the program) while also accessing each other's distribution streams, with their programs shown on each nation's respective networks (e.g., *Sherlock* is produced by both the BBC and PBS and is aired on both networks).[66] Post-9/11, this Anglo-American production of series has only gathered pace.

Further, as this exchange has amplified, so has audience desire to watch programs from the other side of the Atlantic. This has especially been the case for U.S. audiences. While viewers in the U.K. have routinely experienced American programming for years, the opposite was true in the U.S.[67] American television had access to enough resources that it did not require British programming to fill its schedules, and it was assumed that U.S. audiences would not tune into a "foreign" series.[68] As a result, the few British programs shown in America mostly appeared on U.S. public television.[69] However, thanks to the need for programming necessary to sustain streaming services, and due to a younger viewership that is more connected globally than ever before, Americans now have much greater access to British series. There is a decided audience in the U.S. for programs set in the U.K. (e.g., Amazon, Hulu, and Netflix have separate categories of "British" programming for their U.S. subscribers). In this way, U.S. audiences still see British television as "quality" programming, a perception that has held since "the late 1960s, [when] U.K. productions found their way onto the newly established Public Broadcasting service (PBS) network, which, like on other broadcaster, reached the cultural elite in the U.S.A. and hence established evaluative frameworks of what 'good television' at that time was supposed to be like."[70] As a result, it is difficult to speak about current television programming without considering that a sizeable percentage of it comprises co-productions of Anglo-American networks and companies, and that the audience consists of viewers in both American and British markets.

In addition to being connected through 9/11 and television, from a historical perspective, the U.S. and U.K. have necessarily had a long and close, although often tense and fraught, relationship. As Elke Weissmann observes, "[p]arts of these affinities stem from a shared colonial history and a subsequent understanding of each as most valued and trusted allies."[71] After all, the U.S. originated as part of the British Empire, and thus the state apparatuses involved in surveillance and social control—the prison, the police, and the spy agency—were either influenced by or adopted from British models. As a former colony, America inherited much of its cultural and governmental DNA from Britain, and this cultural and governmental connection continued in various ways after the Revolutionary War. Narratives regarding these institutions were also shared on both sides of the Atlantic; for example, Puritan and Barbary captivity narratives were published in both Britain and America and were immensely popular on both shores, and the Sherlock Holmes stories proved as popular in the U.S. as in Britain.[72]

Here, we see a dovetailing of the U.S. and U.K. in various ways: twenty-first century terrorism, television co-production, shared cultural and governmental history, and shared narratives of surveillance, social control, and terror. As a result, it makes sense to speak of these two nations together. This does not mean that the two nations consistently share similar perspectives or agree in their narrating of surveillance and social control; on the contrary, there are ways in which both countries look askance at one another and see each other with as much suspicion as empathy.[73] However, both struggle with the place of surveillance and social control, and they share post-9/11 television narratives about these concerns. We might ask, therefore, how the two nations, through television narratives, might be influencing each other's understanding of their shared apparatuses of surveillance and social control.

As I write this introduction, the U.K. has recently voted to leave the European Union, and this vote, known as "Brexit," reiterates the "special relationship" between Britain and America. Indeed, one factor in the "leave" vote is that many in Britain do not see themselves as European but as a separate entity with more in common with its former colonies (e.g., the U.S.) or current Commonwealth nations (Canada, Australia, New Zealand, etc.).[74] In the vote's aftermath, the Obama administration re-affirmed the special relationship between the U.S. and U.K., although it had urged the U.K. to remain in the E.U. prior to the referendum. *The Financial Times* reported, for instance, that after the Brexit vote, "the White House [went] out of its way to emphasise the enduring links that will remain between the US and the UK."[75] However, prior to the referendum, Obama "travelled to London to warn voters that after Brexit the UK would be at 'the back of the queue' in future trade talks with the United States."[76]

The ramifications of Brexit for U.S.–U.K. television production are difficult to predict. As noted earlier, there has been increased cooperation between the U.S. and U.K. in the last two decades to better fund and distribute programming. However, we should note that the U.K. also receives television funding and support from the E.U.; often, there are multiple finance streams that triangulate between the U.K., the U.S., and E.U., including location filming within E.U. countries using E.U. actors.[77] Without E.U. membership and its role in funding U.K. television, the future of British programming is unclear.[78] Will Brexit mean that the U.K. will need to form even closer connections with the U.S. to fund programs? Or, will U.S. companies now shy away from working with U.K. networks that might no longer have access to subsidies, revenue streams, and locations that membership in the E.U. provides? Some predict dire consequences: the rich vein of British programming over the last two decades that has been distributed around the world (such as *Sherlock* or *Doctor Who*) might be a thing of the past.[79]

In no small part is the Brexit situation driven by a sense of British exceptionalism. The notion of what I will call "Anglo-American" exceptionalism is crucial to understanding the narratives of surveillance, social control, and terror that appear in current television programs. We are already familiar with "American exceptionalism," the metanarrative that the U.S. is a special country superior to other nations because it enshrines civil liberties and democratic government.[80] In this narrative, America is a place where an immigrant finds a better life, and someone can rise from poverty to wealth because of the freedom and opportunity provided by democracy and a capitalist economy. This narrative also assumes a religious cast because it originates in a messianic, divine understanding of America's purpose.[81] For example, John Winthrop, in his Puritan vision of the Massachusetts Bay Colony, envisioned this early American settlement as a "Citty [sic] on a Hill" that would be an example to other nations of a community that is closer to God.[82] While the metanarrative of American exceptionalism has since moved away from such a strictly Christian vision, the idea of the U.S. as "chosen" by God still pervades the myth.

Yet, this notion of a chosen nation can be traced to Britain itself. While the Puritans might have left Britain to form what they believed was a better and more virtuous society than what they left behind, nevertheless, they did not abandon the exceptionalist narrative itself. Britain has long seen itself as morally and governmentally superior to other nations, a view that coalesces around the reverence of Magna Carta.[83] Although this document did not begin democracy as the Whig version of history would have it, it did initiate the concept of civil liberties and a restraint on the power of government. J.C. Holt writes that "[t]he essence of Whig history was to read the present back into the past and to interpret the past in light of selected themes: the growth of liberty, the development of Parliament and, within Parliament, of the House of Commons, the growth of 'nationhood,' and so on."[84] It therefore makes sense to speak of Anglo-American exceptionalism in which both nations see themselves as defenders of civil liberties and government restraint, particularly as opposed to other nations. The idea of British exceptionalism is alive and well can be seen in the Brexit, in which those who want to leave the E.U. have expressed sentiments that Britain has a superior culture and government to those of the European continent.

Since the U.K. joined the E.U. in 1973 as part of what was then titled the European Economic Community, the "special relationship" between the U.S. and U.K. in terms of their ostensible exceptionalism, has admittedly been more of an idealized or imaginative relationship than an actualized one.[85] As part of the E.U., at least until Brexit takes place, the U.K. is far more tied to Europe in terms of laws, regulations, and trade than it is currently to the U.S. Recently, in terms of surveillance, the European Court of Human Rights, to which the U.K. is subject as part of the Council of Europe (which also includes Turkey and Russia), ruled that "British spy agencies broke human rights by conducting mass surveillance without proper oversight or safeguard."[86] As a result, the U.K. is amending their

Investigatory Powers Act.[87] In this way, Europe has critiqued the idea of "British exceptionalism" and checked the U.K.'s ability to mount surveillance in a manner equal to that of the U.S. Therefore, we should be mindful that the connection between the U.S. and U.K. governments and their surveillance apparatuses that plays out on television screens relies more on the perceptions of American and British viewers, writers, and producers than it does on actual legal fact.

Nevertheless, for my purposes, the ongoing metanarrative of Anglo-American exceptionalism and of an Anglo-American special relationship remains important to post-9/11 television. Despite Britain's membership in the E.U., the actions of the U.S. and U.K. governments throughout the war on terror have still called into question the veracity of this narrative in the minds of the British and American publics. The establishment of Guantanamo Bay, the torture of potential terrorist suspects with "enhanced interrogation techniques," the invasion of Iraq on scant evidence, and the expansion of the scope and capabilities of intelligence-gathering networks have led many to believe both nations have forfeited their claim to exceptionalism.[88] The U.K. House of Commons' Environmental Audit Committee confirms that "[t]he appreciation overseas of civilized British values continues to take a battering, especially when U.K. criticism of Guantanamo Bay was so late and so feeble."[89] Critics of American and British exceptionalism cite America's willingness (and Britain's complicity) to send detainees to regimes of non-Western nations to be interrogated, with these nations signifying regimes of demagoguery, totalitarianism, and the absence of civil liberties. This practice was termed "extraordinary rendition" by the U.S. government. Jane Meyer adds that "[t]he most common destinations for rendered suspects [were] Egypt, Morocco, Syria, and Jordan, all of which have been cited for human-rights violations by the State Department and are known to torture suspects."[90] In this way, narratives of American and British exceptionalism often elevate the U.S. and U.K. at the expense of not just mainland Europe, but, more specifically, non-Western, non-white nations which become constructed as barbaric rather than civilized. And yet, U.S. and U.K. actions since 9/11 have for television producers and viewers alike called into question who is truly barbarous.

As the following chapters will show, television narratives post-9/11 have, either overtly or surreptitiously, wrestled and fretted over this problem of Anglo-American exceptionalism, with some programs exposing it as non-existent while others attempt to reassure the audience that such exceptionalism is valid (or, a contradictory mix of the two). Again, however, this book will demonstrate that such wrangling with the exceptionalist myth is not new, and that we in British and American culture have long confronted in literature and popular culture the fear that such exceptionalism is not valid. The state apparatuses of surveillance and control—the prison, the police, and the intelligence agency—have been fodder for narratively questioning Anglo-American exceptionalism since before 9/11 because they can undermine the very civil liberties that are the foundation of the U.S. and the U.K.'s claim to Anglo-American exceptionalism.

WHY STATE APPARATUSES OF SURVEILLANCE AND SOCIAL CONTROL?

Surveillance studies as a focus of inquiry was in place before 9/11 (e.g., Foucault's seminal work on panopticism); and, certainly, the growth of American and British state surveillance in response to terrorism occurred prior to 9/11, such as the proliferation of the CCTV system in the U.K. to foresee and forestall IRA bombings[91] or increased airport security and scrutiny in the U.S. and Europe following the bombing of Pan-Am 103 over Lockerbie, Scotland.[92] Nevertheless, both surveillance studies and state surveillance itself has increased in importance and visibility since 9/11.[93] Many surveillance scholars, such as Ayse Ceyhan, have rightly noted that we should not neglect to focus on the surveillance conducted by corporations such as Google, given that it is marketing that is driving much of the innovation and expansion of surveillance of the populace.[94] Employing Foucault's concept of "biopower," Ceyhan writes that "Google [...] has become the most powerful biopolitical surveillance tool as it gathers, processes and mines large volumes of information about people and groups."[95] Ceyhan observes that "biopower understood in its Foucauldian formulation," is the state's "power over life and the species' body."[96] From this basis, she argues that "biopoliticized surveillance" is "surveillance taking the human body and its movements as focal points."[97] Ceyhan adds, however, that biopower and biopoliticized surveillance are "not the exclusive attribute of the state but can be achieved anywhere by any organization [such as Google] through information gathering and date-management process and tools."[98] In turn, the U.S. and U.K. governments work with companies like Google to purchase the data the tech giants have gathered on citizens and their habits.

The confluence of marketing and government surveillance data and practices reflects Gilles Deleuze's model of surveillance society, what he termed "societies of control."[99] Many surveillance scholars prefer this model, which emphasizes the fluidity and prevalence of surveillance throughout every aspect of life, over the older, panoptic, model put forward by Foucault.[100] In panopticism, the emphasis is on institutions (like the prison, the school, the workplace, and so on), while in Deleuze's societies of control, surveillance and control flow freely without institutional barriers dividing the public and the private. While this book agrees with Deleuze's assessment of modern surveillance (hence, my use of the term "social control"), I nevertheless concur with David Lyon, who insists that we not neglect the role of traditional state apparatuses in our understanding of modern surveillance and control. By "social control," I mean what Deleuze describes as that "which no longer operate[s] by confining people but through continuous control and instant communication"[101] that today's technology facilitates. My argument, however, is that state apparatuses are part of this continuous control through their ability to constantly monitor the population. Lyon concurs that "state forms of surveillance have by no means disappeared, and a world event like 9/11 has shown that they have both power and influence when perceived threats are of a sufficient magnitude."[102] Further, he states that the Deleuzian society of control, which he terms "assemblage," co-exists alongside the panoptic model of surveillance in terms of state apparatuses: "The assemblage and the apparatus are overlapping, even superimposed and mutually informing systems, and the assemblage can still be appropriated by the apparatus."[103] These institutions still comprise the most visible, repressive, and powerful means of monitoring and regulating the public: "The responses to September 11 are a stark reminder that [...] the nation state is still a formidable force, especially when the apparently rhizomic shoots can still be exploited for very specific purposes to tap into the data they carry."[104]

Given the continuing centrality of the state, it should not be surprising that a canvas of historical and current narratives of surveillance, social control, and terror shows they coalesce around the three major apparatuses tasked with monitoring and controlling the population on behalf of the state: the prison, the police, and the national intelligence agency. While there are television programs (such as *Big Brother*) that do address the more Deleuzian aspects of surveillance culture in which the audience itself participates in the process of control, the focus of television narratives is more on the state and its interaction with the public rather than the public's interaction with itself though social media or how it is shaped by corporate surveillance (I will expand further on these issues in the book's conclusion). And, while several scholars have addressed surveillance in relation to film and television,[105] none have specifically focused on the role of state apparatuses in television series, nor have they tackled television surveillance narratives from a historical perspective, which this book aims to do.

It makes sense that television narratives of surveillance, social control, and terror focus on state apparatuses in our post-9/11 world. Years of public and political debate have occurred since 9/11 about how the U.S. and U.K. governments should respond to terrorism, and there have been myriad contradictory and complex demands and arguments. For example, after the attacks, many asked how various government apparatuses, such as the police and spy agencies, could not know the attacks would happen; as a result, they called for strengthening and expanding the capacities of those apparatuses so that such an attack could never happen again.[106] In this sense, the state employs Deleuzian control because it is not merely responding to but attempting to be predictive of terrorism—in other words, risk management. Our governments and ourselves increasingly put faith in technology—data mining, computer algorithms—to prevent future terror events: "As global modernization produces more risks, so more efforts are made to counteract risk, particularly through insurance based on surveillance information."[107] However, the problem is that such algorithms divide populations into groups that are predicted as more likely to commit acts of terror, thus leading to discrimination and increased monitoring of Muslim citizens, for example. Indeed, Shane Harris traces the desire for terror risk management to former National Security Adviser John Poindexter's frustration that the U.S. could not have prevented the Islamic militant terrorist bombing of the Marine barracks in Beirut in 1983.[108]

However, others counterargued that the questionable effectiveness of predictive surveillance was not worth the lessening of civil liberties. Those opposed to expanded surveillance powers pointed to the PATRIOT Act and the broad scope it granted to the National Security Agency (NSA), as well as former NSA employee Edward Snowden's revelations regarding the extent of the agency's intelligence gathering.[109] American police, too, have often been hailed as heroes of 9/11 in their response to the attacks (specifically, the New York Police Department [NYPD]), but they have also been criticized as becoming too powerful and militarized by the war on terror, resulting in attacks on non-white civilians in particular.[110] Finally, the prison has also grown into a site of controversy, specifically regarding Guantanamo Bay, which was opened in the wake of 9/11 to hold indefinitely those suspected of participating in terrorist organizations. Those in favor of Gitmo's continuing operation claim it is necessary to circumvent U.S. laws to "keep enemy combatants off the battlefield" because these detainees would otherwise "slaughter Americans by the thousands if they get the chance."[111] Those against it declare "Guantanamo does the American people more harm than good. It has come to symbolize abuse of Muslim prisoners and serves as a powerful recruiting tool for al-Qaeda. It also undermines vital counterterrorism cooperation from our Western allies, who view the prison as inconsistent with their own and U.S. values," and thus the prison not only violates U.S. law but it also destroys the U.S.'s claim to be a model of freedom and liberty in the world.[112] As a result, the attention toward Gitmo and other post-9/11 prison scandals, such as Abu Ghraib, has shifted focus to the American and British prison systems in general.

Although Britain does not operate Gitmo itself, it has been complicit in its existence. Further, while the U.K. might be less involved in this extra-legal detention center, Britain has still nonetheless been at the forefront of creating and implementing surveillance systems that monitor the U.K. public—systems that are arguably more extensive than those in the U.S. As noted earlier, beginning with the era of IRA terrorism, the U.K. has developed and relied on one of the most extensive CCTV apparatuses in the world, and, through this network and related surveillance technology (such as Automatic Number Plate Recognition or ANPR, which utilizes cameras monitoring roads and cameras onboard police cars to identify suspect vehicles[113]), the British state can observe, police, and control the population. Indeed, *The Telegraph* recently reported that a government privacy watchdog group warns that the U.K. "is the most snooped upon country in the democratic world" and that "the combination of CCTV, biometrics, databases and tracking technologies can be seen as part of a much broader exploration, often funded with support from the US/UK 'war on terror,' of the use of interconnected 'smart' systems to track movements and behaviours of millions of people in both time and space."[114] Thus, there remain similar questions about Britain's ideals of civil liberty and democracy, and how they are or are not expressed in their domestic criminal justice system.

As noted above, numerous post-9/11 television narratives coalesce around these three state apparatuses, and when we return to older narratives of surveillance, social control, and terror, we see the same tendency of storytelling regarding the prison (or captivity), the police, and the intelligence agency (or spycraft generally). It is not within the purview of this book to recite a history of surveillance and social control as part of the modern British and American nation state. Other critics have done this more and ably.[115] However, we should understand that, as scholars like Foucault have noted, the growth of state apparatuses such as the prison, police, and intelligence agency are concomitant with the development of the entity we understand as the modern nation state. For example, Alistair Black, Dave Muddiman, and Helen Plant write that "[i]n the era of modernity, the major agency of surveillance has been the nation state [...]. As it has evolved, the nation state has increasingly involved itself in the collection and manipulation of information on the private citizen and his/her activities, social, political and economic."[116] More to the point, I argue, these apparatuses *are* the state. Black, Muddiman, and Plant agree that "[t]he nation state is [...] essentially an 'information state,' and has been nurturing and performing this role for centuries."[117] Therefore, as the modern state has grown in both countries, the debate between safety and social control on the one hand and civil liberties on the other have accompanied the growth and establishment of the U.S. and U.K. states as we know them today.

Narratives that embody these debates could thus arguably be intrinsic to what we understand as a modern society. I contend we cannot understand our current attitudes and narratives about surveillance and social control without first recognizing that these stories have a history, and, additionally, appreciating where these narratives come from, and why, and whose purpose they serve. Russell Jacoby terms such forgetting "social amnesia": "a forgetting of the past and a pseudohistorical consciousness."[118] In other words, "[s]ocial amnesia is society's repression of remembrance—society's own past. It is a psychic commodity of the commodity society."[119] Jacoby connects this forgetting with capitalism and the status quo, since it works in favor of the narrative of progress and the continual production of the "new": "The intensification of the drive for surplus value and profit accelerates the rate at which past good are liquidated to make way for new goods."[120] For my purposes, I propose we maintain a social amnesia regarding the long narrative history of surveillance and social control prior to 9/11. In forgetting this history, we can believe that 9/11 and our subsequent narration of it was a fundamental break with the past—a break which, as I will argue in the following chapters, can serve to maintain the status quo of Anglo-American dominant culture. As Jacoby notes, social amnesia upholds the status quo because it functions as a reification of the past.[121] However, this book aims to rectify this amnesia by demonstrating that not only do these stories shape current television narratives, but also that television can be a key factor in responding to this forgetting by recalling these older narratives (either by replicating them or by choosing to displace narratives into the past). Yet, television can also continue our obliviousness by crafting simplistic surveillance stories that remain unaware of the complexities and history behind the narrative.

Then as now, the public expects that one of the government's roles is to keep the peace and protect its citizens. However, in Britain and America, both with a history of laws and cultural expectations of civil liberties, the public also expects that the power of these state apparatuses should not exceed what is necessary for a nation's well-being. If narratives of surveillance and control are currently popular and prevalent across various television networks, platforms, and genres, then we can surmise that writers and viewers alike are interested in confronting the challenges and complexities of articulating through narratives the balance between safety and privacy, control and liberty. After all, stories are an important means by which writers, readers, and viewers can work through difficult problems facing a society. Stories can provide catharsis, but they can also offer potential solutions. Sometimes, these solutions might work in favor of the status quo, but this is not always the case. Other times, narratives offer no actual solutions but rather lay before us the various aspects of the problem we are grappling with. Stories are the most palatable means for people to represent to themselves complex and abstract issues in a more concrete way; in television, this might conceivably be more so since programs can visually represent and realize these concepts.

The Prison, the Police, and the Intelligence Agency in Post-9/11 British and American Television

This book seeks to examine the issues outlined in this introduction in the next three chapters, each centered on one of the primary state apparatuses of surveillance and social control: the prison, the police, and the intelligence agency. Chapter 2 focuses on the prison and takes as its central text the Channel 4/National Geographic docuseries program, *Locked Up Abroad,* and its relation to other post-9/11 fictional or documentary prison-themed series, including *Oz* (HBO), *Orange Is the New Black* (Netflix), *Wentworth* (Netflix), *Prison Break* (Fox), *The Night Of…* (HBO),

Strangeways (ITV), *Lockup* (MSNBC), and *Hard Time* (National Geographic). *Locked Up Abroad*, a U.S./U.K. production (titled *Banged Up Abroad* in Britain), has been broadcast since 2004 and is also currently a popular podcast. Its longevity, as well as its viewership in the U.S. and U.K., and its multi-platform presence, suggests there is audience interest in the imprisonment and captivity stories it tells.

Chapter 2 begins by discussing how the overarching narrative of the series, in which Westerners are subjected to poor conditions in non-Western prisons, replicates captivity narratives that were extremely popular in Britain and America from the seventeenth to the nineteenth century. The series specifically reproduces seventeenth-century Puritan and Barbary captivity narratives in which the writer uses his or her imprisonment or captivity to illustrate the differences between the West and the non-Western Other in order to establish Anglo-American culture, law, and morality as superior. *Locked Up Abroad*'s modern take on this narrative constructs the same division by outlining the horrific prison conditions and corrupt legal systems of non-Western nations who disregard the civil liberties of a Westerner (usually an American or British citizen). While the series does not address U.S. and U.K. prisons, the program's implication is that the British and American prison apparatus is by contrast civilized, fair, and humane. This implication is accentuated by the fact that, as in the seventeenth-century narratives, the accused return to their homes after their ordeals more appreciative of British or American culture. In this way, Chap. 2 argues, we see a recapitulation of an older captivity narrative to accomplish a similar goal post-9/11: to reassert British and American exceptionalism during a time of conflict and crisis. In the seventeenth century, the conflict was between Britain and America on the one hand, and Native American societies and Barbary states on the other; in the twenty-first century, it is between the U.S. and U.K. and radical Islamic terrorism. In both the seventeenth and the twenty-first centuries, the struggle pits Anglo-American society against non-Western cultures, with captivity and imprisonment (or prison systems) as the focal point.

While *Locked Up Abroad* attempts to reassure its audience about the integrity of the Anglo-American prison apparatus by comparing it to non-Western prisons, other programs complicate this assessment. Since 9/11, there has been a substantial increase in the number of prison-themed television programs. Television has turned its panoptic and synoptic gaze on the prison to narrate how this apparatus in the U.S. and U.K. can be just as problematic, corrupt, and unjust. We can trace such narrative questioning back to writers like Charles Dickens or the philosopher Jeremy Bentham, who sought prison reform and whose panoptic, rehabilitative prison model was adopted in the U.S. as well as in the U.K. The popularity and number of prison-themed television programs demonstrates a desire on the part of producers and viewers to engage with stories about a key state apparatus of surveillance and social control. While these programs together do not necessarily provide any solutions to how an institution such as a prison should function within a society that also embraces civil liberties, they do demonstrate the variety of narratives circulating then and now about captivity, the prison, and its place in Anglo-American society.

Next, Chap. 3 turns its focus to the institution of the police by focusing specifically on the BBC's global phenomenon, *Sherlock*, and CBS's *Elementary*, and situates both in context with various series that indicate a specific trend in police- or detective-themed television programs post-9/11: programs set in embryonic police and forensic science departments in the nineteenth century. While *Sherlock* and *Elementary* take place in the twenty-first century, they are based on Sir Arthur Conan Doyle's original Sherlock Holmes stories, which were some of the first to narrate the role of police, detection, and forensic science in the nineteenth century. As a result, the two series demonstrate connections between the nineteenth and twenty-first centuries in terms of Anglo-American concerns about the police apparatus. Sherlock Holmes has always been an articulation of the desire for someone who was able to surveil, detect, and track criminals and keep the public safe in ways the police apparatus might fail to do. In this way, Holmes embodies a desire for surveillance and social control, and he signifies a recognition that the police apparatus cannot always be successful. And yet, he also stands as an alternative to the police apparatus because audiences fear how the police can conversely become too powerful and abuse their authority. Holmes is, as he adamantly states in the original tales and in the television series, not part of the police apparatus but an adjacent, adversarial adviser to it; thus, he is neither fully outside nor inside the system.

In post-9/11 Britain and America, the popularity of the two series indicates that audiences are as conflicted about the police today as they were in the late Victorian era. Given that there was originally opposition to the creation of a police force in both Britain and America, it is not surprising that there has been ongoing suspicion regarding its power and scope mixed with a desire for the police to protect against criminals and potential terrorist threats. Programs like *Ripper Street* (BBC1 and 2 and Amazon Prime),

Copper (BBC America), *Whitechapel* (ITV), *The Alienist* (TNT), *Life on Mars* (BBC1 and ABC), *Ashes to Ashes* (BBC1), *The Frankenstein Chronicles* (ITV Encore), *City of Vice* (Channel 4), and, outside of the U.S. and U.K., Canada's *Murdoch Mysteries* (CTV) and Germany's *Babylon Berlin* (Sky 1 Deutschland), all displace current concerns about the police into the past to contend with them. They also serve as a reminder of the problematic nature of the police apparatus well before 9/11 and the current focus on police brutality in the U.S. and U.K. As Chap. 3 explores, in addition to writers such as Conan Doyle, Dickens, Wilkie Collins, and Edgar Allen Poe, the nineteenth-century British and American press played significant roles in developing such narratives, alternatively castigating and praising the police for their work, as can be seen with the Whitechapel murders in London (the focus of *Ripper Street*) or the 1843 Draft Riots in New York (the subject of *Copper*). Such older narratives, which influence and shape the television programs addressed in this chapter, demonstrate that there has been a tension between the public and the police apparatus from its inception as a force of surveillance and social control. Two other series, *Life on Mars* and *Ashes to Ashes*, look back on more recent policing in the 1970s and 1980s rather than the nineteenth and early twentieth centuries, but the same principle applies—the reconsideration of the police apparatus post-9/11 through the lens of the institution's historical role.

On the one hand, we can correctly read these police programs as ones in which writers, producers, and viewers reassure themselves that the police apparatus has improved over time to become more accountable to the public, more observant of civil liberties, and better at detecting and preventing crime and terrorism by inviting the viewer to compare the relatively rough surveillance techniques and actions of early policing to today. On the other hand, these programs speak to a continuing fascination with and desire for rough justice. In a post-9/11 world that instills fear of criminals and terrorists, these series highlight a longing for officers or detectives who break the bureaucratic rules to protect the public. In this way, we can see that viewers, writers, and producers are conflicted about the police apparatus, both desiring yet disdaining the power it can wield.

Finally, Chap. 4 will consider programs that feature the national intelligence or spy agency. This chapter will continue the theme of narratives that return to an earlier time by taking as its focus the series *Turn: Washington's Spies* (TNT). Inspired by recent publications that have reminded us of the role of spycraft in helping the Americans win the Revolutionary War, *Turn* follows Abraham Woodhull and his friends who, in real life, comprised the Culper Spy Ring tasked with spying on British forces and reporting their findings to General Washington. By returning to our American espionage past, the program highlights two issues in our post-9/11 culture: first, the place of espionage and surveillance in a nation founded on the principle of civil liberties; and, second, the contentious relationship between the U.S. and U.K. which is a consistent refrain in post-9/11 television spy dramas.

Whereas spy series in the U.S. and U.K. prior to 9/11 focused on Cold War issues of communism versus capitalism and the Soviet Bloc versus the West, the attention now is on the ethics of surveillance and the division between allies, particularly the "special relationship" of the U.S. and U.K. As noted earlier in this introduction, after 9/11, the power and scope of surveillance by intelligence agencies such as the National Security Agency (NSA), Central Intelligence Agency (CIA), Government Communications Headquarters (GCHQ), and Military Intelligence Sections 5 and 6 (Mi-5 and Mi-6) grew exponentially in response to terrorist threats. As a result, there have been questions raised in both the U.S. and U.K. about the need for surveillance versus maintaining the civil liberties and privacy of citizens. As discussed in the other chapters, one of the ways such questions are considered and worked though is the medium of television drama. *Turn*, by fictionalizing historical accounts of early American spycraft, narrates a complex story in which espionage is revealed to have developed in the U.S. concomitant with the American state itself. In other words, writers, producers, and viewers face an uneasy truth that there has always been a counternarrative to the American exceptionalist story of freedom and civil liberties: that surveillance and social control was a key part of creating and then maintaining a state based on democratic ideals.

Narratively speaking, surveillance and espionage have also been a part of American literature from its beginnings, with novels such as James Fenimore Cooper's *The Spy: A Tale of the Neutral Ground* (1821) establishing a fictional narrative of spycraft in American culture. *Turn* therefore reminds the audience of a long history of concerns about intelligence gathering that pre-date 9/11 and even the Cold War, the era most associated with espionage in our popular culture. In early America, as now, the problem was the ethics and necessity of spying. In the eighteenth century, covert surveillance was deemed "unmanly" because it was secretive, unlike fighting in battle; it was a necessary evil, and that is a theme of post-9/11 narratives as well.

While other recent spy programs and miniseries are not set historically like *Turn*, they likewise contend with the ethics and place of national intelligence: *Person of Interest* (CBS), *Homeland* (Showtime), *Spooks* (*Mi-5*) (BBC1), *Berlin Station* (Epix), *London Spy* (BBC2), *24* (Fox), *The Night Manager* (BBC1/AMC), and *Covert Affairs* (U.S.). *The Americans* (Showtime) like *Turn*, is a historical spy drama, although it takes place during the height of the Cold War in the 1980s. However, rather than focus on Cold War issues, the emphasis, as with *Turn* and other post-9/11 spy dramas, is more on the ethics and implications of surveillance itself. What does espionage do to the participants, and what benefits does it yield? Also, like what we see with police programs, these series articulate a desire for the spectacle and thrill of espionage. Whereas espionage originally was deemed cowardly, the spy narrative has shaped intelligence gathering into a story of adventure and panoptic enjoyment. So, while many of these programs question the place of national surveillance and the intelligence agency, they also often make it a spectacle that is pleasing and desirable because it is an expression of the seductive power of the state.

In addition, these television narratives connect the present era to the past in terms of tension between the U.S. and U.K. Here, these series express how the "special relationship" is not always a close or easy one, and that such strain can be traced to the Revolutionary War. In American programs like *Turn* and *Person of Interest*, it is British agents or former British intelligence officers who are the antagonists. Conversely, in much post-9/11 British spy drama, it is the U.S. intelligence agency that functions either as a political bully or an unwanted interloper in British affairs. Such representation is no doubt an expression of British resentment of being brought by the U.S. into post-9/11 conflicts in Iraq and Afghanistan. We should note that questions about national intelligence overlap into police programs as well, especially *Sherlock* and *Elementary*, given that even in the original Holmes stories, the detective engaged with both the police and government intelligence entities. For example, in *Sherlock*, Holmes maintains a wary relationship with the intelligence agency through his brother, Mycroft, who is often described by critics as a state spymaster.[122] While the program mistrusts the U.K. government, it even more so depicts American intelligence agencies with contempt. Similarly, in *Elementary*, Holmes often works out of necessity with agencies such as the NSA, but, in the program's logic, it is Mi-5 and 6 who are particularly pernicious. They force his brother, Mycroft, to spy for them (in exchange for protecting Sherlock), and Holmes himself leaves New York at the end of season 2 to be a part of Mi-6, again in exchange for protection (this time for his partner, Joan Watson).

As this introduction has pointed out, the television viewer is a participant in these narratives not only by consuming them but also by commenting on and even influencing them through social media. But, we can argue that this panoptic participation in television narratives is an extension of a wider surveillance culture that has developed not necessarily in response to 9/11, but more in tandem with the post-9/11 years, as technology and social media have allowed an increased ability to make oneself and one's affairs public, and to follow, monitor, and comment on each other's actions in real time. Therefore, I will conclude this book in Chap. 5 by emphasizing that viewers are not innocent; they are not forced or coerced into watching narratives about surveillance and social control. Rather, viewers are quite willing participants in the larger surveillance culture, and this fact complicates the issue of television viewing. While the television narratives articulate the conflicted nature of surveillance, social control, and terror post-9/11, and viewers themselves can feel conflicted, nevertheless, they ultimately operate the panopticon/synopticon by watching television and using social media.

In other words, we as viewers enjoy the power of the panopticon/synopticon, and we often seek out its gaze by offering up our lives on social media and reality television for viewing, judgment, and examination. In this way, Foucault is correct that we internalize the panopticon "[s]o to arrange things that the surveillance is permanent in its effects, even if it is discontinuous in its action [...] in short, that the inmates should be caught up in a power situation of which they are themselves the bearers."[123] However, we do more than internalize it; we relish operating it and being the focus of it. John McGrath, the Artistic Director of the Contact Theater (Manchester, U.K.), affirms, "Introducing surveillance-like moments into theatre pieces myself—sequences in which the audience appeared, through video, on stage, or where the stage space itself was interrogated by its reappearance on screen—I found that the audience reaction was often quite gleeful."[124] Perhaps the ultimate post-9/11 narrative of surveillance and social control is our own ordinary lives on social media; like a serial drama, it never reaches a conclusion but plays out episodically, day by day.

We might ask if television programming and its panoptic nature have over time created the need to shape our own lives to be like this drama. Perhaps. However, if we look to the past, we see that of course there has been episodic drama prior to television, such as the nineteenth-century novels, like Dickens's, that were published in installments, or short stories, like Doyle's, published in *The Strand Magazine,* that the Victorian public followed with as much fervor and anticipation as any new episode of *Sherlock.* Further, then as now, there was keen interest in following the lives of celebrities and infamous criminals, as can be attested to by the many print publications from confessional pamphlets by American colonial criminals to contemporary celebrity gossip magazines. Therefore, it is not the public's panoptic/synoptic gaze that is a new development but rather that everyone can participate in this gaze and even become a willing subject of it. Ordinary life is now the focus of notoriety and interest.

Further, while Foucault theorized how the panoptic gaze can regulate and maintain order in a way conducive to the state, this book will argue that this might not always be the case. In many ways, the public's panoptic social media gaze is responsible for bringing to the fore questions about the power and scope of state apparatuses studied in this book. Social media can allow these apparatuses to monitor the people (e.g., *Person of Interest* cheekily hints that sites like Facebook are in fact government projects designed to encourage people to display their lives for easier surveillance). But people can also monitor the state surveillance apparatuses through social media, such as filming police brutality and posting it to Twitter or Facebook to make it visible to the public. However, much surveillance culture is at its heart narcissistic and does not produce anything more than pleasure and desire.[125] In other words, it is voyeurism for voyeurism's sake, and we are a bored James Stewart in *Rear Window*, watching our neighbors for entertainment. It is therefore interesting to see the revival of a program like *The X-Files* in a post-9/11 world. On the one hand, it makes sense to reboot the series, given that its 1990s paranoia of government surveillance and secret programs seems prescient in years after 9/11 when there has been an increase in the scope and power of state apparatuses of surveillance and social control. And yet, there is something quaint about such paranoia when so much surveillance is not only practiced every day but also is even sought after by the public. *The X-Files*'s axiom, "the truth is out there" seems hollow when it is evident to anyone in our surveillance culture that the notion of a "truth" is suspect at best, and that we are not interested so much in the truth but in the pleasure of visibility. I began this introduction with *Person of Interest*'s similar ominous dictum, "you are being watched." For many, the problem, to paraphrase Oscar Wilde, is not in being watched, but in not being watched.

NOTES

1. Some examples of scholarship on the impact of 9/11 on television and film in general include: Jeff Birkenstein, Anna Froula, and Karen Randall, eds., *Reframing 9/11: Film, Popular Culture, and the War on Terror* (New York: Continuum International Publishing, 2010); Aviva Briefel and Sam J. Miller, eds., *Horror after 9/11: World of Fear, Cinema of Terror* (Austin: U of Texas P, 2011); Wheeler Winston Dixon, ed., *Film and Television after 9/11* (Carbondale: Southern Illinois UP, 2004); Phillip Hammond, ed., *Screens of Terror: Representations of War and Terrorism in Film and Television Since 9/11* (Bury St. Edmunds, UK: Arima Publishing, 2011); Stephen Lacey and Derek Paget, eds., *The 'War on Terror': Post 9/11 Television Drama, Docudrama, and Documentary* (Cardiff: U of Wales P, 2015); and Stacey Takacs, *Terrorism TV: Popular Entertainment in Post-9/11 America* (Lawrence: U of Kansas P, 2012).
2. Scholarship on this point includes: Sébastian Lefait, *Surveillance on Screen: Monitoring Contemporary Films and Television Programs* (Lanham, MD: Scarecrow Press, 2013); Peter Marks, *Imagining Surveillance: Eutopian and Dystopian Literature and Film* (Edinburgh: Edinburgh UP, 2015); John E. McGrath, *Loving Big Brother: Performance, Privacy and Surveillance Space* (London: Routledge, 2004); Garrett Stewart, *Closed Circuits: Screening Narrative Surveillance* (Chicago: U of Chicago P, 2015); and Catherine Zimmer, *Surveillance Cinema* (New York: New York UP, 2015).
3. Stephen Lacey and Derek Paget, "Introduction," in *The 'War on Terror': Post 9/11 Television Drama, Docudrama, and Documentary*, eds. Steven Lacey and Derek Paget (Cardiff: U of Wales P), 5.
4. Derek Paget, "Ways of Showing, Ways of Telling: Television and 9/11," in *The 'War on Terror': Post 9/11 Television Drama, Docudrama, and Documentary*, eds. Steven Lacey and Derek Paget (Cardiff: U of Wales P), 26.
5. John Ellis, *Seeing Things: Television in the Age of Uncertainty* (London: I.B. Taurus, 2000).
6. Ibid., 1.
7. Stephen E. Atkins, "International Reactions to September 11," *The 9/11 Encyclopedia: Second Edition* (Santa Barbara, CA: ABC-CLIO), Credo Ebrary.
8. Lacey and Paget, 5.
9. Ellis, *Seeing Things*, 74.
10. In this book, I use the term "Anglo-American" not in the racial and/or class sense (to indicate socially elite whiteness), but as a way of describing television series or narratives that are in some way shared by both the U.S. and U.K.

11. Ellis, 74.
12. "Television and Teaching," interview with Raymond Williams, from *Screen Education* (1979), in Alan O'Connor, *Raymond Williams on Television: Selected Writings* (London: Routledge, 1989), 211.
13. Lynn Spiegel and Jan Olsson, eds., *Television After TV: Essays on a Medium in Transition* (Durham: Duke UP, 2004), 8.
14. Toby Miller, *Television Studies: The Basics* (London: Routledge, 2010), 147.
15. Ibid., 148.
16. T. Miller, 148.
17. See Amanda D. Lotz, ed., *Beyond Prime Time: Television Programming in the Post-Network Era* (London: Routledge, 2009); Lotz, *Redesigning Women: Television after the Network Era* (Urbana: U of Illinois P, 2006); Lotz, *The Television Will Be Revolutionized* (New York: New York UP, 2007); Lotz, "Using 'Network' Theory in the Post-Network Era: Fictional 9/11 U.S. Television Discourse as a 'Cultural Forum'," *Screen*, 45.4 (Winter 2004): 423–439; and Spiegel and Olsson.
18. Lotz, "Using 'Network Theory'," 425.
19. Ibid., 429.
20. Ibid., 430.
21. Spiegel, "Introduction," in *Television After TV: Essays on a Medium in Transition*, eds. Lynn Spiegel and Jan Olsson (Durham: Duke UP, 2004), 2. See also John Hartley, *Digital Futures for Cultural and Media Studies* (Chichester, UK: Wiley-Blackwell, 2012).
22. Ibid., 431–436.
23. Ibid.
24. Examples of such networks mentioned in this book include BBC, ITV, CBS, FX, and AMC among others.
25. See Ien Ang, *Desperately Seeking the Audience* (London: Routledge, 1991); Ellis, *Visible Fictions: Cinema: Television: Video* (London: Routledge, 1982); and Hartley.
26. Ang, 18.
27. Ibid.
28. Hartley, 3.
29. Ibid., 125.
30. Ibid., 126, emphasis original.
31. Henry Jenkins, *Convergence Culture: Where Old and New Media Collide* (New York: New York UP, 2006), 3.
32. Ibid.
33. Sarah Doran, "The Awkward Moment When Peter Capaldi, Steven Moffat, and Mark Gatiss Came Third in a Doctor Who Pub Quiz," *Radio Times*, Nov. 23, 2015, https://www.radiotimes.com/news/2015-11-

23/the-awkward-moment-when-peter-capaldi-steven-moffat-and-mark-gatiss-came-third-in-a-doctor-who-pub-quiz/.

34. Nellie Andreeva, "*The Expanse*: Amazon Picks Up Space Drama Series After Syfy Cancellation," *Deadline*, May 25, 2018, https://deadline.com/2018/05/the-expanse-amazon-picks-up-space-drama-series-season-4-syfy-cancellation-1202398511/.

35. Ellis, *Visible Fictions*, 112.

36. T. Miller, 144.

37. See endnote 2 for a comprehensive list of studies which discuss how television and film depict surveillance.

38. Ellis, *Visible Fictions*, 137.

39. See especially the chapter "Panopticism" in Michel Foucault, *Discipline and Punish: The Birth of the Prison*, 1975, second Vintage Books edition, trans. Alan Sheridan (New York: Vintage, 1991).

40. Thomas Matiesen, "The Viewer Society: Michel Foucault's 'Panopticon' Revisited," *Theoretical Criminology*, 1.2: 215–232.

41. Ellis, *Visible Fictions*, 131.

42. John E. McGrath, "Performing Surveillance," in *Routledge Handbook of Surveillance Studies*, eds. Kristie Ball, Kevin D. Haggerty, and David Lyon (London: Routledge, 2012), 87.

43. David Rosen and Aaron Santesso, *The Watchman in Pieces: Surveillance, Literature, and Liberal Personhood* (New Haven: Yale UP, 2013), 10.

44. Ibid.

45. Ellis, *Visible Fictions*, 112.

46. John Fiske, *Reading the Popular*, 1989 (London: Routledge, 2004).

47. For more on the struggle of writers and producers to balance their own creative instincts with demands from fans posted on sites such as Twitter, see John Jannarone, "When Twitter Fans Steer TV," *The Wall Street Journal*, Sep. 17, 2012, https://www.wsj.com/articles/SB1000087239 63904447728045776234442730016770.

48. Ellis, *Visible Fictions*, 123.

49. Ibid., 14.

50. Jennifer Keishin Armstrong, "How Sherlock Holmes Changed the World," *BBC1*, Jan. 6, 2016, http://www.bbc.com/culture/story/20160106-how-sherlock-holmes-changed-the-world.

51. E.D.H. Johnson, "Dickens and His Readers," *The Victorian Web*, Jan. 2000, http://www.victorianweb.org/authors/dickens/edh/3.html.

52. Ibid.

53. Ibid.

54. Ibid.

55. Paget, "Ways of Showing," 15–16.

56. Ibid.

57. See, for instance, Chap. 3 on policing, in which I discuss the public and media response to the 1843 New York Draft Riots, an event which informs the BBC America series, *Copper*, as well as the fears regarding the Whitechapel murders, which are reflected in the BBC series *Ripper Street* and ITV's *Whitechapel*.

58. Paget and Lacey, "Introduction," 5.

59. For a complete discussion of British and American transatlantic television, see the following: Carlen Lavigne and Heather Marcovitch, eds., *American Remakes of British Television: Transformations and Mistranslations* (Lanham, MD: Lexington Books, 2011); Michelle Hilmes, *A Transnational History of British and American Broadcasting* (New York: Routledge, 2012); Jeffrey S. Miller, *Something Completely Different: British Television and American Culture* (Minneapolis: U of Minnesota P, 2000); Kristine A. Miller, *Transatlantic Literature and Culture After 9/11: The Wrong Side of Paradise* (London: Palgrave Macmillan, 2014); Paul Rixon, *American Television on British Screens: A Story of Cultural Interaction* (London: Palgrave Macmillan, 2006); and Elke Weissmann, *Transnational Television Drama: Special Relations and Mutual Influence Between the U.S. and U.K.* (London: Palgrave Macmillan, 2012).

60. Rixon, 64.

61. Ibid., 69.

62. Ibid.

63. Weissmann, 6.

64. For a more in-depth discussion of the economics of British and American television, see Hilmes, Rixon, and Weissmann.

65. Ibid.

66. Ibid.

67. See especially J. Miller, Rixon, and Weissmann on this point.

68. Ibid.

69. Ibid.

70. Weissmann, 11–12.

71. Ibid., 4.

72. On publications of Barbary and Puritan narratives in America and Britain, see Paul Baepler, "The Barbary Captivity Narrative in American Culture," *Early American Literature*, 39.2 (2004): 217–246; Baepler, "The Barbary Captivity Narrative in Early America," *Early American Literature*, 30 (1995): 95–120; Jacob Rama Berman, "The Barbarous Voice of Democracy: American Captivity in Barbary and the Multicultural Specter," *American Literature: A Journal of Literary History, Criticism, and Bibliography* 79.1 (2007): 1–27; Linda Colley, *Captives: Britain, Empire, and the World 1600–1850* (New York: Anchor Books, 2007);

Kathryn Zabelle Derounian, "The Publication, Promotion, and Distribution of Mary Rowlandson's Indian Captivity Narrative in the Seventeenth Century," *Early American Literature*, 23.3 (1988): 239–261; and Amy Schrager Lang, "Introduction to *A True History of the Captivity and Restoration of Mrs. Mary Rowlandson*," in *Journeys in New Worlds: Early American Women's Narratives*, eds. William L. Andrews et al. (Madison: U of Wisconsin P, 1990): 11–26.

73. See especially Chaps. 3 and 4, in which I discuss television series about policing and spy agencies which reflect this tension between Britain and America.

74. For a full discussion of the British identity and relationships between the U.S., Britain, and Europe, see Tim Oliver and Michael John Williams, "Special Relationships in Flux: Brexit and the Future of the US–EU and US–UK relationships," *International Affairs*, 92.3 (May 2016): 547–567, and Sofia Vasilopoulou, "UK Euroscepticism and the Brexit Referendum," *The Political Quarterly*, 87.2 (April–June 2016): 219–227.

75. Geoff Dyer, Demetri Sevastopulo, and David J Lynch, "UK-US Special Relationship Shaky Following Brexit Vote," *Financial Times*, June 26, 2016, https://www.ft.com/content/0c71dc88-3b8b-11e6-9f2c-36b487ebd80a.

76. Harold D. Clarke, Matthew Goodwin, and Paul Whiteley, "Why Britain Voted for Brexit: An Individual-Level Analysis of the 2016 Referendum Vote," *Parliamentary Affairs*, 70 (2017): 439–464.

77. See the following on the possible ramifications of Brexit on the U.K. television and film industry: Stewart Clarke, "Britain Calls for Continued European Access for Broadcasters Post-Brexit," *Variety*, Mar. 2, 2018, https://variety.com/2018/tv/news/britain-theresa-may-brexit-tv-channels-broadcasters-europe-1202715473/; Niall Duffy, "Ask the Experts: The Brexit Effect on UK production," *Screen Daily*, Sep. 12, 2017, https://www.screendaily.com/features/ask-the-experts-the-brexit-effect-on-uk-production/5122456.article; and Ray Snoddy, "Brexit: What Leaving the EU Could Mean for the Broadcast Industry," *IBC*, Nov. 17, 2017, https://www.ibc.org/production/brexit-what-leaving-the-eu-could-mean-for-the-broadcast-industry/2545.article.

78. Ibid.

79. Ibid.

80. For more on the idea, definition, and history of American exceptionalism, see Seymour Martin Lipset, *American Exceptionalism: A Double-Edged Sword* (New York: Norton, 1996); Charles Lockhart, *The Roots of American Exceptionalism: Institutions, Culture and Policies* (London: Palgrave Macmillan, 2003); and Deborah L. Madsen, *American Exceptionalism* (Jackson: U of Mississippi P, 1998).

81. See especially Lipset and Madsen. Additionally, see Steven G. Calabresi, "A Shining City on a Hill: American Exceptionalism and the Supreme Court's Practice of Relying on Foreign Law," *Boston University Law Review*, 86 (2006): 1335–1416; and James W. Ceaser, "American Exceptionalism: Is It Real, Is It Good? The Origins and Character of American Exceptionalism," *American Political Thought*, 1.1 (Spring 2012): 3–28.

82. John Winthrop, *A Modell of Christian Charity*, 1630, Collections of the Massachusetts Historical Society, Boston, 1838, 3rd series 7:31–48, Hanover Historical Texts Collection, scanned by Monica Banas, August 1996, https://history.hanover.edu/texts/winthmod.html.

83. For a nice summation of British exceptionalism in general, see Simon Tilford, "The British and Their Exceptionalism," *The Centre for European Reform*, May 3, 2017, https://www.cer.eu/insights/british-and-their-exceptionalism. For the connection between British exceptionalism and Magna Carta, see Judi Atkins, "(Re)imagining Magna Carta: Myth, Metaphor and the Rhetoric of Britishness," *Parliamentary Affairs*, 69.3 (July 2016): 603–620.

84. J.C. Holt, *Magna Carta*, 3rd edition (Cambridge: Cambridge UP, 2015), 39.

85. I am indebted to my manuscript reader for this observation.

86. David Meyer, "Top European Court Says British Spies Broke Human Rights Rules with Their Mass Surveillance Tactics," *Fortune*, Sep. 13, 2018, http://fortune.com/2018/09/13/european-court-human-rights-uk-gchq-mass-surveillance/.

87. Ibid.

88. See, for example, *The New York Times* editorial, "On Torture and American Values," Oct. 7, 2007, https://www.nytimes.com/2007/10/07/opinion/07sun1.html; "Guantánamo Remains a Stain on America's Reputation," *The Economist*, Jan. 14, 2017, https://www.economist.com/international/2017/01/14/guantanamo-remains-a-stain-on-americas-reputation; Scott Beauchamp, "Ignoring Guantanamo Won't Make It Go Away," *The Atlantic*, Dec. 17, 2015, https://www.theatlantic.com/politics/archive/2015/12/ignoring-guantanamo-wont-make-it-go-away/420795/; John Clossick, "British Values, Western Barbarity," *The Socialist Review*, Jan. 2017, http://socialistreview.org.uk/420/british-values-western-barbarity; Afua Hirsch, "Secret Evidence Imperils the Core Values of British Justice," *The Guardian*, July 16, 2009, https://www.theguardian.com/commentisfree/libertycentral/2009/jul/16/secret-evidence-detention-guantanamo-security.

89. *Trade, Development, and the Environment: The Role of the FCO [Foreign and Commonwealth Office]: Fifth Report of the Session 2006–07* (The House of Commons, 2007): E16.

90. Jane Meyer, "Outsourcing Torture: The Secret History of America's 'extraordinary rendition' Program," *The New Yorker*, Feb. 14, 2005, https://www.newyorker.com/magazine/2005/02/14/outsourcing-torture.

91. For more on how the CCTV system in the U.K., and, in particular, London, originated in response to IRA (Irish Republican Army) terrorism, see Jon Coaffee "Fortification, Fragmentation and the Threat of Terrorism in the City of London in the 1990s," in *Landscapes of Defence*, eds. John Robert Gold and George Revill (London: Routledge, 2000): 114–129; Coaffee, "Rings of Steel, Rings of Concrete and Rings of Confidence: Designing Out Terrorism in Central London Pre and Post September 11th," *International Journal of Urban and Regional Research*, 28.1 (March 2004): 201–211; Pete Fussey, "Observing Potentiality in the Global City: Surveillance and Counterterrorism in London," *International Criminal Justice Review*, 17.3 (2007): 171–192; and Jade Moran, "A Brief Chronology of Photographic and Video Surveillance," in *Surveillance, Closed Circuit Television and Social Control*, eds. Clive Norris and Jade Moran (London: Routledge, 2016): 277–287.

92. For further discussion of the response of Western nations to the Lockerbie terrorist bombing, see Jens Hainmüller and Jan Martin Lemnitzer, "Why Do Europeans Fly Safer? The Politics of Airport Security in Europe and the US," *Terrorism and Political Violence*, 15.4 (2003): 1–36; David Lyon, "Airports as Data Filters: Converging Surveillance Systems after September 11th," *Journal of Information, Communication and Ethics in Society*, 1.1 (2003): 13–20; Manoj S. Patankar and Louis Holscher, "Accessibility Vs Security: The Challenge to Airport Security Systems," *Security Journal*, 13.2 (2000): 7–19; Kathleen Sweet, *Aviation and Airport Security: Terrorism and Safety Concerns* (New York: CRC Press, 2008); and Paul Wilkinson and Brian Jenkins, *Aviation Terrorism and Security* (London: Routledge, 2013).

93. While the following is not a comprehensive list of all surveillance studies scholarship, it should give an idea of the breadth and scope of the field since 2001: Julia Angwin, *Dragnet Nation: A Quest for Privacy, Security, and Freedom in a World of Relentless Surveillance* (New York: Henry Holt, 2014); Kristie Ball, Kevin D. Haggerty, and David Lyon, eds., *Routledge Book of Surveillance Studies* (London: Routledge, 2012); Clay Calvert, *Voyeur Nation: Media, Privacy, and Peering in Modern Culture* (Boulder, CO: Westview Press, 2004); John Gilliom and Torin Monahan, *SuperVision: An Introduction to the Surveillance Society* (Chicago: U of Chicago P, 2013); Shane Harris, *The Watchers: The Rise of America's Surveillance State* (New York: Penguin, 2010); David Lyon, *Surveillance after September 11* (Cambridge, UK: Polity, 2003); Lyon, *Surveillance*

Studies: An Overview (Cambridge, UK: Polity, 2007); Christian Parenti, *The Soft Cage: Surveillance in America from Slavery to the War on Terror* (Cambridge, MA: Basic Books, 2003); J.K. Peterson, *Introduction to Surveillance Studies* (New York: CRC Press, 2013); and William G. Staples, *Everyday Surveillance: Vigilance and Visibility in Postmodern Life*, 2nd edition (Lanham, MD: Rowan and Littlefield, 2014).

94. Ayse Ceyhan, "Surveillance as Biopower," in *Routledge Handbook of Surveillance Studies*, eds. Kristie Ball, Kevin D. Haggerty, and David Lyon (London: Routledge, 2012): 38–46.

95. Ibid., 42.

96. Ibid., 38.

97. Ibid.

98. Ibid.

99. Gilles Deleuze, "Postscript on Control Societies," in *Negotiations: 1972–1990*, by Gilles Deleuze, trans. Martin Joughin (New York: Columbia UP, 1995): 177–182.

100. See especially William Bogard, "Simulation and Post-panopticism," *Routledge Handbook of Surveillance Studies*, eds. Kristie Ball, Kevin D. Haggerty, and David Lyon (London: Routledge, 2012): 31–38; Greg Elmer, "Panopticon—Discipline—Control," *Routledge Handbook of Surveillance Studies*, eds. Kristie Ball, Kevin D. Haggerty, and David Lyon (London: Routledge, 2012): 21–30; and Gilliom and Monahan.

101. Gilles Deleuze, "Control and Becoming," in *Negotiations: 1972–1990*, by Gilles Deleuze, trans. Martin Joughin (New York: Columbia UP, 1995), 174.

102. Lyon, *Surveillance After September 11*, 32.

103. Ibid.

104. Ibid., 33

105. See endnotes 1 and 2.

106. See Lyon, Bogard, Ceyhan, and Gilliom and Monahan for further discussion of the expansion of surveillance by the state in hopes of being able to predict and anticipate terror attacks.

107. Lyon, *Surveillance after September 11*, 28.

108. Harris, *The Watchers*, 24–25. Interestingly, a film about terrorism in Lebanon, *Beirut* (titled *The Negotiator* in the U.K.), was recently released in 2018. Starring Jon Hamm, it is set in 1982 and focuses on Mason Skiles (Hamm), who is asked to negotiate for the release of a CIA officer abducted by a terror group. I would argue that the fact this film was made post-9/11 and during the current war on terror is no coincidence; it reflects an effort to remember the history of terrorism in the Middle East that precipitated 9/11 and subsequent terror attacks on Western nations.

109. It would be impossible to list all sources of criticism of the PATRIOT Act. However, the following two are a good beginning for understanding opposition to it: Susan Herman, *Taking Liberties: The War on Terror and the Erosion of American Democracy* (Oxford: Oxford UP, 2014) and Jeffrey Rosen and Benjamin Wittes, eds., *Constitution 3.0: Freedom and Technological Change* (Washington, DC: The Brookings Institute, 2011). For scholarly sources on Edward Snowden and his NSA disclosures, see Loch K. Johnson, ed., "An INS Special Forum: Implications of the Snowden Leaks," *Intelligence and National Security*, 29.6 (2014): 793–810; and Susan Landau, "Making Sense from Snowden: What's Significant in the NSA Revelations," *IEEE Security & Privacy*, 11.4 (2013): 54–63. For the connection between Snowden's disclosures and the PATRIOT Act, see Casey J. McGowan, "The Relevance of Relevance: Section 215 of the USA PATRIOT Act and the NSA Metadata Collection Program," *Fordham Law Review*, 82 (2014): 2399.

110. For more on the militarization of the police and connections with race in the U.S., see Olugbenga Ajilore, "The Militarization of Local Law Enforcement: Is Race a Factor?," *Applied Economics Letters*, 22.13 (2015): 1089–1093; Radley Balko, *The Rise of the Warrior Cop: The Militarization of America's Police Forces* (New York: Public Affairs, 2013); Peter B. Kraska, "Militarization and Policing—Its Relevance to 21st Century Police," *Policing: A Journal of Policy and Practice*, 1.4 (January 2007): 501–513; and Daryl Meeks, "Police Militarization in Urban Areas: The Obscure War Against the Underclass," *The Black Scholar*, 35.4 (2006): 33–41.

111. Clifford D. May qtd. in "Should Guantanamo Bay Be Closed?," *Council on Foreign Relations*, Jan. 20, 2010, https://www.cfr.org/expert-roundup/should-guantanamo-bay-be-closed. For other voices advocating that Guantanamo Bay should continue operating, see "Ignore Obama's Grandstanding and Keep Gitmo Open," *The National Review*, Feb. 24, 2016, https://www.nationalreview.com/2016/02/keep-guantanamo-bay-open/; and Jennifer Daskal, "Don't Close Guantánamo," *The New York Times*, Jan. 10, 2013, https://www.nytimes.com/2013/01/11/opinion/dont-close-guantanamo.html. At the time of writing, the Trump administration recently issued an executive order to keep the facility open "after pledging during the campaign to 'load it up with some bad dudes'," Scott Neuman, "Trump Signs Order to Keep Prison at Guantanamo Bay Open," *NPR News*, Jan. 31, 2018, https://www.npr.org/sections/thetwo-way/2018/01/31/582033937/trump-signs-order-to-keep-prison-at-guantanamo-bay-open.

112. John B. Bellinger III qtd. In "Should Guantanamo Bay Be Closed?," *Council on Foreign Relations*, Jan. 20, 2010, https://www.cfr.org/

expert-roundup/should-guantanamo-bay-be-closed. For further voices advocating the closing of Guantanamo Bay, see Katrina Vanden Heuvel, "Why We Must Close Guantanamo Bay Now," *The Washington Post*, Mar. 1, 2016, https://www.washingtonpost.com/opinions/why-we-must-close-guantanamo-now/2016/03/01/fe829b80-df0a-11e5-846c-10191d1fc4ec_story.html?utm_term=.fce5ad6b6fe9; American Civil Liberties Union (ACLU), "Close Guantánamo," *ACLU*, https://www.aclu.org/feature/close-guantanamo; and Kya Palomaki, "It's Time to Close Guantanamo Bay," *International Policy Digest*, Mar. 11, 2017, https://intpolicydigest.org/2017/03/11/time-to-close-guantanamo-bay/.

113. According to *The Guardian*, "There are Now More Than 8,000 Cameras in the [ANPR] Network," in Nick Hopkins, "CCTV Cameras on Britain's Roads Capture 26 million Images Every Day," *The Guardian*, Jan. 23, 2014, https://www.theguardian.com/uk-news/2014/jan/23/cctv-cameras-uk-roads-numberplate-recognition.

114. Phillip Johnston, "Britain: The Most Spied on Nation in the World," *The Telegraph*, Nov. 2, 2006, https://www.telegraph.co.uk/news/uknews/1533054/Britain-the-most-spied-on-nation-in-the-world.html.

115. Often, sources focus specifically on espionage in terms of the history of surveillance and the nation state (especially, the foundation of the American nation state). For example, see: Terry Crowdy, *The Enemy Within: A History of Spies, Spymasters and Espionage* (Oxford, UK: Osprey Publishing, 2006); Colonel John Hughes-Wilson, *The Secret State: A History of Intelligence and Espionage* (New York: Pegasus Books, 2016); Nathan Miller, *Spying for America: The Hidden History of U.S. Intelligence* (New York: Paragon House, 1989); Alexander Rose, *Washington's Spies: The Story of America's First Spy Ring* (New York: Bantam, 2006); Michael Smith, *The Spying Game: The Secret History of British Espionage* (London: Politico's Publishing, 2004); Michael J. Sulick, *Spying in America: Espionage from the Revolutionary War to the Dawn of the Cold War* (Georgetown: Georgetown UP, 2012); Ernest Volkman, *The History of Espionage: The Clandestine World of Surveillance, Spying and Intelligence from Ancient Times to the Post-9/11 World* (London: Carlton Books, 2007); Michael Warner, *The Rise and Fall of Intelligence: An International Security History* (Georgetown: Georgetown UP, 2014). For a more general look at the connection between the development of the nation state and surveillance, see Alistair Black, Dave Muddiman, and Helen Plant, *The Early Information Society: Information Management in Britain before the Computer* (London: Routledge, 2016); Keith Laidler, *Surveillance Unlimited: How We've Become the Most Watched People on Earth* (Cambridge, UK: Icon Books Ltd., 2008); David Lyon, "A Short History

of Surveillance and Privacy in the United States," in *Engaging Privacy and Information Technology in a Digital Age*, eds. James Waldo, Herbert S. Lin, and Lynette I. Millett (Washington, DC: National Academies Press, 2007): 349–365.

116. Black, Muddiman, and Plant, 12.

117. Ibid.

118. Russell Jacoby, *Social Amnesia: A Critique of Contemporary Psychology* (London: Routledge, 2018): iii.

119. Ibid., 5.

120. Ibid., 4.

121. Ibid.

122. See, for example, Brian McClusky, "221B-9/11: Sherlock Holmes and Conspiracy Theory," in *Transatlantic Literature and Culture After 9/11: The Wrong Side of Paradise*, ed. Kristine A. Miller (London: Palgrave Macmillan, 2014): 50–67 and Matthew Sweet, "Sherlock: How It Became a Global Phenomenon," *The Telegraph*, Dec. 27, 2013, https://www.telegraph.co.uk/culture/tvandradio/10501730/Sherlock-how-it-became-a-global-phenomenon.html.

123. Foucault, *Discipline and Punish*, 201.

124. McGrath, *Loving Big Brother*, 4.

125. See especially McGrath on the pleasure of surveillance.

BIBLIOGRAPHY

Ajilore, Olugbenga. "The Militarization of Local Law Enforcement: Is Race A Factor?" *Applied Economics Letters*, 22.13 (2015): 1089–1093.

The Alienist. Executive produced by Hossein Amini, E. Max Frye, and Steve Golin. Starring Daniel Brühl, Dakota Fanning, and Luke Evans. Based on the novel *The Alienist* by Caleb Carr. Aired in 2018 on TNT.

American Civil Liberties Union (ACLU). "Close Guantánamo." https://www.aclu.org/feature/close-guantanamo.

The Americans. Created by Joseph Weisberg. Starring Keri Russell, Matthew Rhys, and Keidrich Sellati. Aired from 2013 to 2018 on FX.

Andreeva, Nellie. "*The Expanse*: Amazon Picks Up Space Drama Series after Syfy Cancellation." *Deadline*, May 25, 2018. https://deadline.com/2018/05/the-expanse-amazon-picks-up-space-drama-series-season-4-syfy-cancellation-1202398511/.

Ang, Ien. *Desperately Seeking the Audience*. London: Routledge, 1991.

Angwin, Julia. *Dragnet Nation: A Quest for Privacy, Security, and Freedom in a World of Relentless Surveillance*. New York: Henry Holt, 2014.

Armstrong, Jennifer Keishin. "How Sherlock Holmes Changed the World." *BBC1*, Jan. 6, 2016. http://www.bbc.com/culture/story/20160106-how-sherlock-holmes-changed-the-world.

Ashes to Ashes. Created by Matthew Graham and Ashley Pharoah. Starring Philip Glenister, Keeley Hawes, and Dean Andrews. Aired from 2008 to 2010 on BBC1.

Atkins, Judi. "(Re)imagining Magna Carta: Myth, Metaphor and the Rhetoric of Britishness." *Parliamentary Affairs*, 69.3 (July 2016): 603–620.

Atkins, Stephen E. "International Reactions to September 11." *The 9/11 Encyclopedia: Second Edition*. Santa Barbara, CA: ABC-CLIO, 2011. Credo Ebrary.

The Avengers. Created by Sidney Newman. Starring Patrick Macnee, Diana Rigg, and Honor Blackman. Aired from 1961 to 1969 on ITV and ABC.

Babylon Berlin. Created by Tom Tykwer, Achim von Borries, and Henk Handloegten. Starring Volker Bruch and Liv Lisa Fries. Aired in 2017 on Sky 1 Deutschland and Netflix.

Baepler, Paul. "The Barbary Captivity Narrative in American Culture." *Early American Literature*, 39.2 (2004): 217–246.

———. "The Barbary Captivity Narrative in Early America." *Early American Literature*, 30 (1995): 95–120.

Balko, Radley. *The Rise of the Warrior Cop: The Militarization of America's Police Forces*. New York: Public Affairs, 2013.

Ball, Kristie, Kevin D. Haggerty, and David Lyon, eds. *Routledge Book of Surveillance Studies*. London: Routledge, 2012.

Beauchamp, Scott. "Ignoring Guantanamo Won't Make It Go Away." *The Atlantic*, Dec. 17, 2015. https://www.theatlantic.com/politics/archive/2015/12/ignoring-guantanamo-wont-make-it-go-away/420795/.

Berlin Station. Created by Olen Steinhauer. Starring Richard Armitage, Leland Orser, Michelle Forbes, and Mina Tander. Aired from 2016 to 2019 on Epix.

Berman, Jacob Rama. "The Barbarous Voice of Democracy: American Captivity in Barbary and the Multicultural Specter." *American Literature: A Journal of Literary History, Criticism, and Bibliography*, 79.1 (2007): 1–27.

Birkenstein, Jeff, Anna Froula, and Karen Randall, eds. *Reframing 9/11: Film, Popular Culture, and the War on Terror*. New York: Continuum International Publishing, 2010.

Black, Alistair, Dave Muddiman, and Helen Plant. *The Early Information Society: Information Management in Britain before the Computer*. London: Routledge, 2016.

Bogard, William. "Simulation and Post-panopticism." *Routledge Handbook of Surveillance Studies*. Eds. Kristie Ball, Kevin D. Haggerty, and David Lyon. London: Routledge, 2012: 31–38.

Briefel, Aviva and Sam J. Miller, eds. *Horror after 9/11: World of Fear, Cinema of Terror*. Austin: U of Texas P, 2011.

Calabresi, Steven G. "A Shining City on a Hill: American Exceptionalism and the Supreme Court's Practice of Relying on Foreign Law." *Boston University Law Review*, 86 (2006): 1335–1416.

Calvert, Clay. *Voyeur Nation: Media, Privacy, and Peering in Modern Culture*. Boulder, CO: Westview Press, 2004.

Ceaser, James W. "American Exceptionalism: Is It Real, Is It Good? The Origins and Character of American Exceptionalism." *American Political Thought*, 1.1 (Spring 2012): 3–28.

Ceyhan, Ayse. "Surveillance as Biopower." *Routledge Handbook of Surveillance Studies*. Eds. Kristie Ball, Kevin D. Haggerty, and David Lyon. London: Routledge, 2012: 38–46.

City of Vice. Directed by Justin Hardy and Dan Reed. Written by Clive Bradley and Peter Harness. Starring Ian McDiarmid and Iain Glen. Aired in 2008 on Channel 4.

Clarke, Harold D., Matthew Goodwin, and Paul Whiteley. "Why Britain Voted for Brexit: An Individual-Level Analysis of the 2016 Referendum Vote." *Parliamentary Affairs*, 70 (2017): 439–464.

Clarke, Stewart. "Britain Calls for Continued European Access for Broadcasters Post-Brexit." *Variety*, Mar. 2, 2018. https://variety.com/2018/tv/news/britain-theresa-may-brexit-tv-channels-broadcasters-europe-1202715473/.

Clossick, John. "British Values, Western Barbarity." *The Socialist Review*, Jan. 2017. http://socialistreview.org.uk/420/british-values-western-barbarity.

Coaffee, Jon. "Fortification, Fragmentation and the Threat of Terrorism in the City of London in the 1990s." *Landscapes of Defence*. Eds. John Robert Gold and George Revill. London: Routledge, 2000: 114–129.

———. "Rings of Steel, Rings of Concrete and Rings of Confidence: Designing Out Terrorism in Central London Pre and Post September 11th." *International Journal of Urban and Regional Research*, 28.1 (March 2004): 201–211.

Colley, Linda. *Captives: Britain, Empire, and the World 1600–1850*. New York: Anchor Books, 2007.

Copper. Created by Tom Fontana, Barry Levinson, and Will Rokos. Starring Tom Weston-Jones, Kyle Schmid, and Anastasia Griffith. Aired from 2012–2013 on BBC America.

Covert Affairs. Created by Matt Corman and Chris Ord. Starring Piper Perabo, Christopher Gorham, and Kari Matchett. Aired from 2010 to 2015 on USA.

Crowdy, Terry. *The Enemy Within: A History of Spies, Spymasters and Espionage*. Oxford, UK: Osprey Publishing, 2006.

Daskal, Jennifer. "Don't Close Guantánamo." *The New York Times*, Jan. 10, 2013. https://www.nytimes.com/2013/01/11/opinion/dont-close-guantanamo.html.

Deleuze, Gilles. "Postscript on Control Societies." *Negotiations: 1972–1990*. By Gilles Deleuze. Trans. Martin Joughin. New York: Columbia UP, 1995: 177–182.

———. "Control and Becoming." *Negotiations: 1972–1990*. By Gilles Deleuze. Trans. Martin Joughin. New York: Columbia UP, 1995: 169–176.

Derounian, Kathryn Zabelle. "The Publication, Promotion, and Distribution of Mary Rowlandson's Indian Captivity Narrative in the Seventeenth Century." *Early American Literature*, 23.3 (1988): 239–261

Dixon, Wheeler Winston, ed. *Film and Television After 9/11*. Carbondale: Southern Illinois UP, 2004.

Doran, Sarah. "The Awkward Moment When Peter Capaldi, Steven Moffat, and Mark Gatiss Came Third in a Doctor Who Pub Quiz." *Radio Times*, Nov. 23, 2015. https://www.radiotimes.com/news/2015-11-23/the-awkward-moment-when-peter-capaldi-steven-moffat-and-mark-gatiss-came-third-in-a-doctor-who-pub-quiz/.

Duffy, Niall. "Ask the Experts: The Brexit Effect on UK Production." *Screen Daily*, Sep. 12, 2017. https://www.screendaily.com/features/ask-the-experts-the-brexit-effect-on-uk-production/5122456.article.

Dyer, Geoff, Demetri Sevastopulo, and David J. Lynch. "UK-US Special Relationship Shaky Following Brexit Vote." *Financial Times*, June 26, 2016. https://www.ft.com/content/0c71dc88-3b8b-11e6-9f2c-36b487ebd80a.

Elementary. Created by Robert Doherty. Starring Johnny Lee Miller and Lucy Liu. Aired from 2012 to present on CBS.

Ellis, John. *Seeing Things: Television in the Age of Uncertainty*. London: I.B. Taurus, 2000.

———. *Visible Fictions: Cinema: Television: Video*. London: Routledge, 1982.

Elmer, Greg. "Panopticon—Discipline—Control." *Routledge Handbook of Surveillance Studies*. Eds. Kristie Ball, Kevin D. Haggerty, and David Lyon. London: Routledge, 2012: 21–30.

Fiske, John. *Reading the Popular*. 1989. London: Routledge, 2004.

Foucault, Michel. *Discipline and Punish: The Birth of the Prison*. 1975. Second Vintage Books edition. Trans. Alan Sheridan. New York: Vintage, 1991.

The Frankenstein Chronicles. Benjamin Ross and Barry Langford. Starring Sean Bean and Anna Maxwell-Martin. Aired from 2015 to present on ITV Encore and Netflix.

Fussey, Pete. "Observing Potentiality in the Global City: Surveillance and Counterterrorism in London." *International Criminal Justice Review*, 17.3 (2007): 171–192.

Gilliom, John and Torin Monahan. *SuperVision: An Introduction to the Surveillance Society*. Chicago: U of Chicago P, 2013.

"Guantánamo Remains a Stain on America's Reputation." *The Economist*, Jan. 14, 2017. https://www.economist.com/international/2017/01/14/guantanamo-remains-a-stain-on-americas-reputation.

Hainmüller, Jens and Jan Martin Lemnitzer. "Why Do Europeans Fly Safer? The Politics of Airport Security in Europe and the US." *Terrorism and Political Violence*, 15.4 (2003): 1–36.

Hammond, Phillip, ed. *Screens of Terror: Representations of War and Terrorism in Film and Television Since 9/11*. Bury St. Edmunds, UK: Arima Publishing, 2011.

Hard Time. Produced by part2 pictures. Starring Thurston Moore. Aired from 2009 to present on National Geographic Channel.

Harris, Shane. *The Watchers: The Rise of America's Surveillance State*. New York: Penguin, 2010.

Hartley, John. *Digital Futures for Cultural and Media Studies*. Chichester, UK: Wiley-Blackwell, 2012.

Herman, Susan. *Taking Liberties: The War on Terror and the Erosion of American Democracy*. Oxford: Oxford UP, 2014.

Hilmes, Michelle. *A Transnational History of British and American Broadcasting*. New York: Routledge, 2012.

Hirsch, Afua. "Secret Evidence Imperils the Core Values of British Justice." *The Guardian*, July 16, 2009. https://www.theguardian.com/commentisfree/libertycentral/2009/jul/16/secret-evidence-detention-guantanamo-security.

Holt, J.C. *Magna Carta*. 3rd edition. Cambridge: Cambridge UP, 2015.

Homeland. Developed by Alex Gansa and Howard Gordon. Starring Claire Danes, Mandy Patinkin, and Damian Lewis. Based on the Israeli series *Prisoners of War* by Gideon Raff. Aired from 2011 to 2019 on Showtime.

Hopkins, Nick. "CCTV Cameras on Britain's Roads Capture 26 million Images Every Day." *The Guardian*, Jan. 23, 2014. https://www.theguardian.com/uk-news/2014/jan/23/cctv-cameras-uk-roads-numberplate-recognition.

Hughes-Wilson, John, Colonel. *The Secret State: A History of Intelligence and Espionage*. New York: Pegasus Books, 2016.

"Ignore Obama's Grandstanding and Keep Gitmo Open." *The National Review*, Feb. 24, 2016. https://www.nationalreview.com/2016/02/keep-guantanamo-bay-open/.

Jacoby, Russell. *Social Amnesia: A Critique of Contemporary Psychology*. London: Routledge, 2018.

Jannarone, John. "When Twitter Fans Steer TV." *The Wall Street Journal*, Sep. 17, 2012. https://www.wsj.com/articles/SB10000872396390444772804577623444273016770.

Jenkins, Henry. *Convergence Culture: Where Old and New Media Collide*. New York: New York UP, 2006.

Johnson, E.D.H. "Dickens and His Readers." *The Victorian Web*, Jan. 2000. http://www.victorianweb.org/authors/dickens/edh/3.html.

Johnson, Loch K., ed. "An INS Special Forum: Implications of the Snowden Leaks." *Intelligence and National Security*, 29.6 (2014): 793–810.

Johnston, Phillip. "Britain: The Most Spied on Nation in the World." *The Telegraph*, Nov. 2, 2006. https://www.telegraph.co.uk/news/uknews/1533054/Britain-the-most-spied-on-nation-in-the-world.html.

Kraska, Peter B. "Militarization and Policing—Its Relevance to 21st Century Police." *Policing: A Journal of Policy and Practice*, 1.4 (January 2007): 501–513.

Lacey, Stephen and Derek Paget. "Introduction." *The 'War on Terror': Post 9/11 Television Drama, Docudrama, and Documentary*. Eds. Steven Lacey and Derek Paget. Cardiff: U of Wales P, 2015: 1–10.

————, eds. *The 'War on Terror': Post 9/11 Television Drama, Docudrama, and Documentary*. Cardiff: U of Wales P, 2015.

Laidler, Keith. *Surveillance Unlimited: How We've Become the Most Watched People on Earth*. Cambridge, UK: Icon Books Ltd., 2008.

Landau, Susan. "Making Sense from Snowden: What's Significant in the NSA Revelations." *IEEE Security & Privacy*, 11.4 (2013): 54–63.

Lang, Amy Schrager. "Introduction to A True History of the Captivity and Restoration of Mrs. Mary Rowlandson." *Journeys in New Worlds: Early American Women's Narratives*. Eds. William L. Andrews et al. Madison: U of Wisconsin P, 1990: 11–26.

Lavigne, Carlen and Heather Marcovitch, eds. *American Remakes of British Television: Transformations and Mistranslations*. Lanham, MD: Lexington Books, 2011.

Lefait, Sébastian. *Surveillance on Screen: Monitoring Contemporary Films and Television Programs*. Lanham, MD: Scarecrow Press, 2013.

Life on Mars. (UK Version). Created by Matthew Graham, Tony Jordan, and Ashley Pharoah. Starring John Simm, Philip Glenister, and Liz White. Aired from 2006 to 2007 on BBC1.

————. (US Version). Developed by Josh Appelbaum, André Nemec, and Scott Rosenberg. Starring Jason O'Mara, Harvey Keitel, and Jonathan Murphy. Aired from 2008 to 2009 on ABC.

Lipset, Seymour Martin. *American Exceptionalism: A Double-Edged Sword*. New York: Norton, 1996.

Locked Up Abroad (Banged Up Abroad). Created by Bart Layton. Aired from 2007 to present on National Geographic Channel and Channel 5.

Lockhart, Charles. *The Roots of American Exceptionalism: Institutions, Culture and Policies*. London: Palgrave Macmillan, 2003.

Lockup. Created by Rasha Drachkovitch. Aired from 2005 to 2017 on MSNBC.

London Spy. Created by Tom Rob Smith. Starring Ben Whishaw, Jim Broadbent, and Edward Holcroft. Aired in 2015 on BBC2.

Lotz, Amanda D., ed. *Beyond Prime Time: Television Programming in the Post-Network Era*. London: Routledge, 2009.

————. *Redesigning Women: Television after the Network Era*. Urbana: U of Illinois P, 2006.

————. *The Television Will Be Revolutionized*. New York: New York UP, 2007.

————. "Using 'Network' Theory in the Post-Network Era: Fictional 9/11 U.S. Television Discourse as a 'Cultural Forum'." *Screen*, 45.4 (Winter 2004): 423–439.

Lyon, David. "Airports as Data Filters: Converging Surveillance Systems after September 11th." *Journal of Information, Communication and Ethics in Society*, 1.1 (2003): 13–20.

———. "A Short History of Surveillance and Privacy in the United States." *Engaging Privacy and Information Technology in a Digital Age*. Eds. James Waldo, Herbert S. Lin, and Lynette I. Millett. Washington, DC: National Academies Press, 2007: 349–365.

———. *Surveillance After September 11*. Cambridge, UK: Polity, 2003.

———. *Surveillance Studies: An Overview*. Cambridge, UK: Polity, 2007.

Madsen, Deborah L. *American Exceptionalism*. Jackson: U of Mississippi P, 1998.

The Man from U.N.C.L.E. Created by Sam Rolfe. Starring Robert Vaughn, David McCallum, and Leo G. Carroll. Aired from 1964 to 1968 on NBC.

Marks, Peter. *Imagining Surveillance: Eutopian and Dystopian Literature and Film*. Edinburgh: Edinburgh UP, 2015.

Matiesen, Thomas. "The Viewer Society: Michel Foucault's 'Panopticon' Revisited." *Theoretical Criminology*, 1.2 (1997): 215–232.

McClusky, Brian. "221B-9/11: Sherlock Holmes and Conspiracy Theory." *Transatlantic Literature and Culture After 9/11: The Wrong Side of Paradise*. Ed. Kristine A. Miller. London: Palgrave Macmillan, 2014: 50–67.

McGowan, Casey J. "The Relevance of Relevance: Section 215 of the USA PATRIOT Act and the NSA Metadata Collection Program." *Fordham Law Review*, 82 (2014): 2399.

McGrath, John E. *Loving Big Brother: Performance, Privacy and Surveillance Space*. London: Routledge, 2004.

———. "Performing Surveillance." *Routledge Handbook of Surveillance Studies*. Eds. Kristie Ball, Kevin D. Haggerty, and David Lyon. London: Routledge, 2012: 83–90.

Meeks, Daryl. "Police Militarization in Urban Areas: The Obscure War Against the Underclass." *The Black Scholar*, 35.4 (2006): 33–41.

Meyer, David. "Top European Court Says British Spies Broke Human Rights Rules with Their Mass Surveillance Tactics." *Fortune*, Sep. 13, 2018. http://fortune.com/2018/09/13/european-court-human-rights-uk-gchq-mass-surveillance/.

Meyer, Jane. "Outsourcing Torture: The Secret History of America's 'extraordinary rendition' Program." *The New Yorker*, Feb. 14, 2005. https://www.newyorker.com/magazine/2005/02/14/outsourcing-torture.

Miller, Jeffrey S. *Something Completely Different: British Television and American Culture*. Minneapolis: U of Minnesota P, 2000.

Miller, Kristine A. *Transatlantic Literature and Culture After 9/11: The Wrong Side of Paradise*. London: Palgrave Macmillan, 2014.

Miller, Nathan. *Spying for America: The Hidden History of U.S. Intelligence*. New York: Paragon House, 1989.

Miller, Toby. *Television Studies: The Basics*. London: Routledge, 2010.

Mission: Impossible. Created by Bruce Geller. Starring Peter Graves, Barbara Bain, and Greg Morris. Aired from 1966–1973 on CBS.

Moran, Jade. "A Brief Chronology of Photographic and Video Surveillance." *Surveillance, Closed Circuit Television and Social Control*. Eds. Clive Norris and Jade Moran. London: Routledge, 2016: 277–287.

Murdoch Mysteries. Developed by R.B. Carney, Cal Coons, and Alexandra Zarowny. Starring Yannick Bisson, Hélène Joy, and Thomas Craig. Based on the novels by Maureen Jennings. Aired from 2008 to present on Citytv and CBC.

Neuman, Scott. "Trump Signs Order to Keep Prison at Guantanamo Bay Open." *NPR News*, Jan. 31, 2018. https://www.npr.org/sections/thetwo-way/2018/01/31/582033937/trump-signs-order-to-keep-prison-at-guantanamo-bay-open.

The Night Manager. Screenplay by David Farr. Directed by Susanne Bier. Starring Tom Hiddleston, Hugh Laurie, and Olivia Colman. Based on the novel *The Night Manager* by John le Carré. Aired 2016 on BBC 1 and AMC.

The Night of .... Created by Richard Price and Steve Zaillian. Starring John Turturro and Riz Ahmed. Aired in 2016 on HBO.

O'Connor, Alan. *Raymond Williams on Television: Selected Writings*. London: Routledge, 1989.

"On Torture and American Values." *New York Times*, Oct. 7, 2007. https://www.nytimes.com/2007/10/07/opinion/07sun1.html.

Orange Is the New Black. Created by Jenji Kohan. Starring Taylor Schilling, Danielle Brooks, and Taryn Manning. First released in 2013 by Netflix.

Oz. Created by Tom Fontana. Starring Ernie Hudson, J.K. Simmons, and Lee Tergesen. Aired from 1997 to 2003 on HBO.

Paget, Derek. "Ways of Showing, Ways of Telling: Television and 9/11." *The 'War on Terror': Post 9/11 Television Drama, Docudrama, and Documentary*. Eds. Steven Lacey and Derek Paget. Cardiff: U of Wales P, 2015: 11–32.

Palomaki, Kya. "It's Time to Close Guantanamo Bay." *International Policy Digest*, Mar. 11, 2017. https://intpolicydigest.org/2017/03/11/time-to-close-guantanamo-bay/.

Parenti, Christian. *The Soft Cage: Surveillance in America from Slavery to the War on Terror*. Cambridge, MA: Basic Books, 2003.

Patankar Manoj S. and Louis Holscher. "Accessibility Vs Security: The Challenge to Airport Security Systems." *Security Journal*, 13.2 (2000): 7–19.

Person of Interest. Created by Jonathan Nolan. Starring Jim Caviezel, Michael Emerson, and Taraji P. Henderson. Aired from 2011 to 2016 on CBS.

Peterson, J.K. *Introduction to Surveillance Studies*. New York: CRC Press, 2013.

Prison Break. Created by Paul Scheuring. Starring Dominic Purcell, Wentworth Miller, and Amaury Nolasco. Aired from 2005–2009 and in 2017 on Fox.

Ripper Street. Created by Richard Warlow. Starring Matthew Macfadyen, Jerome Flynn, Adam Rothenberg, and MyAnna Buring. Aired from 2012 to 2016 on BB1, BBC2, and Amazon Video.

Rixon, Paul. *American Television on British Screens: A Story of Cultural Interaction*. London: Palgrave Macmillan, 2006.

Rose, Alexander. *Washington's Spies: The Story of America's First Spy Ring*. New York: Bantam, 2006.

Rosen, David and Aaron Santesso. *The Watchman in Pieces: Surveillance, Literature, and Liberal Personhood*. New Haven: Yale UP, 2013.

Rosen, Jeffrey and Benjamin Wittes, eds. *Constitution 3.0: Freedom and Technological Change*. Washington, DC: The Brookings Institute, 2011.

Sherlock. Created by Steven Moffat and Mark Gatiss. Starring Benedict Cumberbatch and Martin Freeman. Aired from 2010 to 2017 on BBC1 and PBS.

"Should Guantanamo Bay Be Closed?" *Council on Foreign Relations*, Jan. 20, 2010. https://www.cfr.org/expert-roundup/should-guantanamo-bay-be-closed.

Smith, Michael. *The Spying Game: The Secret History of British Espionage*. London: Politico's Publishing, 2004.

Snoddy, Ray. "Brexit: What Leaving the EU Could Mean for the Broadcast Industry." *IBC*, Nov. 17, 2017. https://www.ibc.org/production/brexit-what-leaving-the-eu-could-mean-for-the-broadcast-industry/2545.article.

Spiegel, Lynn. "Introduction." *Television After TV: Essays on a Medium in Transition*. Durham: Duke UP, 2004: 1–34.

Spiegel, Lynn and Jan Olsson, eds. *Television After TV: Essays on a Medium in Transition*. Durham: Duke UP, 2004.

Spooks (Mi-5). Created by David Wollstencroft. Starring Peter Firth, Hugh Simon, and Nicola Walker. Aired from 2002 to 2011 on BBC1.

Staples, William G. *Everyday Surveillance: Vigilance and Visibility in Postmodern Life*. 2nd edition. Lanham, MD: Rowan and Littlefield, 2014.

Stewart, Garrett. *Closed Circuits: Screening Narrative Surveillance*. Chicago: U of Chicago P, 2015.

Strangeways. Produced by Wild Pictures. Aired in 2011 on ITV.

Sulick, Michael J. *Spying in America: Espionage from the Revolutionary War to the Dawn of the Cold War*. Georgetown: Georgetown UP, 2012.

Sweet, Kathleen. *Aviation and Airport Security: Terrorism and Safety Concerns*. New York: CRC Press, 2008.

Sweet, Matthew. "Sherlock: How It Became A Global Phenomenon." *The Telegraph*, Dec. 27, 2013. https://www.telegraph.co.uk/culture/tvandradio/10501730/Sherlock-how-it-became-a-global-phenomenon.html.

Takacs, Stacey. *Terrorism TV: Popular Entertainment in Post-9/11 America*. Lawrence: U of Kansas P, 2012.

Tilford, Simon. "The British and Their Exceptionalism." *The Centre for European Reform*, May 3, 2017. https://www.cer.eu/insights/british-and-their-exceptionalism.

Trade, Development, and the Environment: The Role of the FCO [Foreign and Commonwealth Office]: Fifth Report of the Session 2006–07. The House of Commons, 2007.

Traffic Cops. Produced by Craig Duncan. Starring Jamie Threakston. Aired from 2003 to present on BBC1, BBC2, and Channel 5.

Turn: Washington's Spies. Created by Craig Silverstein. Starring Jamie Bell, Heather Lind, and Samuel Roukin. Aired from 2014 to 2017 on AMC.

Vanden Heuvel, Katrina. "Why We Must Close Guantanamo Bay Now." *The Washington Post*, Mar. 1, 2016. https://www.washingtonpost.com/opinions/why-we-must-close-guantanamo-now/2016/03/01/fe829b80-df0a-11e5-846c-10191d1fc4ec_story.html?utm_term=.fce5ad6b6fe9.

Vasilopoulou, Sofia. "UK Euroscepticism and the Brexit Referendum." *The Political Quarterly*, 87.2 (April–June 2016): 219–227.

Volkman, Ernest. *The History of Espionage: The Clandestine World of Surveillance, Spying and Intelligence from Ancient Times to the Post-9/11 World*. London: Carlton Books, 2007.

Warner, Michael. *The Rise and Fall of Intelligence: An International Security History*. Georgetown: Georgetown UP, 2014.

Weissmann, Elke. *Transnational Television Drama: Special Relations and Mutual Influence Between the U.S. and U.K*. London: Palgrave Macmillan, 2012.

Wentworth (Wentworth Prison). Created by Lara Radulovich and Reg Watson. Starring Kate Atkinson, Celia Ireland, and Robbie Magasiva. First released in 2013 by SoHo (Australia) and Netflix.

Whitechapel. Created by Ben Court and Caroline Ip. Starring Rupert Penry-Jones, Phil Davis, and Steve Pemberton. Aired from 2009 to 2013 on ITV.

Wilkinson, Paul and Brian Jenkins. *Aviation Terrorism and Security*. London: Routledge, 2013.

Williams, Michael John. "Special Relationships in Flux: Brexit and the Future of the US–EU and US–UK Relationships." *International Affairs*, 92.3 (May 2016): 547–567.

Williams, Raymond. "Television and Teaching." Interview by Richard Collins, James Donald, Simon Frith, and Jim Grealy (uncredited). *Screen Education*, 31 (Summer 1979): 5–14.

Winthrop, John. *A Modell of Christian Charity*. 1630. Collections of the Massachusetts Historical Society, Boston, 1838. 3rd series 7:31–48. Hanover Historical Texts Collection. Scanned by Monica Banas. August 1996. https://history.hanover.edu/texts/winthmod.html.

Zimmer, Catherine. *Surveillance Cinema*. New York: New York UP, 2015.

CHAPTER 2

Captive Viewing: Prisons, Surveillance, and Social Control

In this chapter, I will examine post-9/11 British and American television programs about one of the least understood apparatuses of surveillance and social control, the prison, as well as the historical imprisonment and captivity narratives on which these programs draw and by which they are inspired. We must appreciate these sources because they influence how we tell modern stories about the place and purpose of the prison in the U.S. and U.K. and how this apparatus pertains to our own need to surveil the ways in which the state uses the prison to regulate and monitor its citizens. Since, as Jan Alber observes, "most people lack first-hand experience of the prison and gain their 'knowledge' through indirect means, it is of primary importance to deal with fictional representations of the prison to get an understanding of how the prison has entered the cultural subconscious."[1] Further, for my purposes, given that Foucault's foundational theory of government and social surveillance is based on the structure and function of the panoptic prison, it is well that we begin our discussion of television programs about surveillance and social control here.

Pre-9/11 Prison Series, Surveillance, and Social Control

As noted in Chap. 1, transatlantic television programs about the prison were sparse until after 9/11. Before 2001, a few fictional prison programs ran mainly in the U.K. and Australia. One, a comedy, *Porridge*, was a

© The Author(s) 2019   55
D. Rives-East, *Surveillance and Terror in Post-9/11 British and
American Television*,
https://doi.org/10.1007/978-3-030-16900-8_2

popular staple on BBC1 from 1974–1977, with a revival series in 2017. Another, the soap-opera *Prisoner*, began as an Australian production on Network Ten, and, retitled in the U.K. and the U.S. as *Prisoner: Cell Block H*, ran from 1979–1986. This series should not be confused with *The Prisoner* (ITV, U.K.; CBS, U.S.) (1967–1968), created by and starring Patrick McGoohan as a retired spy confined by a mysterious entity to an island until he reveals the reason for his resignation from espionage. While this program does focus on surveillance and imprisonment, I will not discuss it in this chapter in favor of those drama and docuseries, such as *Prisoner: Cell Block H*, which depict prison realism. *Prisoner* was based on the British drama *Within These Walls*, a drama centered on prison staff rather than prisoners, which appeared on ITV from 1974–1979. This lack of Anglo-American television series about the prison can be attributed in part to the abject nature of the apparatus: it is a place whose goal, in part, is to "incapacitate" those whom society has deemed "deviant" and "dangerous criminals."[2] In this way, the state, via the prison, controls and monitors the public by separating out populations that are productive from those who are considered unproductive and, moreover, unsafe: "Whatever else, incarceration serves to remove a potential offender from the community."[3]

Because narrating the prison means telling the stories of those whom viewers might deem offensive or unworthy because of their crimes, such series can require viewers both to identify and to empathize with the very people they wish to ignore or believe deserve to be ignored. Overcoming this antipathy can be a tough proposition for writers and producers who wish to explore the prison apparatus and pitch their series to a wary broadcast network dependent on ad revenue. As Bradford Winters, a writer for HBO's prison drama *Oz*, states, the prison is not "a sacred space" like the hospitals, court rooms, and police precincts of other, more common dramas which focus on institutions that also monitor and control populations.[4] Certainly, this disinterest in prison television series is evident by their lack prior to 9/11.

An analysis of *Porridge* and its comedic take on prison life could occupy an entire volume in and of itself.[5] Important for my purposes is Julien Pettifer's argument that the comedy allows for the real and often dire conditions of prisons to be glossed over so that the prison becomes more palatable for the audience. Pettifer writes that "[i]t is a measure of the success of Ronnie Barker [the lead actor] and scriptwriters Dick Clement and Ian La Frenais that they have been able to take a situation as profoundly disturbing and unfunny as imprisonment and make it very, very amusing and unthreatening."[6] To support his contention that British prisons are problematic, Pettifer refers to a BBC *Panorama* program on the bleak incarceration conditions in the U.K. He cites interviews in that program in which inmates relate that they feel treated like "animals" and that incarceration has not led to reformation, but to a desire for "revenge" for having been locked away.[7] Further, inmates refer to a "state of war" between the "cons" (inmates) and the "screws" (the prison officers).[8] By contrast, Pettifer comments that "[a]ccording to Tom Mangold [investigative journalist for BBC's *Panorama*], prison officers thoroughly approve of *Porridge*, and in this view it does a very useful public relations job for them by distracting the public from the reality and magnitude of the crisis inside."[9] In other words, according to Pettifer, the comedy of *Porridge* makes prison seem innocuous and affable, rather than a punitive state surveillance apparatus. In this way, *Porridge* works similarly to several of the post-9/11 prison programs I discuss in this chapter, in that it can reconcile the audience to the prison apparatus; to put another way, the prison, particularly in the U.S. and U.K., is made out to be a relatively enlightened space (particularly in comparison with prisons in non-Western nations). But, like many post-9/11 prison programs, *Porridge* distracts from very real issues in U.S. and U.K. prisons, such as prison overcrowding (which is still a major problem for both nations, particularly the U.S.).

Further, while pre-9/11 series like *Prisoner* depict real issues associated with incarceration, it is notable that most involve women in prison, apart from *Porridge*'s comedic take on prison life. That is, before 9/11, only women's imprisonment was presented dramatically and with grittier realism. This gender disparity suggests how, prior to 9/11, viewers and networks alike did not take seriously the larger cultural issues raised by the existence of the prison, including its purpose, given that prisons are frequently unsuccessful at either deterring crime or rehabilitating inmates, the two often stated primary goals of the modern penal institution[10]; instead, it became a space for voyeurism of female sexuality.

The appeal of female incarceration for viewers is a prurient one in which women's bodies become available for surveillance and are placed within not only confining, but also homoerotic contexts—something that would be less acceptable if those bodies were male. Rob Cope notes that Grundy Television [Australia] "tried to launch an all-male version [of *Prisoner*] called *Punishment*, but it failed despite featuring a youthful Mel Gibson."[11] I would contend that its failure was due to discomfort with homosocial, homoerotic, and homosexual relations between male prisoners, which is not constructed by Western culture as "reclaimable" as is lesbian sexuality. Further, female bodies have long been the subject of the male-dominated cultural gaze, not male ones. A prison drama like HBO's *Oz* overturns this script so that male bodies become the focus of surveillance and policing— to wit, male bodies become feminized and thus disempowered. Therefore, it is not surprising that it was not until *Oz*—a pay-cable program rather than one on a more widely viewed network channel—that a serious prison drama about men was successfully produced.

By fusing sexuality, criminality, and surveillance (both within the program and on the part of the viewer), female-focused prison dramas reinforce the criminality of female sexuality and its threatening nature, as well as the cultural norm that sexuality is something only "bad" girls express. At the same time, an argument can be made that *Prisoner: Cell Block H* at least made lesbian sexuality visible during the still-closeted 1980s. For example, Rose Collis writes, "During the past year alone, British audiences have seen multi-dimensional (i.e., non-predatory) lesbians in episodes of 'Golden Girls,' 'Kate and Allie,' and 'Hill Street Blues.' And let's not forget the surprise cult hit of the year, Australia's 'Prisoner: Cell Block H'."[12] Collins describes how the program has become popular among lesbian viewers because, despite its prurient aspect, the series still makes queer women feel seen and acknowledged. She cites two women who founded a *Prisoner* fan club who contend that "'The Frankie Doyle character (a Butch prisoner, shot on the run) broke so much new ground. […] Sure, the series is trashy but it is actually really well-researched. We think it has the best portrayal of lesbians ever seen on the small screen'."[13] Here, even the program's fans in the 1980s acknowledged the exploitative, voyeuristic nature of the program (i.e., its "trashiness"), but it still offered ways for lesbian viewers to have their sexuality recognized and validated by the drama.

Such surveillance of female bodies and queer sexuality becomes pleasurable and enticing, yet safe because it is displaced onto a prison background. The prison setting further allows viewers to voyeuristically experience BDSM sexuality, with dominance and submission taking place between and among prisoners and prison guards. That is, the audience can enjoy a kind of prurient female sexuality and suggestion of kink within regulated bounds, given that the confines of the prison within the narrative not only contains the inmates but also, narratively, the sexuality as well. We, as viewers, could therefore "visit" the prison, engage momentarily in kink or lesbian sexuality, and then leave again, to resume our supposedly "normal" heterosexual, monogamous sexual lives.

Despite their voyeurism, programs like *Prisoner: Cell Block H* do offer an account of prison space and the issues of incarceration. *Prisoner* and *Porridge* both visualize the panoptic nature of the prison, in which everyone is involved in a surveillance culture within the prison apparatus: guards watch prisoners, prisoners watch prisoners, and prisoners watch guards. Rob Cope, for instance, remarks on the claustrophobic atmosphere of *Prisoner*: "What set the series apart from its contemporaries was that the central characters were in a no escape situation, they couldn't catch a plane or move to another town, so the tensions were always a little short of boiling point, where the only threat greater than that of a fellow inmate was the presence of a handful of warders,"[14] and Bernard Davies similarly writes of *Porridge*, "What is [...] remarkable, however, is the way in which they [the writers] managed this claustrophobic atmosphere of their locale. Prison is by definition an enclosed place."[15] All actions, bodies, and sexualities are monitored within the fictional prison space as well by the voyeuristic eye of the viewer. In this way, the television prison in these series anticipate a more nuanced model of contemporary surveillance. For Foucault, the panoptic model of surveillance and social control involves the guards watching the prisoners; however, *Prisoner* and *Porridge* narrate a more complex version of the prison in which everyone monitors everyone else—the guards are watched as much as the prisoners. This model is much more like the surveillance society we currently participate in, a synoptic-panoptic mode in which state apparatuses monitor citizens, citizens monitor the state, and citizens monitor one another.[16] In these television narratives, the guards and the prisoners are more intertwined in their actions and relationships than in Foucault's model, and this is true outside the television space as well: the state apparatus and the public are interconnected in daily life and have reciprocal relationships, from the police and intelligence services who depend on information from the public to the public who films and disseminates the actions of state apparatuses over social media, thus forcing those apparatuses to function in different ways.

GUANTANAMO BAY, ANGLO-AMERICAN EXCEPTIONALISM, AND THE RISE IN PRISON SERIES POST-9/11

It is this last point that I argue explains a recent increase in television series about the prison and captivity more generally. As Jacob Rama Berman notes, "[t]he figure of the captive has emerged again at the crux of present contestations over the meaning of American democracy, playing a role in claims used alternately to justify and castigate the U.S. military mission against an Islamic enemy."[17] Following 9/11, the U.S. and U.K. reacted to the threat of al-Qaeda by participating in extra-legal imprisonment of potential terror suspects at the U.S. Naval base in Guantanamo Bay, Cuba.[18] Because Guantanamo Bay, nicknamed Gitmo, functions outside the official legal jurisdiction of the U.S. (and U.K.) justice system, these suspected terrorists could be held without recourse to the constitutional requirements of habeas corpus and the right to a speedy trial. In other words, they could be incarcerated indefinitely without due process. The rationale behind Gitmo was that extraordinary times called for extraordinary measures. Terror suspects needed to be found and imprisoned for American and British national safety, and the legal system was too slow and could potentially allow suspects to go free for lack of evidence.

While in the immediate wake of 9/11, public fear in large part allowed the Bush administration to commit such extra-legal actions, as the years wore on, the public and critics alike began to resist the creation and sustainment of Gitmo (which is still currently operating). For these critics, this military prison stood and still stands as an affront to the narrative of American and British exceptionalism; that is, if such exceptionalism is based on an exemplary Anglo-American system of justice, then Gitmo tarnished this reputation for these nations whose legal systems were supposedly more just and rational than those in countries with more totalitarian regimes. Berman writes that "[d]ebates about the moral justifications for captivity have become global, with Arabic television networks and some European networks juxtaposing U.S. complaints about war crimes committed against American soldiers with images and discussions of the indefinite incarceration of Muslim prisoners at the U.S. naval base at Guantanamo Bay, Cuba."[19] To wit, the U.S. and U.K. were becoming like the same regimes (such as those of Iraq or Iran) they feared and wanted to defeat. However, Gitmo has remained open because the debate between national safety and civil liberties is still contentious 17 years later. Those in Congress who want to keep it open have done so out of concern that the Gitmo inmates will return to their ostensible terror organizations to carry out attacks if released.

Therefore, I trace the rise in prison and captivity-themed programs since 9/11 to concern and unease regarding the nature of imprisonment in the U.S. and U.K. Instead of narrating Gitmo specifically, these post-9/11 programs have instead turned a panoptic eye onto the prison apparatus in developing world nations, as well as within Britain and America, in both fictional and docuseries programs. I argue this panoptic gaze is driven by a desire on the part of writers, producers, and viewers to see, monitor, and examine the prison system at home and abroad in the years after the establishment of Gitmo. The series and their viewers seek to understand if our prison apparatus is as just as the American and British exceptionalist narratives would have us believe. Further, they want to understand the following questions about the Anglo-American prison apparatus: "What are prisons for? What purposes do they serve? In what conditions should the prisoners be held? What are prisoners obliged to do, and to forfeit?"[20] Therefore, the television series since 9/11 have narrated captivity in various and complex ways, in which there is both reassurance but also criticism of Anglo-American prison systems which can function in harsh, punitive ways that do not rehabilitate but merely house and/or exacerbate the issues that have led inmates to commit crimes in the first place—or, as with Gitmo, there are those held unjustly by the system. These critical narratives question the exceptionalist nature of the U.S. and U.K. prison and justice systems, and they suggest that spaces such as Gitmo might be more of an extension, rather than an aberration, of these systems and their methods of social control. However, the questioning of this exceptionalism via prison and captivity narratives is not a new in either Britain or America. Imprisonment and captivity have long been spaces in which to wrestle with the idea of Anglo-American exceptionalism and with what it means for the Anglo-American state to monitor and regulate its population. For example, Catherine Scott, in writing about captivity narratives produced by American embassy employees held hostage in 1980 by Iranian university students, comments that such accounts "provid[e] important insights into wider cultural concerns about American [and Western] power and standing in the world, relations with other countries, reactions to Third World revolutions, and the continuing vitality of American mythologies about its exceptionalism and mission."[21] Scott succinctly sums up the idea of American exceptionalism that resides at the core of written and visual prison and captivity narratives: "Fundamental to these formulations is the notion of American [and Western] specialness [...], its basic goodness."[22] In other words, because of its exceptionalism, the Anglo-American state can supposedly be trusted to surveil and imprison in humane ways and for just and fair reasons.

Captivity Narratives and Anxieties About
Exceptionalism, Slavery, and Social Control

Such formulations can be traced to captivity narratives written in the seventeenth century by British and British-American former captives and prisoners who were held by nations or groups with whom Britain and other European powers were in conflict, such as the Barbary States of the north coast of Africa (which were, in turn, part of the Muslim Ottoman Empire) and Native American societies in northeast America. To truly understand the connections between modern captivity and prison television series and these older texts, it is first necessary to take the time to appreciate the basic aspects and narrative arc of Puritan and Barbary captivity narratives and their similarities to those of modern series about captivity and imprisonment. Therefore, I will first discuss the connections between captivity narratives, then and now, before returning to how both served and continue to assist in narrating state surveillance and social control as it relates to imprisonment.

As Benjamin Mark Allen and Dahia Messara point out, the line between incarceration and captivity is a blurred one: "When dealing with captivity narratives, scholars tend to cross back and forth between actual physical captivity or imprisonment [...] and the various nuances and interpretations of the different aspects of that captivity" which include "not only the physical but rather psychological and cultural dimensions as well."[23] Therefore, it makes sense that post-9/11 prison narratives should find their roots in stories of captivity that existed beyond formal prison walls and cells, but which were, like incarceration at Gitmo, political in nature, given that captives were often taken as hostages or spoils in times of war and conflict. We should note that these Barbary and Puritan captivity narratives were transatlantic best-sellers, with readership in Britain, the British-American colonies, and beyond.[24] These narratives tell similar accounts of a British or British-American citizen taken captive by either Barbary corsairs or Native Americans, and they narrate the writer's story of their survival during imprisonment. The narratives often contrast a civilized, structured, and rationally controlled state based on religious Christian morals (i.e., Britain or the British colonies), with those that are conversely barbaric, non-Christian, and disorganized (i.e., Native Americans or Muslim Barbary states). My purpose here is not to enter into a close study of Puritan and Barbary captivity narratives, which has been done better and more ably by other scholars.[25] Rather, I am interested in the captivity narrative's account of the space and function of imprisonment that sets the stage for wrangling with Anglo-American exceptionalism in prison and captivity television series in the years post-9/11.

As other scholars have noted, both older and modern captivity and prison narratives employ what Edward Said termed "Orientalism." For example, in discussing the modern captivity narrative of Private Jessica Lynch during the Iraq War, Stacey Takacs nicely summarizes Orientalism as a Western ideology "predicated upon the distinction between the West (the Occident) and the East (the Orient). The Orient is both a material space and an imaginary construct whose purpose is to give coherence to the image of the West [...]. Specifically, Orientalism seeks to identify the West with civilization by coding the East as barbaric."[26] In this way, the Orientalist captivity or prison narrative, which is seemingly about the non-Western Other, is in truth about "standard beliefs about American [and Western] identity."[27] Even in early Puritan and Barbary captivity stories, when American identity was nascent, the purpose was still to frame what it meant to be an American colonist or a British citizen: "[T]he image of the Arab [and the Native American] became the exotic vehicle through which Anglo-Americans navigated anxieties [...] inherent in the formation of early American citizenship."[28] Such anxiety included contradictions to the ostensibly exceptionalist British and early American states and their actions with regard to social control.

For example, the Arab and Native populations were constructed as uncivilized in their treatment of their captives or prisoners. In captivity narratives, we read depictions of the brutal treatment of captives, such as Mary Rowlandson's account of Narragansett warriors smashing babies' heads ("a sucking Child, they knocked on the head")[29] or supposedly celebrating the death of a pregnant woman and her child ("[they] gathered a great company together about her, and stript her naked, and set her in the midst of them; and when they had sung and danced about her (in their hellish manner) as long as they pleased; they knockt [sic] her on the head, and the child in her arms with her").[30] Further, captives are often not allowed food or rest, and are abused physically, psychologically, and verbally. Rowlandson attributes this treatment to Natives' non-Christian and non-white status, which de facto makes them demonic and barbaric in her cultural lens. For instance, she consistently employs descriptors such as "heathen," "hellish," "barbarous creatures," and "infidels," implying that her own Puritan community is the opposite.

The latter term, "infidel," is significant, given that it demonstrates Berman's point that the Barbary captivity narratives conflated Native

American with Muslim Arabs to construct both as uncivilized compared with their American Christian captives: "[In his narrative, Dr. Jonathon] Cowdery [a former captive] pushes these Arabized Berbers, or berberized Arabs, into the literal and figurative 'back country.' They are backward in relation to civilization, described, as were Natives of the American frontier, as existing on the fringe of the modern world."[31] In addition, Berman makes the interesting point that the Berbers of the Barbary states were often also constructed as simultaneously European [i.e., not Anglo-American] "in their degeneracy and decadence."[32] This oppositional positioning of Muslim Arabs allowed the Barbary narratives to thus "[clear] the space between savagery and overcivilization for American identity to flourish."[33] Like Goldilocks, America was "just right": it was civilized enough without losing any physical vigor and vitality. In this way, America crafted its exceptionalist image as tough and bold, yet fair and just, one that appeals to Americans still.

We see in these narratives the creation of an opposition between what today we would call Western and non-Western culture (included here would be Native American societies which reside outside Eurocentric culture even if located geographically in the West). For example, while Rowlandson terms the Narragansetts as "infidels" and "heathens," she clearly demarcates herself and her fellow white Puritans as "Christians," which, in her paradigm, connotes all that is civilized and godly. In such ways, the Puritan and Barbary narratives present the West as enlightened, and it is constructed as such through how non-Westerners behave and treat their prisoners. In this way, imprisonment becomes a means of narrating Anglo-American exceptionalism; the implication is that Anglo-Americans would not treat their captives or prisoners in comparable ways.

And yet, the anxiety about Anglo-American identity that pervades the captivity narratives can be traced back in part to not-so-enlightened practices of imprisonment and punishment meted out by the Anglo-American state. This is not to argue that writers like Rowlandson or Cowdery were thinking consciously of the state's punitive methods when crafting their narratives. Rather, former captives could have formed, following their own brutal imprisonment, unspoken concerns about the harsh and often unjust practices of their own societies in controlling inmates and punishing those who broke the law—especially since such practices could undermine their own beliefs in Anglo-American superiority over those cultures that were non-white and non-Christian.

Certainly, as Baepler writes, Barbary captivity narratives led some British-American citizens to "question America's decision to encourage human bondage."[34] Slavery, whether in Barbary or in America, was a form of state-sanctioned imprisonment, and, as some recognized, if it was wrong for Americans to be enslaved in Barbary, then it was equally wrong for Africans to be enslaved in America. Baepler notes that Puritan judge Samuel Sewell, who worked to free American Joshua Gee from Barbary captivity, wrote an anti-slavery tract in 1707 in which he "suggests that the colonists are complicit in Barbary captivity by holding African slaves in America."[35] Slavery was not the only imprisonment that contradicted claims to Anglo-American exceptionalism, however. Prior to calls for prison reform in the late seventeenth century, "[p]unishment in English criminal law [which would have regulated the American colonies initially as well] was intended to be quick and public to serve as a deterrent to crime."[36] As Edward M. Peters points out, imprisonment in the late seventeenth and early eighteenth centuries could include a "wider category of physical punishments that restrict an individual's freedom of movement" than simply being confined to cells.[37] As such, imprisonment and punishment by the state would include using public surveillance by putting wrongdoers on "shaming display" through "the pillory, mutilation, branding, public stocks, and ducking stools" and public capital punishments like "hanging, drowning, burning, burial alive, or decapitation."[38]

In this way, the populace functioned as part of the state surveillance apparatus to watch and censure fellow citizens. Actual prisons themselves were unpleasant, in which common rooms housed prisoners without separating inmates according to age, gender, or severity of crime. Further, prisons often housed debtors who were incarcerated for not being able to make their loan payments. In these ways, imprisonment and captivity in Britain and the American colonies was certainly not more "enlightened" than the treatment captives received among Native people or Barbary pirates. As such, we can draw a parallel between the anxieties regarding state use of imprisonment and punishment among British and British-Americans of the late seventeenth and early eighteenth centuries and similar concerns for U.S. and U.K. citizens about their own government's use of surveillance, imprisonment, and punishment in the name of "homeland security" in the years following 9/11.

SURVEILLANCE AND A COVENANT WITH GOD

The Puritan and Barbary captivity narratives surveilled non-Western captors and their methods of imprisonment in order to find evidence of their uncivilized and uncontrolled natures. The same was true post-9/11, during which the pervading rhetoric framed Islamic extremist groups in similar terms. For example, President George W. Bush characterized al-Qaeda in ways analogous to the captivity narratives' construction of Native Americans and Barbary States by describing the organization as similarly barbaric, immoral, and unregulated. In his speech shortly after 9/11, Bush characterized the nations aligned with the U.S. against al-Qaeda as the "civilized world,"[39] while terrorists were "the enemies of freedom," and the "mafia," who were "plot[ting] evil and destruction," thus demarcating America from radical Islam as Rowlandson, Cowdery, and other writers did so between the U.S. and Native Americans and Barbary States. This speech, like the captivity narratives, performs a similar erasure of why al-Qaeda, like Native peoples or Berbers, might feel the need to attack America and the West. In the most famous paragraph from his speech, Bush claims, "Americans are asking, why do they hate us? They hate what we see right here in this chamber—a democratically elected government. Their leaders are self-appointed. They hate our freedoms—our freedom of religion, our freedom of speech, our freedom to vote and assemble and disagree with each other."[40] Takacs further notes that the media often "strategically framed [9/11] in ways that made the U.S. seem like an innocent victim of a senseless act. Political elites, likewise, decontextualized terrorism, describing it as a 'cowardly' act born of 'hatred,' 'jealousy,' and 'evil,' rather than politics."[41] In other words, "they" hate "us" for the Anglo-American exceptionalism we possess and which they do not.

What is not mentioned is the long history of U.S. and British interference in the Middle East and other Muslim nations. For example, there were the numerous wars in Afghanistan. These include the three Anglo-Afghan wars in which Britain was involved: (1839–1842), (1878–1881), and 1919; and the U.S. participation in the Soviet-Afghan war (1979–1989), which, as a result of the U.S. employment of Mujahedeen fighters and its military and financial support of Mujahedeen leader Osama bin-Laden during that war, led to the creation of al-Qaeda. In addition, in 1953, there was the CIA/British-supported overthrow of Prime Minister Mohammad Mosaddegh in Iran to further the interests of British Petroleum. Further, during the Reagan administration, there occurred the

U.S. military backing of Iraq while covertly sending arms to Iran during the Iran-Iraq war (culminating in the Iran-Contra scandal). And, finally, there remains the ongoing U.S. support of the Israeli state. All of these examples of interference gave and continue to give cause for many Muslim to see the U.S. and its allies as enemies of their freedom to determine their own lives, thus justifying violent action against America and the West.

Similar erasures of Western responsibility occur in the earlier Puritan and Barbary captivity narratives. For example, in the 1682 preface to Rowlandson's narrative, the preface's author (widely believed to be Increase Mather[42]) writes that there was "causeless enmity of these Barbarians against the English," even though the author next states that "The Narrhagansets [sic] were now driven quite from their own country."[43] Here, the Puritans do not connect the enmity of Native people and their forcible removal from their land; instead, the Natives attacked simply because they were "'wolves,' 'hellhounds,' 'ravenous bears' [...] [for] [r]ejecting the light of the Gospel, the Indians were allied with the forces of Satan; failing to cultivate the land, they were, in the biblical phrase, 'not a People'."[44] Likewise, the writers of Barbary narratives often fail to acknowledge that their captivity was the result of a long-standing schism between Christianity and Islam that had followed European settlers to the America colonies.[45] This schism, which in truth derived from the economic concerns of trade and shipping, "had been framed in Europe as a fight between Christian knights and Islamic pirates in which both sides justified enslaving each other."[46] As a result of this mutual antagonism, in speaking about Christian captives of Barbary Muslims, famed Puritan minister Cotton Mather deems the latter "Hellish Pirates" and "barbarous Negroes,"[47] instead of understanding the deeper reasons why the Barbary states might have taken captives.

We can compare such language in captivity narratives regarding Native people and Muslims to Bush's own descriptions of radical Islamic terrorists as similarly inhuman: they are "evil-doers," "evil people," "evil folks," and they practice a "kind of barbarism."[48] Tellingly, Bush also referred to the fight against terrorists as a "crusade," thus (whether deliberate or not) connecting the current war on terror to the medieval Crusades to "take back" Jerusalem from Muslim control.[49] Bush's use of adjectives and his earlier statement about "freedom" exemplifies the notion of American (and British) exceptionalism—that it is the idea of freedom, particularly as enshrined in the Anglo-American justice system, that is the cause of jealousy among other nations. Both Baepler and Berman connect the Bush administration's rhetoric to the Barbary narratives, going so far as to argue that these narratives laid the foundation for the construction of the Muslim world post-9/11. For example, Baepler writes, "To what degree, we might ask, is the portrayal of the Muslim terrorist predicated on the Barbary pirate? [...] As the United States formally enters into the war on terrorism, these questions become even more relevant."[50] Berman concurs, noting that "scholars have compared the United States' engagement in the Barbary Wars [...] with the nation's current 'war on terrorism,' which once again pits the United States against stateless Muslim actors and the Islamic states that give them harbor. Indeed, the two eras have striking parallels."[51] Similarly, the captivity narratives construct Native and Barbary nations as wanting to destroy the superior Anglo-American culture out of a kind of innate hatred of anything moral, correct, and well regulated.

In this way, the captivity narratives explicitly link this exceptionalism to being God's chosen people, particularly within a Puritan context in early America. Again, this chapter will not discuss in depth the concept of American exceptionalism and its relationship to Christianity, as it has been analyzed elsewhere.[52] But, we should note how John Winthrop, in his speech to fellow Puritans prior to sailing for what would become the Massachusetts Bay Colony, declared that the new colony "shall be as a Citty [sic] upon a hill."[53] It would be an example to other nations of good Christian government, in which the colony had "entered into [a] Covenant with [God],"[54] much like the Biblical Israelites. This notion of exceptionalism as tied to a covenant with or promise to God might not be as explicit in modern versions of Anglo-American exceptionalism, but the sense of being a "chosen people" certainly remains, as can be seen in Bush's post-9/11 rhetoric. Above all, the existence of a covenant is held in place by divine surveillance: God is watching to make sure that his chosen ones comply with the promise they have made to uphold the highest standards of morality and faith.

The belief in a covenant with God certainly plays a role in the narrative arc of the captivity tales, particularly in those written by British colonists in America. Some scholars have argued that, through a Puritan lens, the brutal British wars with Narragansetts and other Native tribes were viewed not so much as the result of taking over Native lands as of punishment for breaking the covenant, given that members of the colony had become less certain of their Puritan faith over time. For example, Amy Schrager Lang writes that "the American-born colonists were showing themselves to be a different breed from their English immigrant fathers."[55] Not only was church membership down, but, by the 1660s, "[t]he spiritual failings of the new generation were fully matched by their material ambitions. Land hunger led the American-born colonists away from the churches, both spiritually and physically. And it led them into contact—and conflict— with the Indians, whose land they coveted as a source of wealth."[56] In other words, like the Biblical Israelites, the Puritans saw themselves as being punished for not observing the religious principles as outlined by Winthrop in describing their covenant with God.

We can see this attitude in Rowlandson's narrative in which she frequently describes her captivity as retribution from God for lapsing in her religious mindset. For instance, she notes how she did not keep the Sabbath and smoked tobacco, and how her sister, who was killed in an attack, even questioned the existence of God. Rowlandson writes, on the death of her sister, "I hope she is reaping the Fruit of her good Labours, being faithful to the Service of God in her Place. In her younger years she lay under much trouble upon Spiritual accounts, till it pleased God to make that precious Scripture take hold of her Heart."[57] Regarding her own spiritual lapses, Rowlandson recalls, "The next day was the Sabbath: I then remembered how careless I had been of God's holy time; how many Sabbaths I had lost and mispent [sic], and how evilly I had walked in God's sight."[58] Later in her narrative, she addresses her Puritan community, who evidently accused her of having her husband send her tobacco for her own use, rather than as currency during her captivity: "It was a great mistake in any who thought I sent for *Tobacco*: for, through the favour of God, that desire [to smoke it] was overcome."[59] Nevertheless, during her captivity, she finds solace in prayer and in reading a Bible given to her by one of her captors. Rowlandson remembers, "I cannot but take notice of the wonderful mercy of God to me in those afflictions, in sending me a Bible: one of the *Indians* that came from Medfield fight, and had brought some plunder; came to me, and asked if I would have a Bible, he had got one in his Basket. [...] So I took the Bible."[60] Indeed, Rowlandson continually comments on God's chastisement, followed by His compassion, throughout her narrative. For example, she remarks, "Yet the still Lord shewed [sic] mercy to me, and upheld me; and as he wounded me with one hand, so he healed me with the other."[61] In this way, she describes how God by turns allows her to be traumatized and then saved, thus demonstrating His power.

Rowlandson therefore makes plain that she believes God is surveilling her actions; like the prison guard at the center of the panopticon, He can observe her at all times and mete out punishment as needed. At the end of her narrative, she emphasizes that her captivity was orchestrated by God so that she could become a better, more grateful woman: "And I hope I can say in some measure, as *David* did, *It is good for me that I have been afflicted*. The Lord hath shewed [sic] me the vanity of these outward things [...]. That we must rely on God himself, and our whole dependence must be upon him."[62] God used captivity as a crucible to purify her, but this purification takes place through surveillance that then Rowlandson internalizes, in accordance with Foucault's panoptic model. After her captivity, she can and will regulate herself to be a better, more moral, and faithful subject—both of God and of the Puritan state. Similarly, in the Barbary narratives, captives write about gaining a stronger belief in a Christian God in the face of conversion to Islam, and how they find a new appreciation for their lives and a renewed faith after their ordeal.[63] In their expressions of faith, these captivity narratives draw on their precursor, the providence tale, which aims to prove the existence of God through God's deliverance of the writer or subject through extreme difficulties and challenges.[64] The captivity narratives in turn build on providence tales by using God's surveillance, along with the space of imprisonment, to reassure both authors and readers that they remain God's chosen people. He continues to watch over them and to watch out for them. We can argue that, in this way, captivity narratives normalized the use of surveillance in regulating behavior so that the end result, as Foucault argues, is a productive citizen who behaves according to the mandates and needs of the state and society.

Post-9/11 Captivity Docuseries and Surveillance of the Non-Western Prison Apparatus

This strategy of constructing exceptionalism through imprisonment or captivity continues post-9/11 on television in the British-American, Channel 5/National Geographic program *Locked Up Abroad*, titled *Banged Up Abroad* in the U.K.[65] The series, created by executive producer Bart Layton, began airing in the U.S. in 2006, five years after 9/11 and at the height of criticism regarding the role of the U.S. and U.K. in creating Gitmo and holding prisoners without due process. The series is successful, as evidenced by the fact that National Geographic continues to air new episodes, and there is now a podcast version of the show. Further, Layton comments that the program has "a weird cult following in the U.S."[66]

However, I would argue that this cult status is not strange; the timing of the series' debut is important because in recapitulating the Puritan and Barbary captivity narratives, *Locked Up Abroad* functions similarly to its spiritual predecessors by constructing Anglo-American surveillance, justice, and imprisonment as enlightened through its depiction of the supposed failures and barbarity of non-Western prisons and systems of justice. Meanwhile, *Locked Up Abroad*, like many captivity narratives, turns a limited (if at all present) panoptic eye on the Anglo-American prison apparatus.

The premise of the docuseries is that the narrator, a man or a woman usually from the U.S. or U.K., tells the story of how they became imprisoned in a non-Western nation, most often in attempting to smuggle drugs back into the U.S. or U.K. Like captivity narratives, each episode is narrated from a first-person perspective, and, with few exceptions (there are episodes featuring imprisonment in Western nations, such as the U.S. and Australia) they detail the hellish, brutal conditions in squalid developing world prisons,[67] as well as the experience of being sentenced via draconian law in what are portrayed as non-democratic justice systems. Often, the story arc is one in which the Anglo-Americans are able, through the work of friends and governments in their home county, to obtain an early release and are welcomed back home, much wiser and more thankful for their lives. The coda to this narrative often depicts the success that the narrator has achieved since their imprisonment, through which they have learned to embrace their life in the U.S. or U.K.

As we can see from this rough outline, *Locked Up Abroad*'s arc is nearly identical to that of the original Puritan and Barbary captivity narratives: the narrator, who has fallen from a moral path, is then observed and consequently punished by God with imprisonment among barbaric people and then, by God's grace, is eventually redeemed, literally and spiritually, to return home a better, and more productive, member of society. In recapitulating this arc, the docuseries also reiterates the captivity narrative's ideological implications. While *Locked Up Abroad* is secular in its outlook, there remains an echo from the captivity narratives of a broken covenant with God that must be punished. Here, the "broken covenant" is with governments, rather than God, by engaging in the illegality and supposed immorality of drug smuggling. Surveillance, too, plays a key role; although, it is not the eye of God that observes and punishes, but the airport or border security in non-Western nations, as well as the viewers themselves who observe, judge, and find guilty the errant narrator(s). Likewise, restoration—release from prison—must be accompanied by repentance. For example, in the 2008 episode "Thailand," Sandra Gregory, a young woman from Britain, wants to return home after living in Thailand for three years, but she does not have the funds to do so. As a result, she agrees to smuggle heroin from Thailand into Tokyo for a fellow British national as an easy way to make the money she needs. She is caught by surveillance at the Bangkok airport, where one of the customs officials mockingly smiles at her and says, in English, "You heroin, you bad, in Thai you die," and proceeds to mimic putting a gun to his head, thus warning her that in Thailand, the punishment for drug smuggling is death. She proceeds to spend three years in Yao Women's Prison, which she describes as having "sleeping conditions like sardines in a tin, except that sardines have more room."[68] She herself describes her experience in biblical language, noting that her decision to smuggle drugs was "pride before the fall."[69] Then, following her imprisonment and subsequent pardon by the King of Thailand, Sandra returns home, earns a degree in geography at Oxford University, and, in her words, "Finally, I have done something to make my father proud."[70]

In these echoes of earlier captivity narratives, *Locked Up Abroad* incorporates the idea of Anglo-American exceptionalism in its desire for American and British subjects to internalize the panoptic eye of God and government in order to abide by the law and be productive citizens, not drug smugglers in contact with non-Western nations. In its secularization of captivity narratives, *Locked Up Abroad* links restoration and repentance with Western subjects eschewing illegal activity and interactions with non-Western nations, which are presented as instigating the moral downfall of the Anglo-American narrators. For instance, many of these narrators initially crave adventure and the exotic. In Sandra's case, she initially found Britain boring and drab, and, on a whim, decided to live in Thailand when visiting there on holiday with friends. She eschewed contact with family back home and, in her words, "My life just drifted on by as I became the stereotypical beach bum."[71] Similarly, in the episode "Peruvian Prison Nightmare," Krista Barnes and Jennifer Davis are two young California women who make money promoting parties; both enjoy the Hollywood lifestyle and are intrigued by an offer from a friend to take an all-expense paid vacation to Peru in exchange for smuggling back to the U.S. "a little bit of cocaine."[72] In the episode "Uganda: Death in the Jungle," Mark Ross is not a drug smuggler, but, like the other narrators, he is someone who nevertheless felt lured away from the West to an exotic land—in Mark's case, it is Africa, which he has dreamed about since boyhood and made good on that dream by becoming a safari guide in the Bwindi Forest on the border between Uganda and Rwanda.[73] As a result, they travel to non-Western nations, and, according to the program's logic, end up paying the price for abandoning a covenant with the laws and mores of their home nations.

In this way, the program firmly divides West from non-West in that it does not highlight the experiences of non-Westerners within their own nations' prisons, nor non-Westerners within the Anglo-American judicial system. The "abroad" of the title rarely refers to Western nations; instead, most often, "abroad" signifies the "Other" and "elsewhere" that is outside the boundaries of what is considered Western society. "Abroad" becomes a space where lawless things happen within unregulated governments. This othering of the non-West is underscored by the fact that the program is shown in the U.S. on the National Geographic Channel. National Geographic and its network aim to depict both wildlife and human culture for its readers and viewers. However, the magazine of the same name recently acknowledged that it has othered non-Western societies. In April 2018, *National Geographic* published "The Race Issue," which not only addressed race in terms of culture and biology, but also issued an apology for the magazine's past racist depiction of non-Western people.[74] Nevertheless, the pervading lens of National Geographic continues to be one which depicts cultures that are decidedly non-Western within the context of non-human animals and geography—in other words, constructing non-Western people as things to be surveilled and studied, not considered as equals with white Western culture.

Taken with the program's narrative arc, *Locked Up Abroad* and its network placement emphasizes Anglo-American exceptionalism. It makes sense that such a television series would appear in the years following 9/11 and in light of imprisonment controversies ranging from Guantanamo Bay to Abu Ghraib to "enhanced interrogation." In their time, captivity narratives served to justify the encroachment of the British on Native lands and Western power in the Mediterranean. These narratives did so by erecting a division between a civilized West and a barbaric non-West; one, the West, chosen and observed by God and made exceptional, while the other, the non-West, remained primitive and evil. Likewise, *Locked Up Abroad* resurrects the same rift in the wake of problematic actions by the U.S. and U.K. after 9/11. It reinforces a sense of Anglo-American exceptionalism by reiterating the brutality of the non-West. In other words, the docuseries implicitly upholds the U.K. and U.S. justice systems by making it seem that Gitmo is an aberration, not an extension, of the existing Anglo-American prison apparatus.

Due to its visuals, the program works even more powerfully than do the written captivity narratives. Certainly, the writers of these narratives craft vivid descriptions of the supposed savagery of the Native groups and the Barbary States. For example, Rowlandson describes the Narragansetts' "outrageous roaring and hooping,"[75] and the squalid, starving conditions in which she lived, such that she was willing to grab food from a Native child and to eat bear fat and other offal that before had seemed disgusting to her. Rowlandson recalls, "[t]here came an Indian to them at that time with a Basket of Horse-liver. I asked him to give me a piece. What, (says he) can you eat Horse-liver? I told him I would try."[76] After wrestling part of the horse liver away from others who tried to take it from her before she could cook it, she claims she "was fain to take the rest, and eat it as it was, with the blood in my mouth, and yet a savoury bit it was to me; for to the hungry soul every bitter thing is sweet."[77] Here, Rowlandson implies through vivid imagery, such as having blood in her mouth, that her conditions are making her as "savage" as her captors. Similarly, she suggests the same in detailing stealing a morsel from a captive child: "The Squaw was boiling horses [sic] feet; then she cut me off a little piece, and gave one of the English Children a piece also: Being very hungry, I had quickly eat [sic] up mine."[78] However, when the young child could not eat the morsel because "it was so tough and sinewy [that the child] lay sucking, gnawing, chewing, and slobbering in the mouth and hand; then I took it [the horse foot] of [sic] the Child, and eat [sic] it myself; and savoury it was to my taste."[79] At this point, it does not matter to Rowlandson that the child is British, like herself; she is so desperate that she is willing to take from anyone—young, old, British, or Native—in order to survive.

In *Locked Up Abroad*, similar "repulsive" details are magnified through the reenactments of the narrator's stories, particularly the striking visuals of the abhorrent conditions in non-Western prisons. Further, in the lead up to the narrator's incarceration, the series includes establishing shots of the non-Western country that emphasize poverty, violence, and danger, with the narrating subject an often terrified one who must navigate this foreign landscape. In these ways, we as viewers surveil, and find wanting, justice systems in non-Western nations. Further, the narrator also occupies the subject position of the viewer: we are situated as the wayward Westerner, and we are given no other point of view, such as that of anyone who lives in the country or who is part of that state's prison apparatus. The docuseries' visual surveillance also concentrates on scenes of non-white law enforcement behaving in menacing and inscrutable ways when arresting and imprisoning the narrating subject. The same is true of the captivity narratives, in which the first-person narration means we have, at best, a limited perspective of either the Native Americans' or the Barbary pirates' motivations. This limits our empathy and scope as readers and viewers, such that we are forced to adopt the Western perspective of the Other.

Further, *Locked Up Abroad* visually lingers on the squalid conditions of the foreign prison: dirty, overcrowded, and in disrepair. The camera also focuses on such images in a way that its surveillance is voyeuristic and disturbingly pleasurable. As noted earlier, there is a kind of sado-masochistic pleasure that operates in the visuals of a program like *Prisoner: Cell Block H*, specifically, the punishment of women's sexuality. Likewise, in *Locked Up Abroad*, there exists a similar sado-masochistic desire in witnessing the punishment of wrongdoing on the part of the narrating subject. While we are in the subject position of the narrator, we are simultaneously panoptically observing the prisoner's actions. Like both a prison guard and judge, our surveillance via the camera allows us to watch and pronounce judgment on the narrating subject who is being punished for breaking the law, and, within the narrative of Anglo-American exceptionalism, being disciplined for abandoning Western values and society. If, in the Puritan and Barbary narratives, God rebukes his followers for abandoning their faith, in the docuseries, the penalty is for abandoning Western culture and breaking the law.

Additionally, we as viewers can witness and pass judgment through the camera, without that panoptic lens turning on ourselves and our own actions, nor on the prison and justice apparatus within the U.S. and U.K. We can panoptically assess both *Locked Up Abroad*'s narrating subject and the non-Western Other, and find both wanting, as did readers of the original captivity narratives. Through the older captivity narratives, readers could similarly witness and pass judgment without scrutinizing themselves or their own Anglo-American culture. For example, certain passages in Rowlandson's narrative point to criticisms or insinuations that were made by her Puritan community regarding her captivity. Earlier, I noted Rowlandson's response to those who believed she had sent for tobacco for her own use; but she also addresses apparent suggestions that she might have either been sexually assaulted by or willingly had sex with her captors for favors. Rowlandson clarifies, "And I cannot but admire at the wonderful power and goodness of God [...] [that] yet not one of them [the Narragansetts] offered the least imaginable miscarriage to me,"[80] and "[t]hen he [Rowlandson's captor] called for me; I trembled to hear him, yet I was fain to go to him; and he drunk to me, shewing [sic] no incivility [...] but, having an old Squaw, he ran to her; and so, through the Lord's mercy, we were no more troubled with him that night."[81] In both instances, Rowlandson indicates to her Puritan community that God preserved her from assault, as well as refutes any implication that she had inappropriate relations with her captor(s). Takacs observes how modern American media were similarly obsessed with the possibility that Private Jessica Lynch had been sexually assaulted during her time in Iraqi hands. Takacs writes, "[l]acking access to information about Lynch's injuries, the documentaries [about Lynch] simply assume she was violated in captivity."[82]

Whether post-9/11 America and Britain or Puritan New England, women who are taken hostage or captive, as civilians or members of the armed forces, must face questions about their sexual behavior and status that men do not. For instance, at no point in John Williams's 1707 Puritan captivity narrative, *The redeemed captive, returning to Zion*,[83] does the Puritan minister ever feel compelled to address his bodily integrity during captivity as Rowlandson does. Similarly, speculations about rape and sexual assault are not asked of modern male P.O.W.s as they were of Lynch. And yet, male captives certainly face rape and sexual assault (e.g., both the 1962 David Lean film *Lawrence of Arabia* and T.E. Lawrence's own autobiography, *Seven Pillars of Wisdom*, hint that Lawrence was assaulted when captured by the Turks during World War I). In this way, there was and continues to exist a gender divide in our considerations of captivity and imprisonment; this divide mirrors that which I addressed earlier in terms of prison dramas that refuse to address issues of male sexuality in prison. Imprisoned women, their bodies, and their sexuality can be publicly judged and displayed while men's imprisoned bodies and sexuality are made invisible and impervious to social critique and interrogation (with the notable exception of *Oz*).

This, I argue, is part of the power of the captivity narrative, then and now: it is the ability to watch, surveil, and critique others—particularly female captives' or inmates' actions and morality—while not being watched oneself. Here, the captivity narratives and the docuseries comply with Foucault's model of the panoptic prison, as well as the synoptic model of surveillance: we, the numerous viewers/readers, are the guards who watch the few without ourselves or our culture being seen or studied. The structure of the captivity narrative allows the reader to be both in the position of the captive but also in the position of God, the silent judge and observer of all things who yet remains inscrutable. It is therefore not surprising that the Puritan and Barbary narratives involve the notion of God as judge, since He would represent the ultimate panoptic power. This point is understood by Foucault and other theorists, such as Jacques Lacan and Slavoj Žižek, who both describe the "big Other" (the symbolic order) as a constructed, rather than a natural, disciplinary force by its position as a constant source of authority and surveillance. According to Žižek "[t]he big Other" is "somewhat the same as God according to Lacan (God is not dead today He was dead from the very beginning, except He didn't know it…): it never existed in the first place, i.e., the 'big Other's' inexistence is ultimately equivalent to Its being the symbolic order, the order of symbolic fictions which operate at a level different from direct material causality."[84] However, in the captivity narrative, this surveillance power transfers to the human reader, just as in our modern society, the power to surveil has become not so much God but government apparatuses and ourselves. This is possible because, as Žižek notes, the "big Other does not exist"—the symbolic order or authority is a cultural construct and, therefore, it could be invested in different forms at different times. He writes that the big Other "does not exist as a consistent, closed order" and that it is "contingent."[85] In other words, we have become the "big Other" in part through texts, but especially through visual narratives that allow us the ability to actually see and assess the actions of others.

As noted earlier, one of the issues with Foucault's model of panoptic power and discipline is that it does not account for the mutual practice of surveillance between prison guard and prisoner. *Locked Up Abroad* likewise does not fully account for this multivalent aspect of surveillance in its depiction of the non-Western prison and justice apparatus. We do not see at length interactions among prison guards, officials, and prisoners; rather, the guards and the entire apparatus itself remain remote and enigmatic. Were it otherwise, it might be difficult to judge the non-Western prison so easily if we were to know more about the complex relationships at play. Similarly, while Layton's other docuseries, *Fugitive Chronicles* (A&E), focuses on imprisonment in the U.S. and does incorporate both "the voice of the fugitive and the voice of law enforcement,"[86] Layton leaves little doubt regarding the stance of the program: "I think we have to be very careful in the way that we present that and we need to be careful and avoid giving them [fugitives] a platform for apologizing for their actions. […] It is really an account rather than an opportunity for them to explain themselves or excuse their actions."[87] *Locked Up Abroad* likewise skirts complexities about its narrating subjects (other than they did wrong to engage with strange people in strange nations) and about the law enforcement apparatus of the non-Western nation. By casting escapees from U.S. prisons as "villains," the prison itself cannot but be constructed as "good" in this dichotomy. As with *Locked Up Abroad*, there is little questioning of the U.S. prison system and why someone might want to escape from it, other than simply to gain liberty.

While *Locked Up Abroad* does not engage in complexity, interestingly, the original captivity narratives do, although perhaps not intentionally. For example, Rowlandson's narrative addresses how she interacted with her Native captors. She writes of how there was a bartering economy within her captivity situation, in which she would perform services such as sewing in return for food and shelter from various members of the tribe. Rowlandson chronicles many instances of this bartering economy. In one example, she remembers, "Then came an Indian to me with a pair of Stockings which were too big for him, and he would have me ravel them out, and knit them fit for him. [...] Then I went along with him, and he gave me some roasted Ground nuts, which did again revive my feeble stomach."[88] Some Narragansetts honored the bartering system, but others did not. As she describes, "Sometimes I met with Favour, and sometimes with nothing but Frowns."[89] Rowlandson attributes this unpredictability to God showing his power by sometimes allowing her to suffer but, at other times, moving the Native people to kindness. For example, she recalls a time she was starving, "[t]his distressed condition held that day and half the next; and then the Lord remembered me, whose mercies are great," and God granted that a Native man took pity on her and gave her some food.[90] However, she rarely attributes these actions to the Native people themselves. Nevertheless, despite her unwillingness to acknowledge the agency of her captors, the narrative illuminates complex two-way relationships and surveillance between captor and captive. We as readers see that the captives are watching the captors as much as they themselves are being watched. In a notable scene of mutual panoptic observation, Rowlandson remarks that "they [the Narragansetts] gathered all about me, I sitting alone in their midst; I observed they asked one another Questions, and laughed, and rejoyced [sic] over their Gains and Victories."[91] At this moment, Rowlandson becomes despondent at the failure of the British army to overcome the Narragansetts and rescue her. One of the Narragansetts notices her tears, and he asks her why she is crying. She recalls, "I could hardly tell what to say; yet I answered, they would kill me:

No, he said, none will hurt you."[92] In this way, Rowlandson continually observes and describes Narragansett behavior and culture, and, though she characterizes them as savage, she nevertheless demonstrates how panoptic power is shared and multifaceted in her situation.

Further, she critiques her own culture in a way that *Locked Up Abroad* does not. Rowlandson closes her narrative by turning her panoptic eye on the British-American colonial army and chastises it for failing to find and liberate the captives because they lack the skills and mobility of the Native people. In this instance, she adopts the viewpoint of her captors regarding the ineffectiveness of the British-Americans, since the Narragansetts were also carefully surveilling and judging the army: "I cannot but remember how the Indians derided the slowness and dullness of the English Army in its setting out: For, after the desolations at Lancaster and Medfield, as I went along with them, they asked me when I thought the English Army would come after them? I told them I could not tell."[93] Rowlandson adds, "But what shall I say? God seemed to leave his People to themselves, and ordered all things for his holy ends."[94] Here again, Rowlandson attributes this failure to God's will, but her criticism of Anglo-American exceptionalism still stands. Thus, while the captivity narrative gives the modern program *Locked Up Abroad* a basis for its narrative arc in re-establishing Anglo-American exceptionalism following the failures of 9/11 and subsequent problematic actions by the U.S. and U.K., the original narratives often demonstrate more complexity in their use of captivity and imprisonment as an articulation of both surveillance and Anglo-American exceptionalism.

QUESTIONING THE ANGLO-AMERICAN PRISON APPARATUS IN POST-9/11 TELEVISION

While that complexity might be lacking in *Locked Up Abroad*, other post-9/11 fictional dramas and docuseries about prisons and captivity in the U.S. and U.K. do highlight these issues. As mentioned, one of the fascinating aspects of Rowlandson's narrative is that she does turn the panoptic lens on the British army to note the ways in which British power was not necessarily superior to that of the Native groups. In a similar post-9/11 critique of the U.S. military, Takacs notes how the rescue of Private Lynch "took on larger-than-life proportions, however, as the vested interests of the military and commercial media coalesced around the need for a good story to clarify the moral stakes of the war in Iraq."[95] As Takacs observes, even though it was not clear that Lynch was ever truly a "captive," rather than simply a patient at the Iraqi hospital, the military and television dramatizations, such as NBC's movie, *Saving Jessica Lynch*, portrayed her as such so that the U.S. army's rescue of her could be constructed as heroic, daring, and effective. In other words, while Rowlandson used her captivity to critique the abilities of the colonial army as compared to the Narragansetts, American media and military used the idea of a woman in captivity to bolster the image of the U.S. army and to justify the presence of the military in Iraq following 9/11. In *Locked Up Abroad*, one key moment when the program does admit that being locked up in the U.S. can be just as traumatic as being locked up elsewhere is in the "Peruvian Prison Nightmare" episode in which a caption notes that in Peru, the mandatory sentence for drug smuggling is six years, while in the U.S., the minimum sentence is ten.[96] This is an example of when the docuseries opens up a space for criticism of Anglo-American incarceration.

Nevertheless, whereas *Locked Up Abroad* might in general avoid critique of American or British prisons, there have been an increased number of programs since Gitmo and other post-9/11 prison scandals that surveil the prison apparatus in America and Britain to understand how incarceration occurs in these nations and if it is in line with the ideals of Anglo-American exceptionalism. For example, the landmark HBO program *Oz* anticipated this need prior to 9/11 and, after 9/11, the drama's creators were acutely aware of how closely the program's focus on the relations between Muslim inmates and other prisoners could be connected with the terrorist attack. Indeed, writer and producer Tom Fontana states that he deliberately avoided grappling with 9/11 directly in the series for fear of minimizing its meaning. For instance, he recalls that he "wasn't ready to write about September 11. I saw the second tower fall with my own eyes, so I could not emotionally go there."[97] As a result, he did not want to "trivialize" or "exploit" the terror attack that he witnessed first-hand.[98] Fontana adds that he was concerned that if he did include 9/11 in the program, it would no doubt "take over the show [...] it would be all that we could really deal with. Because it was such a monumental event, at the moment."[99] As a result, within the fictional world of the series, Fontana decided that September 11 simply did not happen.[100]

First airing in 1997, nearly four years before 9/11, *Oz* is a dense, intricate drama set in a men's prison. What makes this program so significant in terms of television (or even print) prison narratives is that it treated the subject with a serious approach to outlining and considering the complicated relationships of power, discipline, and surveillance within a prison, and it did so before questions were raised about the U.S. prison system after 9/11 and Gitmo. In this program, the viewer is denied a kind of prurient look and gaze that *Cell Block H* or *Locked Up Abroad* fosters. Instead, the viewer's panoptic eye must witness horrible brutality among prisoners; between guards and prisoners; and even among guards themselves. Many television critics initially condemned the program for its level of violence: "'I am starting to think that some of the violence is excessive,' wrote the *Baltimore Sun*'s David Zurawik. '[A]re its sociological themes anything more than window dressing for lurid prison scenes?' asked Caryn James for *The New York Times*. 'The show is as dehumanizing as the prison system it attacks,' said *USA Today*'s Dinitia Smith."[101] It is true that *Oz*'s violence is often hard to watch, but this is the point of the series: the viewer cannot remain complacent or feel pleasure in his or her panoptic viewing. *Oz* forces the viewer to reckon with how the prison system in the U.S. functions and gives rise to violence, considering that Fontana had experience with real prison facilities in the U.S.: "I went to a lot of prisons—maximum security, medium security [...] the actual incidents, a lot of them were based on [real] things. I interviewed a lot of men in prison and also COs [correctional officers]."[102]

As such, it makes sense that this program aired on HBO at a time when the network turned from showing movies to developing more original programming. Given that the major networks must answer to advertisers, who can be pressured by viewers to deny funding to programs that might be too controversial in content, a series that visually articulated the brutal conditions of U.S. prisons would not work on American network television. *Oz* graphically depicts prison violence, rape, drug use, drug smuggling, verbal abuse, gangs, and the true power dynamic between prisoners and guards. Unlike Bentham's prison model, prisoners conduct all kinds of illegal activities, often with the guards' consent and even participation. It is not clear, therefore, who is truly "in charge" of the prison, since power shifts from moment to moment among guards, prisoners, and prison administrators. Crucially, this series implies that the prison is not truly different from the "outside," although viewers might initially want to believe the two realms are separate. The prison, as *Lockup* (MSNBC) executive producer and creator Rasha Drachkovitch argues, is "a microcosm of society" where there is "currency, relationships," and shifting power dynamics between citizens (the inmates) and the government (the prison staff).[103] Albers cites Charles Dickens as making the same point in *Little Dorrit*, a novel which "undermines the distinction between the prison and the 'free world',", by an "imputation of corruption to society," given that criminality and goodness exist on both sides of the prison wall.[104] The ambiguities regarding who is watching whom, who controls whom, and who is criminal and who is lawful is highlighted by *Oz*'s first season, culminating in a prison riot in the episode, "A Game of Checkers."[105] This prisoner revolt reflects actual ones that have occurred in the U.S. and U.K., from Attica to Strangeways, in response to what prisoners see as unfair treatment and conditions within the prison. These prison take-overs have often led to changes in prison structure and administration, thus showing how panoptic power does not flow in one direction.

In this way, *Oz* utilizes television drama to give insight into the true power valences of the Anglo-American prison apparatus that viewers would otherwise be denied if limited to news coverage. For example, while a prison uprising like Attica might be well known, many Americans are likely unaware that inmates at 17 different prisons organized a three-week, nation-wide prison strike "to protest unfair treatment in the [U.S.] criminal justice system" from August 21 to September 9, 2018.[106] During the strike, inmates "conduct[ed] work stoppages, hunger strikes, and [...] boycotts," to demand better treatment of prisoners, especially of those who are non-white, and an end to "an exemption in the 13th Amendment allowing them to be forced to work for pennies a day."[107] However, this prison strike garnered little attention in the mainstream U.S. media. Other riots in 2018 which also went largely ignored in the U.S. media included those at South Carolina's Lee Correctional Institution, on April 15, during which seven inmates were killed; and at California's Sierra Conservation Center (a prison camp), on July 14, during which five inmates were injured. But it was these uprisings that in part inspired the nation-wide prison strike beginning in August. Given the dearth of reportage on the prison apparatus, television drama becomes an important means of narrating that space and the complexity of how and who practices surveillance and social control within it—whether through fictional drama or docuseries.

While I agree with cultural critic Brendan Gallagher's assessment that "[t]he prison industrial complex is an incredibly outsized aspect of American life," given that it "houses 22 percent of the world's prisoners despite [the U.S.] having just 4 percent of the world's population," I would strongly disagree that "the prison occupies an outsized place in American entertainment," and thus "[t]he average American TV or film viewer probably has a solid grasp (or at least thinks they have a solid grasp) on various aspects of the criminal justice system just from their media diet."[108] Indeed, audiences are drawn to dramas focused solely on the prison, like *Oz*, *Orange Is the New Black* (Netflix, U.S.), *The Night of …* (HBO, U.S.), *Wentworth* (SoHo/Showcase, Australia; Netflix, U.S.), or docuseries such as *Lockup* (MSNBC, U.S.), *First and Last* (Netflix, U.S.), *Prison: First and Last 24 Hours* (Sky 1 U.K.; Amazon Prime, U.S.), and *Back to The Joy* (RTÉ, Ireland; Amazon Prime, U.S.) primarily because this apparatus of surveillance and social control is still mysterious to many viewers.

For instance, Drachkovitch notes that many of our prisons are often "in the middle of nowhere,"[109] and so are physically distant from where most citizens live. In addition, given the nature of prison—that it separates offenders from the general population—the physical structure is meant to keep out non-offenders unless they work there or are approved to visit inmates. Therefore, most of us simply do not see into the physical space of the prison, let alone understand how the apparatus functions within. In these ways, the location and the structure of the prison makes it an apparatus that is both prevalent (at least in American society) yet obscure. Further, Drachkovitch notes that there is lack of fictional prison dramas because prison life is mostly tedium punctuated by moments of violence or chaos, and, by their nature, television dramas must "limit the amount of boredom" in order to tell a compelling story.[110] That is not to say that the violence depicted in programs like *Oz* or *Orange Is the New Black* is inaccurate, but they cannot truly represent the monotony of prison life.

Even docuseries like *Lockup* cannot focus solely on the routine of the prison without sacrificing a narrative arc that captures the viewer. Drachkovitch emphasizes, for instance, that the *Lockup* film crew embeds within a prison for four months, during which time they get to know the inmates and are able to find interesting inmate stories or record moments of drama and violence in order to tell a compelling narrative.[111] He also points out that it takes four months not only to garner enough material for a series, but also to allow inmates time to feel comfortable enough with a film crew to behave naturally and to be willing to share their stories and experiences with the crew.[112] However, Netflix's latest prison docuseries, *First and Last*, filmed inside Georgia's Gwinnett County Jail, does especially well highlighting the tedious and claustrophobic aspect of imprisonment, with tight camera shots of the endless waiting in overcrowded holding cells during the first 48 hours after arrest to those who count down the final 24 hours of their sentences by playing interminable card games or having lengthy conversations with cellmates.[113] Docuseries like *Lockup* and *First and Last* are also less prevalent than those that follow other apparatuses of surveillance and social control (such as the police ride-alongs discussed in Chap. 3) because it is "very difficult to film in prisons" given that few prison administrators give permission to do so, and thus "very few producers have the access."[114] Nevertheless, as Drachkovitch asserts, these fictional and docuseries programs about prisons are often the only means by which most viewers will ever see inside a prison facility, and so there is a "fascination" with being "able to see something as a viewer you never get to see."[115]

And, unlike *Locked Up Abroad*, what we surveil in these fictional programs and docuseries about the Anglo-American prison apparatus post-9/11 is not necessarily reassuring. For instance, what proves especially provocative about *Oz* is its ideological implication: the U.S. prison system can be problematic and unjust like the non-Western prisons depicted in *Locked Up Abroad*. Having spent time filming in prisons in the U.S. and other nations, Drachkovitch cautions us to not equate the American prison system with some, like those in *Locked Up Abroad*; but, he also notes that our prison apparatus certainly has many problems to grapple with, including high rates of recidivism, overcrowding, gang violence, and incarceration of non-white males: "While our prisons are not the model of the world, they are still not as bad as in other places."[116] Drachkovitch cites in particular Israel and Norway as having prison systems where there is less recidivism, and that fact seems to correlate with a "humanistic and holistic way of looking at prisoners."[117] For example, he observes that prison in Norway "is amazing" with "softer environments and color palates," cells "are not steel and cold," and where "inmates are treated with more respect [and] given more opportunities to get a degree" or other qualifications for post-prison life.[118] By contrast, he also notes systems that are worse than those in the U.S., such as the frightening atmosphere of "gulag-like" prisons in Russia, as well as of those in China, where his film crew was detained and almost not allowed to leave the country.[119]

While there may be other nations with prison systems more problematic than that of the U.S., *Oz* nevertheless turns the lens of surveillance back on the U.S. prison apparatus to show the ways in which the American correctional facility (and this is true of the U.K. prison apparatus as well) too often fails at rehabilitation (the purpose of Bentham's panoptical prison) and becomes mostly a place of incarceration. Certainly, the U.K. and Ireland, like the U.S., experience high rates of recidivism, as is discussed frequently throughout episodes of the British prison docuseries *Prison: First and Last 24 Hours* and the Irish docuseries *Back to The Joy*.

The violence and questionable ethics depicted in *Oz* anticipates by four years Guantanamo Bay and its treatment of inmates, both physically and emotionally, and the way it skirts around U.S. constitutional law. Here, we see how a television program, though fictional, predicted the ability of the U.S. to create an extra-legal prison facility. Unlike *Locked Up Abroad*, *Oz* explicitly demonstrates that the panoptic lens of the Anglo-American public should be directed toward its own prison apparatus, not that of others.

Similar fictional "prison realism" Anglo-American programs that have aired in the years following 9/11 have included *Orange Is the New Black* (*OITNB*) (Netflix, U.S.) and *Wentworth*[120] (SoHo, Australia), the latter a grittier reboot/prequel to *Prisoner: Cell Block H*, which is broadcast in the U.S. and U.K. on Netflix and BBC1, respectively. The latter, especially, has been compared with *Oz* in terms of its unflinching look at a women's prison: "*Wentworth* doesn't just veer into dark territory every once in a while; it resides there. Sure, there are flashes of humor, [but] the show's gritty violence is more in line with *Breaking Bad* or *Oz* than it is with *Orange* [*Is the New Black*]. Any single episode could feature a combination of gang beatings, mutilations, rape or murder."[121] Critics note that *OITNB* is less challenging in its presentation of violence. For instance, Liz Rafferty and Sadie Gennis write that "the ladies of Litchfield [the prison in *OITNB*] make prison life seem fairly bearable,"[122] whereas Duncan Lindsay comments that *Wentworth*, as opposed to *OITNB*, "shows life inside a prison, warts and all, never avoiding harsher scenes and [story]lines."[123] Still, in both *OITNB* and *Wentworth*, incarcerated women's bodies are not present for the viewer's panoptic pleasure; rather, the programs, like *Oz*, illustrate the brutality that can occur within the Anglo-American prison apparatus. While lesbian sexuality is certainly a part of both series, that sexuality is not for the viewer's gaze, but, rather, it functions as an illustration of the complex relationships within a prison. In other words, the focus on women is not prurient; it demonstrates how the problems of the Anglo-American prison apparatus do not change because of gender. Prison conditions can be as tough and inhumane in a women's facility, and incarceration can dehumanize women as well as men.

All three prison dramas, *Oz*, *OITNB*, and *Wentworth*, further complicate our surveillance of the Anglo-American prison apparatus by creating, as an entry point into the prison, a main character who could be "like us"—an everyday citizen, not a career criminal, who nevertheless commits a crime and is incarcerated. Albers argues that the danger in such a character is that it can further separate us as viewers (or readers) from the prison apparatus. He writes that "[o]ur identificatory figures [...] are often prisoner-heroes who are wrongfully imprisoned," such as Andy Dufresne in Frank Darabont's *The Shawshank Redemption* (1994).[124] As a result, while we as viewers "question the legitimacy of the central protagonists incarceration," we are still encouraged to "tacitly accept imprisonment when it comes to the other prisoners who are usually represented as the 'real' criminals."[125] However, *Oz*, *OITNB*, and *Wentworth*, like Dickens's *Little Dorrit*, blur the lines between the outside and inside of the prison by refusing to make the identifying character any less criminal or flawed than the other inmates. In *Oz*, for example, viewers can uncomfortably identify with Tobias Beecher, an otherwise law-abiding, successful, white attorney who drives drunk and kills a nine-year-old girl; or, in *Orange Is the New Black*, with Piper Chapman, a young, white, middle-class woman about to get married who is arrested for an instance of drug smuggling she committed 10 years previously (much like the narrators in *Locked Up Abroad*); or, in *Wentworth*, with Bea Smith, a white, middle-class, devoted mother who is sentenced for the attempted murder of her abusive husband, Harry. In all three cases, the character initially believes, sometimes with the encouragement of friends and family, that they can do their time while remaining untouched by the prison apparatus. However, all three are altered and not necessarily for the better. They each find themselves capable of doing things they never believed they could because the apparatus affects them with its violence and punitive systems. They become dehumanized not only by the guards and the prison administration who treat them as less than human, but also by other prisoners, who vie for what power can be had within the system of the prison.

In other words, the need for power pervades all levels of the system, and one cannot remain outside the paradigm—much like the world outside the prison walls. In blurring the line between prison and public, the series also ask us to consider how we are surveilled and controlled outside of the prison, given that the penitentiary is not necessarily differently structured or regulated than the supposed "free" world the viewers inhabit. These dramas beg the question if incarceration in any form can truly be "civilized." As Foucault suggests, incarceration is a form of state control no matter its appearance, and even if U.S. and U.K. penitentiaries have the veneer of cleanliness and orderliness, this veneer masks the social problems of poverty, violence, and drugs that require the need for control and incarceration of the Anglo-American population in the first place. Indeed, as Jean Baudrillard writes, "prisons are there to hide that it is the social in its entirety, in its banal omnipresence, that is carceral."[126]

In so doing, the programs question Anglo-American exceptionalism at various levels. In the prison, we see conditions that are not far removed from those at Gitmo, which stands supposedly as an aberration in terms of the treatment of prisoners within the American judicial system. But the programs suggest that an Anglo-American culture that can be so undemocratic, power-seeking, and pitiless outside of the prison as well as inside of it can be "exceptional." The surveillance culture that can breed such violence in its various forms is in our own living rooms as well as within the prison apparatus. Winters, as one of *Oz*'s writers, adds that the difficulty regarding fictionalized prison dramas is that viewers must empathize with the characters, given that those characters remain from episode to episode, which often is not the case with real-life prisoners interviewed in docuseries.[127] Identifying with those considered abject or deviant by society can be an uncomfortable experience because it forces viewers in the U.S. and U.K., especially those who are white and middle class, to consider if they might be one false step from prison, and therefore, not so different from the inmate who is non-white and poor.

The jailing of vulnerable populations of the poor, disadvantaged, and mentally ill in Anglo-American prisons is highlighted in *Oz*, *OITNB*, and *Wentworth*. The U.S. dramas, in particular, grapple with the mass incarceration of African Americans and African American men, specifically. In so doing, the series emphasize that in the U.S., justice and punishment are not exceptional because they are not applied equally across race and class. More non-whites are incarcerated than whites, and often do more and harsher time than their white counterparts. For example, African Americans make up 13.2% of the U.S. population, but constitute 35.4% of the inmates in state and federal facilities.[128] Further, 48.3% of African Americans inmates have life sentences, while 56.4% have life without parole.[129] Compare these statistics with those for whites: whites are 62.1% of the U.S. population, but constitute just 33.6% of inmates incarcerated in state and federal prisons. In addition, whites are less likely to be sentenced to life (33.4%) or life without parole (33.5%).[130] With casts of mainly black and Latinx characters, *Oz* and *OITNB* demonstrate the racism and classism of American society both inside and outside prison walls. The prison is not separate from society, but a reflection of its identity, and the facilities in these series paint an undemocratic picture of America. The panoptic eye here does not function to reassure the audience but to ask the audience to look at themselves and their society. It disturbs the passivity and complacency that television can engender, as noted in Chap. 1, or the feeling of total power and judgment, as it can manifest in *Locked Up Abroad*.

This lack of reassurance might explain why the most successful American network representation of imprisonment to date was *Prison Break* (FOX, U.S.). *Prison Break* was popular enough to warrant renewal for four seasons, from 2005–2009, plus an additional fifth in 2017. The drama centers on structural engineer Michael Scofield, who deliberately commits armed robbery so he can be sentenced to the same prison as his brother, Lincoln Burrows, who has been wrongly sentenced to death for the murder of Terrance Steadman, the brother of the U.S. Vice President. Michael does so in order to use his engineering skills to help his innocent brother escape from prison. In this way, *Prison Break* was more of a thriller than a serious, complex portrayal of the American prison apparatus. That is not to say *Prison Break* does not touch on the problems of the U.S. justice system, such as the danger of sentencing innocent people to death. This latter issue is magnified by the fact that in the U.S. "since 1973, 163 people have been exonerated and freed from death row."[131] Indeed, one of the primary rationales for ending capital punishment in the U.S. is that there is always the possibility that innocent men and women could be put to death (while a life sentence would at least prevent the state from carrying out wrongful death).

But in *Prison Break*, the camera's eye and the drama's narrative do not delve deeply into such dilemmas. Therefore, it is possible for the audience to remain untouched by the prison apparatus because the show's over-the-top premise of a prison escape based on plans elaborately tattooed on Michael's body moves the action from the realm of stark reality into a fantasy space that can be dismissed by the viewer. The same is true for the short-lived program *Alcatraz* (ABC, U.S.), in which long-dead prisoners from Alcatraz's dark past keep manifesting in the present. The program does not realistically address the harsh conditions there that gave rise to the prison's infamous escape attempts and near riots, such as the Battle of Alcatraz in 1946. During this incident, five inmates attempted to escape, and, as a result of their plan (which included taking prison guards hostage), two guards and two of the escapees were killed, and 11 guards and one uninvolved inmate were injured. Instead, the program displaces that history into a science fiction realm about time-travel that again makes it easy for the audience to take the prison apparatus less seriously. By contrast, *Oz*, *OITNB*, and *Wentworth* do not allow the reader or viewer to enter a fantasy space—the prison remains firmly real and a testament to the problematic enactment of the values of Anglo-American society.

While fictional television representations of the prison have been few even post-9/11, docuseries about prisons in the U.S. and U.K. have been more prevalent. These programs include the aforementioned *Lockup*, *First and Last*, *Prison: First and Last 24 Hours*, *Back to The Joy*, *Strangeways* (ITV, U.K.), *Hard Time* (National Geographic Channel, .U.S.), *Las Vegas Jailhouse* (truTV, U.S.), and several *Frontline* (PBS, U.S.) episodes on issues of imprisonment in the U.S.[132] These nonfiction series, like their fictional counterparts, do allow the audience a panoptic view of the harsh realities of prison life, including overcrowding, lack of funding to maintain facilities, and inequities in incarceration. However, they also do not implicate the viewer as do the fictional programs because we are given neither the time nor opportunity, as Winters notes above, to identify and empathize with subjects in a docuseries as we are with characters in an ongoing dramatic narrative. In other words, the docuseries allow their audience to maintain a distance in their panoptic gaze even while that gaze witnesses the problems of U.S. and U.K. prisons. Rather than identify with the subjects, we are positioned with the camera crew that follows prisoners and guards around during their daily life, and, who, at the end of the day, leave the prison behind. Some of the docuseries, like *Lockup*, even give cameras to the prisoners so that they can film themselves in a kind of confessional setting that is then included for our panoptic consumption.

The increase in prison docuseries is in part economical, at least on the part of networks and streaming services; any kind of docuseries is much less expensive to produce than dramas that must pay for sets, actors, costumes, and so on. However, the fact that these very different networks have chosen to film within prisons speaks to an interest, as Drachkovitch comments above, on the part of both audiences and producers to see what prisons are like. This can in part be fueled by a voyeuristic desire to see a world that the viewer, especially one who is white and middle class, might be able to congratulate him or herself on not being a part of. The viewer can in this way feel superior to those who are incarcerated for robbery or murder, something the viewer might believe he or she would never commit. On the other hand, as Drachkovitch argues, audiences also consider what if they would do if they became one of the Beechers, Chapmans, or Smiths: "Watching from the comfort of my own living room, I can think: how would I survive? And, so, the audience projects a lot of themselves into the show."[133] But the popularity of the docuseries can also speak to a larger cultural desire to think about the prison apparatus in the wake of Gitmo and charges that America and Britain are not living up to their exceptionalist image. Therefore, the docuseries can function, from the viewer's perspective, as surveillance of the U.S. and U.K. prison systems to either question the apparatus or to reassure him or herself that it is functioning properly.

To their credit, these docuseries depict a complicated image of the U.S. and U.K. prison apparatus. On the one hand, we see shots that are not comforting and that are reminiscent in many ways of visuals of the ostensible barbaric prisons in *Locked Up Abroad*. In U.S. programs like *Lockup*, for instance, we witness dilapidated conditions, overcrowded prison cells, or spaces not originally meant for housing that have been repurposed to handle the overflow of inmates. These images speak to the high incarceration rates in the U.S., as noted earlier by Gallagher, that far surpass those of other Western nations. Further, U.S. docuseries like *Lockup* and *Frontline* examine the administration of capital punishment, a policy that also sets America apart from other Western nations, in their interviews of prisoners on death row. They also show the violence that erupts within the prison system between inmates and the force used by guards who must perform cell extractions and other procedures to deal with unruly prisoners. One *Lockup* episode, for instance, highlighted the issue of the use of solitary confinement, particularly for months or even years, to quell intractable inmates.

Indeed, many of the docuseries, through interviews with administrators, suggest that those who work in prisons are doing their best to uphold the law and provide adequate conditions, given state budget cuts and harsh sentencing practices. Drachkovitch, for instance, comments on the enormous respect he has for correctional officers (COs): "We [the *Lockup* film crew] have found that it [being a CO] is a thankless, and dangerous, and draining job. You are surrounded by inmates—some with severe emotional or psychological issues—and these are your co-workers, and you have to make sure everybody is getting along."[134] The panoptic eye of such docuseries is therefore both critical yet sympathetic to the issues plaguing U.S. and U.K. prisons. Albers concurs: "Most [modern] prison narratives [...] critique and legitimate the prison at the same time. More specifically, they tend to condemn 'traditional' prisons based on discipline but simultaneously legitimate rehabilitative incarceration."[135] He cites bell hooks's observation that a text "may have incredibly revolutionary standpoints merged with conservative ones."[136] From the prison administrators' point of view, these series are a means of showing the public the difficult situation that U.K. and, especially, U.S. prisons are in. Administrators want to reassure audiences they know there are significant problems but also that they recognize and are trying to cope with those difficulties exacerbated by larger social ills: racism, poverty, drug and alcohol addiction, and (in the U.S.) gun violence. In this way, the Anglo-American prison is, as noted before, an extension or reflection of society itself, rather than merely the activities within prison apparatus.

Likewise, the docuseries *Las Vegas Jailhouse*, which aired on the truTV network in the U.S., works to soothe the viewer that the American prison system is measured in the means it uses to control inmates. On the one hand, the advertisements for the program were flamboyant, and they highlighted the entertainment value of watching newly arrested people out of control, as if the point was to laugh or be amused by the antics of those brought to the jail. However, on the other hand, the jail administrators' decision to give permission to producers to film in the Clark County Detention Center indicates that those officials wanted to convince the audience that if police and intake officers use force, it is because they are contending with citizens with significant mental health issues, drug and alcohol addictions, and other problems. *Las Vegas Jailhouse* tries to persuade the viewer that aggressive tactics, such as restraint chairs, are not dehumanizing, such as those used at Gitmo or at Abu Ghraib, but, rather, a necessary and judicial use of force. This docuseries, as do others like *Lockup*, also show guards filming themselves as evidence of what they do. This visual thus testifies to prison officials' own willing participation in panoptic monitoring as evidence there is nothing to hide regarding the maneuvers and devices they use. *Las Vegas Jailhouse* aside, the presence of these programs mostly on networks such as MSNBC and National Geographic also lends an air of authenticity and journalistic reportage for these docuseries, since these channels can be considered mainstream news and information networks. Drachkovitch states, for instance, that MSNBC's mandate to *Lockup* was "not to answer questions" about the prison apparatus but to use a "straightforward approach from a news point of view" and to "hold up a mirror" to the prison system.[137]

Given that British networks have also aired several docuseries about prisons, we can see that, like the U.S., the U.K. has faced questions about its own prison apparatus, even though the U.K. has a lower incarceration rate than the U.S. and does not engage in capital punishment. According to Norval Morris, "a substantial reason for the doubling and redoubling of incarceration rates in the United States in the period from 1970 to 1994 [and in the following years] was a profound change in sentencing practices."[138] Such practices included sending more offenders to prison (versus placing them on probation or assigning them community service) for longer sentences.[139] Overall, the increased American incarceration rates reflects the "tough on crime" approach in which, during the 1980s and 1990s, "[i]t was almost a competition among [state] legislatures of both parties to show how tough they could be on crime,"[140] particularly drug and gang crime, which also led to higher incarceration rates for African American and Latino men. As Morris argues, "many of the prisons and jails of the United States, particularly the larger, maximum-security institutions, appear to be institutions designed to segregate from society a young black and Hispanic male underclass."[141]

Nevertheless, the U.K. has not been immune from the tendency to institute more punitive sentencing practices. Morris writes that during the same period from the 1970s to the 1990s, "[t]here were similar increases [in incarceration rates] for a time in England and Wales, but nothing like the deluge in the United States."[142] Further, since Britain for the moment is still part of the European Union, three men serving life sentences in the U.K. have brought lawsuits against the British government for their prison terms in the European Court of Human Rights.[143] They claim that "the denial of a parole option does not allow them to claim they have changed. They further argue that the assignment of these sentences is arbitrary—some convicted killers get them, others do not."[144] Therefore, although the prison sentencing situation in Britain is more lenient than in the U.S., there are still questions in the U.K. regarding its current sentencing practices and its prison facilities that lead to viewer interest in documentaries that make visible this apparatus.

For example, *Strangeways* (ITV), like *Lockup* and other programs in the U.S., gives a behind-the-scenes view of how Her Majesty's Prison Service manages its facilities. Here, the setting is significant, since Strangeways—the nickname of H.M. Prison in Manchester—was, in 1990, the site of one of the worst prison uprisings in U.K. history. The riot was instigated by the unfair and harsh treatment of prisoners, as well as desultory conditions and services within the prison. The docuseries is promoted as an update on how Strangeways now operates as a modern U.K. prison facility. As with the American reality programs, this docuseries presents a complex portrait of problems (such as recidivism, poverty, and drug and alcohol addiction) but also of better regulations and more human treatment than was the policy in the past. As Albers notes, such a "contrast between the traditional and the more progressive prison […] implies that prisons today are not as bad as they used to be," which, he warns, can also lead to complacency on the part of the audience: "Viewers are drawn into believe that penal reform has already taken place" when there is still considerable work to be done to make Anglo-American incarceration truly rehabilitative rather than simply punitive.

Given the host of uncomfortable issues raised by realistic prison dramas and docuseries, it should therefore not be too surprising that the prison-type programming most popular in both countries consists of "reality" programs like *Big Brother* or *Survivor*, which involve a kind of willing captivity. Here, contestants choose to be confined to an island or a house to participate in competitive games as a means of being watched synoptically by millions and of becoming famous, even if it is for a short period of time. This voluntary captivity does not involve government surveillance and social control. Rather, the series encourages surveillance and social control by ordinary citizens: viewers who watch and judge the participants and their actions. The viewer can be completely free in his or her panoptic power over these participants because they are people who desired incarceration in return for fame, money, and notoriety. As a result, the audience remains free from observing a prison apparatus that is representative of the failings of U.S. or U.K. to live up to their exceptionalist ideals. However, that is not to say that such reality programs are not indicative of a larger extension of the mechanisms of the state prison apparatus into our post-9/11 identity. Leveling our panoptic gaze at fellow citizens to judge, scrutinize, and control embodies the surveillance culture in which we currently live and to which we have all, in a sense, become willing captives.

Notes

1. Jan Alber, *Narrating the Prison: Role and Representation in Charles Dickens' Novels, Twentieth-Century Fiction, and Film* (Youngstown, NY: Cambria Press, 2007), 1.
2. Norval Morris and David J. Rothman, "Introduction," in *The Oxford History of the Prison: The Practice of Punishment in Western Society,* eds. Norval Morris and David J. Rothman (New York: Oxford UP, 1998), Kindle.
3. Ibid.
4. Bradford Winters, interviewed by Darcie Rives-East at Dordt College, Sioux Center, Iowa, Oct. 28, 2017.
5. See Richard Weber, Dick Clement, and Ian Le Frenais, *Porridge: The Inside Story* (London: Headline, 2001) for the program writers' account of their unique television approach to prison.
6. Julien Pettifer, "Preview," *Radio Times,* 26 Feb.–Mar. 4 (1977): 15.

7. Ibid.
8. Ibid.
9. Ibid.
10. Morris and Rothman, "Introduction."
11. Rob Cope, "The Wild, Wild Women of Wentworth," *Classic Television*, 4.1–4 (1988): 15.
12. Rose Collis, "Soap Opera Comes Clean," *City Limits*, Oct. 6–13 (1988): 20–21.
13. Ibid.
14. Cope, 22.
15. Bernard Davies, "One Man's Television," *Broadcast*, 4 (April 1977): 20.
16. For more information and sources regarding the differences between panoptic surveillance and synoptic surveillance, please refer to Chap. 1, "Introduction: Surveillance and Terror in Post-9/11 British and American Television."
17. Jacob Rama Berman, "The Barbarous Voice of Democracy: American Captivity in Barbary and the Multicultural Specter," *American Literature: A Journal of Literary History, Criticism, and Bibliography*, 79.1 (2007), 2.
18. For further information and sources regarding the cultural and political response to Guantanamo Bay, please refer to Chap. 1, "Introduction: Surveillance and Terror in Post-9/11 British and American Television."
19. Berman, 2.
20. Morris and Rothman, "Introduction."
21. Catherine Scott, "'I Had Left One America and Come Home to Another One': First-Person Accounts of Captivity During the Iranian Hostage Crisis," *Journal of American Culture*, 27.1 (2004), 27.
22. Ibid.
23. Dahia Messara, "Introduction," *The Captivity Narrative: Enduring Shackles and Emancipating Language of Subjectivity*, eds. Benjamin Mark Allen and Dahia Messara (Newcastle upon Tyne, UK: Cambridge Scholars Publishing, 2012), xiv and xiii.
24. See, for instance, Lisa Voigt, *Writing Captivity in the Early Modern Atlantic: Circulations of Knowledge and Authority in the Iberian and English Imperial Worlds* (Chapel Hill: U of North Carolina P, 2009) for a wonderful study of Spanish and Portuguese captivity narratives and how those narratives, set in both South America and the Barbary states, helped to craft Spanish and Portuguese identity in the sixteenth and seventeenth centuries.
25. In addition to Allen and Messara, Berman, Scott, and Voigt, see also Paul Baepler, "The Barbary Captivity Narrative in Early America," *Early American Literature*, 30 (1995): 95–120; Baepler, "The Barbary Captivity Narrative in American Culture," *Early American Literature*,

39.2 (2004): 217–246; Kathryn Zabelle Derounian-Stodola, "Captivity, Liberty, and Early American Consciousness," *Early American Literature*, 43.3 (2008): 715–724; James D. Hartman, "Providence Tales and the Indian Captivity Narrative: Some Transatlantic Influences on Colonial Puritan Discourse," *Early American Literature*, 32.1 (1997): 66–81; Elise Marienstras, "Depictions of White Children in Captivity Narratives," *American Studies International*, 40.3 (2002): 33–45; Nabil Matar, "English Accounts of Captivity in North Africa and the Middle East: 1577–1625," *Renaissance Quarterly*, 54.2 (2001): 553–572; Matar, "The Traveler as Captive: Renaissance England and the Allure of Islam," *Literature Interpretation Theory*, 7.2–3 (1996): 187–196; Andrew Newman, "Captive on the Literacy Frontier: Mary Rowlandson, James Smith, and Charles Johnston," *Early American Literature*, 38.1 (2003): 31–65; Colin Ramsey, "Cannibalism and Infant Killing: A System of 'Demonizing' Motifs in Indian Captivity Narratives," *CLIO: A Journal of Literature, History, and the Philosophy of History*, 24.1 (1994): 55–68; Audra Simpson, "From White into Red: Captivity Narratives as Alchemies of Race and Citizenship," *American Quarterly*, 60.2 (2008): 251–257; Stacy Takacs, "Jessica Lynch and the Regeneration of American Identity and Power Post-9/11," *Feminist Media Studies*, 5.3 (2005): 297–310.

26. Takacs, 300.
27. Scott, 27.
28. Berman, 4.
29. Mary Rowlandson, *A True History of the Captivity and Restoration of Mrs. Mary Rowlandson*, 1682, in *Journeys in New Worlds: Early American Women's Narratives*, eds. William L. Andrews et al. (Madison: U of Wisconsin P, 1990), 27.
30. Ibid, 39.
31. Berman, 7.
32. Ibid.
33. Ibid.
34. Baepler, "The Barbary Captivity Narrative," 112.
35. Ibid., 113.
36. Edward M. Peters, "Prison Before the Prison: The Ancient and Medieval Worlds," in *The Oxford History of the Prison: The Practice of Punishment in Western Society*, eds. Norval Morris and David J. Rothman (New York: Oxford UP, 1995), Kindle.
37. Ibid.
38. Ibid.
39. George W. Bush, "Address to the Nation," Washington, DC, Sep. 20, 2001.
40. Ibid.

41. Takacs, 297.
42. See editor Amy Schrager Lang's footnote 6 in Rowlandson, 31.
43. "Preface" to Rowlandson, 28.
44. Amy Schrager Lang, "Introduction to *A True History of the Captivity and Restoration of Mrs. Mary Rowlandson*," in *Journeys in New Worlds: Early American Women's Narratives*, eds. William L. Andrews et al. (Madison: U of Wisconsin P, 1990), 13.
45. Baepler, "Barbary Captivity Narrative," 219.
46. Ibid.
47. Cotton Mather, *The Glory of Goodness: The Goodness of God Celebrated; In Remarkable Instances and Improvements Thereof; And More Particularly in the Redemption Remarkably Obtained for English Captives, Which have been Languishing under the Tragical, and the Terrible and the Most Barbarous Cruelties of Barbary* (Boston: Printed by T. Green, for Benjamin Eliot, 1703), 33, https://quod.lib.umich.edu/cgi/t/text/text-idx?c=evans;cc=evans;view=toc;idno=N00939.0001.001.
48. Manuel Perez-Rivas, "Bush Vows to Rid the World of 'evil-doers'," *CNN*, Sep. 16, 2001, http://edition.cnn.com/2001/US/09/16/gen.bush.terrorism/.
49. Ibid.
50. Baepler, "Barbary Captivity Narrative," 240.
51. Berman, 1.
52. See, for example, Matthew Costello, "The Pilgrimage and Progress of George Bailey: Puritanism, *It's a Wonderful Life*, and the Language of Community in America," *American Studies*, 40 (1999): 31–52; V. Bradley Lewis, "American Exceptionalism," *America*, 205.9 (October 3, 2011): 19–22; Deborah L. Madsen, *American Exceptionalism* (Jackson: U of Mississippi P, 1998); Deborah L. Madsen, "The Sword or the Scroll: The Power of Rhetoric in Colonial New England," *American Studies*, 1992: 45–61; Mark A. Noll, *Religion and American Politics: From the Colonial Period to the 1980s* (New York: Oxford UP, 1990); David Hoogland Noon, "Cold War Revival: Neoconservatives and Historical Memory in the War on Terror," *American Studies*, 2007: 75–99; John D. Wilsey, *American Exceptionalism and Civil Religion* (Downers Grove, IL: InterVarsity Press, 2015).
53. John Winthrop, *A Modell of Christian Charity*, 1630, Collections of the Massachusetts Historical Society, Boston, 1838, 3rd series 7:31–48, Hanover Historical Texts Collection, scanned by Monica Banas, Aug. 1996, https://history.hanover.edu/texts/winthmod.html.
54. Ibid.
55. Lang, 15.
56. Ibid.

57. Rowlandson, 33.
58. Ibid., 35.
59. Ibid., 57, emphasis original.
60. Ibid., 38, emphasis original.
61. Ibid., 35.
62. Ibid., 65 (emphasis original).
63. See Baepler and Berman on this point.
64. See Hartman for more on the providence tale.
65. I will refer to the series from here on by its U.S. title, *Locked Up Abroad*.
66. Jim Halterman, "Interview: *Fugitive Chronicles* Executive Producer Bart Layton," *The Futon Critic*, Apr. 1, 2010, http://www.thefutoncritic.com/interviews/2010/04/01/interview-fugitive-chronicles-executive-producer-bart-layton-35152/20100401_fugitivechronicles/. The interview itself focuses on another of Layton's docuseries, *Fugitive Chronicles* (U.S., A&E), which Halterman states "spends an hour each week on a true story about an often-dangerous criminal being chased by law enforcers."
67. Examples of countries highlighted in the docuseries include: Peru, Thailand, Uganda, Venezuela, Iraq, Iran, and so on.
68. *Locked Up Abroad*, "Thailand," season 1, episode 8, written by Bart Layton, aired Apr. 21, 2008, on National Geographic Channel.
69. Ibid.
70. Ibid.
71. Ibid.
72. *Locked Up Abroad*, "Peruvian Prison Nightmare," season 1, episode 1, directed by Katinka Newman, written by Bart Layton, aired July 24, 2007, on National Geographic Channel.
73. *Locked Up Abroad*, "Uganda: Death in the Jungle," season 2, episode 2, written and directed by Paul Berczeller, aired July 7, 2008, on National Geographic Channel.
74. Susan Goldberg, "For Decades, Our Coverage Was Racist. To Rise Above Our Past, We Must Acknowledge It," *National Geographic*, Apr. 2018, https://www.nationalgeographic.com/magazine/2018/04/from-the-editor-race-racism-history/.
75. Rowlandson, 37.
76. Ibid., 52, emphasis original.
77. Ibid.
78. Ibid.
79. Ibid.
80. Ibid., 44.
81. Ibid., 58.
82. Takacs, 303.

83. John Williams, *The Redeemed Captive, Returning to Zion. A Faithful History of Remarkable Occurrences, in the Captivity and the Deliverance of Mr. John Williams; Minister of the Gospel, in Deerfield, Who, in the Desolation Which Befel That Plantation, by an Incursion of the French & Indians, was by Them Carried Away, with His Family, and His Neighbourhood, unto Canada.: Whereto There is Annexed a Sermon Preached by Him, upon His Return, at the Lecture in Boston, Decemb. 5. 1706. On Those Words, Luk. 8. 39. Return to Thine Own House, and Shew How Great Things God Hath Done unto Thee* (Boston: Printed by B. Green, for Samuel Phillips, at the brick shop, 1707), https://quod.lib.umich.edu/cgi/t/text/text-idx?c=evans;cc=evans;view=toc;idno=N01123.0001.001.

84. Slavoj Žižek, "The Big Other Doesn't Exist," *Journal of European Psychoanalysis*, Spring–Fall (1997), http://www.lacan.com/zizekother.htm.

85. Žižek, "From Reality to the Real," in *Cultural Theory and Popular Culture: A Reader*, ed. John Storey, 4th edition (Harlow, UK: Pearson Education, 2009), 344.

86. Halterman.

87. Ibid.

88. Rowlandson, 49, emphasis original.

89. Ibid., 45.

90. Ibid., 49.

91. Ibid., 42.

92. Ibid.

93. Ibid., 59.

94. Ibid., 59.

95. Takacs, 297.

96. "Peruvian Prison Nightmare."

97. Tom Fontana qtd. in Elon Green, "The Legacy of *OZ*: A Chat with Tom Fontana," *The Toast*, Aug. 11, 2015, http://the-toast.net/2015/08/11/the-legacy-of-oz-chat-with-tom-fontana/.

98. Ibid.

99. Ibid.

100. Ibid.

101. Qtd. in Green.

102. Ibid.

103. Rasha Drachkovitch, interviewed by Darcie Rives-East via telephone, July 12, 2018.

104. Albers, 50.

105. *Oz*, "A Game of Checkers," season 1, episode 8, directed by Jean de Segoznac, written by Tom Fontana, aired Aug. 25, 1997, on HBO.

106. Jennie Neufeld, "A Mass Incarceration Expert Says the 2018 Prison Strike Could Be 'one of the largest the country has ever seen'," *Vox*, Aug. 22, 2018, https://www.vox.com/2018/8/21/17721874/national-prison-strike-2018-13th-amendment-attica.
107. Ibid. The issue of a "loophole" in the 13th Amendment outlawing slavery—one that allows for forced prison labor—is the subject of the documentary, *13th*, written and directed by Ava Duvernay, released Oct. 7, 2016, on Netflix.
108. Brendan Gallagher, "Netflix's 'First and Last' Offers a Fascinating Look at the American Prison System," *The Daily Dot*, Sep. 17, 2018, https://www.dailydot.com/upstream/netflix-first-and-last-review/.
109. Drachkovitch, telephone interview.
110. Ibid.
111. Ibid.
112. Ibid.
113. *First and Last*, executive produced by Jeanne Begley, released Sep. 7, 2018, on Netflix.
114. Ibid.
115. Ibid.
116. Ibid.
117. Ibid.
118. Ibid.
119. Ibid.
120. Titled *Wentworth Prison* in Australia and in the U.K.
121. Liz Rafferty and Sadie Gennis, "9 Reasons You Need to Watch *Wentworth* on Netflix ASAP," *TV Guide*, Mar. 13, 2015, https://www.tvguide.com/news/wentworth-netflix-reasons-to-watch/.
122. Ibid.
123. Duncan Lindsay, "10 Reasons *Wentworth Prison* is better than *Orange Is the New Black*," *Metro*, July 22, 2015, https://metro.co.uk/2015/07/22/10-reasons-wentworth-prison-is-better-than-orange-is-the-new-black-5307336/.
124. Albers, 109–110.
125. Ibid., 111.
126. Jean Baudrillard, *Simulacra and Simulation*, trans. Sheila Faria Glaser (Ann Arbor: U of Michigan P, 1994), 12.
127. Winters, personal interview.
128. Alison Walsh, "The Criminal Justice System is Riddled with Racial Disparities," *Prison Policy Initiative*, Aug. 15, 2016, https://www.prisonpolicy.org/blog/2016/08/15/cjrace/.
129. Ibid.
130. Ibid.

131. Death Penalty Information Center (DPIC), "Fact Sheet," Mar. 12, 2019, https://deathpenaltyinfo.org/documents/FactSheet.pdf.
132. These *Frontline* episodes, all aired on PBS, include: "Last Days of Solitary" (Apr. 18, 2017); "Life on Parole" (July 18, 2017); "The New Asylums" (May 10, 2005); "Prison State" (Apr. 29, 2014); "The Released" (Apr. 28, 2009); "Second Chance Kids" (May 2, 2017); "Solitary Nation" (Apr. 22, 2014); "Stickup Kid" (Dec. 17, 2014); and "When Kids Get Life" (May 8, 2007).
133. Drachkovitch, telephone interview.
134. Ibid.
135. Albers, 117.
136. bell hooks cited in Albers, 117.
137. Drachkovitch, telephone interview.
138. Norval Morris, "The Contemporary Prison: 1965-Present," in *The Oxford History of the Prison*, eds. Norval Morris and David J. Rothman (New York: Oxford UP, 1998), Kindle.
139. Ibid.
140. The Sentencing Project Director Mark Mauer quoted in Kate Dailey, "Why the U.S. Locks Up Prisoners for Life," *BBC News*, June 16, 2013, https://www.bbc.com/news/magazine-22912075.
141. Morris, "The Contemporary Prison: 1965-Present."
142. Ibid.
143. Dailey, "Why the U.S. Locks Up Prisoners for Life."
144. Ibid.

Bibliography

13th. Written and directed by Ava Duvernay. Released Oct. 7, 2016, on Netflix.

Alber, Jan. *Narrating the Prison: Role and Representation in Charles Dickens' Novels, Twentieth-Century Fiction, and Film*. Youngstown, NY: Cambria Press, 2007.

Alcatraz. Created by Steven Lilien, Elizabeth Sarnoff, and Bryan Wynbrandt. Starring Sarah Jones and Sam Neill. Aired in 2012 on ABC.

Back to the Joy. Produced by Poolbeg Productions. Aired in 2018 on RTÉ (Ireland).

Baepler, Paul. "The Barbary Captivity Narrative in American Culture." *Early American Literature*, 39.2 (2004): 217–246.

———. "The Barbary Captivity Narrative in Early America." *Early American Literature*, 30 (1995): 95–120.

Baudrillard, Jean. *Simulacra and Simulation*. Trans. Sheila Faria Glaser. Ann Arbor: U of Michigan P, 1994.

Berman, Jacob Rama. "The Barbarous Voice of Democracy: American Captivity in Barbary and the Multicultural Specter." *American Literature: A Journal of Literary History, Criticism, and Bibliography*, 79.1 (2007): 1–27.

Bush, George W. "Address to the Nation." Washington, DC, Sep. 20, 2001.

Collis, Rose. "Soap Opera Comes Clean." *City Limits*, Oct. 6–13 (1988): 20–21.

Cope, Rob. "The Wild, Wild Women of Wentworth." *Classic Television*, 4.1–4 (1988): 15.

Costello, Matthew. "The Pilgrimage and Progress of George Bailey: Puritanism, *It's a Wonderful Life*, and the Language of Community in America." *American Studies*, 40 (1999): 31–52.

Dailey, Kate. "Why the U.S. Locks Up Prisoners for Life." *BBC News*, June 16, 2013. https://www.bbc.com/news/magazine-22912075.

Davies, Bernard. "One Man's Television." *Broadcast*, 4 (April 1977): 20.

Death Penalty Information Center (DPIC). "Fact Sheet." Mar. 12, 2019. https://deathpenaltyinfo.org/documents/FactSheet.pdf.

Derounian, Kathryn Zabelle. "The Publication, Promotion, and Distribution of Mary Rowlandson's Indian Captivity Narrative in the Seventeenth Century." *Early American Literature*, 23.3 (1988): 239–261.

Drachkovitch, Rasha. Interviewed by Darcie Rives-East via Telephone, July 12, 2018.

First and Last. Executive produced by Jeanne Begley. Released Sep. 7, 2018, on Netflix.

Frontline. "Last Days of Solitary." Season 33, episode 19. Produced and directed by Dan Edge and Lauren Mucciolo. Aired Apr. 18, 2017, on PBS.

———. "Life on Parole." Season 35, episode 14. Written, produced, and directed by Matthew O'Neill. Aired July 18, 2017, on PBS.

———. "The New Asylums." Season 23, episode 13. Produced by Miri Navasky and Karen O'Connor. Aired May 10, 2005, on PBS.

———. "Prison State." Season 32, episode 10. Directed by Dan Edge. Produced by Dan Edge and Lauren Mucciolo. Aired Apr. 29, 2014, on PBS.

———. "The Released." Season 27, episode 13. Produced by Miri Navasky and Karen O'Connor. Aired Apr. 28, 2009, on PBS.

———. "Second Chance Kids." Season 35, episode 11. Written, produced, and directed by Ken Dornstein. Aired May 2, 2017, on PBS.

———. "Solitary Nation." Season 32, episode 9. Directed by Dan Edge. Produced by Dan Edge and Elizabeth C. Jones. Aired Apr. 22, 2014, on PBS.

———. "Stickup Kid." Season 33, episode 50. Written, produced, and directed by Caitlin McNally. Aired Dec. 17, 2014, on PBS.

———. "When Kids Get Life." Season 25, episode 11. Produced by Ofra Bikel. Aired May 8, 2007, on PBS.

Fugitive Chronicles. Created by Bart Layton. Starring Adam Fortner, Martin Garcia, and Kiriakos Stavros. Aired from 2009 to present on A&E.

Gallagher, Brendan. "Netflix's 'First and Last' Offers a Fascinating Look at the American Prison System." *The Daily Dot*, Sep. 17, 2018. https://www.daily-dot.com/upstream/netflix-first-and-last-review/.

Goldberg, Susan. "For Decades, Our Coverage Was Racist. To Rise Above Our Past, We Must Acknowledge It." *National Geographic*, Apr. 2018. https://www.nationalgeographic.com/magazine/2018/04/from-the-editor-race-racism-history/.

Green, Elon. "The Legacy of *OZ*: A Chat with Tom Fontana." *The Toast*, Aug. 11, 2015. http://the-toast.net/2015/08/11/the-legacy-of-oz-chat-with-tom-fontana/.

Halterman, Jim. "Interview: Fugitive Chronicles Executive Producer Bart Layton." *The Futon Critic*, Apr. 1, 2010. http://www.thefutoncritic.com/interviews/2010/04/01/interview-fugitive-chronicles-executive-producer-bart-layton-35152/20100401_fugitivechronicles/.

Hard Time. Produced by part2 pictures. Starring Thurston Moore. Aired from 2009 to present on National Geographic Channel.

Hartman, James D. "Providence Tales and the Indian Captivity Narrative: Some Transatlantic Influences on Colonial Puritan Discourse." *Early American Literature*, 32.1 (1997): 66–81.

Lang, Amy Schrager. "Introduction to *A True History of the Captivity and Restoration of Mrs. Mary Rowlandson*." *Journeys in New Worlds: Early American Women's Narratives*. Eds. William L. Andrews et al. Madison: U of Wisconsin P, 1990: 11–26.

Las Vegas Jailhouse. Created by John Langley and Morgan Langley. Aired from 2010–2012 on truTV.

Lewis, V. Bradley. "American Exceptionalism." *America*, 205.9 (October 3, 2011): 19–22.

Lindsay, Duncan. "10 Reasons *Wentworth Prison* is Better Than *Orange Is the New Black*." *Metro*, July 22, 2015. https://metro.co.uk/2015/07/22/10-reasons-wentworth-prison-is-better-than-orange-is-the-new-black-5307336/.

Locked Up Abroad. "Peruvian Prison Nightmare." Season 1, episode 1. Directed by Katinka Newman. Written by Bart Layton. Aired July 24, 2007, on National Geographic Channel.

———. "Thailand." Season 1, episode 8. Written by Bart Layton. Aired on Apr. 21, 2008, on National Geographic Channel.

———. "Uganda: Death in the Jungle." Season 2, episode 2. Written and directed by Paul Berczeller. Aired July 7, 2008, on National Geographic Channel.

Lockup. Created by Rasha Drachkovitch. Aired from 2005 to 2017 on MSNBC.

Madsen, Deborah L. *American Exceptionalism*. Jackson: U of Mississippi P, 1998.

———. "The Sword or the Scroll: The Power of Rhetoric in Colonial New England." *American Studies*, 33 (1992): 45–61.

Marienstras, Elise. "Depictions of White Children in Captivity Narratives." *American Studies International*, 40.3 (2002): 33–45.

Matar, Nabil. "English Accounts of Captivity in North Africa and the Middle East: 1577–1625." *Renaissance Quarterly*, 54.2 (2001): 553–572.

———. "The Traveler as Captive: Renaissance England and the Allure of Islam." *Literature Interpretation Theory*, 7.2–3 (1996): 187–196.

Mather, Cotton. *The Glory of Goodness: The Goodness of God Celebrated; In Remarkable Instances and Improvements Thereof; And More Particularly in the Redemption Remarkably Obtained for English Captives, Which have been Languishing under the Tragical, and the Terrible and the Most Barbarous Cruelties of Barbary*. Boston: Printed by T. Green, for Benjamin Eliot, 1703: 33. https://quod.lib.umich.edu/cgi/t/text/text-idx?c=evans;cc=evans;view=toc;idno=N00939.0001.001.

Messara, Dahia. "Introduction." *The Captivity Narrative: Enduring Shackles and Emancipating Language of Subjectivity*. Eds. Benjamin Mark Allen and Dahia Messara. Newcastle upon Tyne, UK: Cambridge Scholars Publishing, 2012: xiii–xviii.

Morris, Norval. "The Contemporary Prison: 1965–Present." *The Oxford History of the Prison*. Eds. Norval Morris and David J. Rothman. New York: Oxford UP, 1998. Kindle.

Morris, Norval, and David J. Rothman. "Introduction." *The Oxford History of the Prison: The Practice of Punishment in Western Society*. Eds. Norval Morris and David J. Rothman. New York: Oxford UP, 1998. Kindle.

Neufeld, Jennie. "A Mass Incarceration Expert Says the 2018 Prison Strike Could Be 'one of the largest the country has ever seen'." *Vox*, Aug. 22, 2018. https://www.vox.com/2018/8/21/17721874/national-prison-strike-2018-13th-amendment-attica.

Newman, Andrew. "Captive on the Literacy Frontier: Mary Rowlandson, James Smith, and Charles Johnston." *Early American Literature*, 38.1 (2003): 31–65.

The Night of …. Created by Richard Price and Steve Zaillian. Starring John Turturro and Riz Ahmed. Aired in 2016 on HBO.

Noll, Mark A. *Religion and American Politics: From the Colonial Period to the 1980s*. New York: Oxford UP, 1990.

Noon, David Hoogland. "Cold War Revival: Neoconservatives and Historical Memory in the War on Terror." *American Studies*, 48 (2007): 75–99.

Orange Is the New Black. Created by Jenji Kohan. Starring Taylor Schilling, Danielle Brooks, and Taryn Manning. First released in 2013 by Netflix.

Oz. "A Game of Checkers." Season 1, episode 8. Directed by Jean de Segoznac. Written by Tom Fontana. Aired Aug. 25, 1997, on HBO.

Peters, Edward M. "Prison Before the Prison: The Ancient and Medieval Worlds." *The Oxford History of the Prison: The Practice of Punishment in Western Society*. Eds. Norval Morris and David J. Rothman. New York: Oxford UP, 1995. Kindle.

Pettifer, Julien. "Preview." *Radio Times*, Feb. 26–Mar. 4, 1977: 15.

Porridge. Created by Dick Clement and Ian La Frenais. Starring Ronnie Barker, Richard Beckinsale, and Fulton Mackay. Aired on BBC 1 from 1974 to 1977.

Prison Break. Created by Paul Scheuring. Starring Dominic Purcell, Wentworth Miller, and Amaury Nolasco. Aired from 2005–2009 and in 2017 on Fox.

Prison: First and Last 24 Hours. Produced by STV Productions and Motion Content Group. Narrated by Siobhan Redmond and Gavin Mitchell. Aired from 2015 to 2016 on Sky 1 (UK).

The Prisoner. Created by Patrick McGoohan and George Markstein. Starring Patrick McGoohan. Aired from 1967 to 1968 on ITV and CBS.

Prisoner (Prisoner: Cell Block H). Created by Reg Watson. Starring Elspeth Ballantyne, Betty Bobbitt, and Sheila Florance. Aired from 1979 to 1986 on Network Ten (Australia).

Rafferty, Liz and Sadie Gennis. "9 Reasons You Need to Watch *Wentworth* on Netflix ASAP." *TV Guide*, Mar. 13, 2015. https://www.tvguide.com/news/wentworth-netflix-reasons-to-watch/.

Ramsey, Colin. "Cannibalism and Infant Killing: A System of 'Demonizing' Motifs in Indian Captivity Narratives." *CLIO: A Journal of Literature, History, and the Philosophy of History*, 24.1 (1994): 55–68.

Rowlandson, Mary. *A True History of the Captivity and Restoration of Mrs. Mary Rowlandson.* 1682. *Journeys in New Worlds: Early American Women's Narratives.* Eds. William L. Andrews et al. Madison: U of Wisconsin P, 1990: 27–66.

Scott, Catherine. "'I Had Left One America and Come Home to Another One': First-Person Accounts of Captivity During the Iranian Hostage Crisis." *Journal of American Culture*, 27.1 (2004): 25–42.

Simpson, Audra. "From White into Red: Captivity Narratives as Alchemies of Race and Citizenship." *American Quarterly*, 60.2 (2008): 251–257.

Strangeways. Produced by Wild Pictures. Aired in 2011 on ITV.

Takacs, Stacy. "Jessica Lynch and the Regeneration of American Identity and Power Post-9/11." *Feminist Media Studies*, 5.3 (2005): 297–310.

Voigt, Lisa. *Writing Captivity in the Early Modern Atlantic: Circulations of Knowledge and Authority in the Iberian and English Imperial Worlds.* Chapel Hill: U of North Carolina P, 2009.

Walsh, Alison. "The Criminal Justice System is Riddled with Racial Disparities." *Prison Policy Initiative*, Aug. 15, 2016. https://www.prisonpolicy.org/blog/2016/08/15/cjrace/.

Weber, Richard, Dick Clement, and Ian Le Frenais. *Porridge: The Inside Story.* London: Headline, 2001.

Wentworth (Wentworth Prison). Created by Lara Radulovich and Reg Watson. Starring Kate Atkinson, Celia Ireland, and Robbie Magasiva. First released in 2013 by SoHo (Australia) and Netflix.

Williams, John. *The Redeemed Captive, Returning to Zion. A Faithful History of Remarkable Occurrences, in the Captivity and the Deliverance of Mr. John Williams; Minister of the Gospel, in Deerfield, Who, in the Desolation Which Befel*

That Plantation, by an Incursion of the French & Indians, was by Them Carried Away, with His Family, and His Neighbourhood, unto Canada.: Whereto There is Annexed a Sermon Preached by Him, Upon His Return, at the Lecture in Boston, Decemb. 5. 1706. On Those Words, Luk. 8. 39. Return to Thine Own House, and Shew How Great Things God Hath Done unto Thee. Boston: Printed by B. Green, for Samuel Phillips, at the brick shop, 1707. https://quod.lib.umich.edu/cgi/t/text/text-idx?c=evans;cc=evans;view=toc;idno=N01123.0001.001.

Wilsey, John D. *American Exceptionalism and Civil Religion.* Downers Grove, IL: InterVarsity Press, 2015.

Winters, Bradford. Interviewed by Darcie Rives-East at Dordt College. Sioux Center, Iowa, Oct. 28, 2017.

Winthrop, John. *A Modell of Christian Charity.* 1630. Collections of the Massachusetts Historical Society, Boston, 1838. 3rd series 7:31–48. Hanover Historical Texts Collection. Scanned by Monica Banas. August 1996. https://history.hanover.edu/texts/winthmod.html.

Within These Walls. Created by David Butler. Starring Googie Withers, Jerome Willis, and Denys Hawthorne. Aired from 1974 to 1978 on London Weekend.

Žižek, Slavoj. "The Big Other Doesn't Exist." *Journal of European Psychoanalysis*, Spring–Fall (1997). http://www.lacan.com/zizekother.htm.

———. "From Reality to the Real." *Cultural Theory and Popular Culture: A Reader.* Ed. John Storey, 4th edition. Harlow, UK: Pearson Education, 2009: 332–348.

CHAPTER 3

Policing, Surveillance, and Terror— and the Return of Sherlock Holmes

In the years after 9/11, film and television viewers in the U.S. and U.K. witnessed the return of the famous detective, Sherlock Holmes. The film *Sherlock Holmes* (2009), set in nineteenth-century London, directed by Guy Ritchie, and starring Robert Downey, Jr., and Jude Law, was the first to revive Sir Arthur Conan Doyle's super sleuth in the twenty-first century. It was followed by a sequel, *Sherlock Holmes: A Game of Shadows*, two years later. Then, in 2010, BBC 1 launched the immensely popular series *Sherlock*, starring Benedict Cumberbatch and Martin Freemen, which was quickly followed by *Elementary*, the American CBS take on the detective, starring Jonny Lee Miller and Lucy Liu. Although this chapter will focus on the aforementioned programs, what binds these film and television iterations of Sherlock Holmes together is that they all began to appear in the years after 9/11 and during what some scholars term our current "Age of Terror."[1]

THE DETECTIVE AS PSYCHOLOGICAL SOLACE: THEN AND NOW

Holmesian scholars, such as Stephen Knight, have long noted how the great detective in Doyle's stories functions for readers as a psychological balm.[2] In other words, Holmes's unsurpassed detective abilities allow his audience, then and now, to feel better about the fearful circumstances in

© The Author(s) 2019
D. Rives-East, *Surveillance and Terror in Post-9/11 British and American Television*,
https://doi.org/10.1007/978-3-030-16900-8_3

which they find themselves because there is a savior who can protect society from potential threats (even if that savior is purely fictional). Certainly, for Victorian readers, Holmes was a "hero" who "assuage[d] the anxieties of a respectable, London-based, middle-class audience. The captivated readers had faith in modern systems of scientific and rational inquiry to order an uncertain and troubling world, but feeling they lacked these powers themselves, they [...] needed a suitably equipped hero to mediate psychic protection."[3] In an age of surveillance, terror, and complex intelligence-gathering technology, the American and British white, dominant middle class in the twenty-first century are no different—it likewise has faith that its technological capabilities can compute and surveil its way to safety in this Age of Terror, but it cannot operate these intricate surveillance and intelligence networks itself. This middle class requires a hero to do this for it, and so we have the reappearance of Doyle's detective.

This social-psychological function of Holmes is supported by the fact that he has been revived many times prior to 9/11 in response to periods of uncertainty in the U.S. and U.K. For instance, Holmes first appeared in 1889 in response to anxieties about the British Empire and possible criminal threats from both within (such as Jack the Ripper) and without (immigrants from British colonies and Eastern Europe) the realm. Again, in the twentieth century, Holmes became popular during World War II, via the 20th Century Fox films starring Basil Rathbone, when both Britain and America had great fears about succeeding against the Axis forces. We can further connect the well-received television versions of Holmes on the BBC in the 1960s with early Cold War fears, particularly in the U.K. Now, in the Age of Terror post-9/11, Holmes once again sleuths across television screens in the aforementioned BBC and CBS series, although, importantly, these dramas re-situate Holmes squarely within a post-9/11 world. Indeed, *Elementary* foregrounds this fact by noting in its pilot episode that the now New York-based Holmes's relationship with the New York Police Department (NYPD) began when, as a Scotland Yard liaison, he assisted with the investigation of the 9/11 attacks.[4] In this way, Holmes works as a particularly modern balm to the current issues of terrorism America and Britain face in the twenty-first century.

However, one of my arguments in this book is that these modern issues, such as terrorism, are not drastically different from those that have come before, and that is why Holmes still works as a psychological solace. If the problems were not similar, the character would not function so well with an audience hungry for a hero who could help us in our time of need.

The character and the narrative must fit a particular necessity. And what Holmes embodies, then and now, is our desire for a scientific and technological surveillance apparatus that can identify, track, and capture those who would hurt innocent civilians before they strike; or, if they do attack, to locate and bring the terrorists to justice. There are certainly other popular post-9/11 heroes who serve as a psychological salve (such as Harry Potter), promising that there is a "chosen one" who can put things right again with his or her special abilities. What makes Holmes somewhat different (although certainly related in his almost preternatural powers) is the character's personification and use of realistic detection and surveillance, rather than magic, to protect society. As such, Holmes can be our entrée to a consideration of the Anglo-American police apparatus, one which in the real world employs Holmesian techniques of surveillance to maintain social order and control. Holmes exemplifies what we as readers or viewers want from a police apparatus—safety and order through continual surveillance. But he also reflects readers' or viewers' anxieties about how the police apparatus operates in the U.S. and U.K. In this chapter, I will consider how white, middle-class British and American hopes and fears regarding policing play out in *Sherlock* and *Elementary*, as well as in other key television series about policing and detection.

CONCERNS REGARDING THE POLICE APPARATUS AND ITS SURVEILLANCE POWERS

Sherlock and *Elementary* both return the master detective to the present, but they also deliberately cite and remind the viewer of the original Doyle stories, albeit reshaped into a modern context. Such literary quotations are too numerous to cite in full, but some examples are various episode titles themselves, such as in *Sherlock*: "A Study in Pink" (for *A Study in Scarlet*); "A Scandal in Belgravia" (for "A Scandal in Bohemia"); "The Sign of Three" (for *The Sign of Four*); and in *Elementary*: "Whatever Remains, However Improbable" (a paraphrase of Holmes's famous aphorism "Once you eliminate the impossible, whatever remains, no matter how improbable, must be the truth"); "The One Percent Solution" (referencing Holmes's "seven percent solution" of cocaine in *The Sign of Four*); and "The Hound of the Cancer Cells" (*The Hound of the Baskervilles*). In so doing, the programs connect the present day with the past, and such connections suggest, deliberately or otherwise, that the problems we experience now are not necessarily new. Britain and America have previously encountered concerns regarding the necessity of a police apparatus while simultaneously ensuring boundaries regarding how far the police can and should go to ensure security. This desire on the part of audiences and producers alike to consider the relationship between the past and present of the police apparatus have resulted in several series in recent years which center on the development of policing in Britain and America. For example, *Ripper Street* (BBC and Amazon), *Copper* (BBC America), *Whitechapel* (ITV), *Murder Maps* (Netflix), *Murdoch Mysteries* (CBC), *City of Vice* (BBC), *Life on Mars* (BBC and ABC), and *Ashes to Ashes* (BBC) are all series whose deliberate purpose is to explore and narrate earlier versions of the police apparatus in the U.S. and U.K. These programs, along with *Sherlock*'s and *Elementary*'s ties to the nineteenth century, enable a dialogue between past and present through which writers, producers, and the audience together work through some of the difficult questions we currently face with the policing, surveillance, and social control.

I would like to pause a moment to clarify what I mean when I say that policing, detection, surveillance, and social control are questions with which the U.S. and U.K. are currently contending. Beginning with 9/11, securing the public from terror attacks was a task conducted not only at a national level (by intelligence agencies, such as the National Security Agency [NSA], Central Intelligence Agency [CIA], or Military Intelligence, Section 5 [Mi-5], or federal law enforcement, such as the Federal Bureau of Investigation [FBI]). Much responsibility was also placed on the police at the state, county, and local levels to surveil potential terror suspects, to be vigilant about attacks that might happen, and to investigate those incidents that did occur. For example, after 9/11, the budget and scope of the NYPD expanded exponentially, such that it now has the capacity of a small nation state in terms of weaponry, technology, and personnel. Indeed, in 2011, New York Mayor Michael Bloomberg bragged that "I have my own army in the NYPD, which is the seventh biggest army in the world."[5] That same year, Police Commissioner Ray Kelly remarked on the U.S. news program *60 Minutes* that the NYPD had the ability to take down a plane,[6] to which Bloomberg responded in a press conference that "the NYPD has lots of capabilities that you [the public] don't know about and won't know about."[7]

Further, as part of the war on terror, the Department of Homeland Security has given police departments paramilitary equipment that for many have made the local police more like a branch of the military than a force designed to keep the peace and investigate provincial criminal matters. As journalist Radley Balko comments, "Since the September 11 attacks, Homeland Security has been handing out anti-terrorism grants like parade candy, giving cities and towns across the country funds to buy military-grade armored vehicles, guns, armor, and other equipment."[8] Balko reminds us, however, that police militarization did not begin with 9/11, but, rather, that this process began in the 1960s, with the creation of the SWAT (Special Weapons and Tactics) unit, in response to the political unrest of that time.[9] In response to the military-style weaponry and tactics employed by the Ferguson, Missouri, police against those protesting the 2015 police killing of Michael Brown, then President Barack Obama signed an executive order curtailing police use of military equipment.[10] However, current President Donald Trump has since pledged to rescind that executive order.[11]

Such paramilitarization in the Age of Terror is certainly more prevalent in the U.S. than in the U.K. Nevertheless, U.K. citizens have also become concerned about the increased weaponization of the British police in the name of counterterrorism, particularly in comparison to the traditional bobbies, armed only with a nightstick.[12] Nicholas Clapham observes that there are "now [2017] 640 more firearms officers in England and Wales than there were this time in 2016," and he quotes Deputy Chief Constable Simon Chesterman as saying, "'Previously the approach was to locate, contain and neutralize. Now it is to locate and confront. Our tactics are more aggressive'."[13] In these ways, a major transatlantic public worry is that the police apparatus is evolving into a domestic military force. In turn, this increased militarization leads to fears regarding how this strengthened force can be used against the public in the manner military juntas might be in totalitarian regimes. In the U.S. and U.K., we have seen this apprehension justified in recent years by the actions of the police in Ferguson against those protesting the killing of Michael Brown, and by the Metropolitan Police firearms officers who killed Mark Duggan in London.

A further public concern is how someone might be tracked and monitored by the police in a way that violates their right to privacy. Post-9/11, the police have access to more technology to conduct surveillance and have also desired, if not been given, a broader scope in its surveillance of citizens. A recent example is the FBI's argument that they should be allowed a "back door" into cell phones that would enable them to access information for investigation (this in response to the December 2015 terrorist incident in San Bernardino). The FBI was supported in this demand by many local and state law enforcement agencies.[14] The police apparatus also utilizes sometimes controversial surveillance methods, including informants, CCTV cameras, patrolling neighborhoods, stop-and-frisk tactics, and communications-monitoring equipment. This last was best exemplified in the HBO series *The Wire*, whose title emphasizes the surveillance aspect of the police apparatus. The series focuses on a fictionalized Baltimore Police Department, in the years after 9/11, conducting audio and visual surveillance by using phone taps and recording devices in suspects' living and work spaces, and the show explores the ethics of this surveillance, particularly when the police proceed with such wiretaps without proper warrants and permission. The program raises questions about the police's pursuit of justice and public safety (against drug rings or corrupt unions) at the expense of civil liberties. In this way, *The Wire* captures the complex nature of the police apparatus without giving easy answers to these questions. Rather, the program's writers encourage viewers to consider these matters for themselves. As Margaret Talbot writes, "*The Wire* débuted in June 2002, looking more or less like a cop show. But the differences were important. [...] [Y]ou didn't see the suspects through the cops' eyes only—you saw them through their own as well. The drug trade emerged as its own intricate bureaucracy, a hierarchy that subtly mirrored that of the police department."[15] As a result, the program questioned if the state-sanctioned police apparatus was fundamentally different from criminal operations in terms of its force and of its tactics.

The Wire's concern regarding the ethics of police surveillance and eavesdropping can be traced back to some of the first novels about policing and detection, such as Wilkie Collins's *The Moonstone* (1868). In the novel, for example, Sergeant Cuff, a London police detective, surreptitiously listens in on various conversations to ascertain the information he wishes to know regarding a jewel theft. Other characters, like the steward, view the sergeant's eavesdropping as dishonest and unmanly, thus pitting an older idea of honor against newer forms of surveillance and social control. The sergeant's methods presage the wiretaps of the modern police apparatus depicted in *The Wire*. Then as now, the police apparatus's ability to breach citizens' privacy and civil liberties are at the root of the viewers'/readers' unease.

In short, many are concerned in this post-9/11 era that the police apparatus has exceeded its scope in terms of brute force and surveillance capabilities. However, this situation is complex because, at the same time, as a public we also desire to be protected from terror attacks and other criminal activity. In this regard, there remains a need and a desire for law enforcement to use physical force and surveillance to keep order and maintain public safety. Thus, overall, we currently have a landscape in the U.S. and U.K. ripe for television narratives that articulate tensions regarding how we can affirm effective law enforcement while also maintaining the civil liberties and privacy of citizens.

Further, the television programs I examine in this chapter serve as reminders that this tension over the role of police in our society has always been present. This is not to minimize the current and valid concerns regarding the police, especially since weaponry and technology are now more advanced and carry with them consequences unimaginable in earlier eras. However, the underlying concern of balancing the need for public safety and protection with the desire for civil liberties and privacy remains consistent. I contend that if we understand the anxieties regarding policing that existed in the past, we can better appreciate how these older narratives or concerns are shaping and influencing our understanding of the police apparatus today.

For example, the programs can remind us that the older narratives of the limitations of policing, detection, and surveillance color our perception of modern police. While one fear has been and continues to be the overreach of the police apparatus, another, seemingly paradoxical concern, has been the worry that the police are incompetent in their role as public guardians. I say "seemingly" because the two perspectives are more interconnected than they might appear. One can fear that the police both enjoy being over-powerful yet remain incompetent at identifying and preventing terror and crime. This paradox is illustrated starkly by the recent Netflix crime docuseries *Making a Murderer* (2015). The series highlights how Steven Avery served 18 years after being wrongfully convicted of sexual assault in Manitowoc County, Wisconsin. The series suggests that, after being exonerated, Avery's later arrest by the same county sheriff's office for murder was a frame-up to disrupt his civil suit against county police and officials. At the same time, the Manitowoc County sheriff's office arrested Avery's nephew, Brendan Dassey, as a co-conspirator. The series charges that Dassey, a mentally vulnerable 16-year-old, was coerced into a confession through intense interrogation.

If, like *Making a Murderer*, the television programs under discussion in this chapter raise concerns regarding police power and ineffectiveness, they can also emulate older narratives (such as Doyle's stories) which introduce characters who compensate for these failings, such as a master detective like Holmes, or a dedicated officer within a police precinct who resists overreach while aiming for success, as we see in *Ripper Street* or *Copper*. In *Making a Murderer*, this role is filled by the docuseries writers and producers Laura Ricciardi and Moira Demos, who brought attention to potential police malfeasance. In fictional crime series, the officer or detective who compensates for the excesses and failings of the apparatus can rehabilitate policing, detection, and surveillance for the audience. They reassure us that good cops remain who ensure that law enforcement strikes the balance we desire between safety and civil liberties. But this comfort also allows the audience off the hook, as it were, in compelling the police force to act as they wish it to function. In other words, these programs about policing can produce a certain passivity, a passivity that is often engendered by the structure of television itself.[16] As viewers, we do not have to do anything about concerns we might have with the police because there are heroes within the force (or, as with Holmes or the aforementioned documentary directors, outside it) who surveil law enforcement, guaranteeing the apparatus is competent without overreaching its mandate.

POST-9/11 TELEVISION AND NINETEENTH-CENTURY CONCERNS ABOUT POLICING

To consider the history of this narrative further, let us examine the press and public's feelings regarding the police in nineteenth-century London and New York; it is a history which influences *Sherlock* and *Elementary* specifically, as well as programs like *Ripper Street, Copper*, and *Whitechapel*. Certainly, *Sherlock* and *Elementary* draw their perspectives on the police from Doyle's stories in which the late nineteenth-century London Metropolitan Police are ignorant and blind, and so require the help of Holmes, a consulting detective, to track and catch criminals. If we examine the British press and public perception of the London police force at this time, it becomes clear how Doyle's narrative originated.

The nineteenth-century British press debated police actions, and newspapers often reveal narratives of a brute force with too much scope and power not guided by intelligence and competence. An example is news coverage of the 1887 Bloody Sunday demonstration in London, so called because of the brutal police and army actions against protesters. The demonstration was organized by the Social Democratic Federation and the Irish National League to protest the Coercion Acts in Ireland, laws which allowed for the arrest of hundreds of Irish, including MPs, in an attempt to quell unrest and political organizing in Ireland. The Liberal newspaper *The Pall Mall Gazette*, in the article "In the Black Hole of Scotland Yard: A Tale of Blows and Bludgeons," characterizes the Metropolitan Police's actions against protestors as an "orgie [sic] of brutality that reigned supreme among our 'admirable police'" and that it was "the 'terror' that reigned in London on that fatal day."[17] The article also claims that it would be up to Londoners to decide "whether the people shall be masters of the police, or the police masters of the people."[18]

Likewise, one year after the protests, in the left-leaning *Reynolds's Newspaper*, the article "The Soldier and The Lawyer: A Comedy" states that one of the reasons for "Bloody Sunday" was that the Chief Commissioner of Scotland Yard at the time, Sir Charles Warren, was trained as a soldier: "A soldier is wholly unqualified for police work, which requires special knowledge, and training, and certain aptitudes seldom found in men who have passed years in the army [...]. The experiment of military commissioners has been tried, and failed."[19] In this way, *Reynolds's Newspaper* echoes post-9/11 concerns about the militarization of the police and the blurring of the boundaries between soldiers and cops. By contrast, the Conservative *St. James's Gazette* viewed the protesters as the brutal ones attacking the police force. The article "The Punishment of the Rioters" constructs protesters as rioters, and it argues that other newspapers, like the *Standard* and the *Daily News*, all agree that the punishment for the leader of the protests was not harsh: "the sentence of five years' penal servitude passed upon George Harrison on Saturday for savage assaults upon the police on the chief day of the Trafalgar-square [sic] riots is not by any means too severe for his offenses, but it is severe enough to spread a wholesome dismay amongst men of the class he represented."[20] These newspaper reports demonstrate that debate was ongoing in the British press about the scope of the police apparatus' power. Then, as now, the press debated if that scope was too wide, and risked violating citizens' rights, or if the scope was not wide enough to ensure national and public safety.

Indeed, even the initial 1829 founding of the police force by Sir Robert Peel was met with much public and journalistic debate and opposition because many feared the police would essentially become a standing army that could run roughshod over the liberties of British citizens. For instance, a poster from 1830 entitled "The New Police" encouraged people to work for the "Abolition of the New Police!" The poster asked several questions, including "Why is the Sword of Justice placed in the hands of a

MILITARY Man?"[21] In so doing, the poster demonstrated the concern about the relationship of the police to a domestic, standing army (given that the first Chief Commissioners of the Met were former soldiers). Further, Clive Emsley cites the radical *Weekly Dispatch* as arguing that the police force would make Britain more like authoritarian France and result in "the exercise of the worst and most odious results attached to the gens d'armrie [sic] system of our French neighbours—the practice of secret denunciations, the destruction of private confidence, the paralyzing of the energies of the people, and the facilitating of every kind of ministerial excess."[22] Even the *Conservative Standard* stated, "The thing is not—never was English."[23]

This same worry about a standing police force was present in New York as well. Inspired by the London Metropolitan Police, New York officials in 1845 founded the Municipal Police (what would eventually become the NYPD). In his comprehensive study of the early years of New York policing, Bruce Chadwick asks, "Why were New Yorkers [in the 1830s] so reluctant to hire a new, armed, trained, and professional police force to quell the city's riots and patrol its streets?"[24] As London was the largest metropolis in Britain, so was New York the largest city in America. As a result, according to Chadwick, the city had been plagued in the 1830s by riots of various kinds, from the political (abolitionist and labor protests) to the merely criminal and hoodlum (such as street gangs rioting on Election Day for or against certain candidates).[25] The constable or night-watch system that was in place was inadequate to deal with these riots as well as rampant crime in areas like the infamous Five Points slum.[26] However, like many in Britain, New Yorkers feared a Metropolitan Police force would be too much like a conquering army: "The British army had occupied several American cities prior to the American Revolution and continued to do so during the conflict. The people hated the British for doing that. That sour feeling continued to be felt for generations, and the people saw the proposed police force as another occupying army, loyal to the mayor and not the residents."[27] Further, Chadwick states that "New Yorkers, and people throughout the country, also feared the enormous cost of a large and professional force."[28]

However, by the 1840s, "the people of New York, fed up with chaos and havoc, finally would begin a strong push for the dismantling of the ragged force of constables and call for professional, trained police."[29] The inadequacy and amateur nature of the previous constable/night-watch system is summed up by John J. Sturtevant, who recalls in his memoirs what the security situation in New York was like prior to the establishment of an official police: "At this early date New York had no police force, but was looked after by constables in the day, serving summons and making arrests when so ordered by any judge; at night we had 'Night Watchmen,' leather-capped guardians, or 'Charlie's Leatherheads.' (Take your choice of names)."[30] Sturtevant notes that this constable/night-watch system was entirely voluntary and was "made up of citizens who wished to add to their daily income who served as a watch on alternate nights on a three-house tour."[31] As such, this ur-police apparatus was an amateur affair, and it was not up to the task of combating the growing problem of crime in an increasingly populated city like New York. Therefore, by 1845, the citizens of New York decided that the benefits to public safety of a professional and organized state surveillance apparatus outweighed the potential risks of the new police apparatus abusing its power.

Meanwhile, in Britain, the press was often quick to report and castigate failures of the police to carry out their duties. One notable example is news stories about the British Detective Inspector Jack Whicher, an inspiration for both Wilkie Collins's Sergeant Cuff in *The Moonstone* and Charles Dickens's Inspector Bucket in *Bleak House*, who was famed for his work at the Met. However, when he fingered Constance Kent for the murder of her half-brother, various newspapers chastised him for so doing, and, eventually, the case was dismissed due to lack of evidence.[32] The newspapers criticized Whicher in part because of a wide-held belief that a woman, let alone a young woman and the victim's half-sister, could be capable of such a vicious murder of a young boy.[33] Another journalistic sensation was the failure of the Met to identify Jack the Ripper.[34] Some specific examples include *The Illustrated London News*, which writes that "[t]he police force at the East End of London is apparently deficient in strength of numbers, considering the large extent of its beats."[35] Here, the newspaper suggests that Her Majesty's government is not funding an extensive enough police apparatus in order to prevent or find criminals like Jack. (On a side note, similar critiques have been made of the current British government's austerity measures that have resulted in less patrols in cities like London and, some say, a concomitant rise in knife and other violent crime.[36]) Further, the paper also argues that "there is something to be said for the institution of a small permanent detective staff, independent of the street patrol, at every police-station in London."[37] In other words, the paper criticizes the Met not only for being short-staffed, but also for not having enough detectives available—an interesting point that reminds us of why, perhaps, a fictional detective like Sherlock Holmes became so popular following the Met's inability to solve the Whitechapel murders. He made up psychologically for what the Met lacked in reality.

The same paper later states that "[t]he repeated horrible murders and mutilations of the dead, perpetrated in the dark nooks and corners of a wretched quarter in the vicinity of Whitechapel and Spitalfields, with the failure of the police either to detect the criminal or to guard against the commission of these atrocities, have excited much alarm."[38] Here, we see the London media calling the British police apparatus to task for its failure to fulfill its raison d'être—to employ its panoptic abilities to protect the public. In a nation where hostility and suspicion toward the creation and existence of the police apparatus ran high, it was unforgivable that the apparatus should fail in its mission despite the government's promises that the advantages (in terms of national security) of instituting this state surveillance apparatus far offset the possible dangers of police power exceeding its mandate.

By contrast, the New York newspapers were generally more favorable in their assessment of the new police apparatus. In particular, the media was appalled at protestors' violent and hostile actions toward the police during the 1863 New York City Draft Riots. These riots occurred in response to the draft implemented by President Lincoln that year to ensure an adequate number of Union troops during the Civil War.[39] The majority of protestors were Irish and working-class men, those whom the draft would affect the most (since they did not have the resources to pay someone else to take their place in the draft, as was allowed at the time). In criticizing these rioters' treatment of the police, the *New York Times* wrote on July 14, 1863, that "[s]oon after the rioting began [Police] Superintendent KENNEDY hurried to the scene in a carriage, and as he alighted a portion of the crowd recognized him, greeting him at first with uncomplimentary epithets and afterwards with blows."[40] The paper goes on to describe more rioters assaulting and nearly killing Kennedy, until one protestor decided to step in to protect the superintendent.[41] At that point, two fellow policemen were able to get to the scene and carry Kennedy to safety.[42] The article continues by relating that while Kennedy was being attacked, "a dispatch was received by the officers of the Broadway Squad in charge of the building [an armory], from Police Headquarters, to the effect that inasmuch as it was impossible to reinforce them, and the attacking party so greatly outnumbered them, they must retire in the best manner they could."[43] The police soon decamped from the armory to safety, with a few assailed by bricks thrown by the rioters.[44] The article concludes that the mood of the protestors toward the police was so violent that officers could not risk being observed by the mob; as such, it was lucky that there was a backdoor to the armory through which they could escape unseen.[45] Likewise, *The New York Tribune* writes of actions elsewhere in the city: "The police at once drew their clubs and revolvers, but after a contest of a few minutes, they were also forced to retreat. [...]. A rush was made at once for the officer [who had fired shots] [...] [the rioters] seized the policeman, knocked him down, and beat him in a fearful manner."[46]

In these ways, the American news media of the time were more willing to praise the work of the police and criticize those—particularly the working class—who did not respect or obey the new apparatus, while their British counterparts were far more critical and wary of police conduct. This difference in tenor we see here between the British coverage of Bloody Sunday or Jack the Ripper and the American coverage of the Draft Riots might be attributed to the fact that the Draft Rioters' violent and destructive attacks on city officials and municipal buildings had an effect on the city not unlike that of 9/11. And, as in the wake of 9/11, the city and its media were grateful for the work the New York police did in protecting the public from what could be considered an early terroristic event.

Certainly, the letters and diaries of Julia Anna Hartness Lay demonstrate the frightening and shocking nature of the riots for those who witnessed it first-hand. Her descriptions of the riots lend credence to the argument that they were a terroristic event in terms of the fear and trauma they precipitated. In her July 13, 1863, entry, Hartness begins thus: "An awful riot commenced today on account of the draft. The Provost Marshall's office was burned and other buildings adjoining. They tore up the railroad tracks, cut down the telegraph wires, entered stores, robbed everything they could get while whole blocks were destroyed."[47] She describes fires cropping up everywhere, including at the armory on Second Avenue. She lived close enough to the riots that she "saw thousands of men pass our house with guns and carbines."[48] These rioters, she claims, ran into various factories and shops to encourage other men there to follow and join the protestors. In a particularly disturbing passage, she writes that "[t]hey [the rioters] hunted the poor negroes, took them from their homes and killed many, hung some, burned their dwellings, destroyed their beds. I saw a pile in the middle of the street burnt and could hear the crockery thrown from the windows and every particle of furniture and clothing entirely gone."[49] Here, Lay is an eyewitness to how the riots were motivated not only by the draft, but also by racism toward African Americans, whom the Irish and other white workers feared would take their jobs. Lay also describes the eventual forceful army response to the riots: "We had cannon placed in the middle of the avenue twice and fired off which scattered the rioters. A large number were killed. I saw them carried past one door cut down in a moment."[50] This military response occurred after the New York police were overwhelmed, and Lincoln was forced to send in regiments fresh off the Civil War battlefield to quell the protestors.

Above all, Lay relates the trauma of what she saw and experienced during what for her were terror attacks on her city: "What dread times. I never wish to see again men with clubs and stones. I saw them thrown and heard the soldiers fire back a whole volley then the screams and groans."[51] She then prays that "the bright sun will shine upon us in the morning and the dreadful sins no longer be persisted in and peace may once more be restored to our beautiful city. [...] I have scarcely slept any for four nights."[52] Her sleeplessness speaks to the horror of what she observed, and it is a common symptom of what we would now characterize as post-traumatic stress disorder,[53] something many experienced after the September 11 attacks.[54] In this way, Lay's painful knowledge of the bloodshed and devastation in New York parallels that of many who were present when the Twin Towers fell in the same area nearly 140 years later. In both situations, the police apparatus was desired in order to protect the general public from those who were bent on terroristic acts. For instance, Lay commends "our military and grand police"[55] in her diary.

Nevertheless, some New York papers did comment that the police and city government were not sufficiently organized or ready for a possible resistance to the implementation of the draft. In fact, the New York police were so overwhelmed that President Lincoln had to eventually send in military regiments from Gettysburg to help suppress the rioting. Regarding the inadequacy of the police, the *Times* writes that "Very few [in the city government] were prepared for the riotous demonstrations which yesterday [...] prevailed almost unchecked in our streets. [...] [N]o one anticipated resistance at so early a stage in the execution of the law, and, consequently, both the City and National authorities were totally unprepared to meet it."[56] Similarly, the *Tribune* criticizes the manner of the police retreat from the rioters, "which they did in good order until near Fortieth street, when one of them [the police officers] discharged his revolver four times into the midst of the throng."[57] Still, these American newspapers' criticisms of the police are much different from those of the British newspapers, since the New York media rebukes the police apparatus for not exercising enough power while the London media criticizes their police for either abusing the apparatus' power or for not adequately using the resources it has.

In this way, we see the beginnings of somewhat divergent attitudes toward the police apparatus in the U.S. and U.K. that continue to the present and, as we will see, inform post-9/11 police dramas and docuseries in both nations. For example, in a study funded by the U.S. Department of Justice about New York public opinion of the police, the authors report that, overall, "[c]itizens' opinions of the police are positive and quite stable over time," despite negative reportage of the American police apparatus.[58] However, this general assessment does not reflect the severe racial divide in the perception of police in the U.S. There is a stark difference between white and black American citizens in terms of trusting the police apparatus: "While a large majority of Americans rate police officers positively on a 0-to-100 'feeling thermometer,' whites and blacks differ widely in their views, including among Democrats, according to a Pew Research Center survey conducted in August."[59] This survey found that "while a clear majority of whites give law enforcement warm ratings (74%), black and Hispanic views of police are more mixed. Just three-in-ten black Americans (30%) express warm attitudes about police officers, while 28% offer a neutral rating. Another 38% give a cold rating, including 30% who give a very cold rating (24 or lower on the 0–100 scale)."[60] At the same, in Britain, while research company Ipsos MORI found that 65% would "generally trust the police,"[61] those trust levels have nevertheless fallen, particularly "since the mid-20th Century. The 1970s and early 1980s were a time of social tensions that boiled over into violent clashes with the police during the miners' strikes and inner-city riots [similar to the Bloody Sunday riots noted earlier in this chapter]. Broader cultural trends may also have played a part—for example British society becoming less deferential to authority in general."[62]

All in all, middle- and upper-class white Americans, as was the case at the time of the Draft Riots, tend to be more supportive of the police apparatus and its work, and, overall, trust more that the apparatus will not overstep its boundaries. However, Americans of color, like the British overall, are leerier of the power this apparatus can wield. This suspicion of police authority has its roots in the nineteenth century, certainly, for African Americans, as the result of slavery (which will be discussed later in this chapter), and, for the British, as the result of police overstep during riots like Bloody Sunday, or failures like the Whitechapel murders.

Perhaps, then, it is not surprising that Doyle's Holmes stories, which are extremely disdainful of law enforcement, emerged in the wake of the aforementioned Whitechapel murders that were never solved, and which represented for much of the press and public a major failure on the part of the Metropolitan Police. For Doyle, as for much of the British press at the time, the police are useful only when brute force is needed to literally physically capture and pin down a criminal. Otherwise, it is only Holmes, not the Met, who can utilize embryonic forensic science techniques to correctly identify the culprit.

However, it is important to point out the complicated response to the Whitechapel murders in the British media. While many London newspapers were definitely critical of the Met, there were some that reminded the public of the difficulty of identifying a culprit amidst the large and itinerant population of the East End. There were even contradictory assessments within the same newspaper. For example, as noted earlier, the *Illustrated London News* criticized the Metropolitan Police's handling of the murders; however, the unnamed author of the paper's "Our Note Book" opinion column writes at length about the capability of the London police and reproaches those in the press and public who brand the police as inadequate: "I am not one of those who cry shame upon the police because they have failed to discover what half the intelligence (and all the folly) of London has failed to disclose."[63] The columnist remarks that no one—certainly not the paper's readers—is any more enlightened as to the Whitechapel murderer's identity than are the Metropolitan police, and so no one is in a position to criticize the Met.[64] He then relates an anecdote in support of the abilities of the London police. The writer describes how he and a friend traveled to the Whitechapel area following the killings. He comments that, without saying a word to a nearby policeman other than to inquire when the next train would depart for Aldgate station, the officer immediately surmised their destination as the Whitechapel scenes of crime and directed them to Mitre Square (the site of Catherine Eddows's murder).[65] The columnist argues that "Mr. Herbert Spencer himself could not have exhibited a greater talent for mental analysis"[66] than did this Metropolitan officer and concludes that the London law enforcement is more than capable of good detective work. No doubt, this particular officer was able to deduce so quickly the friends' destination because he had seen many curious Londoners who had similarly desired to see the infamous Whitechapel district in the wake of the murders. Nevertheless, for this writer, the problem was not the Met but that the public and press did not appreciate how difficult this particular crime was to solve.

In this way, the nineteenth-century London and the New York press were similar to news sources today regarding its reportage of policing. Like contemporary media in the wake of 9/11 and subsequent terrorist attacks, their nineteenth-century counterparts voiced complicated views of the police apparatus following major challenges to public safety: sometimes questioning it, sometimes supporting it, and sometimes remaining ambivalent. In other words, the contemporary press, as well as modern social media, replicate the older narrative of an apparatus that is at once formidable but whose power might not be used equitably or effectively.

One might imagine this nineteenth-century journalistic debate regarding the Met's inability to resolve the Whitechapel murders would be irrelevant to a twenty-first-century public. Yet, its ramifications are such that this most famous of cold cases has inspired two British television series, *Ripper Street* and *Whitechapel*, which wrestle directly with this failure of the police apparatus to protect the public. In *Ripper Street*, the H Division of the Metropolitan Police, centered in the Whitechapel district, is depicted in the years immediately following the infamous murders. The series spends time visualizing from the detectives' point of view the pain resulting from the loss of public confidence in their abilities. *Whitechapel*, meanwhile, returns to the district in the modern day; however, the Met detectives posted there must cope with copycat criminals reenacting crimes from Whitechapel's dark past, from the Ripper murders to the Kray brothers' gangland activities. The fact that the series is explicitly titled *Whitechapel*, and begins season one with a criminal who recreates the Ripper murders, underscores the lingering sting of the London police's most notable defeat.

I argue that these U.K. programs are driven to recapitulate and recuperate Met debacles of the past as the result of similar, ostensible failures of the British police apparatus in the present (from unsuccessfully preventing 7/7 and more recent London terrorist attacks to the killing of Mark Duggan). *Ripper Street*, for instance, addresses the problem narratively by utilizing the psychological balm discussed earlier: a competent detective on the force who counteracts the mediocrity of the apparatus. Interestingly, this detective is based on a real policeman, Inspector Edmund Reid, who investigated the murder of Martha Tabram, a Whitechapel sex worker, a crime which occurred prior to the official Whitechapel killings (although some, then and now, argue that Tabram might also have been the victim of the Ripper). Various police reports by Reid demonstrate his thoroughness in attempting to solve Tabram's murder (unfortunately, he and the Met were unable to do so). His reports also establish that his efforts and those of the Met were not lessened by the fact that the victim was a sex worker. For instance, he writes, "On [the] 9th [Mary Ann] Connelly [Tabram's friend and fellow sex worker] came to Commercial Street Station and stated that she and the deceased were with two soldiers, one a corporal, and the other a private of the Guards from 10 till 11:45 p.m. on Monday 6th walking about Whitechapel. [...] She stated that she should know both men again."[67] As a result, Reid then organized an identity parade of any soldier who was in the area that night in the hope that Connelly could identify the customers she and Tabram had been with the night of the murder.[68] However, Connelly was a no show to the line-up, but, when located again, promised to attend a new identity parade, which Reid then proceeded to arrange.[69] This report demonstrates not only Reid's zeal in his attempt to locate the murderer of Tabram, but also that he took the murder of a sex worker seriously and valued the eyewitness testimony of a sex worker enough to assemble new identity parades when Connelly did not attend previous ones. In this way, the Met demonstrated that they did care about the itinerant population of Whitechapel and worked hard to solve violent crimes against these women. It was not lack of consideration or effort on the part of the police that prevented detection—it was simply that the murders were difficult to solve in a crowded, peripatetic, and volatile neighborhood like Whitechapel.

According to Metropolitan Police records, the real-life Reid was on leave during the actual Whitechapel investigation. Reid's fellow inspector, Joseph Chandler, noted Reid's absence in his police report discussing the crime scene of the Ripper's second victim, Annie Chapman. Chandler writes that "[e]very possible enquiry is being made with a view of tracing the murderer but up to the present without success. Local Inspector Reid being on his annual leave the inquiries have been entrusted to Inspector Chandler."[70] Here, Chandler refutes the London press by demonstrating how the Met were indeed trying their best to determine the Whitechapel culprit. He further mentions Inspector Joseph Abberline, whose name would become synonymous with the investigation and who would eventually bear the brunt of criticism for not locating Jack: "I would respectfully suggest that Inspector Abberline [who] is well acquainted with H. Division be deputed to take up this inquiry as I believe he is already engaged in the case of the Bucks Row murder [that of Mary Ann Nichols, the first victim] which would appear to have been committed by the same person as the one in Hanbury Street [where Chapman's body was found]."[71] This report demonstrates how quickly the Met understood that the three murders—Tabram, Nichols, and Chapman—were related.

This point is significant, given that the idea of what we now call a "serial killer" was not extant at the time.

Reid's real-life absence from the Whitechapel investigation allows *Ripper Street* to in turn fictionalize Reid as a detective untainted by the Met's unproductive efforts and, as such, paint him as a potential hero who might have solved the murders. The program develops Reid into a Holmes-like investigator who successfully adopts and employs nascent forensic science techniques to solve crimes in ways the Victorian police establishment, which is resistant to such new methods, cannot. In a similar vein, *Murdoch Mysteries* (CBC), shown on Netflix and Hulu in the U.S., features the titular police detective William Murdoch who is on the vanguard of forensic science but must work amid the more loutish and brutish police officers of the late nineteenth-century Toronto police.

These narratives about policing, whether newspaper stories from the past or television series of the present, are certainly compelling. However, Metropolitan police documentation of the Whitechapel investigation, housed at the U.K. National Archives, demonstrates the power of such narratives to obscure the complexities of how the police apparatus works. Police reports from the Whitechapel investigation indicate that members of H Division were neither brutal nor incompetent, and yet they still failed to find Jack. For example, as noted earlier, during the Tabram investigation, Reid's reports indicate how he patiently arranged for numerous identity parades for Connelly to identify her and Tabram's customers because Connelly often failed to attend these line-ups.[72] Further, other police reports show that the officers present at the Whitechapel scenes of crime were detailed in their descriptions, much like modern police and forensic technicians would be today. For example, here is the detailed description of Chapman's body and crime scene in Chandler's report: "I at once proceeded to No. 29 Hanbury Street, and in the backyard found a woman lying on her back dead, left arm resting on left breast, legs drawn up, abducted small intestine and flaps of the abdomen lying on right side, above right shoulders [...] [with a] large quantity of blood above the left shoulder [...] [and cut in a] jagged manner right around the throat."[73] Here, Chandler carefully notes the position and state of the body, much as modern law enforcement would do. He also minutely records the state of the crime scene, including location and manner of blood spatter: "In examining the yard I found on the back wall of the house (at the head of the body) and about 18 inches from the ground about 6 patches of blood varying in size from a swooping piece to a point, and [...] on the left of the body near the head patches and smears of blood about 10 inches from the ground."[74] Such blood-spatter analysis would be familiar to any viewer of contemporary forensic docuseries such as *Forensic Files* or fictional dramas like *CSI*.

In other words, the approach to crime scene analysis in the late nineteenth century is not all that different from how police might handle a crime scene today. This report reinforces the point that while modern police do have access to better forensic tools and technology, even contemporary law enforcement might be stumped by the Whitechapel case. After all, the Met police went about their investigation into the Ripper murders as methodically and thoroughly as they could. Indeed, there are untold numbers of cold cases in contemporary police departments despite modern developments in forensics or behavioral science. The presence of technology does not automatically mean that every crime can be solved, no matter what programs like *Forensic Files* or *CSI* might imply.

While modern forensic tools such as DNA and fingerprint analysis could have helped detectives were these available to them, success eluded the Met mainly because useable evidence was simply non-existent. There were no witnesses yet innumerable potential suspects, and the victims were impoverished sex workers who were from a transient population. Add to this the dark, warren-like streets and alleys of Whitechapel, and the situation produces a murderer who could operate invisibly with near impunity. Even today, the same conditions might thwart modern police detection, despite the presence of CCTV surveillance cameras. Further, the reams of reports suggest the Met spent a great deal of time, effort, and care to follow up on potential leads. A report from Inspector Abberline exemplifies how the Met traced any possible lead or suspect, in this case, a butcher named Joseph Isenschmid. Abberline describes in minute detail his findings about Isenschmid, including the suspect's personality, his marriage, his recent stays at a mental institution, and his run-ins with the law.[75] In modern terms, we might say Abberline constructed a "profile" of this possible suspect in his report. For example, Abberline writes of Isenschmid: "He has been in Colney Hatch Lunatic Asylum for ten weeks and was discharged from there […]. He then got employment as Journeyman butcher. […] He has not slept at home for quite two months. […] He is fond of other women, he used to frequent a public house kept by a 'German' named Gerhringer in Wentworth Street Whitechapel. He is known as 'the mad butcher'."[76] Certainly, Abberline's profile of Isenschmid suggests he was someone who could have been capable of eviscerating several women.

In such Met reports from 1888, it is clear the police had cast a wide net for suspects, even outside of London proper, particularly if a homicide happened to resemble in some fashion the signature of the Whitechapel killings. One such murder, that of a woman named Frances Cole, yielded a suspect named Sadler. Sadler's wife cooperated with the police, and in return, they helped protect her from retribution from her violent husband: "Following report of violence against Sarah Sadler. [...] [A] P.C. has been and is now patrolling Danbrook Road in view of Sadler's house to render Mrs. Sadler assistance should occasion arise. Mrs. Sadler expresses her thanks for the attention and courtesy that she has received from the Police. Signed, Frances Boswell, Sergeant."[77] In this way, the Met in their reports attempt to refute their image as one of incompetence or laziness, and their respectful treatment of abused women and sex workers belies the press' construction of the police as an instrument of brute force.

Interestingly, BBC's *Whitechapel* gestures toward this counternarrative of "failure despite competence" in its first season: the "new" Jack the Ripper, despite modern forensics and surveillance technology, still slips out of the Met's grasp. Nevertheless, in subsequent episodes, the modern Whitechapel division rectifies police missteps of the past. For example, in season two, the Whitechapel detectives arrest twins who are revenants of the Kray Brothers. However, they refuse, at great risk to their lives, to be on the payroll of Jimmy and Johnny Kray. As such, they fictionally compensate for the era of London police corruption from the 1960s to the 1980s and so represent the ostensibly better policing of today.

In these ways, I see series like *Ripper Street* and *Whitechapel* offering British writers, producers, and viewers an opportunity to fictionally and narratively make up for the Met's past sins of omission and commission as a means of addressing current concerns about modern police blunders, such as misidentifying the wrong suspect in the wake of the 7/7 bombings. Jean Charles de Menezes, a Brazilian national, was shot eight times and killed by the Metropolitan Police at Stockwell Station in the London Underground after they mistakenly thought he was one of the 7/7 bombers still at large (the shooting took place two weeks after the attacks).[78] This police recuperation appears as a recurring theme in the programs written and produced for British networks (although, as in the case of *Ripper Street*, U.S. platforms such as Amazon often contribute financially). Again, we need to consider the television narrative here as a psychological balm. The narrative solace offered is that policing overall is superior today to that of the past, despite public concern about police overreach or incompetence since

9/11. In other words, police today have greater scientific tools at their disposal to track criminals or prevent crime, including surveillance technologies, such as CCTV, or the ability to monitor phone and internet communications. Further, police must now be more accountable to various rules and regulations regarding conduct and treatment of people so that policing is not as brutal or corrupt as it has been perceived to be in the past. In this way, these series' narratives reassure even as they depict problems with policing, such as violence, unjust arrest, or incompetence.

THE POLICE APPARATUS AND THE VISUAL SPECTACLE OF VIOLENCE

This narrative of the police progress despite ongoing problems also preoccupies the programs *Life on Mars* (both the British and American versions) and *Copper*, although each acknowledge the darker actions of the police apparatus more than *Ripper Street* or *Whitechapel* do. For example, in both the British and American versions of *Life on Mars*, Detective Sam Tyler appears to travel back in time to the 1970s and must survive as a policeman of that era (in the Greater Manchester Police in the U.K. series, and in the NYPD in the U.S. iteration). He is shocked by the rampant corruption, use of violence to coerce confessions or to maintain police power, and the limited abilities or even desire to uncover criminal activity. Interestingly, but not surprisingly, given what I discussed earlier about the American press' and public's more favorable attitudes toward the police, the U.S. version of *Life on Mars* is critical but less so than the U.K. version of 1970s' policing practices. The police commander Lt. Gene Hunt (portrayed by Harvey Keitel) becomes a more sympathetic and humorous character, not to mention a father figure, to Sam Tyler. This is opposed to the analogous character of DCI Gene Hunt (played by Phillip Glenister) in the original U.K. series, who remains a deeply problematic and brutal character throughout the program. Given that American policing incorporates more militarized and brutal police tactics than the British, and, given the greater acceptance of these practices in the U.S. (both in the nineteenth century and today), it should not be unexpected that these factors translate into the U.S. *Life on Mars*'s more benign depiction of 1970s American policing. However, in the BBC version, our subject position is that of Sam Tyler, and so we as viewers are invited to be as equally upset and concerned about the British policing methods of the past.

In a similar way, *Copper* transports the viewer to the Five Points borough of 1864 New York, a rough and cruel neighborhood in which the cops are likewise brutal and pitiless in their methods of dispensing justice and maintaining law and order. Like *Life on Mars*, the series encourages us to consider that the brutal methods of policing are something of the past and that law enforcement has today become a more sophisticated and regulated apparatus. Although in *Copper* some officers, such as protagonist Detective Corky Corcoran, are more interested in justice than others, he is still depicted as a product of his time, ready to use violence and coercion rather than investigative techniques to maintain peace and apprehend criminals. The same is true in *Life on Mars*, where brutality, bribery, and corruption are at par for the course.

As we discussed earlier, the 1863 New York Draft Riots were described as a form of terrorism on the part of wealthier New Yorkers for whom the event was analogous to 9/11 in its traumatic effects; they, along with the city's Republican (and thus loyal to President Lincoln) government, were the target of the mainly Irish working-class dissidents. The rioters did not want to be drafted into the Union army because they believed that they, as working-class men and women, bore an unfair amount of the burden in terms of who was being asked to fight because the wealthy were able to buy their way out of service.[79] However, much of their resistance was also due to blatant racism against African Americans—the New York working class had no wish to end slavery, especially since they viewed African American labor as a threat to their livelihoods.[80] As a result, rioters attacked African Americans, including the murder of Abraham Franklin, a Black New York citizen. In the New York County District Attorney indictment records for the riots, it is clear that many witnesses were deposed regarding violence against African Americans, including Franklin's killing. For example, the grand jury statement concludes that the defendants Mark J. Silva and Dennis Carey "did make an assault [on Franklin] and that they [Silva and Carey] [...] with both their hands and feet then and there [...] did kick and strike and beat the said Abraham Franklin in and upon the head, breast, back, belly, sides and other parts of the body of him [...] of which said mortal strokes, wounds, bruises and contusions [...] [Franklin] did die."[81] In this way, the grand jury left no doubt regarding the brutality of Franklin's murder.

The terroristic violence committed by white New Yorkers against African Americans is made clear in such reports. By situating itself in the aftermath of the Draft Riots, *Copper* reminds us therefore that terroristic violence has occurred in New York before 9/11. This implicit connection between the New York of 1863–1864 and the New York post-9/11 is underscored by a story arc in the episodes "The Hudson River School"[82] and "Better Times Are Coming,"[83] in which Corcoran and other New York Metropolitan officers use surveillance techniques, including undercover operations, to infiltrate what amounts to a Confederate terrorist cell bent on using Greek Fire to incinerate much of New York. In this way, the series' writers counter our cultural amnesia of New York's long history of terroristic violence.

Although *Copper* depicts the New York police as a line of defense against terrorism (as did the New York papers of the time), *Copper*, like *Life on Mars*, still positions viewers as a modern, enlightened audience appalled at the brutality and illegality of past policing methods. This idea that we have "progressed" in our ideas of proper policing is underscored by the cover of the season one DVD of *Copper* which depicts Corcoran and other detectives sporting shotguns over their shoulders, with the tagline, "In 1864, he was New York's finest," implying that, compared to the modern NYPD officer, he was anything but. Here, the DVD cover references how today's NYPD is often termed "New York's finest." The cover therefore creates a distance between what was considered "fine" or "acceptable" in 1864 versus what we today would deem appropriate police methods.

Nevertheless, such images also emphasize a visual spectacle of police violence and brutality that is as seductive as it is shocking. For example, advertisements and images for *Copper* emphasize this point; one features a brass knuckle with "New York, 1864" stamped on it[84]; and, on the season two DVD cover, a fierce Corcoran glares at us, accompanied by the tagline "New York, 1865. There are no city limits," ostensibly hinting at how there were no checks on what the early New York police could do. Further, scenes in both *Copper* and *Life on Mars* linger on officers' physiques as a literal embodiment of the police apparatus. The male body becomes a brute instrument for contending with potential criminals and coercing them to confess. The seductiveness of the spectacle of violence is created because it achieves results. For instance, if, in the storyline, the police know the culprit but cannot prove it, it is physical force on the part of Tyler or Corcoran that enables them to garner a confession or to force others to rat out the criminal. To put it bluntly, we as viewers have the satisfaction of seeing the baddies get what they "deserve," even if it is at the expense of the rule of law.

Even modern police themselves admit to envying officers like Tyler and Corcoran. For example, in a Channel 4 docuseries, similarly titled *Coppers*, which rides along with real-life modern U.K. police, a Gillingham custody sergeant remarks that offenders often take advantage of the "duty of care" British police are today charged with in terms of making sure those arrested are cared for.[85] For instance, in this particular episode, an offender had pretended to be ill in order to be taken to hospital and so delay his intake into the custody suite.[86] Her frustration with this aspect of modern policing is palatable: "C'mon, all this human rights now … which I think is totally rubbish … sorry."[87] Further, in the episode "C.I.D.," a Mansfield detective laughingly states, "Sometimes I watch *Life on Mars*, and I think, if only it was still like that" because detectives face "no comment" interviews with offenders who refuse to admit to crimes or give the police information.[88] In this way, she wishes she could be like Detective Gene Tyler, who regularly roughs up offenders to gain a confession or information. A fellow detective clarifies that, unlike Tyler, he "has never banged a table, never stood up and slammed a door."[89] Yet another detective half-jokingly laments: "I'm a bit gutted that I wasn't around in the 80s, particularly before the [1984] Police and Criminal Evidence Act because now we've got to, like, abide by the law and stuff."[90] The pleasing visual spectacle of watching evildoers punished is yet another aspect of our conflicting narratives about the police apparatus, ones that both desire to see the police operate within the boundaries of civil liberties and yet demand justice at all costs.

Interestingly, though Doyle characterized Holmes as mostly antithetical to such brute force, given that Holmes represented a newer, more intellectual and scientific approach to police work, the spectacle of the violence is still present in this detective who is ostensibly removed from the ills of the official police apparatus. In the original stories, Holmes is portrayed as simultaneously thin and cerebral, yet surprisingly strong and pugnacious when necessary; for example, in "The Adventure of the Speckled Band," he can straighten out a bent fireplace poker, or, in "The Adventure of the Solitary Cyclist," he can engage in fisticuffs like an expert boxer. This visual spectacle of Holmes as a literal embodiment of justice is adopted by both *Sherlock* and *Elementary*. In *Sherlock*, Holmes can disarm and toss (multiple times) a CIA operative out his 221B window,[91] while a muscular, tattooed, yet wiry Holmes in *Elementary* regularly teaches Watson combat techniques using a dummy and a truncheon. In this way, the original Holmes and his modern interpretations (including Guy

Ritchie' Holmes, who participates in illegal boxing matches) bring together the disparate desires of writers and viewers/readers: a detective who is both an ally of the police yet separate from the apparatus, and a detective who can embody the brute physical power of law enforcement yet can maintain control and return to an intellectual, scientific method of deduction.

SURVEILLING THE POLICE THROUGH REALITY TELEVISION

In our current television landscape, the panoptic view of the police continues beyond the fictional realm into that of documentary television. The aforementioned *Coppers* is only one example of the recent exponential rise of "ride along" programs in which the audience is given an apparent "fly-on-the-wall" position to view the police doing their work in various situations, from traffic stops to quelling domestic disputes to drug busts. Like the prison reality programs discussed in Chap. 2, these police docuseries are cheap to produce and popular among viewers. In both the U.S. and U.K., these programs are prolific, and audiences on both sides of the Atlantic can access either nation's series through platforms such as You Tube, Netflix, or Amazon. As Stuart Heritage of *The Guardian* points out, "Multichannel television means we're now exposed to more global law enforcement than ever before."[92] Heritage then describes the comforting nature of these police docuseries, the British ones in particular: "But despite this giddy spectrum of international crimefighting, there's still nothing that soothes the bones quite like a documentary about British coppers. Less violent than their American equivalents, and with far fewer frizzy haircuts than anything from Australia, you know exactly what to expect with a British cop doc—namely lots of people called Colin doing mundane things in bleak little towns that you barely knew existed."[93] However, since 2011, the nature of criminal and police violence in British police reality series has increased dramatically. In the latest series of *Traffic Cops* and *Police Interceptors*, for instance, we see how drug gangs are moving from larger cities like Leeds, Manchester, or Liverpool into smaller, more rural towns in Yorkshire, bringing with them more violence and the need for U.K. police to respond with greater, more American-style force, including the use of armed response units.

Some examples of similar docuseries in the U.S. are the long-running *Cops* (which, in the wake of 9/11, sported an American flag in the credits, linking the police with the war on terror) and *Alaska State Troopers*

(National Geographic). Police docuseries are especially numerous in the U.K., with *Traffic Cops*, *Motorway Cops*, *Coppers*, and *Police Interceptors* to name just a few. As with prison docuseries, a primary motivating force for networks and production companies in filming these programs is that they are relatively inexpensive to make. However, they also answer viewers' desires to inspect the police and their actions in a panoptic way from their living rooms. Heritage argues that this is the true reason for the production of so many law enforcement reality series—their popularity, not their inexpensive budget: "But people like this sort of documentary. That's why the TV schedules are currently overrun with them. It's not because they're cheap [...]. No, it's because people love them."[94] The audience gains a sense of monitoring the police, reassuring themselves that law enforcement carries out its function as an apparatus in appropriate ways that balance the need for social control with the public's right to civil liberties and privacy.

Certainly, footage can be edited, and so watching the docuseries is not the same as viewing unadulterated surveillance tape of police who are unaware they are being observed (e.g., many incidents of police brutality have been caught on cell phone cameras by bystanders). Therefore, the footage is edited, and all participants are aware of being filmed and thus can be on their best behavior. As such, the docuseries are in many ways a narrative as controlled as those in a fictional series, and the viewers can maintain a false sense of monitoring the apparatus. In actuality, we are only seeing an amended version of that apparatus. Like in prisons, the police in the U.S. and U.K. benefit from these docuseries as well, which is why they grant access to camera crews. The police have the opportunity through these series to explain their actions and point of view to the audience. So, for example, if force is used (such as to restrain a citizen refusing arrest), officers can clarify that such methods are required and minimal. In *Traffic Cops*, for example, we also see how the police use body cams to record their interactions with suspects for proof that there was no excessive use of force. In other words, surveillance via film is doubly used in these series—first, by the police and, second, by the audience. The programs thus work as good PR for the police to assure viewers that the apparatus is working appropriately.

However, the second function of these docuseries, like their fictional counterparts, is surveillance as entertainment and spectacle. Although they might have conflicted feelings about the police and a desire to witness what they do, ultimately, viewers can simply watch for the pleasure of watching, without being asked to do anything further. As with the fictional programs like *Copper* and *Life on Mars*, it can be the spectacle of the police apparatus itself and its power that is alluring. Even if, as opposed to fictional dramas, we do not witness violations of civil rights and violent brutality, the spectacle of the apparatus technologically surveilling and catching criminals can nevertheless be as pleasurable as it is in fictional programs. We can vicariously experience applying force and surveillance by watching the police do it through various panoptic technologies and tools of force. For example, *Traffic Cops* frequently features the onboard police computer that can quickly identify license plates to signal which ones are in violation of U.K. MOT standards; or, in U.S. series like *Cops*, we see the formidable gear of the American police, including guns, Tasers, and military-like body armor. All these effects speak of a seductive power derived through technology and through disciplinary mechanisms and accoutrements.

This docuseries approach to surveilling the police is, as I have discussed regarding recent fictional police dramas set in the past, one that has a long history in print with origins in the nineteenth century. Charles Dickens, for instance, was an admirer of the police and wrote several non-fiction accounts, including "On Duty with Inspector Field," "A Detective Police Party," and "The Metropolitan Protectives," in his *Household Words* periodical that took readers along on expeditions with the police, particularly the detective division of Scotland Yard. Phillip Collins notes that Dickens resembled many viewers of modern crime series in his complex feelings about criminality and policing. On the one hand, Dickens could understand and empathize with offenders: "He readily identified himself, in imagination, with their [offenders'] aggressive activities."[95] On the other hand, he admired and even idolized the growing British police apparatus, and he "would also strongly repudiate this sympathy [with criminals] by extolling their adversaries, the police, and demanding severe punishment for offenders against the law."[96]

Like post-9/11 police docuseries, Dickens panoptically observes the surveillance capabilities of a detective like Inspector Charles Frederick Field, on whom Dickens famously based Inspector Bucket from *Bleak House*. In "On Duty with Inspector Field," for instance, Dickens relates that, like a modern CCTV camera, "Inspector Field's eye is the roving eye that searches every corner of the cellar as he talks."[97] And, like a surveillance camera, Field possesses a seemingly 360 degree range of vision: "He [Fields] sees behind him, without any effort, and exceedingly disturbs one individual far in the rear by coolly calling out, 'It won't do, Mr. Michael! Don't try it!'"[98] In these descriptions of Field's surveillance capabilities, we see what will become Dickens's portrayal of Inspector Bucket's ability to see and observe in an almost machine-like fashion. For example, Dickens writes that Bucket looks at Mr. Snagsby "as if he [Bucket] were going to take his [Snagsby's] portrait"[99]; Bucket "notices things in general"[100]; he locates Gridley by tracking and viewing him through a skylight on a roof[101]; and he is "impossible to be evaded or declined."[102] As with modern police docuseries, we are limited in our view of the police—whether that be the real-life Field or the fictional Bucket—by what Dickens allows us to read. For instance, Dickens is not critical of the police or of Field's methods. Rather, he is awed by the power of the police apparatus, not skeptical of it. Imagining the perspective of a criminal, Dickens writes: "And to know that I *must* be stopped, come what will. To know that I am no match for this individual keenness and energy, or this organised and steady system!"[103] Here, Dickens's use of "organised" and "system" echo Foucault's description of what makes panoptic apparatuses powerful— they are logically ordered structures which allow the state to reach far into the lives of citizens.

In this way, the function of both the modern docuseries and Dickens's writings is the same: to allow the audience a glimpse of this organized surveillance system for reassurance and for pleasure. The fact that the same underlying documentary structure existed in the nineteenth century again underscores the similar reasons why this genre of the police docuseries would become popular: the concern, then as now, is with how the police apparatus operates—its scope and relation to the civil liberties of the public—but, also, we take pleasure in voyeuristically experiencing the power of the apparatus. As such, we are not readers or viewers who are duped or coerced into accepting a narrative about police surveillance; rather, we are readers and viewers who willingly participate in the panoptic pleasure, for comfort and for fun, of watching the police apparatus work. In this subject position, the viewer and reader are not the objects of police surveillance but the observers, if not direct operators, of it. As such, this activity accentuates John Ellis's argument about the passivity of television—that it does not require further political action on the part of the viewer.[104]

I would note, too, how many of the modern docuseries on crime and policing take their cue not only from Dickens, but also from the "penny dreadfuls" of the nineteenth century. These cheap, sensational publications were mostly published in Britain, although there were American versions as well (namely, dime novels and early pulp magazines).[105] The penny dreadfuls were so named because they cost an English penny and were thus inexpensive publications affordable by the general populace, although this does not mean they were read and consumed only by working-class readers. The penny dreadfuls were sensationalist journalism, in which crime was the spectacle not only in terms of the story, but also, like modern crime docuseries, in their visuals which were often explicit and detailed in their gory pictorials of crime scenes and criminal acts. In these publications, the focus was less on the actual police investigation as compared to contemporary docuseries. However, these programs, like their penny dreadful forebears, also present the spectacle of crime along with the display of police investigation. The nineteenth- as well as the twenty-first-century texts are powered by the desire to see crime enacted but then punished by the police apparatus. In this way, in both eras, there is a voyeuristic pleasure on the part of the reader/viewer to experience crime vicariously through the relation of the act and then also to experience the execution of justice by the police apparatus. The reader/viewer as such panoptically observes and experiences both crime and punishment. So, while the audience can enjoy what it might feel and look like to break the boundaries and rules of law and society, it can also pull back from that pleasure to experience the delight of seeing those rules reestablished and order restored and maintained.

Much of the pleasure in surveillance spectacle is watching the methods and technology of the police and detectives, especially the forensic science aspects of investigation. Other critics have more ably spoken in detail about the immense popularity in the last two decades, beginning even before 9/11, of drama and docuseries that present the almost magical qualities of forensic science methods. In particular, these scholars discuss the effect of the worldwide popularity of forensic science programs, both fictional and documentary, on public expectations of investigations and on how juries now demand DNA evidence at trial (what prosecutors term "the *CSI* effect").[106] Certainly, a discussion of all such series in the U.S. and U.K. is beyond the scope of this chapter. However, whether they are docuseries like *Forensic Files* or fictional programs like *CSI* and *Sherlock*, it is the spectacle and power of such surveillance technology that is the draw. These programs make it seem as if forensic science is an esoteric, alchemic process that can yield answers quickly and irrefutably.

However, the appeal of forensic science is not new, since we can witness its power and pleasure at play in the original Doyle stories that can be rightly thought of as the true genesis, if not of detective fiction, then of forensic science spectacle. Here, the phenomenon takes place in print rather than visually, but the descriptions Watson gives of Holmes's methods are nevertheless memorable and powerful. At the time, Holmes's forensic methods were extraordinary and unorthodox in terms of police work, but they are recognizable to us today as early crime scene analysis. For example, Holmes analyzes tobacco ash through smell and texture, or he "dr[aws] out a lens, and [lies] down on [the ground] to have a better view"[107] of footprints in mud, or he "crawl[s]" along floors "swiftly backwards and forwards" with "his lens in his hand" in order to "examin[e] minutely the cracks between the boards"[108] looking for what today would be termed hair and fiber evidence. His actions were as fascinating to a Victorian British and American audience as they are for modern viewers of *Sherlock* and *Elementary*. It is Holmes's peculiar ability to gather and read forensic evidence that makes the detective such a powerful and compelling figure then and now. In this way, the Holmes narratives of the past have primed and shaped our own understanding of detective work today as something that is based in science and reason, and almost magical in its supposed infallibility.

Other scholars have discussed the supernatural aspect of Holmes's forensic science. Anna Neill, for instance, makes an interesting and convincing argument that Holmes is not just a detective who relies on ratiocination, but he is also a genius in that he draws on atavistic, primitive abilities to access the subconscious and, shaman-like, the thoughts and potential actions of others.[109] In this way, the Holmes stories refute the fear of degeneracy in fin de siècle Britain (and America) by arguing that not all "primitive" abilities should be considered undesirable. By making this argument, Neill shows that the Holmes stories are perhaps not as distinct from Doyle's later involvement with and support of Spiritualism.[110] As such, the lure of forensics then and today is a longing to believe that there are nearly supernatural and even superhuman surveillance technologies that could help the police apparatus function optimally and overcome incompetence. The wish is that this technology could make the apparatus prevailing in its reach and scope, and, yet, because of its grounding in science and reason, one that would not overreach or result in erroneous or biased conclusions.

However, television can also provide counternarratives to such influential narratives about forensic science. For example, some docuseries elucidate the problems with forensic science and its function within the police apparatus. These programs, such as PBS's *Frontline* or BBC's *Panorama*, present themselves not as entertainment but as investigative journalism. Rather than amuse through spectacle, such series function as surveillance of the police apparatus in a critical and questioning way. In the U.S., *Frontline* has been one of the major docuseries to highlight the problems of forensic science, as well as the police apparatus generally. For instance, the episode "The Real CSI"[111] in its title directly references and countermands prevalent narratives about the miraculous quality of forensics. In "The Real CSI," *Frontline* tackles how physical crime scene evidence, including fingerprints, is still subject to human interpretation, which can either be faulty or biased. As Judge Douglas Johnson of the Circuit Court in Michigan notes in "The Real CSI," even fingerprint analysis is not foolproof, given that there are no studies that actually confirm that no two fingerprints are alike and that it is up to human interpretation to decide if there is a fingerprint match: "Fingerprint examiners [and the public at large] have been taught that there's only one person in the world who could have left this fingerprint. [However], [t]here's no scientific basis for that."[112] Further, Johnson points out that there are no standards for fingerprint comparison. As he states, the number of points of comparison between a fingerprint on record and one from a crime scene "varies from laboratory to laboratory."[113] Johnson observes that there can be variations from 7 to 16 points of comparison.[114] As a result, he concludes that in terms of fingerprint analysis, "it's really a matter of the individual experience and judgment of the fingerprint examiner."[115] This lack of standardization and reliability is frightening, considering that defendants' very lives could rest on such shaky evidence.

Indeed, this problem with fingerprint analysis was highlighted by the FBI's arrest of Brandon Mayfield, an attorney for Washington County, Oregon, when his fingerprints were determined a match for those found on a bag of detonators at the site of the 2004 Madrid bombings. Mayfield, however, was later determined to be innocent of the charge. Similarly, in an investigation for *Frontline Scotland* (BBC Scotland), correspondent Shelley Joffre investigated the case of Shirley McKie, a detective with Strathclyde, Scotland, police. She was "told her thumbprint had been lifted from the room where the murder victim was found. McKie said that was impossible—she'd never been in the house. But four experts [...] maintained it was her left thumbprint."[116] Later, McKie was exonerated on the basis of examination by alternate fingerprint examiners, and she "made history as the first person in 100 years of fingerprinting to challenge an identification in court successfully."[117] Even DNA can be problematic if the explanation of why DNA is present at a scene is incorrect, or if DNA analysis is not done properly in a lab or is contaminated by another specimen. Meanwhile, in "Policing the Police," *Frontline* (PBS) asks Juvenal's famous question "Quis custodiet ipsos custodets?" ("Who watches the watchers?"). The episode proceeds to consider how we ensure the police apparatus does not operate beyond the scope of its powers.[118]

Interestingly, "Policing the Police," as well as U.K. programs like *Traffic Cops* or *Police Interceptors*, suggests that one way to safeguard against a rogue or excessive police force is through increased surveillance and monitoring of the population, or what police refer to as "intel" or intelligence gathering. As Newark, New Jersey, Mayor Ras Baraka argues in "Policing the Police," intelligence can help police target actual criminals rather than utilize stop-and-frisk programs that can violate not only the Fourth Amendment but also create public mistrust and resentment of the police apparatus: "Intelligence, who is actually somebody you should probably stop, and somebody who's just Ms. Martha's kid going to the store with his hat to the back, right? So, I mean, that's—intelligence gets you that information, not just, like, random stops. That's not how you police."[119] In the U.K., one example of such intelligence gathering emphasized in various docuseries is central control centers that watch everything through an enormous CCTV network, as well as automated programs in which cameras in police cars are linked with computers that can detect through license plate recognition those vehicles that are flagged as stolen or in violation of MOT standards. Further, bodycams, which are cameras that record sound and visuals as the police do their work, are another surveillance mechanism that has been suggested to deter police overreach. The irony here, of course, is that an expansion of the same surveillance technology and techniques that create unease regarding the capability of the police apparatus is the very thing proposed to curb excessive police control.

We can also extend public panoptic viewing of the police apparatus to audience policing of fiction stories about the apparatus. Specifically, fans of programs like *Sherlock* or *Elementary* monitor and critique the series' narratives via online discussion, and so influence the writers' takes on their presentation of policing and detection.[120] As Mark Lawson, television critic for *The Guardian*, observes, "For most of the history of TV drama, fans have been on the outside looking in. [...] More recently, websites and social media have changed beyond recognition the way in which a show is watched, through preview, real-time and review discussion between viewers."[121] Lawson then describes a specific instance of fans influencing the writing of *Sherlock*. He notes that Mark Gatiss, in writing the episode "The Empty Hearse," deliberately incorporated various elaborate fan theories that had been circulating on the internet regarding Holmes's death in season two.[122] While this fan participation in television panopticism does not mean that the viewer or reader gains real-life power over a controlling surveillance apparatus, the point is that the viewer can experience a vicarious panoptic power by being the critical reviewer and influencer of a series, rather than a completely passive subject of it. Such sway is both pleasurable and enjoyable, but it does not change the surveillance culture or state surveillance apparatuses. Moreover, social media monitoring of television narratives can instead become a means of training and accustoming viewers to the practice of surveillance, even if the narrative itself offers spaces to question the place of surveillance in the state and in the culture.

However, this policing of police narratives is not new, since famously it was the thousands of readers of the original Sherlock Holmes stories who eventually convinced Doyle to return to writing Holmes after the author had killed off his creation to move on to other, less lucrative, projects.[123] In this way, the reading audience in the early twentieth century did have real power over their favorite character and his fate. Therefore, surveillance by television viewers of the writers and producers of series like *Sherlock* and *Elementary* is not a recent phenomenon, except that modern technology makes such scrutiny and influence more quick, easy, and widespread. Social media allows viewers to be more involved than ever in the creation and development of a program or narrative as are the writers, producers, and networks.

DEPICTIONS AND FUNCTIONS OF SURVEILLANCE IN *SHERLOCK* AND *ELEMENTARY*

Here, I would like to think further about the versions of Holmes viewers are carefully surveilling in *Sherlock* and *Elementary*. The BBC modernization is arguably the one which hews closest to the Doyle stories in terms of Holmes's relationship to the police and other state apparatuses (such as the intelligence agency). Like his Victorian counterpart, *Sherlock*'s Holmes is an anti-social, cold, and often rude consulting detective. In both the original stories and in *Sherlock*, his consultancy is a position he creates for himself to aid Scotland Yard, whom he characterizes in the episode "A Study in Pink" as nearly always "out of [its] depth."[124] And, as in the original stories, *Sherlock*'s detective resides at 221B in London with his friend and colleague Dr. John Watson, who, like the original Watson, is an army doctor who fought in Afghanistan. By contrast, in *Elementary*, Holmes has relocated from London and 221B to a Brooklyn brownstone, where he assists the NYPD as a consulting detective. In the CBS version, John Watson is now Joan Watson, an Asian American doctor who was formerly a surgeon and who is now a sober companion hired by Sherlock's father to help his son stay off heroin. As with BBC's *Sherlock* (which describes Holmes as both a "high functioning sociopath"[125] and as having Asperger's[126]), *Elementary*'s Holmes is what the program terms "neuroatypical" in his emotional and social responses to others. This term is specifically used in the episode "Ready or Not," in which Holmes develops a relationship with a woman named Fiona Helbron, who is herself autistic/neuroatypical.[127] However, given that the program imagines romances for Holmes, such as the one with Fiona, Jonny Lee Miller's version of Sherlock is a more empathetic one. The CBS series essentially makes the detective a kindlier, gentler Holmes than either the BBC or Doyle version of the character.

However, the BBC Holmes becomes even more of a panoptic machine than Doyle's or *Elementary*'s adaptation, and the visual medium of television helps underscore his surveillance capabilities. Ronald R. Thomas notes that the original Holmes was "the literary embodiment of the elaborate network of visual technologies which revolutionized the art of seeing in the nineteenth century."[128] This embodiment is enhanced further within the television series; for instance, the camera functions as Holmes's eye, demonstrating how, like a lens, he can zoom in on minute details. These visuals increase Sherlock's already machine-like nature, but they also make the audience an extension of his panoptic eye. In this sense, we become doubly panoptic: through Holmes himself and through the television screen. The series also visualizes Holmes's thought processes by displaying his conclusions across the screen. Again, we are panoptic witnesses to the great detective's mental processes of how he is rationally solving a mystery. Viewers, in essence, function like Holmes's bodycam to observe what he does. And, as his own CCTV camera, he can target precisely the people who need to be watched and tracked, avoiding needlessly stopping and searching anyone (as do police) in his search for intel (although, in

"A Study in Pink," Sherlock does erroneously stop a cab thinking the passenger, not the driver, is the sought-after serial killer). We can therefore see that Holmes operates like a police surveillance apparatus without the drawbacks of that apparatus noted earlier.

While *Sherlock* depicts Holmes as a highly technical, twenty-first-century surveillance machine, this linkage between panoptic camera and detective can be traced back before Doyle's Holmes to Dickens's *Bleak House*. For example, as I have touched on earlier, critics have noted how Dickens consistently frames Inspector Bucket in terms of cameras and all-seeing eyes.[129] Thomas explains: "'Appearing to Mr. Snagsby to possess an unlimited number of eyes,' the detective Mr. Bucket seems to those he looks on to 'take' their portraits instantaneously through his powerful [eyeglass] lenses, a perfect description of what only the revolutionary new machine called the camera was capable of doing."[130] We therefore have in *Bleak House* a construction of the detective as a surveillance CCTV camera before photo technology itself was fully developed. Simon Joyce observes that "mystery texts often predicted the invention or use of specific forensic tools ahead of their adoption by the authorities."[131] Joyce's point raises the interesting question of how much the narrative of panoptic police observation preceded the actual technology to carry out that surveillance, such that the camera (like CCTV) became a natural extension of the police apparatus.

In addition, while *Sherlock*'s Holmes possesses a network of informants, his operatives are informal ones comprised of a collection of homeless men and women,[132] as well as a circle of petty criminals that he surveys for signs of an impending event.[133] In *Elementary*, these "irregulars" are likewise a random assortment of people, often experts in their fields, to whom Holmes turns for assistance in various episodes. Both series borrow this idea from Doyle's original stories, in which Holmes maintained a surveillance network of street urchins, whom he termed his "Baker Street Irregulars." The word "irregular" emphasizes the unofficial nature of a surveillance apparatus which is separate from the state. In these ways, Holmes operates both in the original stories and the modern series like the state police apparatus but apparently without the drawbacks of force, incompetence, and overreach.

On the other hand, while Holmes and his surveillance system are not official, nor as pervasive or forceful as the police apparatus, they can still be subversive and lack empathy. It is on this point that the difference between *Elementary*'s Holmes and the *Sherlock*/Doyle Holmes becomes most apparent. Holmes in the original stories is an early version of an undercover police officer; he often tricks people into giving up information by disguising himself and playing a role, and, in the process, he involves innocent and unsuspecting people in this work. The figure of the undercover police officer is an interesting development in terms of police surveillance. As I will discuss in Chap. 4, the idea of spying (which is, essentially, going undercover to gather intelligence by pretending to be someone one is not) was, until the late nineteenth century, considered unjust because it was deceptive. However, one can see a shift in attitudes toward spying and undercover police work in the Holmes stories, since his undercover surveillance operations (where he gains information in disguise) are presented in the stories as amazing and beneficial exploits that demonstrate Holmes's surveillance powers. This is true in *Sherlock* as well. The BBC Sherlock does not dress up as theatrically as his predecessor, but he does alter his personality to achieve results. So, too, does *Elementary*'s Holmes, who often disguises himself on the phone by speaking in other languages or accents.

But in terms of hurting innocent people, the Doyle and BBC Holmes run roughshod over other people's feelings. For example, in Doyle's "The Adventure of Charles Auguts Milverton" and in the *Sherlock* episode "His Last Vow" (based on the Milverton story),[134] Holmes pretends to love a woman to gain from her access to Milverton and his trove of blackmail information without regard for her feelings when he abandons her. It is this callous, even ruthless, nature that can make Holmes problematic. It allows him to remain uncontrolled by the police apparatus, as well as by any other person who might try to claim his loyalties. Since he is loyal, in the end, only to his detective work (and to Watson), he is as much of a free agent as possible. But this callousness can be like the issue that arises for the public regarding the police apparatus—that it, and Holmes, lack empathy for those they would police.

Therefore, it is interesting that in the CBS version of Holmes, he maintains his anti-social nature without completely losing a sense of empathy and justice for his colleagues and for suspects, such as his desire in the episode "Tremors" to make amends with NYPD Detective Bell after Holmes's interference in an arrest results in Bell being shot in the arm.[135] Further, *Elementary*'s Holmes is a much more flawed and, frequently, incorrect detective. For instance, while the Doyle and *Sherlock* Holmes have a history of drug use (Doyle's is cocaine, *Sherlock*'s is heroin), Holmes's addiction in both the series and the stories becomes mostly symbolic of the price the detective pays for his great intellect. But, in *Elementary*, Holmes's heroin addiction is a continuing story arc, with Holmes falling off the wagon at the end of the third season out of guilt for possibly causing the death of a friend.[136] In addition, we learn Holmes's addiction arises out of Moriarty's betrayal of him (*Elementary* transforms Professor Moriarty into a female criminal mastermind, Jaime Moriarty, with whom Holmes fell in love, in her persona as the artist Irene Adler). He initially believes she has been killed, and subsequently falls into a deep depression relieved by heroin abuse.[137] Later, in season one, Holmes discovers the relationship was fabricated by her to gain information about Scotland Yard's movements and out of curiosity for a man who is as intelligent as her.[138] That *Elementary*'s Holmes is truly capable of romantic love, something neither of the other Holmes versions is, speaks again to the complex emotional portrayal of Holmes in *Elementary* and the writers' choice of making his policing and detection not as emotionally cold as that of the other iterations.

ELEMENTARY, SHERLOCK, RACE, AND POLICE SURVEILLANCE PRACTICES

The *Elementary* writers' alteration of Holmes's character can be read as the result of U.S. concerns regarding the American police apparatus since 9/11. In other words, if Holmes stands as a narrative alternative to the police apparatus, then *Elementary*'s detective embodies qualities that reassure an American audience who have been and continue to be witnesses of ongoing police brutality, particularly against African Americans. In *Elementary*, Holmes remains distant from the police and from others, but not to the extent that he himself becomes someone that could trespass boundaries, as the Doyle and BBC versions of Holmes can. And, when he does overreach, the Holmes in this series is subsequently contrite and pained by the hurt he has caused. This is not to say that the U.K. has not had similar issues with the police use of force and police overreach, as I have noted earlier. Nevertheless, the history of police brutality, particularly in relation to African Americans, in the U.S., is one that shapes the formation of Holmes in *Elementary*, his relationship with the NYPD, and the NYPD's depiction in the program.

Here, I would like to pause to discuss briefly this historical background behind the NYPD, race, and policing that I argue influences how *Elementary* portrays Holmes. Whereas many of the British programs discussed in this chapter, including *Sherlock*, have several definite nineteenth-century policing narratives, both fictional (Doyle, Dickens) and non-fictional (penny dreadfuls, newspaper reportage of the Whitechapel murders) to draw from, in the U.S., there are fewer fictional stories about the police from the nineteenth century. Rather, precedents for American fictional policing narratives are historical events, documents, and press coverage involving police actions. For instance, the American police apparatus and its surveillance strategies evolved particularly from the enforcement of slavery in the South, as well as in the North after the 1850 Fugitive Slave Act required Northern states to capture and return any escaped slaves.[139] As a result, police in Northern states and cities, such as New York, were involved in locating and sending fugitive slaves back to the South, and so these departments were crucial in policing and upholding the enslavement of African American men and women in the U.S. This racial aspect of the American police apparatus, during slavery and, later, Jim Crow, stands at the root of problems in the U.S. between the majority white police apparatus and the African American community, and this tension continues to this day. While it is beyond the scope of this book to explore in depth this history, it is important to be aware of this past regarding the U.S. police apparatus and African Americans in order to see how American police and detective narratives like *Elementary* grow out of that history. Even in Northern states that did not have Jim Crow laws, there still existed racist actions against the black community; to this day, in cities like New York, black Americans are stopped, searched, and arrested by the police disproportionately more than are white Americans.[140]

It should be noted here that the terrain of this history becomes more complex regarding the interaction of race and class. For example, as noted earlier, documents from the NYPD records of the 1863 Draft Riots demonstrate that the New York police and fire departments tried to protect African Americans from rampaging groups of Irish and other white working-class New Yorkers. In one of the most horrific incidents of the riots, an angry mob burned down The Orphan Asylum for Colored Children. Members of New York's fire department attempted to save the building and stop the mob, but in vain. The *New York Times*'s description of the incident underscores the magnitude of the racial violence during the riots and the danger New York police and firemen faced to end it. Significantly, the paper notes that this racial violence was not only perpetrated by white men, but also by white women and children. The article begins thus: "The Orphan Asylum for Colored Children was visited by the mob about 4 o'clock. [...] Hundreds, and perhaps thousands of the rioters, the majority of whom were women and children, entered the premises, and in the most excited and violent manner they ransacked and plundered the building from cellar to garret."[141] Fortunately, the African American orphans had been evacuated prior to the rioters' attack. However, despite the best efforts of the New York fire chief and fellow firefighters, "[t]he institution was destined to be burned, and after an hour and a half of labor on the part of the mob, it was in flames in all parts. [...] There is now scarcely one brick left upon another of the Orphan Asylum."[142] In this way, we see that during the riots, the same apparatuses that would later oppress and target people of color in New York were, ironically, the ones defending the city's African American population. As noted earlier, the NYPD sought out those white working-class men and women who lynched, killed, or abused African Americans during the riots in retaliation for what they saw as Black Americans taking their jobs. For example, the following deposition of arresting officers John Gunner and Henry Roberts was taken at the court hearing of Silva and Carey, the men who murdered Abraham Franklin: "They [Gunner and Roberts] arrested Mark J. Silva and Dennis Carey, [and] charged [them] with having aided and abetted in feloniously murdering, beating, and hanging a certain colored man whose name deponents have been informed was Abraham Franklin on the Fifteenth day of July 1863."[143]

While the NYPD assisted African Americans during the riots, race then and now nevertheless emerges in American policing as the dominant factor in terms of police bias and use of force. We can see, then, that the history of policing and abuse in the U.S. and U.K. diverges between race and class. In the U.K., until more recently, it was the working class and poor who were the primary targets of police scrutiny and action. We can affirm this divergence in viewing docuseries from the two nations. *Frontline*'s "Policing the Police," for instance, focuses on the relations between African Americans and the police in Newark, New Jersey, while U.K. programs like *The Force: Manchester* reveal it is often white working-class members of the public who feel most singled out and antagonized by the police.

However, race as a factor in U.K. policing has certainly become more prominent in the U.K. after 9/11. For example, Muslim Asian British citizens have become a major focus of surveillance as a result of the Prevent policy, which was "introduced in the UK in 2003 as part of an overall post 9/11 counter-terrorism approach [...] with the aim of preventing the radicalisation of individuals to terrorism."[144] Further, there have been increased "stop and search" actions by the U.K. police (thus paralleling the American police's focus on black and Latino citizens noted earlier).[145] Julian Hargreaves does point out, however, that "[t]he analysis revealed a picture of stop and search that is more complex than that found throughout the literature. However, at least some findings lend support to allegations of state discrimination against British Muslim communities."[146] James Renton argues more emphatically that Muslims have not only become a major focus of British surveillance, but, rather, that Islamophobia itself is the central structuring mechanism of surveillance not only in the U.K., but in the global West: "[T]oday's surveillance order is designed primarily to identify *Muslim* subjects who enter into what is understood to be Muslim politico-*theological* ontology—labelled extremism—that produces terrorism."[147] As such, he contends that Muslims are not simply the most recent in a series of racial and ethnic bogeymen and scapegoats for problems within the U.K. and the global West: "The Muslim surveillance target is not merely the latest form of racism that serves to justify imperialist violence and power—as short of shifting avatar of a racial enemy, which transfigures effortlessly from one form to another."[148] Instead, the British and Western security state has been brought into being by Islamophobia. Therefore, while we can acknowledge that Black British citizens are also similarly subject to higher rates of police use of force and stop-and-search actions,[149] Renton argues that we must also recognize a qualitative difference between the surveillance of British Muslims and that of Black British residents.

Returning to *Elementary* and its relationship to American policing, the program therefore takes care to foreground diverse characters, particularly in the roles of law enforcement. For example, two of the series' principle characters are the African American Detective Bell and Asian American Joan Watson. These characters are ones whose abilities Holmes highly respects, and, indeed, he trains Watson as a detective so that she becomes his partner and equal in their consulting practice. Likewise, Holmes views Detective Bell as talented and values Bell's opinion and input; in fact, in the latest season of *Elementary*, Sherlock recommends Bell for the U.S. Marshals service because Holmes believes Bell is too talented to remain a police detective. In this episode, Holmes says to Bell: "[W]hen I was at Scotland Yard, I was only too happy to watch the moss gather under the policemen I worked with. Only to me, they were just a means of gaining access to people and places that I otherwise couldn't. [...] But it's never been like that with us, has it? No. You're too good a detective. So, I want something better for you. Something ... something more."[150]

Here, Sherlock considers the African American Bell as superior not only in terms of his talent but also in his integrity Bell's to fellow NYPD officers. In this way, the program is aware of the historical and current problems in American policing, and of the NYPD in particular. For example, the NYPD in the 1990s, under New York's then mayor Rudy Giuliani, instituted a major stop-and-frisk program that disproportionately affected Black (mostly male) Americans. Further, in 2014, Eric Garner, an African American man, died from being held in a chokehold by an NYPD officer. These are only a few instances of NYPD's long, problematic relationship with the African American community.[151] In this way, the crucial difference with the American version of Holmes compared to his British counterpart(s) is that while he remains a genius detective, he cannot work alone without the aid and input not only of the NYPD, but also of those who represent minority groups in law enforcement. They help Holmes improve his empathy and compassion for others. As a result, *Elementary*'s Holmes becomes less threatening and more comforting through his acceptance and need of assistance, as well as his ability to see past identity and avoid racism, sexism, and homophobia.

By contrast, the BBC's *Sherlock* hews more closely to the original tales in that no one is Holmes's equal, not Watson and certainly not anyone in Scotland Yard. He lacks almost all compassion and empathy, characterizing himself as a "high-functioning sociopath"[152] and his brain as a computer hard drive.[153] But the series is also closer to the Doyle tales in its treatment of race and gender in policing. Very few characters of color appear in the series, one exception being Scotland Yard Sargent Sally Donovan, who is Black and female, and is not an assistant of Holmes but his vocal adversary. In addition, television critics have commented on the unfavorable way women have been portrayed in the series, notably the character of Irene Adler in the episode "A Scandal in Belgravia" (based on Doyle's "A Scandal in Bohemia").[154] Further, in a Christmas special, "The Abominable Bride,"[155] set in Victorian London, Holmes discovers a group of terrorists who are radical feminists, and both Holmes and his brother, Mycroft, express some sympathy for their cause (although, as historian Fern Ridell has noted in her work on the Suffragette movement, the Suffragettes did use violence and terror tactics in their campaign for the right to vote).[156] *Sherlock* also replicates troubling racial tropes that appear in the original stories, such as criminal gangs from Asia who threaten the British public.[157] In this sense, the Holmes of Doyle and *Sherlock* persists as a potential troubling figure in his assistance to the British police apparatus in carrying out surveillance and social control, and one who, like the British police, draws on the experience of British methods of surveillance and control practiced in British colonies such as India. In this way, Britain, like America, traces the origin of its disciplinary tools and techniques to policing non-white populations. However, the American connection between modern policing and the control of enslaved African Americans is more direct and prevalent than that between Britain and its former colonies because it took place on American soil.[158] *Sherlock*'s reiteration of racist and sexist narratives thus demonstrates the tenacity of older narratives that surround policing and its relationship to race, gender, class, and surveillance. Nevertheless, while *Sherlock* seems to repeat these narratives, *Elementary* is more aware of and responds to that history of the police apparatus.

WE ARE WATSON: WATCHING THE DETECTIVE

While it is crucial to understand the series' interpretation of Holmes and his relationship to the police apparatus, we cannot ignore Watson's function in both programs. Other critics have argued that in the original stories, Watson resembles the reader: he is capable but not a genius like Holmes.[159] In other words, Watson is the character with whom we can relate and who mediates for us our contact with the cold, distant, brilliant Holmes. However, as I have argued elsewhere,[160] Watson also performs a powerful role in terms of surveillance. In the stories, Watson embodies the middle-class British sensibility of Doyle's readers; while he might sometimes break the law with Holmes (in the name of justice), he subscribes to a more conventional life than his friend does and follows the Victorian socially prescribed rules of etiquette. As a representative of British Victorian middle-class virtue, he functions as the monitor of Holmes. On behalf of the readers, he watches Holmes, records his actions, and tempers the detective's more eccentric or even dangerous habits (such as his cocaine addiction).

Watson overall possesses great power because it is he who writes the stories (within the fiction of the narrative). Indeed, Holmes often argues with Watson about the way his friend tells the stories as being more dramatic than educational. For example, in "The Adventure of the Copper Beeches," Holmes admonishes Watson for focusing on the sensational details of their cases, rather than the rational and scientific aspects of detection: "Crime is common. Logic is rare. Therefore, it is upon the logic rather than upon the crime that you should dwell. You have degraded what should have been a course of lectures into a series of tales."[161] Here, we see that it is Watson who creates and shapes the narrative. He serves as British society's panoptic eye on Holmes, and, through the doctor, we as readers also monitor the great detective and either condone or condemn his actions. As noted earlier, Doyle's readers gained so much control over Holmes that Doyle was in a sense forced to resurrect the detective after killing him off at Reichenbach Falls. This power reflects how the stories prime readers to assume a panoptic position regarding the detective, a position that continues into *Sherlock* and *Elementary* to an even greater extent.

As viewers of *Sherlock* and *Elementary*, however, we possess a panoptic eye that exceeds Watson's. First, we can observe and judge Watson's actions as much as those of Holmes. In Doyle's stories, Holmes is the clear subject of our panoptic gaze. By contrast, Watson, because he is writing in the first person, forces us to identify with him and occupy his space, such that we do not objectively observe the doctor. However, in the television programs, the camera grants us a more distanced, third-person perspective, so that we can watch both Holmes and Watson in a more detached way. This signifies that the panoptic power in *Sherlock* and *Elementary* shifts to the viewer; if anything, we are more like Mycroft in *Sherlock* surveying Watson through CCTV cameras or the NSA who occasionally drop in on Holmes and Watson's investigations in *Elementary*. In other words, our surveillance capability becomes more formidable than that of Holmes and Watson combined. We are privy to scenes or clues before Holmes, thus allowing us to become the detective by putting together clues and scenes possibly before Holmes does. In this way, the television format of the two series allows the viewer more surveillance facility than do the original stories, and it is a power that can equal or rival that of Holmes himself. We as viewers thus become, like Holmes, a curb on the police apparatus— as well as the consulting detective.

Elementary adopts this idea in its characterization of Watson not as a chronicler of Holmes's adventures (as Watson is in the original stories and in *Sherlock*, where he blogs about Holmes's exploits) but as an equal sharer in them: Sherlock recognizes Joan's potential and trains her to be a detective. She even operates her own detective agency for a time, which she then integrates back into Sherlock's when he returns after having been fired from Mi-6. Holmes leaves New York at the end of season two to work with Mi-6 in exchange for his brother, Mycroft, being given a new identity and protection by the agency, which is necessitated by Mycroft's espionage work involving dangerous criminal gangs.[162] Beginning in season three, Watson transforms into a detective and represents the viewer's potential to become one as well. She even succeeds where Holmes fails, particularly in her ability to outmaneuver and apprehend Moriarty. Specifically, in "Heroine," the final episode of season one, Joan anticipates that Moriarty/Irene Adler's love for Sherlock will not allow her to resist visiting Holmes if his life is in danger; therefore, Watson plans a scheme in which Holmes fakes a heroin overdose in order to lure Moriarty to Sherlock's hospital room, where Moriarty confesses her involvement in a murder and is subsequently arrested by awaiting NYPD officers. In this way, Watson shares with the viewer the capability to become Holmes's peer as well as a surveillance restraint on the police apparatus. The series thus moves the viewer from ordinary citizen to this panoptic operator more fully than do either *Sherlock* or Holmes's original stories.

Despite our identification with Watson, the third-person perspective of both television series lets us understand that the doctor bears as much monitoring as Holmes, since he/she is more unconventional and dangerous than is Watson in the original stories. In *Sherlock*, for instance, Watson is also an Afghan war veteran, but, unlike Doyle's version, the modern doctor still enjoys the thrill of combat, and it is this desire that drives him to work with Holmes. Indeed, in "A Study in Pink," Mycroft observes that Watson is "not haunted by the war" but, rather, that the doctor "misses it."[163] Further, Watson's military training allows him to be a crack shot, and he kills a man to protect Holmes in "A Study in Pink," something the original Watson never did. Similarly, Holmes trains Joan in *Elementary* to be a dangerous adversary in combat, and her sexual desires might be as unconventional as Holmes's, as the detective points out that a typical relationship might not suit her. In the CBS series, unlike in the original stories, Holmes does engage in sex, but only with sex workers in order to avoid intimate, emotional relationships. For instance, in the "Pilot" episode, Sherlock states, "I actually find sex repellent. All those fluids and odd sounds. But my brain and my body require it to function at optimum levels, so I feed them as needed."[164] Holmes claims that Joan is likewise sexually unconventional and is perhaps more asexual, like himself. In "Hemlock," for example, Watson feels confused regarding her relationship with Andrew Mittal, a businessman; while he seems perfect, Joan feels disinterested in him. Holmes observes, "The man's always been something of a 'placeholder' for you [...]. You've also, in all the time you've dated, never displayed even a hint of the intoxication which accompanies new love [...]. You know, you might have to accept the fact that whatever your relationship with Andrew means, you just don't want it."[165]

In these ways, Watson becomes less like the typical viewer in certain respects, such that the audience must keep a panoptic eye on Watson as well as Holmes. Again, this alteration emphasizes how the television medium transforms aspects of the original stories to allow even more surveillance capacity on the part of the viewer. If we as viewers remain detached and distanced because the first-person narration is absent, we can become the ultimate operator of the panopticon because we watch Holmes, Watson, and the police, yet remain apart from all three, just as we desire Holmes to remain apart from the police apparatus. However, the television medium does not require us to act on this panoptic power; instead, it is simply pleasurable to have this power as well as to feel that we can view and monitor the police apparatus in addition to those who, within the narrative, assist and keep that apparatus in check.

One ongoing challenge of the police apparatus that requires monitoring is corruption, and *Elementary* seems more alert to historical issues of vice within the NYPD as opposed to BBC's *Sherlock*, in which the Yard might be incompetent but is not necessarily on the take. *Sherlock*, like its nineteenth-century counterpart, presents the Yard as bumbling rather than troubling in its actions. *Elementary*, as well as other American series such as *Person of Interest* (also on CBS) and *Copper*, all by contrast do reckon with police corruption in the NYPD and present this exploitation of police power as both a historical and potentially ongoing issue. While *Elementary*'s Holmes has respect for members of the NYPD, such as Bell and Captain Tommy Gregson (whose name is based on Tobias Gregson, a Yard inspector in the original Holmes stories), various episodes over several seasons are nevertheless devoted to Holmes and Watson rooting out corruption within the NYPD. Such vice includes officers on the take from Russian mobs or the Mafia, as well as some who tamper with crime scenes to continue their dishonest practices. In terms of a narrative arc, one might argue that this ongoing storyline can perpetuate a satisfying ending for the audience in which a hero who can cleanse the police apparatus provides a fictional balm to a real problem within that apparatus (e.g., *Frontline*'s "Policing the Police" notes how one Newark gang unit officer was fired for demanding sexual favors in return for letting a suspect go). On the other hand, *Elementary* does acknowledge this issue and so connects the series with the history of the NYPD corruption scandals from Tammany Hall (which is depicted in *Copper*) to its coziness with the Mafia and other criminal organizations.[166]

SHERLOCK, ELEMENTARY, SURVEILLANCE, AND TERRORISM

However, if *Elementary* probes more the faults of the NYPD and American policing, *Sherlock* connects further with the central issue that has brought about the revival of the storied detective in the first place: terrorism. This difference is interesting because in the pilot episode of *Elementary*, the premise for Holmes working in New York with the NYPD is that "a few months after 9/11," Sherlock "was assigned by Scotland Yard to observe their [the NYPD's] counterterrorism bureau."[167] After a stint in rehab, Holmes "decide[s] to resume [his] work as a consultant" with the NYPD. Therefore, the entire foundation of the series is 9/11 and the need for a detective genius like Holmes to be present in unsettled times. Yet, subsequent *Elementary* episodes neither address the threat of terrorism nor depict Holmes working to prevent such attacks. In two episodes, one involving a plane ("Flight Risk")[168] and another involving a potential lethal virus ("The Red Team"),[169] the threats turn out not to be terrorists but, rather, personal rivalries among colleagues.

By contrast, *Sherlock*, while not overtly situated in relation to 9/11 like *Elementary*, includes three episodes involving terrorism in some form. For example, Holmes works to prevent a major terrorist attack on the Houses of Parliament in "The Empty Hearse," and, as mentioned earlier, he uncovers what amounts to an underground terrorist cell of early feminists in "The Abominable Bride." However, only in "A Scandal in Belgravia" is there a direct mention of radical Islamic terror groups, these groups being the main cause for concern among the public in the U.S. and U.K. In that episode, we learn that Moriarty has been working with such an organization to help them carry out a terrorist attack in the U.K., but the Islamic terrorist group itself is not present as actors within the episode. The other two episodes, "The Empty Hearse" and "The Abominable Bride," connect to earlier historical events that, through a modern lens, could be considered terrorism. For example, in "The Empty Hearse," a British MP, working as an operative for North Korea, attempts to replicate the Gunpowder Plot to blow up Parliament. The original Gunpowder Plot was devised by what might today be termed a homegrown "terrorist cell" of English Catholics, led by Robert Catesby. In this case, however, the terror plot consists not of barrels of gunpowder placed beneath Parliament but a Tube carriage full of explosives, and Sherlock and Watson foil the plot just in time.

Sherlock here shares similarities with *Whitechapel* in revisiting an older criminal event from British history. In this way, *Sherlock* reminds us that terror attacks are not a new phenomenon—certainly not for the U.K.—but that we now name and categorize such attacks as "terrorism" in the wake of 9/11. As noted earlier, Renton contends that this shift in the definition of terrorism is due to the construction of a modern British and global West security and surveillance state as a specific response to Islamophobia.[170] Interestingly, Doyle never involved Holmes directly in investigating what the Victorian English might have considered the "terrorism" of their day, including anarchists and groups like the Fenians, often referred to as the Irish Brotherhood, who used bombings as a means of persuading Britain to grant Ireland independence. This is curious since, as John Greenfield notes, *The Strand*, the magazine in which the Holmes stories were originally published, often featured stories and articles related to the Victorian public's fears of domestic terrorism, such as "an article on 'Dynamite and Dynamiters,' the first segment in the 'Crimes and Criminals' series, and with a story by Eugene Moret titled 'The Anarchist.'"[171]

Indeed, in a foreshadowing of the Irish Republican Army (IRA) bombings of the twentieth century and the 7/7 attacks on the London Underground, in 1883, Fenians exploded bombs at Praed Street (near Paddington Station, 62 people were injured) and in the tunnel between Charing Cross (now Embankment) and Westminster stations; in 1885 at Gower Street (now Euston) station; and in 1897 at Aldersgate (now Barbican) station, injuring 60 and killing one. While Doyle's Holmes does not investigate such domestic terrorism, he does confront foreign spies, or British citizens who spy for enemy nations, in stories such as "The Second Stain," "The Bruce-Partington Plans," "The Naval Treaty," and "His Last Bow." In so doing, he prevents other nations from sowing chaos within Britain or drawing the U.K. into war. As a result, Doyle, like the *Sherlock* series, avoids confronting terrorism too directly, yet still allows the super-sleuth to provide readers a sense that Holmes is protecting national security.

Further emphasizing the similarities between the nineteenth and twenty-first centuries, the *Sherlock* Christmas special deliberately links the original Doyle stories with the modern BBC version by setting the action in Victorian London with Victorian versions of Holmes, Watson, and other recurring characters in the modern series. And, given the episode's inclusion of terrorism, it does suggest that the show's writers are considering how the older Holmes stories reflect certain concerns that persist today regarding surveillance, terrorism, and the police apparatus. Indeed, both *Elementary* and *Sherlock* intentionally play with either elements of or entire storylines from the original stories by refashioning them into ones that suit a modern setting. Certainly, doing so on the writers' part is largely simply a homage to Doyle's work by demonstrating a love and knowledge for those stories; these references likewise appeal to those in the audience who are fans of the original material. However, the viability and popularity of two series featuring a twenty-first-century Holmes, both of which draw heavily from Doyle's work, demonstrate how well much of his Victorian-era stories and ideas still work in our contemporary society.

This underscores how underlying issues or concerns about policing, surveillance, crime, and terrorism remain similar despite the passing of years and the advancement of technology. Of course, the issue of terrorism as we define it today is not as explicit in the original Holmes stories, but there are several tales in which Holmes, like his modern versions, must deal with criminal organizations that terrorize individuals who will not bend to their will, such as the Ku Klux Klan (KKK) in "The Five Orange Pips," a Chicago criminal gang in "The Adventure of the Dancing Men," and the Mafia in "The Adventure of the Red Circle." Interestingly, in each of these stories, the criminal/terrorist organizations all originate in the U.S. and bring their felonious activities to Britain (and are threats to British homeland security which Holmes must eliminate). In addition, as noted earlier, he also solves crimes that involve the theft of national secrets that could be passed into the hands of Britain's enemies.

To return to "The Abominable Bride," the episode was controversial in its portrayal of a feminist terror group who seek to advance the position of Victorian-era women. These women retain few rights within marriage, are denied the vote, and cannot work in their desired professions (e.g., in this episode, Holmes's colleague Molly disguises herself as a man in order to be a forensic medical examiner). Some television critics criticized *Sherlock* writer and producer Steven Moffat for his portrayal of women in the episode and in the series as a whole, noting that Doyle often created more independent, intelligent, and interesting women characters in his stories.[172] They considered it risible that Holmes and his brother, Mycroft, were the ones at the end of the episode to "mansplain" the rationale for the women's terroristic actions. As Jamison Cox aptly puts it, "Of course, the culmination of the show's interaction with the [Suffragette] movement is a speech in which Sherlock bemoans the injustice of the whole thing while a room of women stands silent around him."[173]

One could argue, by contrast, that Moffat wrote the episode in response to previous criticism of the lack of women and women's issues in seasons one and two. As a result, he drafted a plot in which Holmes and Watson empathize with the early feminist fight for women's rights. However, for my purposes, what is more interesting is that these early feminists are portrayed as a clandestine organization designed to spread terror among Victorian men. This construction is not without historical truth. Some terror attacks in late nineteenth-century Britain were perpetrated by Suffragettes using homemade bombs,[174] and one of these devices is currently on display at the City of London Police Museum. Whether with early suffragettes, the Gunpowder Plot, or criminal gangs, *Sherlock* references a history of terror in the U.K. In these episodes, Holmes is the only one who can assist the police and the national intelligence apparatuses to conduct the surveillance necessary to prevent or end the attacks to restore public order and safety. In this way, although 9/11 and 7/7 do not emerge directly in *Sherlock*, echoes of these attacks in displaced form do appear in the series, and Holmes is present narratively as the solution to the perceived inadequacies of these two surveillance apparatuses.

Undoubtedly, it would be difficult for the writers of *Elementary* or *Sherlock* to directly incorporate into their story lines police surveillance of radical Islamic terrorism groups such as the Islamic State in Iraq and Syria (ISIS) or al-Qaeda. First, espionage series that do so directly, such as *Spooks (MI-5)*, *24*, or *Homeland* (each covered more in depth in Chap. 4), involve more realistic plots and settings. *Sherlock* and *Elementary*, like the original Doyle stories, are more fantasy even though they retain a semblance of verisimilitude. Their fantastic aspect arises from the idea that one person can solve the shortcomings of the police and intelligence apparatuses. As noted earlier, this is a powerful idea that can be narratively satisfying for the reader or viewer. However, readers and viewers are still aware that this is not a realistic solution to the issue; the narrative is pleasurable to watch, read, and experience, but we who consume it understand that it exists within a fantasy space. Therefore, to bring into this space characters based on actual terrorist groups such as ISIS or to focus at length on real terror events like 7/7 or 9/11 would disrupt the fantasy.

This was true even of the original Holmes stories. Given that most were written after the Whitechapel murders, Doyle could have conceivably written a narrative in which Holmes tackles this serial killer whom the Met failed to catch. While contemporary writers of pastiche Holmes novels and stories have done this,[175] at the time, the Whitechapel murders, and the failure of the police apparatus to find him, would have been too recent. And, so, like actual terror attacks today, the murders would have disrupted the fantasy space of the Holmes stories by having real events intrude on the narrative. This point can further explain why *Elementary* introduces 9/11 as a backstory for Holmes but does not return to this attack nor address the NYPD's involvement in counterterrorism surveillance. As a framework, 9/11 allows the audience to link Holmes and the terror attack without disrupting the fantasy space of a genius who compensates for surveillance inadequacies of the police and intelligence apparatuses; 9/11 serves as an impetus for the return of the great detective without dealing with the narrative consequences of having Holmes involved in real events.

Further, another issue for the series' writers would be the response of viewers to the portrayal of Muslim terrorists, as well as the use of actual terror events that could be regarded as inappropriate or inflammatory. Because of 9/11 and later terrorist attacks, Muslim communities in the U.S. and U.K. have experienced a great deal of prejudice and violence. Indeed, in the U.S., hate-based attacks against American Muslims have recently risen to levels not seen since the months just after the 9/11, in part due to President Donald Trump's provocative rhetoric and actions (during his presidential campaign and throughout his tenure in office). These include implementing the so-called Muslim ban against immigration and travel from certain Muslim-majority nations.[176] A similar situation exists in the U.K., which is heightened by Brexit anti-immigration rhetoric and those seeking revenge for Islamic fundamentalist car and van terror attacks on pedestrians in London.[177]

As such, writers and viewers are sensitive about the depiction of Muslims as terrorists on television and in film; given the dearth of Muslim characters in series and films, this limited image of Islam in Western narratives perpetuates the dangerous stereotype that all Muslims are terrorists. Programs such as *24*, for example, have been criticized for how they equate Muslims with terrorism,[178] and so writers of other programs have become mindful of this issue. Therefore, to tackle the notion of terrorism in *Sherlock* and *Elementary*, the perpetrators are recast as other groups, such as North Koreans in "The Empty Hearse," early feminists in "The Abominable Bride," Chinese gangsters in "The Blind Banker," or, in a return to a Cold War trope, Russians in various episodes of *Elementary*. And while we should be mindful of Renton's admonition that we must not view Muslims and other racial/ethnic/gender groups as interchangeable in terms of how actual international terrorism and the responsive

Western surveillance order are structured and defined,[179] it is nevertheless clear that television writers, producers, and viewers seem to accept, expect, and rely on such interchangeability. In this way, terrorism is integrated into the programs but also displaced so that the series do not invoke a stereotype that could raise the audience's and critics' ire. Here, we can see the power of viewers, particularly through social media, to shape how these narratives are constructed. That the writers of *Sherlock* in particular are thinking about terrorism can be seen in Moffat's tenure as showrunner on the BBC series *Doctor Who*. In particular, the episodes "The Zygon Invasion"[180] and "The Zygon Inversion"[181] feature the alien Zygons as symbolic of those immigrants who wish to live in peace, and those who eschew assimilation and resort to terrorist actions. The aliens become a means of displacing such concerns and working through them without resorting to stereotypes or disrupting the fantasy space (which is even more true in a science fiction program like *Doctor Who*).

However, the enemy of the state most emphasized in both Holmes revivals (as in countless other film and television interpretations) is the aforementioned arch villain, Moriarty. In *Sherlock*, he is characterized not as a professor but as a "consulting criminal,"[182] and, as such, Holmes's alter-ego; in *Elementary*, Moriarty, like Watson, is re-cast as a woman named Jaime Moriarty. However, whether in the original stories or in these series, Moriarty stands at the center of a web of crime and terrorism. It is not my intent to discuss this relationship in depth; instead, what I wish to illustrate here is how this character functions, then and now, as the ultimate embodiment of threats to national security that Holmes must eradicate, given that the police are oblivious to Moriarty's existence. Although he is depicted in only one story in Doyle's work, "The Final Problem," he nevertheless is described by Holmes in that tale as "the Napoleon of crime [...]. He is the organizer of half that is evil and of nearly all that is undetected in this great city [of London]."[183] Crucially, for my purposes, Moriarty develops a crime syndicate—a kind of terror cell—that carries on after his own death, and one that Holmes must destroy in "The Empty House."

In *Sherlock* and *Elementary*, this syndicate becomes a multinational organization, particularly so in the CBS series. Moriarty in *Sherlock* not only assists radical Islamic terrorists, but is himself a terrorist. However, unlike terror organizations and leaders like ISIS or Osama Bin Laden, Moriarty espouses no political or ideological goals; in "The Great Game," he simply enjoys creating chaos and manipulating Holmes to watch him solve terroristic puzzles he sets for the detective. Indeed, Ellen Burton Harrington argues that the series makes Moriarty an obsessive fan of Sherlock (and, as such, he resembles viewers of the series), rather than a criminal mastermind and terrorist who threatens Britain.[184] Meanwhile, Moriarty in *Elementary* becomes the creator of a global organization of crime and political control and power. She is like Keyser Soze in *The Usual Suspects*—a subtle power behind almost every monetary or political event, reminiscent of conspiracy theories surrounding the Illuminati and other such fictive global cabals. In fact, at the end of the fourth season of *Elementary*, Sherlock's father, Morland, himself a formidable businessman and intellect, takes over Moriarty's organization with the intention of destroying it from within (after Moriarty has been imprisoned for several years).[185]

The structural function underlying all these versions of the infamous villain is that it is easier to consider criminal or terroristic threats to national security if they are embodied in one person, just as it is comforting to think the answer to such problems can be personified in one man or woman like Holmes. This is true even more so today, given that the difficulty with current radical Islamic terror threats is precisely that they are not and cannot be contained within one figure. While Osama Bin Laden was for a time a Moriarty-like face of terrorism, his death demonstrated that terror continues even if the figurehead is gone. While in the original and television versions of the Holmes stories, Moriarty's organization endures despite his death or her incarceration (the latter occurs in *Elementary*), the syndicate is still one that is tightly controlled and requires a leader (such as Morland Holmes or Sebastian Moran), whereas terrorism post-9/11 requires only radicalization by a few without any direction from a central authority. Notably, Moriarty in *Elementary* persists as a much graver threat than in *Sherlock*. *Sherlock*'s Moriarty is unstable, devoted to chaos, and fixated on Holmes. By contrast, in *Elementary*, Moriarty is responsible for orchestrating coups and fixing global markets. In this way, the *Elementary* version hews closer to Doyle's creation, although with a greater and more profound reach. I contend that each version of Moriarty demonstrates a different kind of panoptic power—the personal versus the global. However, we should also reflect that the Moriarty the *Sherlock* and *Elementary* writers imagine for their respective British and American audiences draws on the divergent status of the two nations post-9/11.

While *Sherlock* and *Elementary* are enjoyed on both sides of the Atlantic, we can understand *Sherlock* as having a British perspective and *Elementary* an American one because of the identity of their writers. Notably, the U.S.

is in virtually the same political position as Britain was in Doyle's era, in that the U.S. is the ruling global power with a vast empire; although, rather than one based on physical colonization, the American empire is an economic and cultural one. And, like nineteenth-century Britain, twenty-first-century America feels besieged by threats, particularly terroristic ones, from within and without. The U.S. is anxious that its global power is being challenged. Therefore, it makes sense structurally that the American *Elementary* crafts a Moriarty who is a serious threat to national security and global stability, and one who can personify such widespread and international threats to U.S. hegemony. By contrast, while the U.K. is certainly also under threat of terrorism, the implications for its global status are not the same, given Britain's decline in power and influence since World War II. Therefore, again, it makes sense structurally that *Sherlock*'s Moriarty is a different kind of terrorist, one not intent on political gain but on perpetrating terror simply to instigate disruption.

Nevertheless, whether created from an American or British perspective, Moriarty in *Sherlock* and *Elementary* represents the fear of the threat from within—that the greatest threat to national security is someone who blends in and cannot be distinguished through police or intelligence agency surveillance as the criminal or terrorist that they are. This idea resonates especially with modern U.S. and U.K. audiences, given that after 9/11, many terrorist attacks, including 7/7 or the San Bernardino attack, have been the work of homegrown Islamic radicals—that is, extremists who were born or who have lived several years in the U.S. and U.K. Further, domestic terrorism in both nations encompasses violence beyond that enacted by Islamic extremists: in the U.S., mass shootings by white men and boys at schools and other venues is rampant, while in the U.K., terroristic gang violence has increased in metropolitan areas including London, Manchester, and Birmingham. For instance, Simeon Moore, a former member of the Johnson Crew in Birmingham, openly characterizes the violence he and his gang perpetrated as terrorism: "How bad was I? Bad. I was a terrorist. I'd hear something has happened to someone, put the phone down and go."[186] This issue of domestic terrorism raises the following questions: How should the state apparatuses surveil and monitor the nations' citizens? How can the police apparatus tell the law-abiding citizen from the potential threat?

These problems are at the heart of surveillance issues in terms of balancing privacy and civil liberties with public safety, and this is the line the police apparatus must walk. That Holmes can detect such a person instantaneously, with only a brief glance, is one of the major qualities that make him a comforting panoptic figure. However, significantly, Holmes in both *Sherlock* and *Elementary* is at first unaware of such a domestic threat and his/her organization. In *Sherlock*, Holmes only begins to discover hints about Moriarty from other criminals he catches, and, in *Elementary*, Holmes is Moriarty's lover until he discovers much later her true criminal identity. These depictions underscore the limits of even Holmes's panoptic abilities, and, by extension, of the police apparatus, to identify the enemy within. While Holmes eventually comes to the rescue of national security, his inability to detect the homegrown threat within the contemporary television programs illustrates a significant divergence from Doyle's "The Final Problem" (in which Holmes is already aware of Moriarty and his organization at the beginning of the story) that speaks to the difficulty of surveillance in our era.

This complication might be why *Sherlock* in particular revisits the original stories' habit of seeking threats that can be identified through visual surveillance. One danger Doyle's stories depict again and again is the threat from the racial and ethnic Other who arrives in Britain from outside the realm, a return of the repressed to exact vengeance on the colonizer. In the original stories, some of these threats could be considered homegrown, in that they are white British men "corrupted" by their time in the East, such as Grimsby Roylott in "The Adventure of the Speckled Band" or Jonathan Small in *The Sign of Four*. However, Holmes locates these dangers more easily because of their colonial past, which instantly indicates they are a potential threat. But, in other cases, the criminal presents himself or herself as visually not white or not British, whether it is the black bodyguard Steve Dixie who menaces Holmes in "The Adventure of the Three Gables" or the dark-complected Italian Beppo in "The Adventure of the Six Napoleons." However, these non-white/British threats are less present in the original stories than the constant motif of the corrupted white British male. Nevertheless, they form the basis for the *Sherlock* episode "The Blind Banker" that presents an overtly Orientalist narrative in which a Chinese tong (gang) is imperiling London and exacting revenge against the corrupt white British men who have stolen from the tong whom they were trafficking for.

In "The Blind Banker," the series recalls such "yellow peril" narratives in Doyle's oeuvre, especially in *The Sign of Four*, that seep into the present and express fears of the economic might of China or the terrorism of Middle Eastern radical groups like ISIS and al-Qaeda. This episode comes

closest in either *Sherlock* or *Elementary* to depicting a terrorist-like group
that is Asian, although, here, the Chinese function as a stand-in for radical
Islamic terrorists. This link is emphasized by the opening scenes of the
episode in which a turbaned man with a scimitar, a Western stereotype of
a person from the Middle East, fights Holmes when the detective refuses
to recover a diamond for this potential client. This episode is problematic
in its Orientalist implications, in which the East or the "Orient" is painted
with a broad swath as being a threat to Britain and the West. This
Orientalism is accentuated by the fact that the tong is disguised as a
Chinese circus, complete with Fu Manchu-like costuming and heavily
accented English. Further, one of the tong's assassins is characterized like
Tonga, the exotic and treacherous Andaman Islander in *The Sign of Four*,
thus emphasizing the assassin's racial Otherness. In these ways, the episode demonstrates the similar political and cultural situations in nineteenth-century Britain and twenty-first-century U.K.; in the current
post-9/11 British culture, there exist comparable levels of suspicion, fear,
and Othering of those who hail from the Middle East and other Asian
nations. That Holmes returns as an answer to such perceived non-Western
threats, which have fueled much rhetoric around Brexit, make even more
sense since the same narrative structures that would have appealed to
white, middle-class audiences then would appeal to them now.

Elementary, however, largely avoids this Orientalist narrative, and,
indeed, appears conscious of it, not only with its inclusion of the Asian
American Joan Watson, but also with its addition of other Asian American
characters, such as Joan's half-sister, Lin Wen. Further, the program does
so in ways in which these characters' racial identity is not the defining trait
of who they are or how they function in the series' narrative. Rather, the
major threat that emerges in the second season, and one on which
Sherlock's brother, Mycroft (played by Rhys Ifans), helps Mi-6 surveil and
gather intelligence, is a French criminal organization, Le Milieu, operating
in both the U.S. and U.K.[187] That *Elementary* would center its pseudo-
terrorist syndicate around a European ally can be attributed to the writers
wishing to avoid the kind of problematic Orientalist depiction found in
Sherlock; it is less risky to displace criminality and terror onto other
Westerners. However, this choice also points to the tension among current
allies, particularly the differences among how the U.K., France, and the
U.S. police and intelligence apparatuses have handled terrorism. After all,
France was infamously on the U.S.'s bad side during the George W. Bush
administration for its refusal to support the war in Iraq. In this way,

Elementary recalls the original Holmes narratives when Britain was not allied with other European nations, and those nations were still potential threats, as is the case in "The Adventure of The Second Stain" and "The Adventure of the Bruce-Partington Plans." It is a reminder that America's and Britain's current alliances do not necessarily have a long history and are more tenuous than they might seem.

The same is true for the rocky history of the Anglo-American alliance. The ongoing animosity between Britain and America arises in both *Elementary* and *Sherlock*, and I will discuss this antagonism at greater length in Chap. 4. While there has existed a special relationship between the U.S. and U.K. since World War II, there has been rivalry and conflict going back to America's War of Independence. This Anglo-American relationship became strained in the years after 9/11 as many citizens in Britain opposed the Blair government's willingness to follow the U.S.'s lead in the war on terror,[188] and the writers of the two programs are aware of this. For example, in "A Scandal in Belgravia," *Sherlock*'s Holmes assaults the brutish CIA operative who threatens the detective and Mrs. Hudson. Similarly, in numerous Doyle stories, the villains and/or those who cause chaos in Britain are Americans. Such tales include *A Study in Scarlet* (Mormons), "A Scandal in Bohemia" (the opera singer Irene Adler), "The Five Orange Pips" (the KKK), "The Adventure of the Noble Bachelor" (an American gold rush heiress), "The Yellow Face" (an American woman and her mixed-race child), "The Adventure of the Dancing Men" (a Chicago criminal gang), and "The Adventure of the Three Garridebs" (an escapee from an American prison). By contrast, in *Elementary*, it is the British who, in the shape of Mi-6, emerge as a disruptive force (although they, like the Americans, wish to dismantle the French criminal organization Le Milieu). In these ways, the two series reflect current global tensions in the years since 9/11, and, in so doing, mirror similar frictions woven into the original Holmes stories over a hundred years earlier.

In this chapter, I have discussed connections among post-9/11 police and detective television series, their nineteenth-century predecessors, and concerns then and now about the surveillance powers of the police apparatus. I would like to end with a particular nineteenth-century narrative, Dickens's *Our Mutual Friend* (1865) and how this novel anticipates and maps out questions regarding a burgeoning culture of surveillance. *Our Mutual Friend* is not about the police per se, but it does depict the desire to track people and ascertain their whereabouts using techniques that would be employed by the growing police apparatus, and which also speak to the need for surveillance methods to police an increasing population. In the novel, two men, Bradley Headstone and Eugene Wrayburn, are obsessed with locating the whereabouts of Lizzie Hexam. Both are in love with Lizzie, but she disappears from society so that she does not suffer the consequences of being involved with either man. In a pre-Victorian world, she might have been successful in slipping away quietly. However, in an increasingly modern and technological London teeming with people and at the beginning of a surveillance culture, Wrayburn determines Lizzie's current location through her return address on an envelope. Meanwhile, Headstone constantly spies on Wrayburn, following him wherever he goes to see if Wrayburn might lead him to Lizzie.

In writing these scenes, Dickens maps a changing world. Before the term "stalking" became common parlance, Dickens foresees the ability to surveil and trace people through markers such as addresses and other codes. According to Foucault, these disciplinary techniques are meant to fix people in place, so that the various state apparatuses, including the police, can find people when necessary.[189] As Foucault argues, in the mid to late nineteenth century, surveillance becomes necessary for the state, including the police apparatus, to manage a modern population that is both greater than before and more mobile, thanks to advances in transportation. In *Our Mutual Friend*, Dickens anticipates two mechanisms of surveillance and social control that would later be thoroughly adopted by state apparatuses: markers of identity (like social security numbers or addresses) and constant surveillance (in police work, tailing a suspect physically, like Headstone; or using technology and crime scene evidence to track down a suspect).

Therefore, we see the nascence of surveillance culture in *Our Mutual Friend*, not only in terms of the police and other state apparatuses, but also among citizens in daily life. That Lizzie is a victim of stalking is obvious to us as modern readers, given that the danger of being unwillingly surveilled and traced by someone (physically and online) is a situation many routinely face today. Here, Dickens, though a supporter of the police apparatus, still makes clear the perils of the panopticon: if one can be tracked, one can be harmed. *Our Mutual Friend* thus records the beginnings of surveillance culture not only on the level of the state, but also on the level of the individual. Indeed, police in *Traffic Cops* and *Coppers* complain that they are under surveillance and scrutiny for their actions not only by higher-ups in the police apparatus but also by ordinary citizens with cell phone cameras.[190] As Dickens envisaged, the panopticon is operated by everyone and at every level, and we all have the chance to play Sherlock Holmes.

NOTES

1. Some examples of scholarly work in various disciplines which employ this term are Joseph M. Conte, "Don Delillo's *Falling Man* and the Age of Terror," *MFS: Modern Fiction Studies*, 57.3 (Fall 2011): 557–583; Stuart Croft and Cerwyn Moore, "The Evolution of Threat Narratives in the Age of Terror: Understanding Terrorist Threats in Britain," *International Affairs*, 86.4 (July 2010): 821–835; Mimi Thi Nguyen, "The Biopower of Beauty: Humanitarian Imperialisms and Global Feminisms in an Age of Terror," *Signs: Journal of Women in Culture and Society*, 36.2 (Winter 2011): 359–383; Gregory F. Treverton, *Intelligence for an Age of Terror* (Cambridge, UK: Cambridge University Press, 2009); and Benjamin Wittes, *Law and the Long War: The Future of Justice in the Age of Terror* (New York: Penguin, 2008).
2. See Stephen Knight's landmark *Form and Ideology in Crime Fiction* (Bloomington: Indiana UP, 1980). In particular, see chapter 3, "'a great blue triumphant cloud'—*The Adventures of Sherlock Holmes.*"
3. Ibid., 67.
4. *Elementary*, "Pilot," season 1, episode 1, written by Robert Doherty, directed by Michael Cuesta, aired September 27, 2012, on CBS.
5. Tana Ganeva and Laura Gottesdiener, "Nine Terrifying Facts about America's Biggest Police Force," *Salon*, Sep. 28, 2012, https://www.salon.com/2012/09/28/nine_terrifying_facts_about_americas_biggest_police_force/.
6. Ibid.
7. Ibid.
8. Radley Balko, *Rise of the Warrior Cop: The Militarization of America's Police Forces* (New York: Public Affairs, 2013), 253–254.
9. Ibid.
10. "Does Militarization of Police Make Us Less Safe?" *The Week*, Aug. 31, 2017, https://www.theweek.co.uk/us/88104/does-the-militarisation-of-police-make-us-less-safe.
11. Ibid.
12. Nicholas Clapman, "Here's When British Police Are Legally Allowed to Shoot under a New Policy on Lethal Force," *The Conversation*, Apr. 28, 2017, https://theconversation.com/heres-when-british-police-are-legally-allowed-to-shoot-under-a-new-policy-on-lethal-force-76666. See also Michael Fisher, "Crossing the Line—Is the Militarisation of British Police Reasonable?," *LinkedIn*, Mar. 10, 2017, https://www.linkedin.com/pulse/crossing-line-militarisation-british-police-michael-fisher, and Andrew Gilligan, "How the British Bobby Turned into Robocop," *The Spectator*, Aug. 4, 2016, https://blogs.spectator.co.uk/2016/08/military-style-policing-creeping-everyday-life/.

13. Ibid.
14. See Joe Nelson, "State, Federal Law Enforcement Agencies File in Support of FBI in Apple Battle," *San Bernardino County Sun*, Mar. 30, 2016, https://www.sbsun.com/2016/03/03/state-federal-law-enforcement-agencies-file-in-support-of-fbi-in-apple-battle/, and Christi Smythe, Selina Wang, and Tiffany Kary, "Apple Goes to Washington Fresh from Big Boost in iPhone Fight." *Bloomberg*, Mar. 1, 2016, https://www.bloomberg.com/news/articles/2016-03-01/apple-goes-to-washington-with-some-wind-in-its-sails.
15. Margaret Talbot, "Stealing Life: The Crusader behind *The Wire*," *The New Yorker*, Oct. 22, 2007, https://www.newyorker.com/magazine/2007/10/22/stealing-life.
16. John Ellis, *Visible Fictions: Cinema: Television: Video* (London: Routledge, 1982), 112.
17. "In the Black Hole of Scotland Yard: A Tale of Blows and Bludgeons," *The Pall Mall Gazette*, Dec. 1, 1887: 1, The British Newspaper Archive.
18. Ibid.
19. "The Soldier and The Lawyer: A Comedy," *Reynolds's Newspaper*, Nov. 18, 1888: 4, The British Newspaper Archive.
20. "The Punishment of the Rioters," *St. James's Gazette*, Dec. 19, 1887: 12, The British Newspaper Archive.
21. "The New Police," 1830, U.K. National Archives, http://www.nationalarchives.gov.uk/education/candp/prevention/g08/g08cs2s3.htm.
22. Clive Emsley, *Policing and Its Context, 1750–1870* (London: Macmillan, 1983), 59.
23. Ibid.
24. Bruce Chadwick, *Law and Disorder: The Chaotic Birth of the NYPD* (New York: St. Martin's Press, 2017), 25.
25. Ibid.
26. Ibid.
27. Ibid.
28. Ibid.
29. Ibid.
30. John J. Sturtevant, memoir, MssCol 2915, New York Public Library Manuscripts and Archives Division.
31. Ibid.
32. See Kate Summerscale, *The Suspicions of Mr. Whicher: A Shocking Murder and the Undoing of a Great Victorian Detective* (New York: Bloomsbury, 2008).
33. Ibid.
34. See, for instance, L. Perry Curtis, Jr., *Jack the Ripper and the London Press* (New Haven: Yale UP, 2001) for a comprehensive analysis of 14 newspapers' coverage of the murders at the time.

35. "A Spitalfields Lodging-House," *Illustrated London News*, Saturday, Sep. 22, 1888, Issue 2579: 350, British Library Newspaper Archives.

36. For more on the debate regarding connections between the rise of violent crime and the reduction of police in the U.K., see Will Bedingfield, "Why It's So Hard to Blame a Rise in UK Knife Crime on Police Cuts," *Wired*, Mar. 7, 2019, https://www.wired.co.uk/article/uk-knife-crime-london-statistics; Benjamin Mueller, "U.K. Knife Crime Rises. Are Budgets to Blame?," *The New York Times*, Mar. 6, 2019, https://www.nytimes.com/2019/03/06/world/europe/uk-knife-crime-austerity.html; and Matthew Weaver, "Police Chief Says Rise in Knife Crime in England is National Emergency," *The Guardian*, Mar. 6, 2019, https://www.theguardian.com/uk-news/2019/mar/06/police-chief-says-rise-in-knife-crime-in-england-is-national-emergency.

37. Ibid.

38. "Outcasts at the East-End," *Illustrated London News*, Oct. 13, 1888: 421+, British Library Newspaper Archives.

39. For a comprehensive discussion of what the riots were, who participated in them, and the circumstances which fueled them, see Ivar Bernstein, *The New York City Draft Riots: Their Significance for American Society and Politics in the Age of the Civil War* (New York: Oxford UP, 1990).

40. "The Mob in New York," *The New York Times*, July 14, 1863: 1, *The New York Times* Digital Archives, https://timesmachine.nytimes.com/timesmachine/1863/07/14/90521933.html?action=click&contentCollection=Archives&module=LedeAsset&region=ArchiveBody&pgtype=article&pageNumber=1.

41. Ibid.

42. Ibid.

43. Ibid.

44. Ibid.

45. Ibid.

46. "The Draft: The Riot in the Ninth Congressional District," *The New York Tribune*, July 14, 1863: 1, NewseumED Digital Collections, https://newseumed.org/tools/artifact/newspaper-coverage-1863-new-york-city-draft-riots.

47. Julia Anna Hartness Lay, diary, ZL-450, New York Public Library Manuscripts and Archives Division.

48. Ibid.

49. Ibid.

50. Ibid.

51. Ibid.

52. Ibid.

53. See National Center for PTSD, "Sleep and PTSD," U.S. Department of Veterans Affairs, https://www.ptsd.va.gov/understand/related/sleep_ptsd.asp.

54. See Anemona Hartocollis, "10 Years and a Diagnosis Later, 9/11 Demons Haunt Thousands," *The New York Times*, Aug. 9, 2011, https://www.nytimes.com/2011/08/10/nyregion/post-traumatic-stress-disorder-from-911still-haunts.html; Yuval Neria, Laura DiGrande, and Ben G. Adams, "Posttraumatic Stress Disorder Following the September 11, 2001, Terrorist Attacks: A Review of the Literature Among Highly Exposed Populations," *American Psychology*, 66.6 (September 2011): 429–446; and Romeo Vitelli, "PTSD in Survivors of 9/11," *Psychology Today*, Oct. 15, 2018, https://www.psychologytoday.com/us/blog/media-spotlight/201810/ptsd-in-survivors-911.

55. Julia Anna Hartness Lay, diary.

56. "The Mob in New York."

57. "The Draft: The Riot in the Ninth Congressional District."

58. Joel Miller et al., "Public Opinions of the Police: The Influence of Friends, Family, and News Media," National Criminal Justice Reference Service (NCJRS), document no. 205619, May 2004, https://www.ncjrs.gov/pdffiles1/nij/grants/205619.pdf.

59. Hannah Fingerhut, "Deep Racial, Partisan Divisions in Americans' Views of Police Officers," Pew Research Center, Sep. 15, 2017, http://www.pewresearch.org/fact-tank/2017/09/15/deep-racial-partisan-divisions-in-americans-views-of-police-officers/.

60. Ibid.

61. Simon Maybin, "Do the Public Still Trust the Police?," *BBC News*, Mar. 25, 2014, https://www.bbc.com/news/magazine-26730705.

62. Ibid.

63. "Our Note Book," *Illustrated London News*, Oct. 13, 1888: 418, British Library Newspaper Archives.

64. Ibid.

65. Ibid.

66. Ibid.

67. Inspector Edmund Reid, "Murder, Aug. 16, 1888, H Division," MEPO 140–142, U.K. National Archives.

68. Ibid.

69. Ibid.

70. Inspector Joseph Chandler, "Met Police Report No. 6 (Special Report), Sept. 8, 1888, H Division," MEPO 140–142, U.K. National Archives.

71. Ibid.

72. Reid, "Murder, Aug. 16, 1888, H Division."

73. Chandler, "Met Police Report No. 6 (Special Report), Sept. 8, 1888, H Division."
74. Ibid.
75. Inspector Joseph Abberline, "Report: re: Man Detained at Holloway re: Murders H Division, 19th Sept. 1888," MEPO 140–142, U.K. National Archives.
76. Ibid.
77. Sergeant Frances Boswell, "Report: Clapham Division, Dec. 16, 1888," MEPO 140–142, U.K. National Archives.
78. For further details, see the Independent Police Complaints Commission report, "Stockwell One: Investigation into the Shooting of Jean Charles de Menezes at Stockwell Underground Station on 22 July 2005," *BBC News*, http://news.bbc.co.uk/2/shared/bsp/hi/pdfs/08_11_07_stockwell1.pdf.
79. See Bernstein, *The New York City Draft Riots*.
80. Ibid.
81. New York County District Attorney Indictment Records, Aug. 4, 1863–Aug. 11, 1863, Roll 119, New York City Municipal Archive.
82. *Copper*, "The Hudson River School," season 1, episode 7, story by Will Rokos and Tom Fontana, teleplay by Frank Pugliese, directed by Larysa Kondracki, aired Sep. 30, 2012, on BBC America.
83. *Copper*, "Better Times Are Coming," season 1, episode 8, story by Will Rokos and Tom Fontana, teleplay by Sara B. Cooper, directed by Larysa Kondracki, aired Oct. 7, 2012, on BBC America.
84. *Copper*, "New York, 1864," print advertisement, https://thepopbreak.com/2012/08/20/tv-review-copper/.
85. *Coppers*, "Custody," series 1, episode 1, directed by Anthony Phillipson, aired Nov. 1, 2010, on Channel 4.
86. Ibid.
87. Ibid.
88. *Coppers*, "C.I.D.," series 2, episode 1, directed by Anthony Phillipson, Jan. 9, 2012, on Channel 4.
89. Ibid.
90. Ibid.
91. *Sherlock*, "A Scandal in Belgravia," episode 1, season 1, written by Steven Moffat, directed by Paul McGuigan, aired Jan. 1, 2012, on BBC1.
92. Stuart Heritage, "Which Cop Docs Are Worth Watching?," *The Guardian*, Aug. 15, 2011, https://www.theguardian.com/tv-and-radio/tvandradioblog/2011/aug/15/cop-docs-worth-watching.
93. Ibid.
94. Ibid.

95. Phillip Collins, *Dickens and Crime*, 1962, 3rd edition (London: Macmillan, 1994), 1.
96. Ibid.
97. Charles Dickens, "On Duty with Inspector Field," *Household Words*, June 14, 1851: 266, Dickens Journals Online.
98. Ibid., 267.
99. Charles Dickens, *Bleak House*, 1853 (Kindle edition, 2012), 201.
100. Ibid., 203.
101. Ibid., 230.
102. Ibid., 232.
103. Ibid., 268.
104. Ellis, 112.
105. For further discussion of penny dreadfuls and related American publications, see Kevin Carpenter, *Penny Dreadfuls and Comics: English Periodicals for Children from Victorian Times to the Present Day* (London: Victoria and Albert Museum, 1983); Pete Haining, ed., *The Penny Dreadful: Or, Strange, Horrid & Sensational Tales!* (London: Orion Publishing Group, 1975); Robert J. Kirkpatrick, *From the Penny Dreadful to the Ha'penny Dreadfuller: A Bibliographical History of the British Boys' Periodical 1762–1950* (London: British Library, 2013); and John Springhall, *Youth, Popular Culture, and Moral Panics: Penny Gaffs to Gangsta-Rap, 1830–1996* (New York: St. Martin's Press, 1998).
106. See, for example, Roland Bal, "How to Kill with a Ballpoint: Credibility in Dutch Forensic Science," *Science, Technology, & Human Values*, 30.1 (2005): 52–75; Cate Curtis, "Public Perceptions and Expectations of the Forensic Use of DNA: Results of a Preliminary Study," *Bulletin of Science, Technology & Society*, 29.4 (2009): 313–324; Ellen Burton Harrington, "Nation, Identity, and the Fascination with Forensic Science in Sherlock Holmes and *CSI*," *International Journal of Cultural Studies*, 10.3 (2007): 365–382; Julie Johnson-McGrath, "Speaking for the Dead: Forensic Pathologists and Criminal Justice in the United States," *Science, Technology & Human Values*, 20.4 (1995): 438–459; Michael Lynch and Sheila Jasanoff, "Contested Identities: Science, Law and Forensic Practice," *Social Studies of Science*, 28.5–6 (1998): 675–686; Helena Machado and Felipe Santos, "Popular Press and Forensic Genetics in Portugal: Expectations and Disappointments Regarding Two Cases of Missing Children," *Public Understanding of Science*, 20.3 (2009): 303–318; Monica L. P. Robbers, "Blinded by Science: The Social Construction of Reality in Forensic Television Shows and Its Effect on Criminal Jury Trials," *Criminal Justice Policy Review*, 19.1 (2008): 84–102; and Mark Seltzer, "Murder/Media/Modernity," *Canadian Review of American Studies*, 38.1 (2008): 11–41.

107. Sir Arthur Conan Doyle, "The Boscombe Valley Mystery," 1891, in *The Adventures of Sherlock Holmes* (New York: Penguin, 1981), 91.
108. Ibid., "The Adventure of the Speckled Band," 1891, in *The Adventures of Sherlock Holmes* (New York: Penguin, 1981), 181.
109. Anna Neill, "The Savage Genius of Sherlock Holmes," *Victorian Literature and Culture*, 37.2 (2009): 611–626.
110. Ibid.
111. *Frontline*, "The Real CSI," season 30, episode 10, written and produced by Andres Cediel and Lowell Bergman, aired Apr. 17, 2012, on PBS.
112. Ibid.
113. Ibid.
114. Ibid.
115. Ibid.
116. Shelley Jofre, "Falsely Fingered," *The Guardian*, July 9, 2001, https://www.theguardian.com/media/2001/jul/09/mondaymediasection4.
117. Ibid.
118. *Frontline*, "Policing the Police," season 34, episode 12, written and produced by James Jacoby and Anya Bourg, aired June 28, 2016, on PBS.
119. Ibid.
120. For a complete discussion of fandom and its relationship to BBC's *Sherlock* specifically, see Louisa Stein and Kristina Busse, eds., *Sherlock and Transmedia Fandom: Essays on the BBC Series* (Jefferson, NC: McFarland, 2012).
121. Mark Lawson, "*Sherlock* and *Doctor Who*: Beware of Fans Influencing the TV They Love," *The Guardian*, Jan. 3, 2016, https://www.theguardian.com/tv-and-radio/tvandradioblog/2014/jan/03/sherlock-doctor-who-fans-influencing-tv.
122. Ibid.
123. For further discussion of Doyle, his ambivalence toward his creation, and his reasons for bringing back the great detective, see Martin Booth, *The Doctor and the Detective: A Biography of Sir Arthur Conan Doyle* (New York: Minotaur Books, 2000); John Dickson Carr, *The Life of Sir Arthur Conan Doyle*, 1949 (New York: Carroll & Graf Publishers, 2003); Jon Lellenberg, Daniel Stashower, and Charles Foley, eds., *Arthur Conan Doyle: A Life in Letters* (New York: HarperPress, 2007); Andrew Lycett, *The Man Who Created Sherlock Holmes: The Life and Times of Sir Arthur Conan Doyle* (New York: Free Press, 2008); Russell Miller, *The Adventures of Arthur Conan Doyle: A Biography* (New York: Thomas Dunne Books, 2008); Pierre Nordon, *Conan Doyle: A Biography* (New York: Holt, Rinehart and Winston, 1967); Ronald Pearsall, *Conan Doyle: A Biographical Solution* (Worthing, UK: Littlehampton Book Services Ltd., 1977); and Daniel Stashower, *Teller of Tales: The Life of Arthur Conan Doyle* (New York: Penguin Books, 2000).

124. *Sherlock*, "A Study in Pink," series 1, episode 1, written by Steven Moffat, directed by Paul McGuigan, aired July 25, 2010, on BBC1.
125. Ibid.
126. *Sherlock*, "The Hounds of Baskerville," series 2, episode 2, written by Mark Gatiss, directed by Paul McGuigan, aired Jan. 8, 2012, on BBC1.
127. *Elementary*, "Ready or Not," season 4, episode 18, written by Robert Doherty and Bob Goodman, directed by Christine Moore, aired Mar. 27, 2016, on CBS.
128. Ronald R. Thomas, "Making Darkness Visible: Capturing the Criminal and Observing the Law in Victorian Photography and Detective Fiction," in *Victorian Literature and the Victorian Visual Imagination*, eds. Carol T. Christ and John O. Jordan (Berkeley: U of California P, 1995), 135.
129. See, for example, David Ben-Merre, "Wish Fulfillment, Detection, and the Production of Knowledge in *Bleak House*," *Novel*, 44.1 (2011): 47–66; Robin L. Fetherston, "Tailing Inspector Bucket: Dickens's Progeny in Hammett's Hard-Boiled Detective Fiction," *International Journal of Arts and Sciences*, 7.1 (2014): 275–290; Ronald R. Thomas, "The Dream of the Empty Camera: Image, Evidence, and Authentic American Style in 'American Photographs' and 'Farewell, My Lovely'," *Criticism*, 36.3 (Summer 1994): 415–457; and Thomas, "Making Darkness Visible."
130. Thomas, "Making Darkness Visible," 137.
131. Simon Joyce, "Reviewed Work: *Detective Fiction and the Rise of Forensic Science* by Ronald R. Thomas," *The Journal of English and Germanic Philology*, 101.4 (October 2002): 587.
132. *Sherlock*, "The Great Game," series 1, episode 3, written by Mark Gatiss, directed by Paul McGuigan, aired Aug. 8, 2010, on BBC1.
133. *Sherlock*, "The Empty Hearse," series 3, episode 1, written by Mark Gatiss, directed by Jeremy Lovering, aired Jan. 1, 2014, on BBC1.
134. *Sherlock*, "His Last Vow," series 3, episode 3, written by Steven Moffat, directed by Nick Hurran, aired Jan. 12, 2014, on BBC1.
135. *Elementary*, "Tremors," season 2, episode 10, written by Liz Friedman, directed by Aaron Lipstadt, aired Dec. 5, 2013, on CBS.
136. *Elementary*, "A Controlled Descent," season 3, episode 24, written by Robert Doherty, directed by John Polson, aired May 14, 2015, on CBS.
137. *Elementary*, "M.," season 1, Episode 12, written by Robert Doherty, directed by John Polson, aired Jan. 10, 2013, on CBS.
138. *Elementary*, "The Woman," season 1, episode 23, written by Robert Doherty and Craig Sweeny, directed by Seth Mann, aired May 16, 2013, on CBS; and *Elementary*, "Heroine," season 1, episode 24, written by Robert Doherty and Craig Sweeny, directed by John Polson, aired May 16, 2013, on CBS.

139. In particular, see Christian Parenti's excellent study, *The Soft Cage: Surveillance in America From Slavery to the War on Terror* (New York: Basic Books, 2003), for a fascinating (and disheartening) discussion of how much American policing—including its surveillance tools and techniques—evolved from the policing, surveillance, and controlling of slaves in antebellum America.

140. For more on statistics and reasons for this disproportionality, see Joshua Chanin, Megan Walsh, and Dana Nurge, "Police Use Traffic Stops as a Form of 'catch and release' to Disproportionately Target Black Americans," London School of Economics, U.S. Centre, Oct. 18, 2018, https://blogs.lse.ac.uk/usappblog/2018/10/18/police-use-traffic-stops-as-a-form-of-catch-and-release-to-disproportionately-target-black-americans/; Michael A. Fletcher, "For Black Motorists, A Never-Ending Fear of Being Stopped," *National Geographic*, Mar. 12, 2018, https://www.nationalgeographic.com/magazine/2018/04/the-stop-race-police-traffic/; Sharon LaFraniere and Andrew W. Lehren, "The Disproportionate Risk of Driving While Black," *The New York Times*, Oct. 24, 2015, https://www.nytimes.com/2015/10/25/us/racial-disparity-traffic-stops-driving-black.html; Kim Soffen, "The Big Question about Why Police Pull over So Many Black Drivers," *The Washington Post*, July 8, 2016, https://www.washingtonpost.com/news/wonk/wp/2016/07/08/the-big-question-about-why-police-pull-over-so-many-black-drivers/?utm_term=.3012ac744b8d; and Richard Winton, "Black and Latino Drivers are Searched Based on Less Evidence and Are More Likely to Be Arrested, Stanford Researchers Find," *The Los Angeles Times*, June 19, 2017, https://www.latimes.com/local/lanow/la-me-ln-stanford-minority-drive-disparties-20170619-story.html.

141. "The Mob in New York."

142. Ibid.

143. New York Municipal Archive, NY County DA Indictment Records, Aug. 4, 1863–Aug. 11, 1863, Roll 119.

144. Fahid Qurashi, "The Prevent Strategy and the UK 'war on terror': Embedding Infrastructures of Surveillance in Muslim Communities," *Palgrave Communications*, 4, Article number: 17 (2018), https://www.nature.com/articles/s41599-017-0061-9.

145. Julian Hargreaves, "Police Stop and Search Within British Muslim Communities: Evidence from the Crime Survey 2006–2011," *The British Journal of Criminology*, 58.6 (October 2018): 1281–1302.

146. Ibid., 1281.

147. James Renton, "The Global Order of Muslim Surveillance and Its Thought Architecture," *Ethnic and Racial Studies*, 41.12 (2018): 2127.

148. Ibid., 2128.

149. See Damian Gayle, "Structural Racism at the Heart of British Society, Human Rights Panel Says," *The Guardian*, Apr. 27, 2018, https://www.theguardian.com/world/2018/apr/27/racism-british-society-minority-ethnic-people-dying-excessive-force; and Catherine Wylie, "Black People 'nine times as likely' as Whites to Be Stopped and Searched by Police in England and Wales," *The Independent*, Oct. 14, 2018, https://www.independent.co.uk/news/uk/home-news/stop-search-black-people-white-police-racism-new-study-a8583051.html.

150. *Elementary*, "Meet Your Maker," season 6, episode 12, written by Robert Doherty, Robert Hewitt Wolfe, and Kelly Wheeler, directed by Ron Fortunato, aired July 23, 2018, on CBS.

151. For more on the NYPD and stop and frisk, see Ryan Devereaux, "New York's Stop-and-frisk Trial Comes to a Close with a Landmark Ruling," *The Guardian*, Aug. 12, 2013, https://www.theguardian.com/world/2013/aug/12/stop-and-frisk-landmark-ruling; and Chris Smith, "The Controversial Crime-Fighting Program That Changed Big-City Policing Forever," *New York Magazine*, Mar. 2, 2018, http://nymag.com/intelligencer/2018/03/the-crime-fighting-program-that-changed-new-york-forever.html; and the U.S. Commission on Civil Rights, "Police Practices and Civil Rights in New York City: Chapter 5, Stop, Question, and Frisk," Aug. 2018, https://www.usccr.gov/pubs/nypolice/main.htm. For more on the death of Eric Garner, see Al Baker, J. David Goodman, and Benjamin Mueller, "Beyond the Chokehold: The Path to Eric Garner's Death," *The New York Times*, July 13, 2015, https://www.nytimes.com/2015/06/14/nyregion/eric-garner-police-chokehold-staten-island.html; Conor Friedersdorf, "Eric Garner and the NYPD's History of Deadly Chokeholds," *The Atlantic*, Dec. 4, 2014, https://www.theatlantic.com/national/archive/2014/12/context-for-the-punishment-free-killing-of-eric-garner/383413/; and Michael R. Sisek, "NYPD Officer will Face Disciplinary Trial in Eric Garner Chokehold Death," *PBS News Hour*, Dec. 6, 2018, https://www.pbs.org/newshour/nation/nypd-officer-will-face-disciplinary-trial-in-eric-garner-chokehold-death.

152. "A Study in Pink."

153. "The Great Game."

154. See, for example, Sophie Gilbert, "The Troublesome Women of *Sherlock*," *The Atlantic*, Jan. 5, 2017, https://www.theatlantic.com/entertainment/archive/2017/01/sherlocks-women/512141/; Jane Clare Jones, "Is *Sherlock* Sexist? Steven Moffat's Wanton Women," *The Guardian*, Jan. 3, 2012, https://www.theguardian.com/commentisfree/2012/jan/03/sherlock-sexist-steven-moffat; and Helen Lewis, "Does Steven Moffat Have a Problem with Women?" *New Statesman America*, Jan. 9,

2012, https://www.newstatesman.com/blogs/helen-lewis-haste-ley/2012/01/moffat-sherlock-women.

155. *Sherlock*, "The Abominable Bride," series 4, episode 0, written by Steven Moffat and Mark Gatiss, directed by Douglas Mackinnon, aired Jan. 1, 2016, on BBC1.

156. Fern Ridell, "The 1910s: 'We have sanitised our history of the suffragettes'," *The Guardian*, Feb. 6, 2018, https://www.theguardian.com/lifeandstyle/2018/feb/06/1910s-suffragettes-suffragists-fern-riddell; Ridell, *Death in Ten Minutes: Kitty Marion. Actress. Arsonist. Suffragette* (London: Hodder and Stoughton, 2018); and Ridell, "Suffragettes, Violence and Militancy," The British Library, Feb. 6, 2018, https://www.bl.uk/votes-for-women/articles/suffragettes-violence-and-militancy.

157. See Darcie Rives-East, "Watching the Detective: *Sherlock*, Surveillance, and British Fears Post-7/7," *The Journal of Popular Culture*, 48.1 (Feb. 2015): 44–58, for an in-depth analysis of the similarities between how Doyle constructs Asians and those British who have lived in Asia as criminals in *The Sign of Four* (1890), and how Asians are represented in the *Sherlock* episode, "The Blind Banker," series 1, episode 2, written by Stephen Thomson, directed by Euros Lynn, aired Aug. 1, 2010, on BBC1.

158. For more on the links between the British police apparatus and British surveillance and control of colonized people, see Georgina Sinclair, ed., *Globalising British Policing* (Farnham, UK: Ashgate Publishing, 2011).

159. See Paul Barolsky, "The Case of the Domesticated Aesthete," *Virginia Quarterly Review*, 60.3 (1984): 438–452; Fred Erisman, "If Watson Were a Woman: Three (Re)Visions of the Holmesian Ménage," *Clues: A Journal of Detection*, 22.1 (2001): 177–188; James Krasner, "Watson Falls Asleep: Narrative Frustration and Sherlock Holmes," *English Literature in Translation*, 40.4 (1997): 424–435; and Rives-East, "Watching the Detective."

160. See Rives-East, "Watching the Detective."

161. Sir Arthur Conan Doyle, "The Adventure of the Copper Beeches," 1891, in *The Adventures of Sherlock Holmes* (New York: Penguin, 1981), 261.

162. This reintegration happens over several episodes in season three, but see especially *Elementary*, "Enough Nemesis to Go Around," season 3, episode 1, written by Robert Doherty and Craig Sweeny, directed by John Polson, aired Oct. 30, 2014, on CBS; and *Elementary*, "The Five Orange Pipz," season 3, episode 2, written by Bob Goodman, directed by Larry Teng, aired Nov. 6, 2014, on CBS.

163. "A Study in Pink."

164. *Elementary*, "Pilot."

165. *Elementary*, "Hemlock," season 3, episode 13, written by Robert Doherty, Arika Lisanne Mittman, and Jeffrey Paul King, directed by Christine Moore, aired Feb. 5, 2015, on CBS.
166. For more on problems with corruption in the NYPD, see Steven V. Gilbert and Barbara A. Gilbert, *Police Corruption in the NYPD: From Knapp to Mollen* (Boca Raton, FL: CRC Press, 2015); Leonard Levitt, *NYPD Confidential: Power and Corruption in the Country's Greatest Police Force* (New York: Macmillan, 2009); Graham Rayman, *The NYPD Tapes: A Shocking Story of Cops, Cover-ups, and Courage* (New York: Macmillan, 2018); Thomas Reppetto and James Lardner, *NYPD: A City and Its Police* (New York: Henry Holt and Company, 2000); and Bernard Whalen and Jon Whalen, *The NYPD's First Fifty Years: Politicians, Police Commissioners, and Patrolmen* (Lincoln, NE: Potomac Books, 2015).
167. *Elementary*, "Pilot."
168. *Elementary*, "Flight Risk," season 1, episode 6, written by Corinne Brinkerhoff, directed by David Platt, aired Nov. 8, 2012, on CBS.
169. *Elementary*, "The Red Team," season 1, episode 13, story by Jeffrey Paul King and Craig Sweeny, teleplay by Jeffrey Paul King, directed by Christine Moore, aired Jan. 31, 2013, on CBS.
170. Renton, 2128.
171. John Greenfield, "Arthur Morrison's Sherlock Clone: Martin Hewitt, Victorian Values, and London Magazine Culture, 1894–1903," *Victorian Periodicals Review*, 35.1 (Spring 2002): 29–30.
172. For articles critiquing "The Abominable Bride" and its portrayal of the Suffragette movement specifically, see, for example, Jamieson Cox, "In '*Sherlock*: The Abominable Bride,' Holmes Is the Worst Kind of Superhero," *The Verge*, Jan. 4, 2016, https://www.theverge.com/2016/1/4/10704192/sherlock-the-abominable-bride-review; Mary Kate McAlpine, "'The Abominable Bride' Is Moffat's Biggest Feminist Failure," *Medium*, Dec. 3, 2017; https://medium.com/@marykatemcalpine/the-abominable-bride-is-moffats-biggest-feminist-failure-9e3bc8ba3a65; and Todd VanDerWerff, "The *Sherlock* Special 'The Abominable Bride' Was Terrible. Has This Show Completely Lost Its Way?," *Vox*, Jan. 2, 2016, https://www.vox.com/2016/1/2/10700800/sherlock-special-recap-pbs-abominable-bride.
173. Cox, "In '*Sherlock*: The Abominable Bride,' Holmes Is the Worst Kind of Superhero."
174. See endnote 156 in this chapter for sources on the suffragettes' use of bombs and terror tactics.
175. There are numerous modern pastiche novels based on Holmes working on the Whitechapel case; see, for example, Michael Dibdin, *The Last*

Sherlock Holmes Story (London: Jonathan Cape, 1978); Lindsay Faye, *Dust and Shadow: An Account of the Ripper Killings by Dr. John Watson* (New York: Simon & Schuster, 2009) (this novel has the distinction of having been given the blessing of the Conan Doyle family); and Edward B. Hanna, *The Whitechapel Horrors: A Sherlock Holmes Novel* (New York: Carroll & Graf, 1993).

176. See Katayoun Kishi, "Assaults against Muslims in U.S. Surpass 2001 Level," Pew Research Center, Nov. 15, 2017, http://www.pewresearch.org/fact-tank/2017/11/15/assaults-against-muslims-in-u-s-surpass-2001-level/; Brian Leven, "Explaining the Rise in Hate Crimes against Muslims in the US," *The Conversation*, July 19, 2017, https://theconversation.com/explaining-the-rise-in-hate-crimes-against-muslims-in-the-us-80304; and Eric Lichtblau, "Hate Crimes Against American Muslims Most Since Post-9/11 Era," *The New York Times*, Sep. 17, 2016; https://www.nytimes.com/2016/09/18/us/politics/hate-crimes-american-muslims-rise.html.

177. See Lizzie Dearden, "Street Attacks on Muslims Rocket in UK as Perpetrators 'emboldened' by Terror Attacks and Political Rhetoric, Report Finds," *The Independent*, July 23, 2018, https://www.independent.co.uk/news/uk/home-news/attacks-muslims-uk-terror-islam-hate-crime-brexit-tell-mama-a8457996.html; Emma Hanes and Stephen Machin, "Hate Crime in the Wake of Terror Attacks: Evidence from 7/7 and 9/11," *Journal of Contemporary Criminal Justice*, 30.3 (2014): 247–267; Yonette Joseph, "'Punish a Muslim Day' Letters Rattle U.K. Communities," *The New York Times*, Mar. 11, 2018, https://www.nytimes.com/2018/03/11/world/europe/uk-muslims-letters.html; and "Rise in Hate Crime in England and Wales," *BBC News*, Oct. 17, 2017, https://www.bbc.com/news/uk-41648865.

178. See, for example, Rolf Halse, "The Muslim-American Neighbour as Terrorist: The Representation of a Muslim Family in *24*," *Journal of Arab & Muslim Media Research*, 5.1 (Nov. 20, 2012): 3–18; Faiza Hirji, "Through the Looking Glass: Muslim Women on Television—An Analysis of *24*, *Lost*, and *Little Mosque on the Prairie*," *Global Media Journal: Canadian Edition*, 4.2 (2011): 33–47; and Abu Sadat Nurullah, "Portrayal of Muslims in the Media: '24' and the 'Othering' Process," *International Journal of Human Sciences*, 7.1 (2010): 1020–1046.

179. Renton, 2128.

180. *Doctor Who*, "The Zygon Invasion," series 9, episode 7, written by Peter Harness, directed by Daniel Nettheim, aired Oct. 31, 2015, on BBC1.

181. *Doctor Who*, "The Zygon Inversion," series 9, episode 8, written by Peter Harness and Steven Moffat, directed by Daniel Nettheim, aired Nov. 7, 2015, on BBC1.

182. "The Great Game."
183. Sir Arthur Conan Doyle, "The Final Problem," *Sherlock Holmes: The Complete Collection* (Kindle edition, 2015).
184. Ellen Burton Harrington, "Terror, Nostalgia, and the Pursuit of Sherlock Holmes in *Sherlock*," in Sherlock *and Transmedia Fandom: Essays on the BBC Series*, eds. Louisa Stein and Kristina Busse (Jefferson, NC: McFarland, 2012): 70–84.
185. *Elementary*, "A Difference in Kind," season 4, episode 24, written by Robert Doherty and John Tracey, directed by John Polson, aired May 8, 2016, on CBS.
186. Simeon Moore quoted in Caroline Gall, "Ex-gang Members Speak Out on Birmingham Gun Crime," *BBC News*, Mar. 28, 2018, https://www.bbc.com/news/uk-england-birmingham-43570280.
187. *Elementary*, "The Man with the Twisted Lip," season 2, episode 21, story by Steve Gottfried, teleplay by Craig Sweeny and Steve Gottfried, aired Apr. 24, 2014, on CBS; *Elementary*, "Paint It Black," season 2, episode 22, written by Robert Hewitt Wolfe, directed by Lucy Liu, aired May 1, 2014, on CBS; and *Elementary*, "Art in the Blood," season 2, episode 23, written by Bob Goodman, directed by Guy Ferland, aired May 8, 2014, on CBS.
188. See Chap. 1, "Introduction: Surveillance and Terror in Post-9/11 British and American Television," for a further discussion of the British public's response to Blair's decision to enter the U.K. into the Iraq War and operations in Afghanistan.
189. See Michel Foucault, *Discipline and Punish: The Birth of the Prison*, 1975, Trans. Alan Sheridan (New York: Vintage, 1995).
190. In the *Traffic Cops* episode "Selling a Line," police are filmed and accused of assaulting a drunk driver. Meanwhile, in the *Coppers* episode "Saturday Night," the police are filmed while they contend with drunk and violent citizens outside of pubs. *Traffic Cops*, "Selling a Line," series 4, episode 3, aired June 6, 2006, on BBC1; and *Coppers*, "Saturday Night," series 1, episode 4, aired Nov. 22, 2010, on Channel 4.

Bibliography

24. Created by Joel Surnow and Robert Cochran. Starring Kiefer Sutherland. Aired from 2001 to 2010 and 2014 on Fox.
Abberline, Joseph, Inspector. "Report: re: Man Detained at Holloway re: Murders H Division, 19th Sept. 1888." MEPO 140–142. U.K. National Archives.
Alaska State Troopers. Produced by Michael Welsh and Brian Jones. Narrated by Marc Graue. Aired from 2009 to 2015 on National Geographic Channel.
Ashes to Ashes. Created by Matthew Graham and Ashley Pharoah. Starring Philip Glenister, Keeley Hawes, and Dean Andrews. Aired from 2008 to 2010 on BBC1.

Baker, Al. J., David Goodman, and Benjamin Mueller. "Beyond the Chokehold: The Path to Eric Garner's Death." *The New York Times*, July 13, 2015. https://www.nytimes.com/2015/06/14/nyregion/eric-garner-police-chokehold-staten-island.html.

Bal, Roland. "How to Kill with a Ballpoint: Credibility in Dutch Forensic Science." *Science, Technology, & Human Values*, 30.1 (2005): 52–75.

Balko, Radley. *Rise of the Warrior Cop: The Militarization of America's Police Forces*. New York: Public Affairs, 2013.

Barolsky, Paul. "The Case of the Domesticated Aesthete." *Virginia Quarterly Review*, 60.3 (1984): 438–452.

Bedingfield, Will. "Why It's So Hard to Blame a Rise in UK Knife Crime on Police Cuts." *Wired*, Mar. 7, 2019. https://www.wired.co.uk/article/uk-knife-crime-london-statistics.

Ben-Merre, David. "Wish Fulfillment, Detection, and the Production of Knowledge in *Bleak House*." *Novel*, 44.1 (2011): 47–66.

Bernstein, Ivar. *The New York City Draft Riots: Their Significance for American Society and Politics in the Age of the Civil War*. New York: Oxford UP, 1990.

Booth, Martin. *The Doctor and the Detective: A Biography of Sir Arthur Conan Doyle*. New York: Minotaur Books, 2000.

Boswell, Frances, Sergeant. "Report: Clapham Division, Dec. 16, 1888." MEPO 140–142. U.K. National Archives.

Carpenter, Kevin. *Penny Dreadfuls and Comics: English Periodicals for Children from Victorian Times to the Present Day*. London: Victoria and Albert Museum, 1983.

Carr, John Dickson. *The Life of Sir Arthur Conan Doyle*. 1949. New York: Carroll & Graf Publishers, 2003.

Chadwick, Bruce. *Law and Disorder: The Chaotic Birth of the NYPD*. New York: St. Martin's Press, 2017.

Chandler, Joseph, Inspector. "Met Police Report No. 6 (Special Report), Sept. 8, 1888, H Division." MEPO 140–142. U.K. National Archives.

Chanin, Joshua, Megan Walsh, and Dana Nurge. "Police Use Traffic Stops as a Form of 'catch and release' to Disproportionately Target Black Americans." London School of Economics, U.S. Centre, Oct. 18, 2018. https://blogs.lse.ac.uk/usappblog/2018/10/18/police-use-traffic-stops-as-a-form-of-catch-and-release-to-disproportionately-target-black-americans/.

City of Vice. Directed by Justin Hardy and Dan Reed. Written by Clive Bradley and Peter Harness. Starring Ian McDiarmid and Iain Glen. Aired in 2008 on Channel 4.

Clapman, Nicholas. "Here's When British Police are Legally Allowed to Shoot under a New Policy on Lethal Force." *The Conversation*, Apr. 28, 2017. https://theconversation.com/heres-when-british-police-are-legally-allowed-to-shoot-under-a-new-policy-on-lethal-force-76666.

Collins, Phillip. *Dickens and Crime*. 1962. 3rd edition. London: Macmillan, 1994.

Conte, Joseph M. "Don Delillo's *Falling Man* and the Age of Terror." *MFS: Modern Fiction Studies*, 57.3 (Fall 2011): 557–583.

Copper. "Better Times Are Coming." Season 1, episode 8. Story by Will Rokos and Tom Fontana. Teleplay by Sara B. Cooper. Directed by Larysa Kondracki. Aired Oct. 7, 2012, on BBC America.

———. "The Hudson River School." Season 1, episode 7. Story by Will Rokos and Tom Fontana. Teleplay by Frank Pugliese. Directed by Larysa Kondracki. Aired Sep. 30, 2012, on BBC America.

———. "New York, 1864." Print Advertisement. https://thepopbreak.com/2012/08/20/tv-review-copper/.

Coppers. "C.I.D." Series 2, episode 1. Directed by Anthony Phillipson. Jan. 9, 2012, on Channel 4.

———. "Custody." Series 1, episode 1. Directed by Anthony Phillipson. Aired Nov. 1, 2010 on Channel 4.

———. "Saturday Night." Series 1, episode 4. Directed by Anthony Phillipson. Aired Nov. 22, 2010, on Channel 4.

Cops. Created by John Langley and Malcolm Barbour. Narrated by Harry Newman. Aired from 1989 to present on Fox, Spike, and Paramount Network.

Cox, Jamieson. "In '*Sherlock*: The Abominable Bride,' Holmes is the Worst Kind of Superhero." *The Verge*, Jan. 4, 2016. https://www.theverge.com/2016/1/4/10704192/sherlock-the-abominable-bride-review.

Croft, Stuart and Cerwyn Moore. "The Evolution of Threat Narratives in the Age of Terror: Understanding Terrorist Threats in Britain." *International Affairs*, 86.4 (July 2010): 821–835.

CSI: Crime Scene Investigation. Created by Anthony E. Zuiker. Starring William Petersen, Marg Helgenberger, and Ted Danson. Aired from 2000 to 2015 on CBS.

Curtis, Cate. "Public Perceptions and Expectations of the Forensic Use of DNA: Results of a Preliminary Study." *Bulletin of Science, Technology & Society*, 29.4 (2009): 313–324.

Curtis, L. Perry, Jr. *Jack the Ripper and the London Press*. New Haven: Yale UP, 2001.

Dearden, Lizzie. "Street Attacks on Muslims Rocket in UK as Perpetrators 'emboldened' by Terror Attacks and Political Rhetoric, Report Finds." *The Independent*, July 23, 2018. https://www.independent.co.uk/news/uk/home-news/attacks-muslims-uk-terror-islam-hate-crime-brexit-tell-mama-a8457996.html.

Devereaux, Ryan. "New York's Stop-and-frisk Trial Comes to a Close with a Landmark Ruling." *The Guardian*, Aug. 12, 2013. https://www.theguardian.com/world/2013/aug/12/stop-and-frisk-landmark-ruling.

Dibdin, Michael. *The Last Sherlock Holmes Story*. London: Jonathan Cape, 1978.

Dickens, Charles. *Bleak House*. 1853. Kindle edition, 2012.

———. "On Duty with Inspector Field." *Household Words*, June 14, 1851: 265–270. Dickens Journals Online.

———. *Our Mutual Friend*. 1865. Project Gutenberg, Apr. 27, 2006. https://www.gutenberg.org/files/883/883-h/883-h.htm.

Doctor Who. "The Zygon Invasion." Series 9, episode 7. Written by Peter Harness. Directed by Daniel Nettheim. Aired Oct. 31, 2015, on BBC1.

———. "The Zygon Inversion." Series 9, episode 8. Written by Peter Harness and Steven Moffat. Directed by Daniel Nettheim. Aired Nov. 7, 2015, on BBC1.

"Does Militarization of Police Make Us Less Safe?" *The Week*, Aug. 31, 2017. https://www.theweek.co.uk/us/88104/does-the-militarisation-of-police-make-us-less-safe.

Doyle, Sir Arthur Conan. "The Adventure of the Copper Beeches." 1891. *The Adventures of Sherlock Holmes*. New York: Penguin, 1981: 260–285.

———. "The Adventure of the Speckled Band." 1891. *The Adventures of Sherlock Holmes*. New York: Penguin, 1981: 165–190.

———. "The Boscombe Valley Mystery." 1891. *The Adventures of Sherlock Holmes*. New York: Penguin, 1981: 75–99.

———. "The Final Problem." 1893. *Sherlock Holmes: The Complete Collection*. Kindle edition, 2015.

———. *The Sign of Four*. 1890. *Sherlock Holmes: The Complete Collection*. Kindle edition, 2015.

"The Draft: The Riot in the Ninth Congressional District." *The New York Tribune*, July 14, 1863: 1. NewseumED Digital Collections. https://newseumed.org/tools/artifact/newspaper-coverage-1863-new-york-city-draft-riots.

Elementary. "Art in the Blood." Season 2, episode 23. Written by Bob Goodman. Directed by Guy Ferland. Aired May 8, 2014, on CBS.

———. "A Controlled Descent." Season 3, episode 24. Written by Robert Doherty. Directed by John Polson. Aired May 14, 2015, on CBS.

———. "A Difference in Kind." Season 4, episode 24. Written by Robert Doherty and John Tracey. Directed by John Polson. Aired May 8, 2016, on CBS.

———. "Enough Nemesis to Go Around." Season 3, episode 1. Written by Robert Doherty and Craig Sweeny. Directed by John Polson. Aired Oct. 30, 2014, on CBS.

———. "Flight Risk." Season 1, episode 6. Written by Corinne Brinkerhoff. Directed by David Platt. Aired Nov. 8, 2012, on CBS.

———. "The Five Orange Pipz." Season 3, episode 2. Written by Bob Goodman. Directed by Larry Teng. Aired Nov. 6, 2014, on CBS.

———. "Hemlock." Season 3, episode 13. Written by Robert Doherty, Arika Lisanne Mittman, and Jeffrey Paul King. Directed by Christine Moore. Aired Feb. 5, 2015, on CBS.

———. "Heroine." Season 1, episode 24. Written by Robert Doherty and Craig Sweeny. Directed by John Polson. Aired May 16, 2013, on CBS.

———. "M." Season 1, episode 12. Written by Robert Doherty. Directed by John Polson. Aired Jan. 10, 2013, on CBS.

———. "The Man with the Twisted Lip." Season 2, episode 21. Story by Steve Gottfried. Teleplay by Craig Sweeny and Steve Gottfried. Aired Apr. 24, 2014, on CBS.

———. "Meet Your Maker." Season 6, episode 12. Written by Robert Doherty, Robert Hewitt Wolfe, and Kelly Wheeler. Directed by Ron Fortunato. Aired July 23, 2018, on CBS.

———. "Paint It Black." Season 2, episode 22. Written by Robert Hewitt Wolfe. Directed by Lucy Liu. Aired May 1, 2014, on CBS.

———. "Pilot." Season 1, episode 1. Written by Robert Doherty. Directed by Michael Cuesta. Aired Sep. 27, 2012, on CBS.

———. "Ready or Not." Season 4, episode 18. Written by Robert Doherty and Bob Goodman. Directed by Christine Moore. Aired Mar. 27, 2016, on CBS.

———. "The Red Team." Season 1, episode 13. Story by Jeffrey Paul King and Craig Sweeny. Teleplay by Jeffrey Paul King. Directed by Christine Moore. Aired Jan. 31, 2013, on CBS.

———. "Tremors." Season 2, episode 10. Written by Liz Friedman. Directed by Aaron Lipstadt. Aired Dec. 5, 2013, on CBS.

———. "The Woman." Season 1, episode 23. Written by Robert Doherty and Craig Sweeny. Directed by Seth Mann. Aired May 16, 2013, on CBS.

Ellis, John. *Visible Fictions: Cinema: Television: Video*. London: Routledge, 1982.

Emsley, Clive. *Policing and Its Context, 1750–1870*. London: Macmillan, 1983.

Erisman, Fred. "If Watson Were a Woman: Three (Re) Visions of the Holmesian Ménage." *Clues: A Journal of Detection*, 22.1 (2001): 177–188.

Faye, Lindsay. *Dust and Shadow: An Account of the Ripper Killings by Dr. John Watson*. New York: Simon & Schuster, 2009.

Fetherston, Robin L. "Tailing Inspector Bucket: Dickens's Progeny in Hammett's Hard-Boiled Detective Fiction." *International Journal of Arts and Sciences*, 7.1 (2014): 275–290.

Fingerhut, Hannah. "Deep Racial, Partisan Divisions in Americans' Views of Police Officers." Pew Research Center, Sep. 15, 2017. http://www.pewresearch.org/fact-tank/2017/09/15/deep-racial-partisan-divisions-in-americans-views-of-police-officers/.

Fisher, Michael. "Crossing the Line—Is the Militarisation of British Police Reasonable?" LinkedIn, Mar. 10, 2017. https://www.linkedin.com/pulse/crossing-line-militarisation-british-police-michael-fisher.

Fletcher, Michael A. "For Black Motorists, A Never-Ending Fear of Being Stopped." *National Geographic*, Mar. 12, 2018. https://www.nationalgeographic.com/magazine/2018/04/the-stop-race-police-traffic/.

The Force: Manchester. Produced by Shine TV. Aired from 2015 to present on Sky 1 (UK).

Forensic Files. Created by Paul Dowling. Narrated by Peter Thomas. Aired from 1996 to 2011 on TLC, Court TV, and truTV.

Foucault, Michel. *Discipline and Punish: The Birth of the Prison.* 1975. Trans. Alan Sheridan. New York: Vintage, 1995.

Friedersdorf, Conor. "Eric Garner and the NYPD's History of Deadly Chokeholds." *The Atlantic*, Dec. 4, 2014. https://www.theatlantic.com/national/archive/2014/12/context-for-the-punishment-free-killing-of-eric-garner/383413/.

Frontline. "Policing the Police." Season 34, episode 12. Written and produced by James Jacoby and Anya Bourg. Aired June 28, 2016, on PBS.

———. "The Real CSI." Season 30, episode 10. Written and produced by Andres Cediel and Lowell Bergman. Aired Apr. 17, 2012, on PBS.

Gall, Caroline. "Ex-gang Members Speak Out on Birmingham Gun Crime." *BBC News*, Mar. 28, 2018. https://www.bbc.com/news/uk-england-birmingham-43570280.

Ganeva, Tana and Laura Gottesdiener. "Nine Terrifying Facts about America's Biggest Police Force." *Salon*, Sep. 28, 2012. https://www.salon.com/2012/09/28/nine_terrifying_facts_about_americas_biggest_police_force/.

Gayle, Damian. "Structural Racism at the Heart of British Society, Human Rights Panel Says." *The Guardian*, Apr. 27, 2018. https://www.theguardian.com/world/2018/apr/27/racism-british-society-minority-ethnic-people-dying-excessive-force.

Gilbert, Sophie. "The Troublesome Women of *Sherlock*." *The Atlantic*, Jan. 5, 2017. https://www.theatlantic.com/entertainment/archive/2017/01/sherlocks-women/512141/.

Gilbert, Steven V. and Barbara A. Gilbert. *Police Corruption in the NYPD: From Knapp to Mollen.* Boca Raton, FL: CRC Press, 2015.

Gilligan, Andrew. "How the British Bobby Turned into Robocop." *The Spectator*, Aug. 4, 2016. https://blogs.spectator.co.uk/2016/08/military-style-policing-creeping-everyday-life/.

Greenfield, John. "Arthur Morrison's Sherlock Clone: Martin Hewitt, Victorian Values, and London Magazine Culture, 1894–1903." *Victorian Periodicals Review*, 35.1 (Spring 2002): 18–36.

Haining, Pete, ed. *The Penny Dreadful: Or, Strange, Horrid & Sensational Tales!* London: Orion Publishing Group, 1975.

Halse, Rolf. "The Muslim-American Neighbour as Terrorist: The Representation of a Muslim Family in *24*." *Journal of Arab & Muslim Media Research*, 5.1 (November 20, 2012): 3–18.

Hanes, Emma and Stephen Machin. "Hate Crime in the Wake of Terror Attacks: Evidence from 7/7 and 9/11." *Journal of Contemporary Criminal Justice*, 30.3 (2014): 247–267.

Hanna, Edward B. *The Whitechapel Horrors: A Sherlock Holmes Novel.* New York: Carroll & Graf, 1993.

Hargreaves, Julian. "Police Stop and Search Within British Muslim Communities: Evidence from the Crime Survey 2006–2011." *The British Journal of Criminology*, 58.6 (October 2018): 1281–1302.

Harrington, Ellen Burton. "Nation, Identity, and the Fascination with Forensic Science in Sherlock Holmes and *CSI.*" *International Journal of Cultural Studies*, 10.3 (2007): 365–382.

———. "Terror, Nostalgia, and the Pursuit of Sherlock Holmes in *Sherlock.*" *Sherlock and Transmedia Fandom: Essays on the BBC Series.* Eds. Louisa Stein and Kristina Busse. Jefferson, NC: McFarland, 2012: 70–84.

Hartocollis, Anemona. "10 Years and a Diagnosis Later, 9/11 Demons Haunt Thousands." *The New York Times*, Aug. 9, 2011. https://www.nytimes.com/2011/08/10/nyregion/post-traumatic-stress-disorder-from-911still-haunts.html.

Heritage, Stuart. "Which Cop Docs Are Worth Watching?" *The Guardian*, Aug. 15, 2011. https://www.theguardian.com/tv-and-radio/tvandradioblog/2011/aug/15/cop-docs-worth-watching.

Hirji, Faiza. "Through the Looking Glass: Muslim Women on Television—An Analysis of *24*, *Lost*, and *Little Mosque on the Prairie.*" *Global Media Journal: Canadian Edition*, 4.2 (2011): 33–47.

"In the Black Hole of Scotland Yard: A Tale of Blows and Bludgeons." *The Pall Mall Gazette*, Dec. 1, 1887: 1. The British Newspaper Archive.

Independent Police Complaints Commission. "Stockwell One: Investigation into the Shooting of Jean Charles de Menezes at Stockwell Underground Station on 22 July 2005." *BBC News.* http://news.bbc.co.uk/2/shared/bsp/hi/pdfs/08_11_07_stockwell1.pdf.

Jofre, Shelley. "Falsely Fingered." *The Guardian*, July 9, 2001. https://www.theguardian.com/media/2001/jul/09/mondaymediasection4.

Johnson-McGrath, Julie. "Speaking for the Dead: Forensic Pathologists and Criminal Justice in the United States." *Science, Technology & Human Values*, 20.4 (1995): 438–459.

Jones, Jane Clare, "Is *Sherlock* Sexist? Steven Moffat's Wanton Women." *The Guardian*, Jan. 3, 2012. https://www.theguardian.com/commentisfree/2012/jan/03/sherlock-sexist-steven-moffat.

Joseph, Yonette. "'Punish a Muslim Day' Letters Rattle U.K. Communities." *The New York Times*, Mar. 11, 2018. https://www.nytimes.com/2018/03/11/world/europe/uk-muslims-letters.html.

Joyce, Simon. "Reviewed Work: *Detective Fiction and the Rise of Forensic Science* by Ronald R. Thomas." *The Journal of English and Germanic Philology*, 101.4 (October 2002): 587–589.

Kirkpatrick, Robert J. *From the Penny Dreadful to the Ha'penny Dreadfuller: A Bibliographical History of the British Boys' Periodical 1762–1950.* London: British Library, 2013.

Kishi, Katayoun. "Assaults against Muslims in U.S. Surpass 2001 Level." Pew Research Center, Nov. 15, 2017. http://www.pewresearch.org/fact-tank/2017/11/15/assaults-against-muslims-in-u-s-surpass-2001-level/.

Knight, Stephen. *Form and Ideology in Crime Fiction.* Bloomington: Indiana UP, 1980.

Krasner, James. "Watson Falls Asleep: Narrative Frustration and Sherlock Holmes." *English Literature in Translation,* 40.4 (1997): 424–435.

LaFraniere, Sharon and Andrew W. Lehren. "The Disproportionate Risk of Driving While Black." *The New York Times,* Oct. 24, 2015. https://www.nytimes.com/2015/10/25/us/racial-disparity-traffic-stops-driving-black.html.

Lawson, Mark. "*Sherlock* and *Doctor Who*: Beware of Fans Influencing the TV They Love." *The Guardian,* Jan. 3, 2016. https://www.theguardian.com/tv-and-radio/tvandradioblog/2014/jan/03/sherlock-doctor-who-fans-influencing-tv.

Lay, Julia Anna Hartness. Diary, ZL-450. New York Public Library Manuscripts and Archives Division.

Lellenberg, Jon, Daniel Stashower, and Charles Foley, eds. *Arthur Conan Doyle: A Life in Letters.* New York: HarperPress, 2007.

Leven, Brian. "Explaining the Rise in Hate Crimes against Muslims in the US." *The Conversation,* July 19, 2017. https://theconversation.com/explaining-the-rise-in-hate-crimes-against-muslims-in-the-us-80304.

Levitt, Leonard. *NYPD Confidential: Power and Corruption in the Country's Greatest Police Force.* New York: Macmillan, 2009.

Lewis, Helen. "Does Steven Moffat Have a Problem with Women?" *New Statesman America,* Jan. 9, 2012. https://www.newstatesman.com/blogs/helen-lewis-hasteley/2012/01/moffat-sherlock-women.

Lichtblau, Eric. "Hate Crimes against American Muslims Most Since Post-9/11 Era." *The New York Times,* Sep. 17, 2016. https://www.nytimes.com/2016/09/18/us/politics/hate-crimes-american-muslims-rise.html.

Life on Mars. (UK Version). Created by Matthew Graham, Tony Jordan, and Ashley Pharoah. Starring John Simm, Philip Glenister, and Liz White. Aired from 2006 to 2007 on BBC1.

———. (US Version). Developed by Josh Appelbaum, André Nemec, and Scott Rosenberg. Starring Jason O'Mara, Harvey Keitel, and Jonathan Murphy. Aired from 2008 to 2009 on ABC.

Lycett, Andrew. *The Man Who Created Sherlock Holmes: The Life and Times of Sir Arthur Conan Doyle.* New York: Free Press, 2008.

Lynch, Michael and Sheila Jasanoff. "Contested Identities: Science, Law and Forensic Practice." *Social Studies of Science*, 28.5–6 (1998): 675–686.

Machado, Helena and Felipe Santos. "Popular Press and Forensic Genetics in Portugal: Expectations and Disappointments Regarding Two Cases of Missing Children." *Public Understanding of Science*, 20.3 (2009): 303–318.

Making a Murderer. Written and directed by Laura Ricciardi and Moira Demos. Released in 2015 by Netflix.

Maybin, Simon. "Do the Public Still Trust the Police?" *BBC News*, Mar. 25, 2014. https://www.bbc.com/news/magazine-26730705.

McAlpine, Mary Kate. "'The Abominable Bride' is Moffat's Biggest Feminist Failure." *Medium*, Dec. 3, 2017. https://medium.com/@marykatemcalpine/the-abominable-bride-is-moffats-biggest-feminist-failure-9e3bc8ba3a65.

Miller, Joel et al. "Public Opinions of the Police: The Influence of Friends, Family, and News Media." National Criminal Justice Reference Service (NCJRS). Document No. 205619, May 2004. https://www.ncjrs.gov/pdffiles1/nij/grants/205619.pdf.

Miller, Russell. *The Adventures of Arthur Conan Doyle: A Biography*. New York: Thomas Dunne Books, 2008.

"The Mob in New York." *The New York Times*, July 14, 1863: 1. *The New York Times* Digital Archives. https://timesmachine.nytimes.com/timesmachine/1863/07/14/90521933.html?action=click&contentCollection=Archives&module=LedeAsset&region=ArchiveBody&pgtype=article&pageNumber=1.

Motorway Cops. Produced by Folio Productions. Starring Jamie Threakston. Aired from 2008 to present on BBC1.

Mueller, Benjamin. "U.K. Knife Crime Rises. Are Budgets to Blame?" *The New York Times*, Mar. 6, 2019. https://www.nytimes.com/2019/03/06/world/europe/uk-knife-crime-austerity.html.

Murder Maps. Produced by 3DD Productions. Starring Nicholas Day, Alan Moss, and Donald Rumbelow. First released in 2015 by Netflix.

Murdoch Mysteries. Developed by R.B. Carney, Cal Coons, and Alexandra Zarowny. Starring Yannick Bisson, Hélène Joy, and Thomas Craig. Based on the novels by Maureen Jennings. Aired from 2008 to present on Citytv and CBC.

National Center for PTSD. "Sleep and PTSD." U.S. Department of Veterans Affairs. https://www.ptsd.va.gov/understand/related/sleep_ptsd.asp.

Neill, Anna. "The Savage Genius of Sherlock Holmes." *Victorian Literature and Culture*, 37.2 (2009): 611–626.

Nelson, Joe. "State, Federal Law Enforcement Agencies File in Support of FBI in Apple Battle." *San Bernardino County Sun*, Mar. 30, 2016. https://www.sbsun.com/2016/03/03/state-federal-law-enforcement-agencies-file-in-support-of-fbi-in-apple-battle/.

Neria, Yuval, Laura DiGrande, and Ben G. Adams. "Posttraumatic Stress Disorder Following the September 11, 2001, Terrorist Attacks: A Review of the Literature Among Highly Exposed Populations." *American Psychology*, 66.6 (September 2011): 429–446.

"The New Police." 1830. U.K. National Archives. http://www.nationalarchives.gov.uk/education/candp/prevention/g08/g08cs2s3.htm.

New York County District Attorney Indictment Records. Aug. 4, 1863–Aug.11, 1863. Roll 119. New York City Municipal Archive.

Nguyen, Mimi Thi. "The Biopower of Beauty: Humanitarian Imperialisms and Global Feminisms in an Age of Terror." *Signs: Journal of Women in Culture and Society*, 36.2 (Winter 2011): 359–383.

Nordon, Pierre. *Conan Doyle: A Biography*. New York: Holt, Rinehart and Winston, 1967.

Nurullah, Abu Sadat. "Portrayal of Muslims in the Media: '24' and the 'Othering' Process." *International Journal of Human Sciences*, 7.1 (2010): 1020–1046.

"Our Note Book." *Illustrated London News*, Oct. 13, 1888: 418. British Library Newspaper Archives.

"Outcasts at the East-End." *Illustrated London News*, Oct. 13, 1888: 421+. British Library Newspaper Archives.

Parenti, Christian. *The Soft Cage: Surveillance in America From Slavery to the War on Terror*. New York: Basic Books, 2003.

Pearsall, Ronald. *Conan Doyle: A Biographical Solution*. Worthing, UK: Littlehampton Book Services Ltd., 1977.

Person of Interest. Created by Jonathan Nolan. Starring Jim Caviezel, Michael Emerson, and Taraji P. Henderson. Aired from 2011 to 2016 on CBS.

Police Interceptors. Created by Steve Warr and Bill Rudgard. Aired from 2008 to present on Channel 5.

"The Punishment of the Rioters." *St. James's Gazette*, Dec. 19, 1887: 12. The British Newspaper Archive.

Qurashi, Fahid. "The Prevent Strategy and the UK 'war on terror': Embedding Infrastructures of Surveillance in Muslim Communities." *Palgrave Communications*, 4, Article number: 17 (2018). https://www.nature.com/articles/s41599-017-0061-9.

Rayman, Graham. *The NYPD Tapes: A Shocking Story of Cops, Cover-ups, and Courage*. New York: Macmillan, 2018.

Reid, Edmund, Inspector. "Murder, Aug. 16, 1888, H Division." MEPO 140–142. U.K. National Archives.

Renton, James. "The Global Order of Muslim Surveillance and its Thought Architecture." *Ethnic and Racial Studies*, 41.12 (2018): 2127.

Reppetto, Thomas and James Lardner. *NYPD: A City and Its Police*. New York: Henry Holt and Company, 2000.

Ridell, Fern. "The 1910s: 'We have sanitised our history of the suffragettes'." *The Guardian*, Feb. 6, 2018. https://www.theguardian.com/lifeandstyle/2018/feb/06/1910s-suffragettes-suffragists-fern-riddell.

———. *Death in Ten Minutes: Kitty Marion. Actress. Arsonist. Suffragette.* London: Hodder and Stoughton, 2018.

———. "Suffragettes, Violence and Militancy." The British Library, Feb. 6, 2018. https://www.bl.uk/votes-for-women/articles/suffragettes-violence-and-militancy.

Ripper Street. Created by Richard Warlow. Starring Matthew Macfadyen, Jerome Flynn, Adam Rothenberg, and MyAnna Buring. Aired from 2012 to 2016 on BB1, BBC2, and Amazon Video.

"Rise in Hate Crime in England and Wales." *BBC News*, Oct. 17, 2017. https://www.bbc.com/news/uk-41648865.

Rives-East, Darcie. "Watching the Detective: *Sherlock*, Surveillance, and British Fears Post-7/7." *The Journal of Popular Culture*, 48.1 (February 2015): 44–58.

Robbers, Monica L. P. "Blinded by Science: The Social Construction of Reality in Forensic Television Shows and its Effect on Criminal Jury Trials." *Criminal Justice Policy Review*, 19.1 (2008): 84–102.

Seltzer, Mark. "Murder/Media/Modernity." *Canadian Review of American Studies*, 38.1 (2008): 11–41.

Sherlock. "The Abominable Bride." Series 4, episode 0. Written by Steven Moffat and Mark Gatiss. Directed by Douglas Mackinnon. Aired Jan. 1, 2016, on BBC1.

———. "The Blind Banker." Series 1, episode 2. Written by Stephen Thomson. Directed by Euros Lynn. Aired Aug. 1, 2010, on BBC1.

———. "The Empty Hearse." Series 3, episode 1. Written by Mark Gatiss. Directed by Jeremy Lovering. Aired Jan. 1, 2014, on BBC1.

———. "The Great Game." Series 1, episode 3. Written by Mark Gatiss. Directed by Paul McGuigan. Aired Aug. 8, 2010, on BBC1.

———. "His Last Vow." Series 3, episode 3. Written by Steven Moffat. Directed by Nick Hurran. Aired Jan. 12, 2014, on BBC1.

———. "The Hounds of Baskerville." Series 2, episode 2. Written by Mark Gatiss. Directed by Paul McGuigan. Aired Jan. 8, 2012, on BBC1.

———. "A Scandal in Belgravia." Series 1, episode 1. Written by Steven Moffat. Directed by Paul McGuigan. Aired Jan. 1, 2012, on BBC1.

———. "A Study in Pink." Series 1, episode 1. Written by Steven Moffat. Directed by Paul McGuigan. Aired July 25, 2010, on BBC1.

Sherlock Holmes. Directed by Guy Ritchie. Starring Robert Downey, Jr. and Jude Law. Released in 2009 by Warner Bros.

Sherlock Holmes: A Game of Shadows. Directed by Guy Ritchie. Starring Robert Downey, Jr. and Jude Law. Released in 2011 by Warner Bros.

Sinclair, Georgina, ed. *Globalising British Policing*. Farnham, UK: Ashgate Publishing, 2011.

Sisek, Michael R. "NYPD Officer will Face Disciplinary Trial in Eric Garner Chokehold Death." *PBS News Hour*, Dec. 6, 2018. https://www.pbs.org/newshour/nation/nypd-officer-will-face-disciplinary-trial-in-eric-garner-chokehold-death.

Smith, Chris. "The Controversial Crime-Fighting Program that Changed Big-City Policing Forever." *New York Magazine*, Mar. 2, 2018. http://nymag.com/intelligencer/2018/03/the-crime-fighting-program-that-changed-new-york-forever.html.

Smythe, Christi, Selina Wang, and Tiffany Kary. "Apple Goes to Washington Fresh from Big Boost in iPhone Fight." *Bloomberg*, Mar. 1, 2016. https://www.bloomberg.com/news/articles/2016-03-01/apple-goes-to-washington-with-some-wind-in-its-sails.

Soffen, Kim. "The Big Question about Why Police Pull over So Many Black Drivers." *The Washington Post*, July 8, 2016. https://www.washingtonpost.com/news/wonk/wp/2016/07/08/the-big-question-about-why-police-pull-over-so-many-black-drivers/?utm_term=.3012ac744b8d.

"The Soldier and The Lawyer: A Comedy." *Reynolds's Newspaper*, Nov. 18, 1888: 4. The British Newspaper Archive.

"A Spitalfields Lodging-House." *Illustrated London News*, Saturday, Sep. 22, 1888. Issue 2579: 350. British Library Newspaper Archives.

Springhall, John. *Youth, Popular Culture, and Moral Panics: Penny Gaffs to Gangsta-Rap, 1830–1996*. New York: St. Martin's Press, 1998.

Stashower, Daniel. *Teller of Tales: The Life of Arthur Conan Doyle*. New York: Penguin Books, 2000.

Stein, Louisa and Kristina Busse, eds. *Sherlock and Transmedia Fandom: Essays on the BBC Series*. Jefferson, NC: McFarland, 2012.

Sturtevant, John J. Memoir, MssCol 2915. New York Public Library Manuscripts and Archives Division.

Summerscale, Kate. *The Suspicions of Mr. Whicher: A Shocking Murder and the Undoing of a Great Victorian Detective*. New York: Bloomsbury, 2008.

Talbot, Margaret. "Stealing Life: The Crusader behind *The Wire*." *The New Yorker*, Oct. 22, 2007. https://www.newyorker.com/magazine/2007/10/22/stealing-life.

Thomas, Ronald R. "The Dream of the Empty Camera: Image, Evidence, and Authentic American Style in 'American Photographs' and 'Farewell, My Lovely'." *Criticism*, 36.3 (Summer 1994): 415–457.

———. "Making Darkness Visible: Capturing the Criminal and Observing the Law in Victorian Photography and Detective Fiction." *Victorian Literature and the Victorian Visual Imagination*. Eds. Carol T. Christ and John O. Jordan. Berkeley: U of California P, 1995: 134–168.

Traffic Cops. "Selling a Line." Series 4, episode 3. Aired June 6, 2006, on BBC1.

Treverton, Gregory F. *Intelligence for an Age of Terror*. Cambridge, UK: Cambridge University Press, 2009.

U.S. Commission on Civil Rights. "Police Practices and Civil Rights in New York City: Chapter 5, Stop, Question, and Frisk." Aug. 2018. https://www.usccr.gov/pubs/nypolice/main.htm.

VanDerWerff, Todd. "The *Sherlock* Special 'The Abominable Bride' was Terrible. Has This Show Completely Lost Its Way?" *Vox*, Jan. 2, 2016. https://www.vox.com/2016/1/2/10700800/sherlock-special-recap-pbs-abominable-bride.

Vitelli, Romeo. "PTSD in Survivors of 9/11." *Psychology Today*, Oct. 15, 2018. https://www.psychologytoday.com/us/blog/media-spotlight/201810/ptsd-in-survivors-911.

Weaver, Matthew. "Police Chief Says Rise in Knife Crime in England is National Emergency." *The Guardian*, Mar. 6, 2019. https://www.theguardian.com/uk-news/2019/mar/06/police-chief-says-rise-in-knife-crime-in-england-is-national-emergency.

Whalen, Bernard and Jon Whalen. *The NYPD's First Fifty Years: Politicians, Police Commissioners, and Patrolmen*. Lincoln, NE: Potomac Books, 2015.

Whitechapel. Created by Ben Court, Caroline Ip. Starring Rupert Penry-Jones, Phil Davis, and Steve Pemberton. Aired from 2009 to 2013 on ITV.

Winton, Richard. "Black and Latino Drivers are Searched Based on Less Evidence and are More Likely to be Arrested, Stanford Researchers Find." *The Los Angeles Times*, June 19, 2017. https://www.latimes.com/local/lanow/la-me-ln-stanford-minority-drive-disparties-20170619-story.html.

The Wire. Created by David Simon. Starring Dominic West, Idris Elba, and Sonja Sohn. Aired from 2002 to 2008 on HBO.

Wittes, Benjamin. *Law and the Long War: The Future of Justice in the Age of Terror*. New York: Penguin, 2008.

Wylie, Catherine. "Black People 'nine times as likely' as Whites to be Stopped and Searched by Police in England and Wales." *The Independent*, Oct. 14, 2018. https://www.independent.co.uk/news/uk/home-news/stop-search-black-people-white-police-racism-new-study-a8583051.html.

CHAPTER 4

We Spy: Espionage and the National Intelligence Agency

In this chapter, I will address a final state apparatus of surveillance and social control often depicted in British and American television since 9/11: the national intelligence agency. In the U.S., the two main intelligence agencies are the Central Intelligence Agency (CIA)[1] and the National Security Agency (NSA),[2] which work closely with their U.K. counterparts—Military Intelligence, Section 5 (Mi-5); Military Intelligence, Section 6 (Mi-6)[3]; and the Government Communications Headquarters (GCHQ).[4] The CIA is primarily responsible for foreign intelligence gathering and operations rather than domestic security and intelligence (which are the purview of the Federal Bureau of Investigation [FBI]). In this way, the CIA is comparable to Britain's Mi-6, while the FBI would be more analogous to Mi-5. Meanwhile, the NSA's mandate is to gather, process, and analyze data and intelligence gathered globally for national security purposes. As such, the NSA is comparable to Britain's GCHQ. Collectively, it is these agencies and the ethics of intelligence gathering—particularly as it relates to anticipating and preventing terrorism—that have been an issue of concern for post-9/11 British and American television series.

The history of television shows us that, certainly, spy series are not new and were popular long before 9/11. Especially, the Cold War lent itself to such drama, given that the conflict between the U.S. and the Soviet Union emerged at roughly the same time as television became widely available. Thus, from the 1960s until the fall of the Communist Bloc and the Soviet

© The Author(s) 2019
D. Rives-East, *Surveillance and Terror in Post-9/11 British and American Television*,
https://doi.org/10.1007/978-3-030-16900-8_4

Union in the early 1990s, there were a myriad of programs in the U.S. and U.K. that centered on fictitious British and American spy agencies attempting to outwit Soviet agents and other nefarious actors. Some key examples from U.K. television are *The Avengers* (ITV, 1961–1969), *The Prisoner* (ITV, 1967–1968), and *The Saint* (ITV; 1962–1969). Among such American series are *The Equalizer* (CBS, 1985–1989), *I Spy* (NBC, 1965–1968), *MacGyver* (ABC, 1985–1992), *The Man from U.N.C.L.E.* (NBC, 1964–1968), *Mission: Impossible* (CBS, 1966–1973), and *Scarecrow and Mrs. King* (CBS; 1983–1987). In an interesting nod to the espionage element of the Sherlock Holmes stories, David McDaniel, author of *The Man from U.N.C.L.E.* book series (on which the drama was based), describes T.H.R.U.S.H., the evil entity against which U.N.C.L.E. fights, as an organization founded by Colonel Sebastian Moran, Professor Moriarty's lieutenant, after the latter's death at Reichenbach Falls.[5]

From this brief list, it is apparent that U.S. television had a greater number of Cold War television series than the U.K., which is not surprising given America's position as the rival superpower to the Soviet Union. It is beyond the scope of this chapter, however, to discuss British and American Cold War spy dramas (except for FX's *The Americans*, which is set during the 1980s). Instead, I want to focus on the development of espionage series in the post-9/11 world. Nevertheless, it is important to acknowledge that programs about national intelligence have a long television history, and the Cold War programs do influence how contemporary programs address surveillance and espionage, given there are echoes of the Cold War in post-9/11 spy dramas.

POST-9/11 ANGLO-AMERICAN ESPIONAGE DRAMA AND THE CRITIQUE OF THE INTELLIGENCE AGENCY

In terms of the post-9/11 television landscape, I argue that current espionage programs have turned their focus more inward on the agency itself, its methods, the morality and purpose of espionage, and how the agency interacts with the British and American public. This is a shift from an emphasis on derring-do and outfoxing Communist adversaries that was the primary motivation of programs about national intelligence prior to 9/11. In other words, espionage dramas post-9/11 articulate concerns about the following: the reason for the spy agency, its adherence to the rule of law in the U.S. and U.K., and the extent to which the British and American public are subject to the agency's scrutiny.

This change in series' emphasis arises from disturbing revelations about U.S. and U.K. intelligence agencies following 9/11. For example, in the years after the attack, the public learned that the CIA was authorized by the Bush administration to abduct those subjects suspected to have al-Qaeda terrorist connections and to relocate them to "black sites" in nations which were outside the jurisdiction of U.S. law and which permitted the use of torture to gain information.[6] We also subsequently understood how little useful information was gained through such actions that not only violated the rule of law in the U.S., but also tarnished the exceptionalist image of America held by many within and without the U.S.. For example, in its famous "Report of the U.S. Senate Select Committee on Intelligence Committee Study of the Central Intelligence Agency's Detention and Interrogation Program," the U.S. Senate Select Committee on Intelligence found that "[t]he CIA's use of its enhanced interrogation techniques was not an effective means of acquiring intelligence or gaining cooperation from detainees"; "[t]he CIA's justification for the use of its enhanced interrogation techniques rested on inaccurate claims of their effectiveness"; "[t]he interrogations of CIA detainees were brutal and far worse than the CIA represented to policymakers and others"; and "[t]he conditions of confinement for CIA detainees were harsher than the CIA had represented to policymakers and others."[7] In this way, the American government itself castigated the spy agency for its overreach and lack of ethics in how it sought to gain information about terrorist groups and activities after 9/11.

Further, former NSA employee Edward Snowden, working with journalists from the British newspaper *The Guardian*, including Glenn Greenwald, revealed extensive documentation on how the NSA was given unprecedented latitude by Congress in its surveillance operations through the USA PATRIOT Act. The USA PATRIOT Act stands for "Uniting and Strengthening America by Providing Appropriate Tools Required to Intercept and Obstruct Terrorism." The U.S. Department of Justice (DOJ) defends the Act, contending that "[s]ince its passage following the September 11, 2001 attacks, the Patriot Act has played a key part—and often the leading role—in a number of successful operations to protect innocent Americans from the deadly plans of terrorists dedicated to destroying America and our way of life."[8] The DOJ also claims that the PATRIOT Act does not represent a fundamental change in U.S. law regarding surveillance techniques and tactics.[9] Rather, the DOJ argues that "Congress simply took existing legal principles and retrofitted them to preserve the lives and liberty of the American people from the challenges posed by a global terrorist network."[10]

However, the American Civil Liberties Union (ACLU) argues that the PATRIOT Act was "an overnight revision of the nation's surveillance laws that vastly expanded the government's authority to spy on its own citizens, while simultaneously reducing checks and balances on those powers like judicial oversight, public accountability, and the ability to challenge government searches in court."[11] The ACLU and other critics insist that this act allows the NSA to collect, through metadata sweeps, the communications of U.S. citizens without warrant and with the cooperation of telecommunications companies, such as AT&T.[12] For example, *The New York Times* reported: "After the terrorist attacks of Sept. 11, 2001, AT&T and MCI were instrumental in the Bush administration's warrantless wiretapping programs, according to a draft report by the N.S.A.'s inspector general. The report, disclosed by Mr. Snowden and previously published by *The Guardian*, does not identify the companies by name but describes their market share in numbers that correspond to those two businesses, according to Federal Communications Commission reports."[13]

This development was particularly worrisome, given that the original Foreign Intelligence Surveillance Act of 1978 (FISA), enacted after the revelation of surveillance abuses by the Nixon administration, mandated that government surveillance of foreign or domestic actors required a warrant from the FISA court. This court was established by the 1978 Act to oversee government requests for these warrants.[14] However, FISA's original mandate altered after 9/11 to allow scrutiny of the communications of U.S. citizens without a warrant in order to discover and track potential terrorist networks or cells within the U.S. Then, in response to the Snowden revelations, the 1978 Act was again amended to restrict warrantless wiretaps to non-U.S. citizens: "Section 702 of the Fisa Amendments Act [...] gives the NSA authority to target without warrant the communications of foreign targets who must be non-US citizens and outside the US at the point of collection."[15] This warrantless surveillance was allowed as long as the foreign targets were non-U.S. citizens and outside the U.S. at the time of data collection. Nevertheless, groups like the ACLU contend that Section 702 does not sufficiently protect the U.S. public: "Given our nation's history of abusing its surveillance authorities, and the secrecy surrounding the program, we should be concerned that Section 702 is and will be used to disproportionately target disfavored groups, whether minority communities, political activists, or even journalists."[16] Here, the ACLU worries that despite the supposed limitations to non-U.S. citizens, NSA surveillance could still be used covertly against American citizens, at home or abroad, simply on the basis of their race, gender, sexuality, religion, political ideology, or profession, rather than their actual threat to national security.

Further, a 2013 White House review panel asserted that, as was the case with the failure of CIA torture to yield valuable information, "the bulk collection of Americans' phone records 'was not essential' to thwarting terror attacks."[17] And, as with the CIA's "enhanced interrogation techniques," many in and outside the U.S. became disillusioned that yet another intelligence agency, the NSA, had violated ideals of American exceptionalism: specifically, the values of freedom of speech and freedom to privacy. Shafiqa Ahmadi, assistant professor of clinical education at the University of Southern California's Rossier School of Education, argues, for instance, that "[t]he law has done more damage than good to the reputation of the U.S., especially among young people at colleges and universities. The fear of government surveillance under the law has chilled international intellectual exchange and alienated many foreign students seeking to study at U.S. campuses."[18] Additionally, Alexander J. Martin, technology reporter for Sky News, echoed what many felt: "We thought we were living in the free world, until Edward Snowden began to reveal top secret documents about mass surveillance in 2013."[19] There also occurred a backlash in the U.K. against its principal intelligence agencies because the British intelligence community aided and abetted the U.S. in its extralegal pursuit of terrorist suspects.[20] Further, Snowden's leaked documents revealed that the GCHQ, like the NSA, maintained extensive surveillance of U.K. citizens.[21] Therefore, in the nearly two decades after 9/11, the Anglo-American public has become much more suspicious of the U.S. and U.K. national intelligence agencies and whose interests they truly serve. Of primary concern is how these agencies' surveillance power is being used, and if that power could be deployed against U.S. and U.K. citizens who have no links to terrorism but who might be opposed to government actions. Therefore, while the spy dramas of the Cold War era often portrayed these agencies and their agents as Cold War heroes, that picture is now murkier and more complex.

SPY SERIES AND THE BEGINNINGS OF SURVEILLANCE
IN AMERICA

As in previous chapters, I am interested in how post-9/11 television programs about surveillance return to the past to consider the origins of the state apparatus in question during the turmoil of our current Age of Terror. As a result, I would like to begin by discussing the U.S. AMC series *Turn: Washington's Spies*, which has recently completed its fourth and final season. This espionage program is based on author, historian, and journalist Alexander Rose's *Washington's Spies: The Story of America's First Spy Ring*,[22] an account of George Washington's development of an assemblage of spies, known as the Culper Ring, during the Revolutionary War to gather intelligence about British troop strength and movements. As noted by Caroline Eastman, the "turn" of the television program's title refers to "the revolutionaries' desperate need to turn the tide of the war in their favor."[23] In his book, Rose elucidates how espionage was a key factor in helping the Americans acquire this advantage over a vastly superior adversary in terms of the British army's training, numbers, armaments, and funding. In other words, had the Americans not employed espionage, then the U.S. might not have won its war of independence from the U.K. (despite assistance from France). The British, of course, had their own spies as well, who would attempt to infiltrate American towns or army battalions, for similar reasons—to gather intelligence on American troop movement and plans.

Together, the book and its television counterpart bring attention to a largely forgotten history of espionage in the U.S. Both highlight the irony that the seeds of the U.S. intelligence agency were sown at the same time as a war was fought to create a new nation under idealistic democratic principles, such as free speech and freedom from violations of privacy, as outlined by Thomas Jefferson in the Declaration of Independence. This paradoxical origin of privacy and surveillance is punctuated by the fact that we learn from the series and the book that espionage was at the time considered unseemly and ignoble. It was viewed as "unmanly" because spying was covert and involved lying about one's identity, instead of fighting openly. As *Turn* creator and producer Craig Silverstein observes, "It was not an honorable thing to be a spy at the time. Before [the Culper Ring], a spy was really a scout—somebody who would sneak across enemy lines, crawl up a hill, look down, count troops, run back. To stay behind enemy lines, live a covert life, lie to your neighbors about being loyal to the king, but not really be, was incredibly uncomfortable. Your personal honor was a huge thing back then."[24]

It was only much later, in the twentieth century, that espionage took on the fascinating and seductive James Bond allure during the Cold War. Although, as Eastman points out, spycraft during the Revolutionary War was developing those accoutrements that we view today as romantic and exciting: "Rose's book offers any number of sexy plot developments, including innovations in invisible ink technology, shadowy couriers, female spies, and the arrival of 'gentleman spy' Major John André."[25] Silverstein concurs that "it's fun to hit on those classic things [in spy fiction] of, you know, the Honey Trap, the idea of planting a mole and watching them either get exposed or flipped. Then the gadgets, we're slowly, slowly getting into as they're pioneering them."[26] He also remarks that there is even a "Q character,"[27] referring to the famous quartermaster and gadgeteer from the Bond films, although the one in *Turn* is based on a real person who worked for the American side during the war.[28] Nevertheless, I argue that after 9/11, we have seen a return to a more suspicious view of intelligence gathering, one that resonates with the eighteenth-century idea of it being an unseemly way to operate.

In *Turn*, a young American man, Abraham Woodhull (played by Jamie Bell), short on money becomes involved in spying for Washington's army. Following Woodhall's exploits, the series demonstrates in vivid and stark detail the brutality of the Revolutionary War. A conflict celebrated in America as a glorious event in U.S. history becomes, in the program, a tough and bloody war in which both sides suffer great causalities; the American public suffers particularly, either from lack of food shipments cut off by the fighting or from in-fighting among those who remain deeply divided regarding separating from Britain. For instance, at a press conference for *Turn*, Silverstein "detailed the show's emphasis on the moral complexities of the era. 'It was a kind of wild and unruly time and was not as "flute-and-drum" as some might have it'."[29] In terms of forgotten history, Americans often overlook that the war was complex and difficult to negotiate, and it was one that often tore families apart in terms of their allegiances.

In this respect, the series' depiction of the Revolutionary War resonates with how many today perceive the current war on terror: it is not straightforward in its aims but is complex in terms of understanding and knowing who the enemy is, and how the enemy could be someone within one's own circle of friends and family. Indeed, the program is so aware of how it connects the past and present problems facing the U.S. that its recent ad campaign incorporated this theme, as the show's producers note: "In our promotional campaign for the upcoming season of our Revolutionary War drama, *Turn: Washington's Spies*, we play off the reality of our current fractured political environment by comparing today with the 1770s, when the colonies were split and warring over their relationship with England."[30] Television promos for the series recall that "before there were red states and blue states, there were redcoats and bluecoats" and billboards and bus side ads claim, "America Divided: Now and Then."[31]

In addition to reminding viewers of the connections between America's early history and its contemporary concerns, *Turn* also makes viewers consider the issues of surveillance and espionage we are grappling with today by displacing them into the past. For example, the Culper Ring must spy on fellow Americans to glean information about the British, given that many Americans were Loyalists. From this narrative, we recognize our current quandary regarding the NSA collecting data on millions of Americans as having its roots in the early days of American intelligence gathering regarding the ethics of surveilling fellow citizens. I would argue that the program here is neither supporting nor condemning the surveillance of ordinary citizens, but, rather, it demonstrates that this question is one we as a nation have had to face since the inception of spying as part of an early American government. On the one hand, as the audience, we support Woodhull, Benjamin Tallmadge (played by Seth Numrich), and Caleb Brewster (played by Daniel Henshaw) as they spy for what we know will be a successful cause: American independence from Britain. In this way, we understand their surveillance work as necessary to America's victory.

However, at the same time, the audience witnesses the trials and consequences for the men, their friends, family, and society, from either participating in surveillance or being spied upon, and the subsequent suspicions and problems this surveillance causes. As viewers, we also experience the contradiction between fighting for civil liberties and violating, through spycraft, those same liberties of those who do not support the American cause. In this way, the program articulates within a historical setting the comparable issues we currently confront regarding intelligence gathering. The series echoes in its treatment of the Revolutionary War questions we have about not only our current political divisions but also the war on terror: do surveillance and the information it can provide, with the promise of winning the war on terror, outweigh the public's right to privacy and freedom of thought and speech?

As was true regarding the series discussed in the previous chapters, we witness within a television program like *Turn* a debate between ideals of American exceptionalism on the one hand and the state's desire to remain intact and guarded from threats on the other. In *Turn*, we see the same problem through the lens of the Revolutionary War: on the one hand, espionage is considered a dishonest and unworthy way of waging war, but, on the other, it can provide the advantage needed to fight a strong and well-equipped British adversary. Outlining this conflict historically is a way of reminding us about the narrative history of espionage. The television stories we tell ourselves today about intelligence gathering and surveillance have a long history—for American television, because of *Turn*, this history stretches back to the founding of the U.S. nation itself. As a result, we must acknowledge how the problem of balancing safety and liberty is not one that has appeared only since 9/11, nor even one that has been resolved over the past 200 years of U.S. history. It remains an ongoing negotiation between the two social desires. Further, *Turn* forces us to acknowledge the presence of surveillance as part of the foundation of the U.S. itself and the irony that it was surveillance and espionage that to some degree made possible the civil liberties and freedoms outlined in the Constitution. This is not to argue that surveillance and espionage are morally right, but that they certainly form part of the fabric of the creation of the American nation state. As such, it might not be surprising that we today have television spy dramas pitting surveillance against civil liberties, given that this tension has existed from the very foundation of the U.S.

Of course, espionage and surveillance have existed since as long as the concept of the state, and, so, one can argue surveillance developed alongside the state in order to preserve its power.[32] In the U.K., for example, the early modern British monarchy often employed spies that worked throughout the land and within rival nations.[33] Most famously, Elizabeth I's adviser, Sir Francis Walsingham, maintained an extensive surveillance network.[34] His espionage system monitored ordinary citizens as well as foreign spies for signs of treason against the crown. Therefore, the connection between espionage and technology that has become so prevalent within television and film narratives since the Cold War and the advent of James Bond has not always been the case. In other words, the conflation of technology with spycraft can obfuscate the long and ancient history of espionage, such that it becomes surprising to a modern television audience to think of the existence of intelligence gathering before the advent of computers and other surveillance equipment.

However, Michael Warner cautions us against too easily equating the terms "espionage" and "intelligence": "Spying might be as old as history, but what we call intelligence is much newer."[35] Warner explains that intelligence "came to mean the overall system" that encompasses "the state's espionage (and counterespionage) function, its collection of secrets and nonsecrets for ministers and commanders, its interaction with friendly intelligence services, and the work product of these functions."[36] He concludes that in the twentieth century, such functions and information were "systematized as intelligence, in both a professional and in an institutional sense, and they worked collectively—if not always consciously—for strategic effect."[37] The technology for such "systemized" intelligence has only grown since the twentieth century, and it has allowed the state's surveillance capabilities to become unprecedented in scope post-9/11.

To return to *Turn*, in terms of viewership, the program was renewed for four seasons, and this demonstrates there was an audience for the program. *Turn* is certainly not a blockbuster show on par with the cultural attention paid to some of the other programs discussed in this book, such as *Sherlock*. For instance, the average audience numbers for *Turn* season three were 566,000 viewers and 630,000 for season four.[38] However, like other cable network programs I have discussed, such as *Locked Up Abroad*, the ratings were consistent enough to warrant continued production beyond one season. While *Turn* concludes with season four, it will remain available for purchase on DVD and for streaming on Amazon, Netflix, and other such services. Further, social media suggests there is a confluence between the writers, producers, networks, and viewers regarding the viability of historical American espionage as a television subject. For example, there is an active discussion board on the social media site Reddit dedicated to *Turn*, indicating an interested viewership which debates the program's plotlines and character development.[39] In this discussion board, we see an audience that desires the continuation of the series and finds the topic of espionage during the Revolutionary War fascinating. They have openly petitioned AMC to keep producing the series. Even if the series' viewers do not explicitly discuss post-9/11 concerns about intelligence agencies on such discussion boards, that does not mean this theme does not resonate on some level with an audience interested in a fictionalized portrayal of historical espionage.

U.S. AND U.K. CONFLICT IN POST-9/11 SPY DRAMAS

A further theme that resonates in this series is the conflict between American and British interests that is at the heart of a program about the Revolutionary War. As noted in Chaps. 1 and 3, the post-9/11 relationship between the U.S. and U.K. has been tumultuous. The Blair government supported actions taken by the Bush administration in the years following 9/11, while the British public were in large part adamantly against such cooperation. As a result, there arose a great deal of anti-American sentiment in the U.K. (and Europe) during the Bush presidency. Such antagonism and disagreement between the British and American public regarding how best to handle the aftermath of 9/11 were reminders of the history of conflict between the two nations. While today we often see the U.S. and U.K. as having a "special relationship" born out of World War II, both the British and Americans can forget that the relationship between the U.S. and U.K. has often been fraught. *Turn* thus reminds viewers of the historical animosity between the U.S. and U.K. that still underlies the affiliation between the two nations.

While *Turn* might not be consciously based on early American fictional spy narratives, it nevertheless owes a debt to James Fenimore Cooper's *The Spy: A Tale of the Neutral Ground*. In his novel, Cooper begins to transform spycraft into something heroic, although the titular American spy, peddler Harvey Birch, can never reveal his true loyalty to the Patriot cause; as a result, many believe him to be a spy for the British. As an early secret agent, Birch interestingly foreshadows Sherlock Holmes's surveillance method of donning clever disguises in order to gain information or to escape enemy hands. Cooper published *The Spy* in 1821, enough years after the Revolution to see it retrospectively as a glorious cause, albeit still a divisive war (like *Turn*, the novel emphasizes families and communities torn apart by competing loyalties). As a result, Cooper could afford to write a narrative that puts espionage and surveillance in a more favorable and honorable light, given that spying aided in the Americans winning their independence. Further, *The Spy*, which takes place during the Revolution, like *Turn* foregrounds the antagonism between the U.S. and U.K. Given that the book was written not long after the War of 1812, the state of relations between Britain and American would still have been tense at the time of publication; indeed, the novel concludes with an elderly Birch still working as a spy, bringing Americans information about British troop movements on the Canadian border.

Therefore, the fact that contemporary television dramas about national intelligence agencies also highlight this antagonism between Britain and America might not be as surprising once placed against a long narrative history of this conflict within espionage narratives. For example, *Person of Interest* (CBS), which focuses on the ethics of post-9/11 surveillance, espionage, and national intelligence agencies, develops in its third and fourth seasons the character of Greer (John Nolan), a British ex-Mi-6 agent, as the primary antagonist. Greer is determined to bring online Samaritan, developed by NSA programmer Arthur Claypool (Saul Rubenstein),[40] which is a surveillance artificial intelligence to rival The Machine. The Machine is the central "character" of the program, and it is a sophisticated super-surveillance system which is able to monitor data streams and CCTV cameras to anticipate which American citizens will need the help of The Machine's creator, Harold Finch (Michael Emerson), a friend of Claypool's while they were students at MIT, and his partner, former CIA agent John Reese (Jim Caviezel). While Finch created The Machine for beneficial purposes, Greer's Samaritan will enact shadowy oppression by controlling the world's governments, markets, and citizens through carefully orchestrated surveillance.

Regarding The Machine, in the episode "The Devil's Share,"[41] we learn that Finch initially developed it in order to prevent another attack like 9/11. His friend who helped Harold create The Machine convinces Finch to keep their work away from the U.S. government, which would use it to oppress rather than help people. As a result, the government attempts to kill Harold and his friend (successfully in the latter's case). This backstory explains how and why Finch needs to hide his identity and The Machine's and his own whereabouts from government countersurveillance. And, in order to explain Greer's championing of Samaritan, *Person of Interest* depicts Greer's Mi-6 past, in which viewers learn that his philosophy—that surveillance machines could better orchestrate and oversee society than people—was born out of his disillusioning Cold War espionage experience. In the aptly titled episode "The Cold War," as a U.K. spy in the 1970s and 1980s, Greer witnessed colleagues, including the Mi-6 deputy director, act as double agents for the Soviet Union for money, thus undermining their own country.[42] This deputy director is no doubt meant to conjure memories of the Cambridge Five, Donald Maclean, Guy Burgess, Kim Philby, Anthony Blunt, and John Cairncross, who were a spy ring of British men recruited by the Soviet security agency, the KGB (in English, the Committee for State Security) while they were students at Cambridge University in the 1930s. After they all obtained careers in the

British government, they passed along sensitive information to the Soviets until the 1950s, when Maclean, Burgess, and Philby defected to the Soviet Union. These men were recruited in part because they believed that Communism was the best existing form of government, especially as a deterrent to fascism. More importantly, for my purposes, the revelation of this spy ring caused much suspicion on the part of the U.S. regarding British Intelligence.[43]

To further emphasize this British-American mistrust, *Person of Interest* crafts a story arc in which Greer, in order to convince the U.S. government to use Samaritan to prevent terrorism and solidify social control, instigates and sponsors an American domestic terrorist group, Vigilance, whose mission is to use violence to return America to its core values of civil liberties and freedoms in a post-9/11 surveillance world. In other words, the members of this organization believe they are rebelling against ubiquitous government surveillance and social control, but it turns out they have been created and funded by those who seek to curtail privacy and civil liberties.[44]

In this way, *Person of Interest* presents the interrelationship between civil liberties and surveillance in a complex and paradoxical way: those who are waging war on behalf of civil liberties are dupes of a system that is already rigged against those civil liberties. Furthermore, the characterization of the fight for civil liberties as domestic terrorism is significant when compared with *Turn*, which depicts how the British viewed American Revolutionary combatants in the same light—as domestic terrorists, rather than freedom fighters. This is not to say that *Person of Interest* claims that the struggle for civil liberties is wrong or that it constitutes terrorism, but, rather, that it is playing with narratives that have long circulated in American culture about the heroic struggle for freedom in order to question how straightforward that narrative is.

Clearly, the program sides with the protagonists who wish to maintain the status quo and work with a computer (The Machine) that aids people by using surveillance while not seeking to control and limit citizens' actions. In this sense, the series champions a balance—one between surveillance and civil liberties—and it characterizes extremists on both sides as potentially dangerous and dogmatic. That is, *Person of Interest* encourages viewers to accept surveillance and surveillance culture but only so far as the panopticon does not become oppressive. That the program is aware of Foucault's theory of the panopticon and government surveillance and control is underscored by one episode which is explicitly entitled

"Panopticon." In this episode, Samaritan is activated, and The Machine and its human helpers must go into hiding since Samaritan provides its operators with total surveillance capabilities. In other words, The Machine and its human companions now live in a panoptic system in which they cannot see Samaritan, but Samaritan can see them.[45] Here, Samaritan represents for the writers a panopticon that is no longer beneficial (like The Machine) but, rather, one which is tyrannical.

Further, the fact that a British former espionage agent represents oppression in the form of quashing civil liberties demonstrates how much of the Revolutionary narrative regarding tyrannical British monarchical rule still pervades the American cultural consciousness. Although modern Britain has the same civil liberties as the U.S., there remains for Americans the idea that the U.S. is the only country with such guaranteed privileges. This view, combined with the tension between British and American national intelligence communities in the years after 9/11, creates espionage narratives in which the British are still adversaries of the U.S.

This trend can be seen in other American programs, such as *Elementary*. Although I discussed *Elementary* at length in the previous chapter in terms of the police apparatus, the program also says much about the U.S. and U.K. intelligence apparatuses. Throughout the series, Holmes and Watson contend with both intelligence communities, in particular, the NSA and Mi-6. *Elementary* does not describe these agencies as being as dangerous as they are in *Person of Interest*, but they do interfere with Holmes's pursuit of justice in quest of their respective national interests. Holmes sometimes gains information he needs from the NSA, but, for the most part, he regards the agency with disdain for its panoptical violations of civil liberties, even though he is as much a participant in surveillance as the NSA. The most serious conflict between Holmes and a national intelligence agency, as noted in the previous chapter, arises when the detective discovers that his investigation is disrupting Mi-6's operation to disperse a French crime ring. Further, we learn that his brother, Mycroft, is an agent of Mi-6, and he was recruited for his ability to organize, remember, and synthesize information. In fact, in using Mycroft, Mi-6 hoped to recall Holmes from the U.S. and return him to Britain so that the detective would not interfere with their clandestine operations. Interestingly, after Mycroft's cover is blown and he is forced to go into witness protection with the help of the U.S. government, Holmes himself volunteers to work for Mi-6. He abandons Watson and America because of his own disillusionment with how little he felt in control of events around him when they were already set up and orchestrated by British intelligence.

While Holmes eventually returns to New York in season three after being too independent to abide by the restrictions of Mi-6, it is nonetheless significant that *Elementary* depicts the British and American intelligence agencies working together in that Mi-6 is allowed to operate on U.S. soil to carry out their operations. Here, the British and American agencies are not at odds, but they are both in conflict with Holmes, who embodies the free agent who works in conjunction with yet separate from the various state surveillance apparatuses. Although Holmes is British, in this series, he makes his home in America, and so the program depicts Mi-6 as both ally and interloper in an uneasy characterization. Like *Person of Interest, Elementary* incorporates the disquiet between the two allies, but it also, like *Person of Interest*, pits individuals (like Watson and Holmes) against seemingly monolithic surveillance apparatuses that have their own interests at heart, rather than those of the public. In other words, these trends in American espionage drama reflect a view that whether the intelligence agency is British or American, they are ultimately not distinguishable from one another; instead, these organizations work for their own interests, and not even for those of the state (at least the state understood as the collective wishes of the public). In both *Person of Interest* and *Elementary*, it is a few against the might of state surveillance, and, in this sense, these espionage dramas recapitulate the great American story of a few ragtag freedom fighters holding out against the powerful British Empire.

NOT JAMES BOND: THE PROBLEM OF BRITISH INTELLIGENCE IN U.K. ESPIONAGE SERIES

A similar narrative—the few against the agency—occurs in post-9/11 U.K. espionage series. Here, there are individuals within the intelligence apparatus who subvert the way in which the British government is working counter to the interests of the public. For example, in *Spooks* (BBC), entitled *Mi-5* for the U.S. market, members of the titular agency, such as director Sir Harry Pearce (played by Peter Firth), and agents Tom Quinn (played by Matthew Macfadyen), Adam Carter (played by Rupert Penry-Jones), and Ros Myers (played by Hermione Norris) are portrayed as complex heroes attempting to safeguard the British public against terrorist attacks or other national security threats. This complexity arises because the series often makes us question the motives of the agents themselves. For example, Lucas North (played by Richard Armitage) is an agent who is returned to Britain in a "spy exchange" after he has spent eight years in a Russian prison for espionage. The program makes us continually question the loyalty of North—was he "turned" after so many years in Russia? In this way, North is similar to American gunnery sergeant Nicholas Brody (played by Damian Lewis) in Showtime's *Homeland,* who becomes a sleeper agent for al-Qaeda after being brainwashed by them while he was their prisoner (like North, for eight years) in Damascus. Eventually, viewers learn that North's questionable identity goes further than his loyalties: he is actually John Bateman, an amateur drug smuggler who operated in Senegal, similar to those British and American nationals featured in *Locked Up Abroad* (see Chap. 2). After becoming an inadvertent terrorist by delivering a package to the British Embassy that turns out to be a bomb that kills 17 people, Bateman escapes the country by killing his own friend, Lucas North, and assuming his identity. North was in the final stages of becoming an Mi-5 agent, and so Bateman takes his place as a British spy.

Such unreliability also factors into the Mi-5 agents' inability to prevent terrorist attacks, much as the actual American and British intelligence agencies failed to avert 9/11 and 7/7. For example, the series eerily anticipated the 7/7 attacks and the powerlessness of the intelligence community to thwart them: "By the time the 7/7 bombings took place in London in 2005, the fourth series of *Spooks* had already been recorded. The main plotline? A terrorist bombing central London."[46] Indeed, the resemblances between fiction and real life were so stark, including a device planted at King's Cross station, that "BBC One's head of drama Jane Tranter and controller Peter Fincham were tempted to pull the series. In the end they settled for a prominent disclaimer, warning viewers of the distressing content."[47]

However, in other episodes, agents do succeed in quietly foiling plots at home and abroad. Nevertheless, these agents must often counteract members of the government, or officials in Mi-6 (often presented in the series as a rival organization to Mi-5), who have their own reasons for not wanting certain suspects detained. This is similar to the rivalry and opposition of the CIA and FBI in *Person of Interest,* in which the FBI is presented as being more aligned with the public interest than the CIA, which seems to be a law unto itself. In these ways, we see how the actions of the CIA and Mi-6 in the post-9/11 years have influenced their portrayal as domestic enemies on par with or perhaps even worse than the terrorist organizations they are meant to defeat. This point is echoed in the 2015

BBC/AMC miniseries *The Night Manager*, which updates John le Carré's novel about Cold War weapons trafficking to the twenty-first century. Here, the terrorists are not only Islamic fundamentalists, but also the British government and British citizens. The primary weapons trafficker in the series is Richard Roper, a British national. There are agents in Mi-6 who want to bring him down, such as intelligence officer Angela Burr (played by Olivia Colman), but they are working against the agency itself and the British government who need Roper to fund their own operations.[48] Once again, we see the pattern of a few against the intelligence apparatus that exists for itself rather than for the good of the nation it is meant to protect.

The post-9/11 fear of despotic intelligence agencies and their surveillance capabilities is further underscored in the 2015 BBC miniseries *London Spy*. Here, the main character, Danny (played by Ben Wishaw), who works in an Amazon-like warehouse by day and parties at clubs by night, falls in love with Alex (played by Edward Holcroft), whom he later discovers was someone who worked for British intelligence—specifically, the Secret Intelligence Service/Mi-6—and may have been killed by them. In his pursuit of the truth, Danny discovers that his partner had developed a computer surveillance program that would, through an algorithm, be able to tell definitively whether or not a person is lying—in other words, a faultless polygraph. Alex's program is considered a threat by various major world governments because it would make it impossible to conduct covert surveillance and espionage without the ability to lie. Consequently, all the major Western intelligence agencies work together not only to kill Alex but also to find and destroy his surveillance program and harm Danny by covertly injecting him with HIV. Danny learns the latter through a mysterious American agent who warns him about his condition by handing him what looks like a cough drop but turns out to be an anti-viral drug. Therefore, the Americans clearly have knowledge of and participate in British intelligence's plan to stop the surveillance program from succeeding.

In this series, it is not so much which nation's intelligence agency is in control as it is that all nations' espionage apparatuses place their interests and existence above those of the public, who might possibly benefit, à la The Machine in *Person of Interest*, from this particular program, given its capacity to end covert government surveillance of citizens as well as identify guilty criminals or exonerate those falsely imprisoned for a crime. At the end of the series, only Danny and his lover's mother, Frances—once again, the few—remain to thwart the intelligence apparatuses' near-monolithic power.

If in this way U.K. spy dramas are like those of the U.S., they diverge in their depiction of American power. Whereas in the American narrative the British are treated with suspicion, in U.K. espionage series, it is the CIA or NSA who bullies the U.K. to fall in line with American policy. In British series, it is the U.S. that is the imperial power. Viewers perceive this in the aforementioned *Spooks*, in which the CIA or the American government often conflicts or interferes with British intelligence operations. A similar struggle arises in *Sherlock*, which, although it is more about the police apparatus, often verges into spy drama through the character of Mycroft, who is a major figure in government intelligence operations. In this sense, the BBC series takes literally the description of Mycroft from the original Doyle story "The Bruce-Partington Plans" that Holmes's brother "occasionally [...] *is* the British government" whose "word" has "again and again [...] decided national policy." Regarding Mycroft's unique qualifications to occupy this position, Holmes explains to Watson that "[h]e [Mycroft] has the tidiest and most orderly brain, with the greatest capacity for storing facts, of any man living. The same great powers which I have turned to the detection of crime he has used for this particular business."[49] Mycroft uses his great acumen to advise the government on how various events or nations connect with and affect one another and recommend how the Crown should then proceed in terms of policy.[50] In other words, he is a one-man national intelligence agency.

While *Sherlock*'s Mycroft is not the "one-stop shop" for intelligence as he is in Doyle's stories, he is, nevertheless, still essential in directing government espionage. For example, in "A Scandal in Belgravia," Holmes's investigation disrupts a British intelligence operation, run by Mycroft, in a strikingly similar scenario to the one mentioned earlier in *Elementary*. However, in this episode, Holmes above all upsets the CIA with his actions. They in turn send an agent to visit his flat to force information from Mrs. Hudson, and this agent ends up on the wrong side of Sherlock's anger. In contrast to *Elementary*, it is the CIA, not Mi-6, that is meddling on foreign soil.

JOINT SPYING, JOINT ANGLO-AMERICAN TELEVISION PRODUCTIONS

It is notable that this Anglo-American conflict plays out in a television market increasingly populated by joint U.S.–U.K. productions of programs. That is, the production side of Anglo-American television is becoming evermore connected and intertwined even as, narratively,

Anglo-American antagonism is articulated within many of these series. Of the programs I have discussed so far, *Person of Interest, Spooks,* and *Turn* are not transatlantic co-productions, but *Person of Interest* and *Spooks* have aired in both countries on broadcast, cable, and streaming platforms. For instance, in the U.S., *Spooks* first appeared as *Mi-5* on BBC America, and it now streams on Hulu and Amazon in the U.S. (not to mention it is also available for American audiences on DVD). Likewise, *Person of Interest* was broadcast in the U.K. on Channel 5, although *Turn* has not been shown on a British television network (not surprising given its focus on the American Revolutionary War); it is, however, available for streaming on Amazon Prime U.K.

While the British might be wary of the need for American money, for the most part, those in television production in both nations have seen co-production as more of a boon that allows for greater budgets as well as wider distribution possibilities. *The Radio Times,* for instance, worries, "[I]sn't there an implicit danger here [in co-productions]? If the people holding the purse strings are thousands of miles away [in the U.S.], will creators end up just trying to make series that they can flog abroad rather than focus on UK viewers?"[51] However, Gareth Neame, a British producer on the transatlantic hit series *Downtown Abbey,* a co-production of ITV and PBS, states that Americanization is not a problem: "I'll come back to the example of *Downton Abbey.* You could not find a more expressly British drama if you tried. The story was not changed to make it more appealing internationally, and it was because it had that integrity that it did so well."[52]

In this way, Neame underscores what I discussed more extensively in Chap. 1: television scholars such as Weissman, Rixon, Hilmes, and J. Miller contend that part of the appeal to an American audience of British-themed television *is* its Britishness. Like these scholars, the American Josh Sapan, chief executive for the U.S. channel AMC, argues that in America, "British" is a synonym for "excellence" when it comes to television. In response to *The Radio Times* query of "what does AMC [and other American networks] get out of the deal [of co-production]?"[53] Sapan replies, "It's almost taken for granted here [in the U.S.] that when something is BBC it's extremely well done. [...] [I]n the US, the BBC brand stands for quality drama, and the British connection allows American broadcasters to tell stories that work on a global scale."[54] For example, BBC's *The Night Manager* and *London Spy* were both financed jointly with the American network AMC; as *The Radio Times* notes, "The BBC could never have paid for *The Night Manager* on its own. Instead, the corporation and Ink Factory joined forces with US broadcaster AMC, the network behind *Mad Men* and *Breaking Bad*. Both the BBC and AMC pumped money into the project; both reaped the rewards."[55] For the British, the reward is making a program as they envision it, "and not look cheap by comparison [with U.S. series]."[56] For the Americans, as Sapan points out, the reward is a wider, global viewership, and one that has particular appeal to a U.S. audience which seeks out British programming for its brand excellence. Indeed, while in both *London Spy* and *The Night Manager* the American presence on screen (in terms of actors and scenarios) was either far less or non-existent, the latter certainly played well to American audiences (Netflix, on which *London Spy* was broadcast in the U.S., does not release viewership numbers). According to Deadline, *The Night Manager* "delivered the cabler a total viewership of 1.6 million with 455,000 among adults 18–49 and 554,000 among the 25–54 demo."[57] Further, these two series' depictions of British intelligence as similarly corrupt and autocratic as American intelligence apparatuses can also draw in U.S. viewers who feel comforted that it is not only the U.S. which struggles balancing the desire for national security with the preservation of civil liberties.

In addition, while it is beyond the scope of this chapter to explore the influence of the James Bond films in the U.S., I would note that spy series like *The Night Manager* and *London Spy* also tap into an American audience already primed by the Bond films to associate espionage with Britain. The Bond films have, of course, incorporated American actors and settings, but they do remain primarily centered on British intelligence, with Mi-6's 007 fighting various world villains, with little involvement of U.S. surveillance apparatuses. American viewers enjoy associating espionage with Britain because doing so makes spying suave, intellectual, and sexy. Bond is Sherlock Holmes-like in his combination of strength and sophistication, and this recipe can make surveillance more appealing if it is shown as urbane rather than brutish. The American admiration for the classy British spy extended to 1960s British television programs popular in the U.S., such as *The Avengers*, *The Prisoner*, and *The Saint*. On the other hand, American spies, like *24*'s Jack Bauer, have been portrayed even by U.S. film and television as less erudite and more brutal. As a result, American espionage is presented in *24* (Fox) and similar post-9/11 U.S. spy dramas as less attractive and more revealing of the sheer visceral power behind the intelligence apparatus. For example, in *Person of Interest*, the CIA agent Reese is the muscle while Finch is the brains behind their operation to help fellow citizens through the Machine's surveillance capabilities.

Tellingly, however, in the post-9/11 *London Spy* and *The Night Manager*, even British spies have become increasingly brutal and dangerous. Even the current incarnation of Bond, Daniel Craig, is noticeably more physical and vicious than previous Bonds, in keeping with a shift in the public perception of espionage agents. In fact, many critics have expressed how tired the Bond franchise seems in a post-9/11 world that is more complicated than the Cold War scenarios of the past. For example, *The Guardian* complained, "While the tone of [the Bond film] *Spectre* might have been somewhat lighter than any other Daniel Craig outing, the theme of surveillance gave it some vague roots in reality. [...] It was clearly a post-Snowden Bond film but other than some rather obvious speeches, did the film really do much with it?"[58] Perhaps articulating this change through visualizing spies' bodies and actions as animalistic reflects this shift in perception.

To return to Anglo-American co-productions of spy dramas, these series articulate not only antagonism but also the dependence of both countries on one another, whether for intelligence or for economics. For example, *24*, after its cancellation in 2010, returned in 2014 with a limited miniseries sequel set in both the U.S. and U.K. entitled *24: Live Another Day* (the title, presumably, a play on the Bond film, *Die Another Day*). *24* originally premiered in the wake of 9/11, and its storylines focused on Islamic fundamentalist terrorism—so much so that, as discussed in Chap. 3, the program was criticized for its negative portrayal of Muslim characters and for perpetuating the stereotype, which has persisted since 9/11, which equates Islam with terrorism. In particular, the program was critiqued for narratively supporting the torturing of terrorist suspects.[59] While the series might have intended to illuminate the dark side of the CIA, it nevertheless presented Bauer as gaining valuable information he needed from torture, when, as noted earlier in this chapter, no worthwhile intelligence was truly gained from CIA "enhanced interrogation techniques."

Doug Mataconis argues, however, that *24* did depict the deleterious effects of torture on the agents tasked with carrying it out: "If you look at the final scenes of the eighth season, or the final scenes of the most recent miniseries [*24: Live Another Day*], you certainly can't say that utilizing torture was something that had a positive impact on [Agent Jack] Bauer, or on anyone around him. Indeed, in the end, it seemed as though all it did was help to destroy the things that meant the most to him."[60] In this sense, *24* functions like the police programs addressed in the previous chapter, in that the series exposes the brutality of a state apparatus (in this case, the intelligence agency)—both in terms of its treatment of potential terrorists and of its own agents—and yet encourages viewers to support that brutality if it brings about justice. In *Live Another Day*, this conflicted narrative draws upon the shared American and British experiences with terrorism and, as such, their dependence on one another as allies in the "war on terror." At the same time, setting the action in both London and America appeals to both U.S. and U.K. audiences, as does the incorporation of both British and American actors.

Live Another Day also acknowledges that, since 9/11, most major terrorist attacks have occurred not on American soil, but in the U.K. and in the E.U. (particularly, France). Most significantly, the terrorist attack on London on July 7, 2005 (7/7) has been called the U.K.'s 9/11. As discussed in Chap. 1, this event was one which invoked in the British public similar feelings toward British intelligence as the American public felt regarding the U.S. intelligence community after 9/11. On the one hand, the British intelligence apparatus failed to prevent this attack, just as U.S. intelligence agencies neglected to identify the 9/11 plot before it was carried out. As a result, the British public felt disappointed and let down by the intelligence apparatus as well as the U.K. police apparatus. However, public mistrust of the intelligence apparatus also surfaced once surveillance increased following 7/7. As noted earlier in this chapter, the U.K. intelligence apparatus increased surveillance on U.K. civilians, particularly through the GCHQ, which, like the NSA, was allowed greater latitude by the British government to monitor communications of the U.K., much to the dismay of many Britons.

SURVEILLING THE NATIONAL INTELLIGENCE AGENCIES

As a result, there exist similar conflicted feelings about the intelligence community in both the U.S. and U.K. among viewers of espionage programs, as well as among those who write and produce them. While antagonism might continue between the two allies, there remains, on the part of viewers, writers, and producers, comparable concerns regarding the erosion of civil liberties in both nations. At the same time, both the British and Americans experience concomitant fears of the rise of domestic Islamic fundamentalist terrorism, given that the terror attacks which have occurred in Britain and, more recently, in France, have been the result not of Islamic extremists coming into these countries but of citizens within those countries being radicalized through online extremist Islamic propaganda.[61]

Therefore, it makes sense from a television standpoint to create spy dramas that can take place in both the U.S. and U.K.; doing so mirrors the transatlantic situation in terms of television production and distribution, as well as in terms of related concerns and fears in the wake of terrorism in both nations.

Importantly, in these espionage series, it is the intelligence apparatus and its agents that are surveilled by the television camera, and not so much the terrorist groups themselves. This indicates that the writers, producers, and viewers wish to narratively scrutinize the ethics, morality, and necessity of the intelligence apparatus. In all the series I have discussed so far, from *Turn* to *London Spy*, the camera and script focus on the agents within the intelligence apparatus and the inevitable toll that conducting surveillance takes on them. In attempting to keep to the right side of the law while operating powerful surveillance mechanisms, agents must contend with the moral quandary that they may be ordered to act in ways that are unethical or unlawful. And yet, either these actions might protect national security, or they are actions necessary for agents to adopt in order to fight against an apparatus that could eliminate them if they threaten to expose what the intelligence agency is doing. It is this latter theme that pervades much of post-9/11 espionage drama: the true terrorist is the intelligence apparatus itself. It exists mainly for its own power and cannot afford to have the extent of that influence revealed to the public. Again, this theme reflects the damaging revelations in the post-9/11 years about potential abuses of power and surveillance on the part of U.S. and U.K. intelligence apparatuses.

Indeed, the espionage drama *Berlin Station* (Epix) focuses on just this premise: it is international in its cast and in its locales, and in its first season, it brings together multiple intelligence apparatuses from different nations (including the U.S. and Germany) in a narrative arc about a cover up of CIA abuses that American agent Daniel Miller (played by Richard Armitage) becomes aware of. These abuses involved the "black sites," noted earlier in this chapter, where the CIA used torture in order to extract information from detainees after 9/11. In the first season, Miller's friend and fellow agent, Hector DeJean (played by Rhys Ifans), is revealed to have had been involved in the torture program; guilt-ridden, he has now become an anonymous source leaking information about CIA actions post-9/11. Miller is tasked by the CIA with taking Hector down, but, in the end, Daniel sympathizes with DeJean's cause. Taking its cue from the real-life stories of Julian Assange and Edward Snowden, the series depicts how, in the eyes of the intelligence apparatus, the true threat here is not the Islamic State in Iraq and Syria (ISIS) but internal whistleblowers who can expose the machinations of the intelligence agencies, as well as agents within who might not comply with the apparatus' wishes. In *Berlin Station*, the CIA becomes more concerned with maintaining its control than working for the interests of the public by identifying and neutralizing terrorist threats.

However, series writer Bradford Winters cautions that he and his fellow writing team did not set out to critique the CIA or government surveillance per se. According to Winters, he wants to "present a complex narrative" in order to allow "the audience to think critically about these issues [i.e., surveillance and the intelligence agency]; we want the audience to make up its own mind about this subject, rather than dictate what the audience should think or believe."[62] Nevertheless, Winters acknowledges that the post-9/11 topics of surveillance, spying, and government control were certainly on his and his fellow series writers' minds when developing *Berlin Station*.[63] The fact that the drama is now in its third season signifies that viewers indeed want to engage with and ponder the ethics of government surveillance and intelligence gathering. When asked about viewer ratings for the series, Winters noted that Epix (like Netflix) does not release audience numbers, and that "even he didn't know" what the viewership for *Berlin Station* was.[64] Winters pointed out that as episodic television has diversified into so many different markets, networks, and streaming platforms, traditional Nielsen-style measurements of a program's popularity and viability have become increasingly outmoded. Instead, he observed, networks are more interested today in the "social media buzz" about a series.[65] This statement is borne out by how many series now encourage "live tweeting" of the program in order to demonstrate to the network the show's popularity. Indeed, in December 2018, during the airing of season three, *Berlin Station* engaged in live tweeting of new episodes on Twitter with series actor Leland Orser (who plays Station Deputy Chief Robert Kirsch). Orser encouraged viewers to use the hashtag #berlinstation as a means of ensuring that the drama would "trend" on the social media site.

Given Winters's statements about the intentionality of the spy drama's writers in incorporating concerns about government surveillance, I argue that we as viewers are narratively put in the panoptic position of watching and conducting surveillance on the intelligence community itself. I maintained this was also true of prison and police programs in Chaps. 2 and 3. A program like *Berlin Station* allows viewers to feel as if they are within a shadowy and mysterious world that they otherwise lack access to. On the one hand, this narrative allows the viewer the sensation of power as he or she watches and judges the surveillance apparatus. On the other hand, as with prison and police dramas, this distance also enables the viewer not to be personally implicated in the ethics of intelligence gathering. The espionage programs do allow viewers to panoptically participate in and consider surveillance; but, in looking at the agency from within and at the psychological effects of conducting surveillance, the series at the same time turns away from the problem of international terrorism and its causes. For instance, post-9/11 espionage dramas do not narratively confront how intelligence agencies and their actions were responsible in part for the troubles in the Middle East, Afghanistan, and Pakistan which gave rise to radical Islamic terrorism. American and British intelligence apparatuses, for example, orchestrated coups in Iran and assisted Bin Laden and other mujahedeen in their fight against the Soviet Union's invasion of Afghanistan.

So, while it is commendable that spy dramas interrogating the ethics of surveillance have appeared in the wake of unpleasant revelations since 9/11, this questioning nevertheless emphasizes the impact of ethical quandaries on American and British agents (such as in *Berlin Station*), or on the American and British public, but not the damage done to non-Western people and nations by the Anglo-American intelligence community. For instance, we do not see television depictions of the psychological damage endured by those incarcerated in Guantanamo Bay, or the injuries of those falsely accused of terrorism who were tortured by the CIA to gain information. Further, the programs do not visualize the emotional harm experienced by innocent American or British Muslims who have been stereotyped as terrorists. Even those series that do touch on these kinds of grievances—such as the consequences of arms dealing in *The Night Manager*—do not examine them at length. The panoptic television eye is turned inward, and it cannot face what has been done in the name of the U.S. or U.K. to those living in Muslim nations and communities; in this way, the programs allow viewers to avoid complicity in actions taken by their governments.

This psychological aspect of post-9/11 espionage dramas is particularly noteworthy. We, the audience, panoptically observe the toll surveillance takes on those who enact it. While the series' observations might be directed inward, they do illuminate the problematic nature of operating the panopticon, as well as the morality and ethical questions of what to do with the knowledge and power gained from surveillance. Even *Turn*, which is set before the advent of an official U.S. intelligence agency, nevertheless concentrates most of its focus on considering what it means to become a spy, particularly in an age when espionage is in its infancy and is not respected as a worthy way to conduct war. In many of the series I have discussed in this chapter, the narratives describe the emotional price the agent who must pretend to be something he or she is not pays while gathering information that might possibly hurt their families and friends. Their struggle occurs between their personal well-being and the government apparatus for whom they conduct surveillance. While this psychological focus is not necessarily new to post-9/11 espionage narratives, this focus has enlarged and assumed added importance not only in an age when government surveillance capabilities have increased exponentially, but also when every person has access to surveillance on the individual level through social media. In other words, even if the writers, producers, and viewers are not conscious of the ramifications of government surveillance on individuals, they are certainly aware of the culture of social media surveillance around them. This factor can then play into the narratives regarding surveillance at a national level. If people can notice the cost that surveillance takes on their personal lives lived on Twitter, Facebook, and so on, then it makes narrative sense that this same psychological impact would be incorporated into the lives of agents in espionage dramas.

THE PERSONAL IS THE STATE: SURVEILLANCE AND THE VIEWER

This psychological pressure of surveillance is at the core of *The Americans* on FX. Set in the 1980s during the Cold War, the drama follows two Soviet KGB sleeper spies, Nadezhda, a.k.a. Elizabeth (played by Keri Russell) and Mischa, a.k.a. Phillip Jennings (played by Matthew Rhys), who pretend to be a married American couple with children living in suburban America while awaiting directions from Moscow. Series creator Joe Weisberg maintains that *The Americans* is, at heart, about family: "*The Americans* is at its core a marriage story. International relations is [sic] just an allegory for the human relations. Sometimes, when you're struggling in your marriage or with your kid, it feels like life or death. For Philip and Elizabeth, it often is."[66] I argue that part of this focus on family allows the audience to understand the emotional pressures of surveillance on a personal level and, as such, to identify with the agents who must craft outward identities for survival the way many of us fashion carefully curated personas online for psychological survival in a surveillance culture.

Displacing the action to the Cold War era also permits the series to work through issues of identity and surveillance occurring today that could be difficult for a television audience to negotiate if, say, the drama was about ISIS sleeper agents in the U.S. Indeed, Weisberg was inspired in part by the 2010 Illegals Program scandal, in which a ring of Russian sleeper agents was exposed and deported from the U.S.[67] Weisberg notes that using a modern setting regarding Russian spies would not work: "a modern day [setting] didn't seem like a good idea. [...] People were both shocked and simultaneously shrugged at the [2010] scandal because it didn't seem like we were really enemies with Russia anymore. An obvious way to remedy that for television was to stick it back in the Cold War. At first, the '70s appealed to me just because I loved the hair and the music. But can you think of a better time than the '80s with Ronald Reagan yelling about the evil empire?"[68] With the Cold War now a memory, the drama's action can address the issue of not only the danger of surveillance within a society, but the identity confusion that occurs in carrying out surveillance. For instance, Elizabeth and Phillip must always maintain a façade not only to the outside world, but even within their own home, given that their children have no idea who their parents truly are. This situation wears down the two principle characters, to the point where they cannot distinguish between real and simulacrum anymore.

Here, viewers encounter a stark articulation of the effect of surveillance on the individual: surveillance is damaging not only to those being watched, but also to those who do the watching. The viewer can recognize himself or herself in *The Americans'* Elizabeth and Phillip. The audience, too, understands how exhausting it is to maintain a façade on social media and to keep up with the accounts of friends, family, and co-workers, such that, as with the agents in *The Americans*, it can be difficult to distinguish between one's social media persona and one's own personal existence. One might argue, of course, that the psychological focus of spy dramas like *The Americans* is due to writers and audiences, like Weisberg, wanting to focus more on personal stories, rather than, say, the logistics of surveillance. But I also contend that the psychological element reflects the surveillance landscape in which much of the world finds itself because of the pervasive social media technology that allows us to see and be seen. We ourselves can feel like spies operating a panopticon on social media, and so we are drawn to television programs that explore the outcomes of surveillance on the individual.

The problem, however, with a focus on the psychological and personal within the context of a state surveillance apparatus is that it can distract from the power and pervasiveness of the state itself and the impact of the state on the family and the personal. While I do argue that these programs show how the state can affect people on the individual level, such narratives still too often insist on characterizing troubles as the fault of the person or the family, rather than the state. In other words, concerns about state surveillance in spy dramas are dropped in favor of dysfunction within families or romantic conflicts, and the apparatus becomes simply a backdrop for those entanglements, rather than a direct interrogation of the apparatus itself. For example, in *The Night Manager*, the focus veers toward a love triangle more so than the issue of the illegal arms trade and the complacency of the British state in allowing it to happen. Here, the intelligence apparatus functions as an obstacle to romantic happiness, and the mechanics of how and why its panoptic power exists is less important. The same is true for prison and police dramas. Here, too, the source of problems is often the family or relationships, rather than the state apparatuses. For example, *Elementary* and *Sherlock* relentlessly immerse the viewer in Holmes's complex relationships with family and friends (or lack thereof) and his own internal psyche, rather than the intelligence and police apparatuses with which the detective contends. *The Americans* is one of the few to locate the tensions and problems between the Phillips and their children, Paige and Henry, as rooted in the demands of the Soviet state on its KGB operatives. Nevertheless, due to its focus, the series does not investigate how the American state affects ordinary American families. It is this element—how the American and British state apparatuses shape and influence even our familial or social relationships—that is missing from the various television dramas discussed throughout this book.

In focusing on the personal at the expense of the state, these narratives of state surveillance apparatuses often suggest that if familial or romantic relationships are somehow rectified, then all will be well. In *Anti-Oedipus: Capitalism and Schizophrenia*,[69] theorists Gilles Deleuze and Felix Guattari discuss at length the cultural dominance of this Freudian narrative—the problem of the family—in understanding psychological troubles. Deleuze and Guattari's theory is exceedingly complex and beyond the scope of this chapter to elucidate fully, but the point that is useful for me here is their lament that the Freudian Oedipus narrative has become so ingrained in Western culture as to obscure more important narratives about the impact of the state on the family and the individual. That is not to say that all espionage programs do not consider the relationship of the state and the family or individual. As noted earlier, *The Americans* situates the Phillips family troubles as originating with the Soviet government. Likewise, while *London Spy* begins with a romance narrative, the program illustrates how the British intelligence agencies have destroyed the lives of those it has encountered and those involved in it, from Danny to his mentor, Scottie, to Alex and his family. Some critics argued that the intrusion of the state into the lives of everyday people in *London Spy* smacked of unbelievable conspiracy. For example, Margaret Lyons complains that the series is over-laden with such plot elements: "There are story lines connected to British intelligence services, global terror, the AIDS crisis, the surveillance state in general, seeming criminal conspiracies, and kink."[70] As a result, she argues, these elements interfere with narrative coherency, and, therefore "some-times the show ought to prioritize narrative coherence over atmosphere, so that there's a sense we're moving forward with the solving of our mys-tery. *London Spy* does not do this all that well."[71] Nevertheless, the series attempted to articulate Deleuze and Guattari's argument that the state is intertwined with the family and the individual. By contrast, while dramas like *Spooks* or *24* explore the effect of surveillance on the agents within the apparatus, the programs' narratives take us into a mysterious realm rather than discussing fully how that realm and its surveillance capabilities touch the lives of ordinary citizens.

One example of an earlier narrative that provides a template for consid-ering the interactions between the individual, family, and the state surveil-lance apparatus is Joseph Conrad's *The Secret Agent* (1907), set in 1886 Britain, which not only demonstrates the long history of British espionage and terror narratives, but also follows an ordinary Londoner, Adolf Verloc, who becomes an agent provocateur for the Russians to cause terror attacks within the city to discredit the Bolshevik-anarchist cause. In terms of a Deleuzian narrative that explores the effect of the state on the individual, what is fascinating about the novel is that we follow Verloc through his seedy, working-class life and the politics of his family and friends that have led him to be recruited as an agent. The action of this novel is certainly not that of the typical spy thriller, and perhaps this is one reason why such espionage narratives are rare. It is not full of derring-do or technological gadgets; rather, it is a desperate and depressing look at how ordinary citi-zens' lives can be manipulated and shaped by state surveillance appara-tuses. In this way, the narrative does not provide escapism, but, rather, it tackles connections between the state and personal lives that Deleuze and

Guattari argue are difficult to face. Unlike the Freudian model, this matrix is so vast and intricate that there is no clear way out of such a paradigm.

Finally, I would be remiss if I did not address Showtime's *Homeland*, a program which involves more directly than even *24* the relationship between U.S. government surveillance and Islamic fundamentalist terrorism. In the series' first season, U.S. Marine Sergeant Nicholas Brody, a returning hero from the Iraq War who was held in captivity by al-Qaeda, has been turned by them into a sleeper terror agent. The drama thus narratively expresses a fear that terrorism could come in the guise of someone one might least expect, such as a white American war hero. In this way, the program revives the nineteenth-century narrative anxiety that a white Westerner can become corrupted and altered by contact with a non-white, non-Western culture. Another Conrad novel, *Heart of Darkness* (1899), famously articulates this dread. Brody is a modern-day Kurtz who has been infected, as it were, with non-Western ideology and has become one of "them." It is interesting to see this narrative return in the post-9/11 world. However, it fits with the return of other, earlier Western impirical narratives I have explored in this and previous chapters. It makes sense that *Homeland* incorporates this imperialist plot, given that the current dominate world power is the U.S., and its empire, though not one of land, is one of commerce and cultural clout. Therefore, older narratives re-emerge as there are challenges to the present ruling empire, and Islamic fundamentalist groups represent such an opposition to and breach of American might. Through this narrative, the program voices the unease that the might of the West, specifically, of the U.S., might be vulnerable to those who have suffered because of that power. In *Homeland*, it is not only that the Islamic terrorists succeeded in destroying the Twin Towers, but also that they can convert white Americans to their cause as well.

Playing the role of Charles Marlow to Brody's Kurtz, CIA operative Carrie Matheson (played by Claire Danes) does not believe Brody's façade but instead is convinced he is a covert agent for al-Qaeda. She goes against the directives of the CIA to conduct her own illegal surveillance of Brody in order to discover the truth. It is at this point in *Homeland* that we yet again encounter less of an interrogation of the agency itself and the mechanics of surveillance and more a focus on the personal entanglements and problems of its individual agents. Carrie, for instance, is bipolar—a secret she keeps from the CIA to stay employed there. As part of her surveillance, she becomes romantically involved with Brody and becomes pregnant with his child. Again, we see how this focus on Oedipal-like love triangles seems to plague espionage series. Part of the problem can be that it is hard to depict the inner workings of a surveillance apparatus that is cloaked in secrecy. By their very nature, it is not possible to reveal exactly how the CIA, NSA, and other such surveillance apparatuses work because that information is classified in the name of national security. Instead, writers and producers of these series must in effect guess and imagine their own version of the apparatus, based on the reports and memoirs of those who have worked in the intelligence community.

Despite their secrecy, intelligence agencies welcome and actively promote and assist with films and television shows about them because such visuals can make these agencies look sexy, alluring, and working in the best interests of the British and American public, even if the text is depicting a power that exceeds its mandate.[72] As I noted in the previous chapters, the spectacle of the surveillance power seduces viewers, since they can experience vicariously the thrill of operating a widespread panopticon. In espionage programs, we are treated to amazing visuals of computer programs that can track and decode communications within minutes, as well as devices that are worn on the body to monitor communications. Further, the visuals of computers in intelligence agencies, like those in forensic science investigation programs, imply the capacity to have all knowledge at the touch of a button: we see the whole world monitored, linked, decoded, and processed within seconds with spectacular graphics. Such visuals are compelling. This power can be frightening, but it is also exciting: this control represents the might of the U.S. (or of the U.K.) and, through television visuals, this authority extends to the viewer as well. In other words, the viewer can relate to the panoptic power in the same way he or she might identify with an Olympic athlete representing a country's worth and strength. In this way, the programs can elicit a kind of national pride: this is our capability and influence. Such visuals therefore can compensate for the perceived loss of Anglo-American power in real life in the post-9/11 years. That these programs make surveillance alluring is demonstrated by the fact that programs like ABC's *Alias* and BBC's *Spooks* did result in increased job applications to the CIA and Mi-5.[73]

While such series make spycraft exciting, in the instances when news programs or documentaries, such as Showtime's *Spymasters: CIA in the Crosshairs*[74] or the BBC's *ModernSpies*[75] are allowed behind the scenes of the intelligence agency, the truth is often more sedate. For instance, many intelligence officers are analysts who sift through data in what amounts to a 9 to 5 desk job. Even Andrey Bezrukov, one of the Russian spies arrested and deported in 2010 during the Illegals Program scandal, stated that spycraft is "more like that of a thinktank analyst than a super-spy. 'Intelligence work is not about risky escapades,' he told *Expert* magazine in 2012. 'If you behave like Bond, you'll last half a day, maybe a day. Even if there was an imaginary safe where all the secrets are kept, by tomorrow half of them will be outdated and useless. The best kind of intelligence is to understand what your opponent will think tomorrow, not find out what he thought yesterday'."[76] The fact that there are no "ride along" docuseries for the intelligence agencies as there are for the prison and police apparatuses is, of course, mainly due to the sensitive nature of the material that cannot be shown to viewers. However, another factor would be that, narratively, intelligence gathering is frequently a rather boring affair, action-wise. And this final point results in the ultimate narrative problem with television series interrogating the surveillance work of the intelligence agency. It is hard to fictionalize or narrativize issues like privacy versus civil liberties without resorting to stories that distract from the tedious, but invasive and powerful, work of gathering and sifting citizens' information to focus on those that possess high drama and romantic relationships.

NOTES

1. For more on the history and purpose of the CIA, see Richard H. Immerman, *The Hidden Hand: A Brief History of the CIA* (Hoboken, NJ: John Wiley, 2014).
2. For more on the history and purpose of the NSA, see James Bamford, *Body of Secrets: Anatomy of the Ultra-Secret National Security Agency* (New York: Knopf Doubleday, 2007) and Bamford, *The Puzzle Palace: A Report on America's Most Secret Agency* (New York: Houghton Mifflin, 1982).
3. For more on the history and purpose of Mi-5 and Mi-6, see Gordon Thomas, *Secret Wars: One Hundred Years of British Intelligence Inside Mi-5 and Mi-6* (New York: Palgrave Macmillan, 2010).
4. For more on the history and purpose of GCHQ, see Richard Aldrich, *GCHQ: The Uncensored Story of Britain's Most Secret Intelligence Agency* (New York: HarperPress, 2010).
5. David McDaniel, *The Dagger Affair* (New York: Ace Books, 1965), 89.
6. See Chap. 1, "Introduction: Surveillance and Terror in Post-9/11 British and American Television," for discussion and sources on this point.
7. U.S. Senate Select Committee on Intelligence, "Report of the U.S. Senate Select Committee on Intelligence Committee Study of the Central Intelligence Agency's Detention and Interrogation Program," S. Report

113–288, 113th Congress, 2nd Session, Dec. 9, 2014, https://www.intelligence.senate.gov/publications/committee-study-central-intelligence-agencys-detention-and-interrogation-program.

8. U.S. Department of Justice, "The USA PATRIOT Act: Preserving Life and Liberty," https://www.justice.gov/archive/ll/highlights.htm.
9. Ibid.
10. Ibid.
11. American Civil Liberties Union (ACLU), "Surveillance under the USA/Patriot Act," https://www.aclu.org/other/surveillance-under-usapatriot-act.
12. See Julia Angwin et al., "AT&T Helped U.S. Spy on Internet on a Vast Scale," *The New York Times*, Aug. 15, 2015, https://www.nytimes.com/2015/08/16/us/politics/att-helped-nsa-spy-on-an-array-of-internet-traffic.html; Jason M. Breslow, "How AT&T Helped the NSA Spy on Millions," *PBS Frontline*, Aug. 17, 2015, https://www.pbs.org/wgbh/frontline/article/how-att-helped-the-nsa-spy-on-millions/; Glenn Greenwald, *No Place to Hide: Edward Snowden, the NSA, and the U.S. Surveillance State* (New York: Metropolitan Books, 2014); Michael Gurnow, *The Edward Snowden Affair: Exposing the Politics and Media Behind the NSA Scandal* (Indianapolis, IN: Blue River Press, 2014); and Luke Harding, *The Snowden Files: The Inside Story of the World's Most Wanted Man* (New York: Knopf Doubleday, 2014).
13. Angwin et al., "AT&T Helped U.S. Spy on Internet on a Vast Scale."
14. For more on the 1978 Act and the FISA court, see David B. Cohen and John W. Wells, *American National Security and Civil Liberties in an Era of Terrorism* (London: Palgrave Macmillan, 2004) and Laura K. Donahue, *The Future of Foreign Intelligence: Privacy and Surveillance in a Digital Age* (Oxford: Oxford UP, 2016).
15. James Ball and Spencer Ackerman, "NSA Loophole Allows Warrantless Search for US Citizens' Emails and Phone Calls," *The Guardian*, Aug. 9, 2013, https://www.theguardian.com/world/2013/aug/09/nsa-loophole-warrantless-searches-email-calls.
16. American Civil Liberties Union (ACLU), "Warrantless Surveillance Under Section 702 of FISA," https://www.aclu.org/issues/national-security/privacy-and-surveillance/warrantless-surveillance-under-section-702-fisa.
17. Michael O'Brien, "Obama Task Force Calls for Overhauls to Surveillance Tactics," *NBC News*, Dec. 18, 2013, http://nbcpolitics.nbcnews.com/_news/2013/12/18/21955636-obama-task-force-calls-for-overhauls-to-surveillance-tactics?lite.
18. Shafiqa Ahmadi, "The Patriot Act Gives the U.S. a Bad Reputation," *The New York Times*, Sep. 8, 2011, https://www.nytimes.com/roomfordebate/2011/09/07/do-we-still-need-the-patriot-act/the-patriot-act-gives-the-us-a-bad-reputation.

19. Alexander J. Martin, "How the Edward Snowden Leaks Revealed Unlawful Spying," *Sky News*, June 6, 2018, https://news.sky.com/story/how-the-edward-snowden-leaks-revealed-unlawful-spying-11395290.

20. See Ian Cobain and Ewen MacAskill, "Criticism Mounts over UK's Post-9/11 Role in Torture and Rendition," *The Guardian*, June 28, 2018, https://www.theguardian.com/uk-news/2018/jun/28/criticism-mounts-over-uk-post-9-11-role-in-torture-and-rendition; Cobain and MacAskill, "True Scale of UK Role in Torture and Rendition after 9/11 Revealed," *The Guardian*, June 28, 2018, https://www.theguardian.com/uk-news/2018/jun/28/uk-role-torture-kidnap-terror-suspects-after-911-revealed; and "Former Mi-5 Head: Torture is 'wrong and never justified'," *BBC News*, Sep. 8, 2011, https://www.bbc.com/news/uk-14750998.

21. See Owen Bowcott, "GCHQ Data Collection Regime Violated Human Rights, Court Rules," *The Guardian*, Sep. 13, 2018, https://www.the-guardian.com/uk-news/2018/sep/13/gchq-data-collection-violated-human-rights-strasbourg-court-rules; Nick Hopkins and Julian Borger, "Exclusive: NSA Pays £100m in Secret Funding for GCHQ: Secret Payments Revealed in Leaks by Edward Snowden," *The Guardian*, Aug. 1, 2013, https://www.theguardian.com/uk-news/2013/aug/01/nsa-paid-gchq-spying-edward-snowden; and Nigel Morris, "Edward Snowden: GCHQ Collected Information from Every Visible User on the Internet," *The Independent*, Sep. 25, 2015, https://www.independent.co.uk/news/uk/home-news/edward-snowden-gchq-collected-information-from-every-visible-user-on-the-internet-10517356.html.

22. Alexander Rose, *Washington's Spies: The Story of America's First Spy Ring* (New York: Bantam, 2006). For more on the history of U.S. espionage in general, see Nathan Miller, *Spying for America: The Hidden History of U.S. Intelligence* (St. Paul, MN: Paragon House, 1989) and Michael J. Sulick, *Spying in America: Espionage from the Revolutionary War to the Dawn of the Cold War* (Washington, DC: Georgetown UP, 2012).

23. Caroline Eastman, "The Revolution Takes A *Turn*: AMC's Drama about Washington's Spies Aims for Moral Complexity," *Perspectives on History: The Newsmagazine of the American Historical Association*, Apr. 1, 2014, https://www.historians.org/publications-and-directories/perspectives-on-history/april-2014/the-revolution-takes-a-turn.

24. Eric Goldman, "*Turn* Creator Craig Silverstein on Showing the Origins of the American Spy Game," *IGN*, Apr. 4, 2014, https://www.ign.com/articles/2014/04/04/turn-creator-craig-silverstein-on-showing-the-origins-of-the-american-spy-game.

25. Eastman, "The Revolution Takes a *Turn*."

26. Silverstein quoted in Goldman.

27. Ibid.

28. Ibid.
29. Silverstein quoted in Eastman.
30. Linda Schupack, executive vice president of marketing for AMC and SundanceTV, quoted in Cate Lecuyer Marian, "AMC Taps into Today's Politics to Promote 'Turn: Washington's Spies'," *Promax*, July 4, 2016, http://brief.promaxbda.org/article/amc-taps-into-todays-politics-to-promote-turn-washingtons-spies.
31. Ibid.
32. For more on the history of state espionage and surveillance, see Terry Crowdy, *The Enemy Within: A History of Spies, Spymasters, and Espionage* (Oxford, UK: Osprey Publishing, 2006); Colonel John Hughes-Wilson, *The Secret State: A History of Intelligence and Espionage* (New York: Pegasus Books, 2016); and Ernest Volkman, *The History of Espionage: The Clandestine World of Surveillance, Spying, and Intelligence from Ancient Times to the Post-9/11 World* (London: Carlton Books, 2007).
33. For instance, see the following fascinating range of studies and essays for more on early modern British spycraft: Nadine Akkerman, *Invisible Agents: Women and Espionage in Seventeenth-Century Britain* (Oxford: Oxford UP, 2018); Amy Blakeway, "Spies and Intelligence in Scotland, c. 1530–1550," *Crossing Borders: Boundaries and Margins in Medieval and Early Modern Britain, Essays in Honour of Cynthia J. Neville*, eds. Sara M. Butler and Krista J. Kesselring (Leiden: Brill, 2018), 83–106; Alan Marshall, *Intelligence and Espionage in the Reign of Charles II, 1660–1685* (Cambridge: Cambridge UP, 2003); and Bernard Porter, *Plots and Paranoia: A History of Political Espionage in Britain, 1790–1988* (London: Routledge, 2016).
34. See Stephen Alford, *The Watchers: A Secret History of the Reign of Elizabeth I* (New York: Bloomsbury Publishing USA, 2012); Stephen Budiansky, *Her Majesty's Spymaster: Elizabeth I, Sir Francis Walsingham, and the Birth of Modern Espionage* (New York: Penguin, 2006); John Cooper, *The Queen's Agent: Sir Francis Walsingham and the Rise of Espionage in Elizabethan England* (New York: Open Road Media, 2013); Robert Hutchinson, *Elizabeth's Spymaster: Francis Walsingham and the Secret War that Saved England* (New York: Palgrave Macmillan, 2014); and Derek Wilson, *Sir Francis Walsingham: Courtier in an Age of Terror* (Boston: Little, Brown, 2013).
35. Michael Warner, *The Rise and Fall of Intelligence: An International Security History* (Washington, DC: Georgetown UP, 2014), 1.
36. Ibid., 3.
37. Ibid.
38. *TV Series Finale: Cancelled and Renewed Television Shows*, updated Mar. 26, 2019, https://tvseriesfinale.com/tv-show/amc-network-tv-show-ratings-33643/.

39. See www.reddit.com/r/turn/ for the subreddit dedicated to the AMC program.

40. *Person of Interest*, "Lethe," season 3, episode 11, written by Erik Mountain, directed by Richard J. Lewis, aired on Dec. 17, 2013, by CBS.

41. *Person of Interest*, "The Devil's Share," season 3, episode 10, written by Amanda Segal and Jonathan Nolan, directed by Chris Fisher, aired on Nov. 26, 2013, by CBS.

42. *Person of Interest*, "The Cold War," season 4, episode 10, written by Amanda Segal, directed by Michael Offer, aired on Dec. 16, 2014, by CBS.

43. For more on the Cambridge Five, their activities, and the subsequent political fallout, see Richard Davenport-Hines, *Enemies Within: Communists, the Cambridge Spies and the Making of Modern Britain* (London: HarperCollins UK, 2018); Verne W. Newton, *The Cambridge Spies: The Untold Story of Maclean, Philby, and Burgess in America* (Lanham, MD: Madison Books, 1993); and Nigel West and Oleg Tsarev, eds., *Triplex: Secrets from the Cambridge Spies* (New Haven: Yale UP, 2009).

44. *Person of Interest*, "Deus Ex Machina," season 3, episode 23, written by Greg Plageman and David Slack, directed by Chris Fisher, aired on May 13, 2014, by CBS.

45. *Person of Interest*, "Panopticon," season 4, episode 1, written by Erik Mountain and Greg Plageman, directed by Richard J. Lewis, aired on Sep. 23, 2014, by CBS.

46. "*Spooks*: Five Shocking Moments," *The Telegraph*, Aug. 11, 2011, https://www.telegraph.co.uk/culture/tvandradio/8695492/Spooks-five-shocking-moments.html.

47. Ibid.

48. *The Night Manager*, series 1, episode 5, screenplay by David Farr, based on the novel *The Night Manager* by John le Carré, directed by Susanne Bier, aired on March 20, 2015, by BBC1.

49. Sir Arthur Conan Doyle, "The Adventure of the Bruce-Partington Plans," *Project Gutenberg*, Oct. 23, 2008, http://www.gutenberg.org/files/2346/2346-h/2346-h.htm.

50. Ibid.

51. James Gill, "British Drama, Global Budgets: How Co-productions Are Changing the Way TV Gets Made," *Radio Times*, March 23, 2017, https://www.radiotimes.com/news/2017-03-23/british-drama-global-budgets-how-co-productions-are-changing-the-way-tv-gets-made/.

52. Ibid.

53. Ibid.

54. Qtd. in Gill.

55. Ibid.

56. Ibid.

57. Dominic Patten, "'The Night Manager' Ratings Score Best Ever Debut Live + 3 Rises for AMC," *Deadline*, Apr. 25, 2016, https://deadline.com/2016/04/the-night-manager-ratings-live3-surge-amc-hugh-laurie-tom-hiddleston-1201743872/.
58. Benjamin Lee, "*Spectre*: The Villains, The Women, The Ending—Discuss the Film (with Spoilers!)," *The Guardian*, Oct. 27, 2015, https://www.theguardian.com/film/filmblog/2015/oct/27/spectre-james-bond-villains-women-ending-sam-mendes.
59. See, for example, Adam Green, "Normalizing Torture on *24*," *The New York Times*, May 22, 2005, https://www.nytimes.com/2005/05/22/arts/television/normalizing-torture-on-24.html; Stuart Heritage, "*24* under Trump: Why the Hit Show's Use of Torture Is All-too-relevant," *The Guardian*, Jan. 30, 2017, https://www.theguardian.com/tv-and-radio/2017/jan/30/24-jack-bauer-torture-donald-trump; and Doug Mataconis, "Did '24' Help Make Torture Acceptable?" *The Christian Science Monitor*, Dec. 19, 2014, https://www.csmonitor.com/USA/Politics/Politics-Voices/2014/1219/Did-24-help-make-torture-acceptable.
60. Mataconis, "Did '24' help make torture acceptable?"
61. For more on the radicalization of British, European, and American Islamic youth, see Rik Coolsaet, *Jihadi Terrorism and the Radicalisation Challenge: European and American Experiences* (London: Ashgate, 2011); House of Commons Home Affairs Committee, "Roots of Violent Radicalisation: Nineteenth Report of Session 2010–12, Vol. 1" (London: The Stationery Office, 2012); Michael Kenney, *The Islamic State in Britain: Radicalization and Resilience in an Activist Network* (Cambridge: Cambridge UP, 2018); and Sam Mullins, *'Home-grown' Jihad: Understanding Islamist Terrorism in The U.S. and U.K.* (Singapore: World Scientific, 2015).
62. Personal interview with Bradford Winters, Nov. 2, 2017, at Dordt College, in Sioux Center, Iowa.
63. Ibid.
64. Ibid.
65. Ibid.
66. June Thomas, "A Conversation with *The Americans* Showrunners Joe Weisberg and Joel Fields," *Slate*, Jan. 1, 2013, https://slate.com/culture/2013/01/the-americans-fx-spy-series-creators-joe-weisberg-and-joel-fields.html.
67. For more on this scandal, see Ellen Barry, "'Illegals' Spy Ring Famed in Lore of Russian Spying," *The New York Times*, June 29, 2010, https://www.nytimes.com/2010/06/30/world/europe/30sleepers.html; Jack Barsky and Cindy Coloma, *Deep Undercover: My Secret Life and Tangled Allegiances as a KGB Spy in America* (Carol Stream, IL: Tyndale House,

2017); Thom Patterson, "The Russian Spies Living Next Door," *CNN*, July 19, 2017, https://www.cnn.com/2017/07/19/us/russian-spies-united-states-declassified/index.html; and Shaun Walker, "The Day We Discovered Our Parents were Russian Spies," *The Guardian*, May 7, 2016, https://www.theguardian.com/world/2016/may/07/discovered-our-parents-were-russian-spies-tim-alex-foley.

68. Olivia B. Waxman, "The Real CIA behind 'The Americans'," *Time*, Jan. 30, 2013, http://entertainment.time.com/2013/01/30/qa-the-cia-officer-behind-the-new-spy-drama-the-americans/.

69. See Gilles Deleuze and Felix Guattari, *Anti-Oedipus: Capitalism and Schizophrenia* (Penguin Classics, 2009).

70. Margaret Lyons, "*London Spy* and the Problem with Contemporary 'Good' TV Shows," *Vulture*, Jan. 20, 2016, https://www.vulture.com/2016/01/london-spy-and-the-problem-with-good-tv.html.

71. Ibid.

72. See, for example, Matthew Alford, "Washington DC's Role behind the Scenes in Hollywood Goes Deeper Than You Think," *The Independent*, Sep. 3, 2017, https://www.independent.co.uk/voices/hollywood-cia-washington-dc-films-fbi-24-intervening-close-relationship-a7918191.html; Alford and Robbie Graham, "An Offer They Couldn't Refuse," *The Guardian*, Nov. 13, 2008, https://www.theguardian.com/film/2008/nov/14/thriller-ridley-scott; Tricia Jenkins, *The CIA in Hollywood: How the Agency Shapes Film and Television*, 2nd edition (Austin: U of Texas P, 2016); and Nicholas Schou, "How the CIA Hoodwinked Hollywood," *The Atlantic*, July 14, 2016, https://www.theatlantic.com/entertainment/archive/2016/07/operation-tinseltown-how-the-cia-manipulates-hollywood/491138/.

73. See, for example, "*Alias*' TV Spy Recruits for Real-Life CIA," *Today*, Mar. 10, 2004, https://www.today.com/popculture/alias-tv-spy-recruits-real-life-cia-wbna4499668; and Martin Bright, "*Spooks* Pulls in Recruits for Mi-5," *The Guardian*, May 25, 2002, https://www.theguardian.com/politics/2002/may/26/uk.politicalnews.

74. *Spymasters: CIA in the Crosshairs*, written by Chris Whipple, directed by Gédéon Naudet and Jules Naudet, aired on Nov. 28, 2015, by Showtime.

75. *Modern Spies*, directed by Mike Rudin, aired on April 2, 2012, by BBC2.

76. Walker, "The Day We Discovered Our Parents were Russian Spies."

BIBLIOGRAPHY

24. Created by Joel Surnow and Robert Cochran. Starring Kiefer Sutherland. Aired from 2001 to 2010 on Fox.

24: Live Another Day. Created by Joel Surnow and Robert Cochran. Starring Kiefer Sutherland. Aired in 2014 on Fox.

Ahmadi, Shafiqa. "The Patriot Act Gives the U.S. a Bad Reputation." *The New York Times*, Sep. 8, 2011. https://www.nytimes.com/roomfordebate/2011/09/07/do-we-still-need-the-patriot-act/the-patriot-act-gives-the-us-a-bad-reputation.

Akkerman, Nadine. *Invisible Agents: Women and Espionage in Seventeenth-Century Britain*. Oxford: Oxford UP, 2018.

Aldrich, Richard. *GCHQ: The Uncensored Story of Britain's Most Secret Intelligence Agency*. New York: HarperPress, 2010.

Alford, Matthew. "Washington DC's Role behind the Scenes in Hollywood Goes Deeper Than You Think." *The Independent*, Sep. 3, 2017. https://www.independent.co.uk/voices/hollywood-cia-washington-dc-films-fbi-24-intervening-close-relationship-a7918191.html.

Alford, Matthew and Robbie Graham. "An Offer They Couldn't Refuse." *The Guardian*, Nov. 13, 2008. https://www.theguardian.com/film/2008/nov/14/thriller-ridley-scott.

Alford, Stephen. *The Watchers: A Secret History of the Reign of Elizabeth I*. New York: Bloomsbury Publishing USA, 2012.

"*Alias*' TV Spy Recruits for Real-Life CIA." *Today*, Mar. 10, 2004. https://www.today.com/popculture/alias-tv-spy-recruits-real-life-cia-wbna4499668.

American Civil Liberties Union (ACLU). "Surveillance Under the USA/Patriot Act." https://www.aclu.org/other/surveillance-under-usapatriot-act.

———. "Warrantless Surveillance Under Section 702 of FISA." https://www.aclu.org/issues/national-security/privacy-and-surveillance/warrantless-surveillance-under-section-702-fisa.

The Americans. Created by Joseph Weisberg. Starring Keri Russell, Matthew Rhys, and Keidrich Sellati. Aired from 2013 to 2018 on FX.

Angwin, Julia et al. "AT&T Helped U.S. Spy on Internet on a Vast Scale." *The New York Times*, Aug. 15, 2015. https://www.nytimes.com/2015/08/16/us/politics/att-helped-nsa-spy-on-an-array-of-internet-traffic.html.

The Avengers. Created by Sidney Newman. Starring Patrick Macnee, Diana Rigg, and Honor Blackman. Aired from 1961 to 1969 on ITV and ABC.

Ball, James and Spencer Ackerman. "NSA Loophole Allows Warrantless Search for US Citizens' Emails and Phone Calls." *The Guardian*, Aug. 9, 2013. https://www.theguardian.com/world/2013/aug/09/nsa-loophole-warrantless-searches-email-calls.

Bamford, James. *Body of Secrets: Anatomy of the Ultra-Secret National Security Agency*. New York: Knopf Doubleday, 2007.

———. *The Puzzle Palace: A Report on America's Most Secret Agency*. New York: Houghton Mifflin, 1982.

Barry, Ellen. "'Illegals' Spy Ring Famed in Lore of Russian Spying." *The New York Times*, June 29, 2010. https://www.nytimes.com/2010/06/30/world/europe/30sleepers.html.

Barsky, Jack and Cindy Coloma. *Deep Undercover: My Secret Life and Tangled Allegiances as a KGB Spy in America*. Carol Stream, IL: Tyndale House, 2017.

Berlin Station. Created by Olen Steinhauer. Starring Richard Armitage, Leland Orser, Michelle Forbes, and Mina Tander. Aired from 2016 to 2019 on Epix.

Blakeway, Amy. "Spies and Intelligence in Scotland, c. 1530–1550." *Crossing Borders: Boundaries and Margins in Medieval and Early Modern Britain, Essays in Honour of Cynthia J. Neville*. Eds. Sara M. Butler and Krista J. Kesselring. Leiden: Brill, 2018: 83–106.

Bowcott, Owen. "GCHQ Data Collection Regime Violated Human Rights, Court Rules." *The Guardian*, Sep. 13, 2018. https://www.theguardian.com/uk-news/2018/sep/13/gchq-data-collection-violated-human-rights-strasbourg-court-rules.

Breslow, Jason M. "How AT&T Helped the NSA Spy on Millions." *PBS Frontline*, Aug. 17, 2015. https://www.pbs.org/wgbh/frontline/article/how-att-helped-the-nsa-spy-on-millions/.

Bright, Martin. "*Spooks* Pulls in Recruits for Mi-5." *The Guardian*, May 25, 2002. https://www.theguardian.com/politics/2002/may/26/uk.politicalnews.

Budiansky, Stephen. *Her Majesty's Spymaster: Elizabeth I, Sir Francis Walsingham, and the Birth of Modern Espionage*. New York: Penguin, 2006.

Cobain, Ian and Ewen MacAskill. "Criticism Mounts over UK's Post-9/11 Role in Torture and Rendition." *The Guardian*, June 28, 2018. https://www.theguardian.com/uk-news/2018/jun/28/criticism-mounts-over-uk-post-9-11-role-in-torture-and-rendition.

———. "True Scale of UK Role in Torture and Rendition after 9/11 Revealed." *The Guardian*, June 28, 2018. https://www.theguardian.com/uk-news/2018/jun/28/uk-role-torture-kidnap-terror-suspects-after-911-revealed.

Cohen, David B. and John W. Wells. *American National Security and Civil Liberties in an Era of Terrorism*. London: Palgrave Macmillan, 2004.

Conrad, Joseph. *Heart of Darkness*. 1899. Project Gutenberg. June 18, 2009. https://www.gutenberg.org/files/219/219-h/219-h.htm.

———. *The Secret Agent*. 1907. Project Gutenberg, Dec. 24, 2010. https://www.gutenberg.org/files/974/974-h/974-h.htm.

Coolsaet, Rik. *Jihadi Terrorism and the Radicalisation Challenge: European and American Experiences*. London: Ashgate, 2011.

Cooper, James Fenimore. *The Spy: A Tale of the Neutral Ground*. 1821. Project Gutenberg, Oct. 23, 2003. http://www.gutenberg.org/cache/epub/9845/pg9845-images.html.

Cooper, John. *The Queen's Agent: Sir Francis Walsingham and the Rise of Espionage in Elizabethan England*. New York: Open Road Media, 2013.

Crowdy, Terry. *The Enemy Within: A History of Spies, Spymasters, and Espionage*. Oxford, UK: Osprey Publishing, 2006.

Davenport-Hines, Richard. *Enemies Within: Communists, the Cambridge Spies and the Making of Modern Britain.* London: HarperCollins UK, 2018.

Deleuze, Gilles and Felix Guattari. *Anti-Oedipus: Capitalism and Schizophrenia.* Penguin Classics, 2009.

Donahue, Laura K. *The Future of Foreign Intelligence: Privacy and Surveillance in a Digital Age.* Oxford: Oxford UP, 2016.

Doyle, Sir Arthur Conan. "The Adventure of the Bruce-Partington Plans." *Project Gutenberg*, Oct. 23, 2008. http://www.gutenberg.org/files/2346/2346-h/2346-h.htm.

Eastman, Caroline. "The Revolution Takes A *Turn*: AMC's Drama about Washington's Spies Aims for Moral Complexity." *Perspectives on History: The Newsmagazine of the American Historical Association*, Apr. 1, 2014. https://www.historians.org/publications-and-directories/perspectives-on-history/april-2014/the-revolution-takes-a-turn.

Elementary. Created by Robert Doherty. Starring Johnny Lee Miller and Lucy Liu. Aired from 2012 to present on CBS.

The Equalizer. Created by Michael Sloan and Richard Lindheim. Starring Edward Woodward and Keith Szarabajka. Aired from 1985 to 1989 on CBS.

"Former Mi-5 Head: Torture is 'wrong and never justified'." *BBC News*, Sep. 8, 2011, https://www.bbc.com/news/uk-14750998.

Gill, James. "British Drama, Global Budgets: How Co-productions are Changing the Way TV Gets Made." *Radio Times*, Mar. 23, 2017. https://www.radiotimes.com/news/2017-03-23/british-drama-global-budgets-how-co-productions-are-changing-the-way-tv-gets-made/.

Goldman, Eric. "*Turn* Creator Craig Silverstein on Showing the Origins of the American Spy Game." *IGN*, Apr. 4, 2014. https://www.ign.com/articles/2014/04/04/turn-creator-craig-silverstein-on-showing-the-origins-of-the-american-spy-game.

Green, Adam. "Normalizing Torture on *24*." *The New York Times*, May 22, 2005. https://www.nytimes.com/2005/05/22/arts/television/normalizing-torture-on-24.html.

Greenwald, Glenn. *No Place to Hide: Edward Snowden, the NSA, and the U.S. Surveillance State.* New York: Metropolitan Books, 2014.

Gurnow, Michael. *The Edward Snowden Affair: Exposing the Politics and Media Behind the NSA Scandal.* Indianapolis, IN: Blue River Press, 2014.

Harding, Luke. *The Snowden Files: The Inside Story of the World's Most Wanted Man.* New York: Knopf Doubleday, 2014.

Heritage, Stuart. "*24* under Trump: Why the Hit Show's Use of Torture is All-too-relevant." *The Guardian*, Jan. 30, 2017. https://www.theguardian.com/tv-and-radio/2017/jan/30/24-jack-bauer-torture-donald-trump.

Homeland. Developed by Alex Gansa and Howard Gordon. Starring Claire Danes, Mandy Patinkin, and Damian Lewis. Based on the Israeli series *Prisoners of War* by Gideon Raff. Aired from 2011 to 2019 on Showtime.

Hopkins, Nick and Julian Borger. "Exclusive: NSA Pays £100m in Secret Funding for GCHQ: Secret Payments Revealed in Leaks by Edward Snowden." *The Guardian*, Aug. 1, 2013. https://www.theguardian.com/uk-news/2013/aug/01/nsa-paid-gchq-spying-edward-snowden.

House of Commons Home Affairs Committee. "Roots of Violent Radicalisation: Nineteenth Report of Session 2010–12, Vol. 1." London: The Stationery Office, 2012.

Hughes-Wilson, John, Colonel. *The Secret State: A History of Intelligence and Espionage*. New York: Pegasus Books, 2016.

Hutchinson, Robert. *Elizabeth's Spymaster: Francis Walsingham and the Secret War that Saved England*. New York: Palgrave Macmillan, 2014.

I Spy. Developed by David Friedkin and Morton Fine. Starring Robert Culp and Bill Cosby. Aired from 1965 to 1968 on NBC.

Immerman, Richard H. *The Hidden Hand: A Brief History of the CIA*. Hoboken, NJ: John Wiley, 2014.

Jenkins, Tricia. *The CIA in Hollywood: How the Agency Shapes Film and Television*. 2nd edition. Austin: U of Texas P, 2016.

Kenney, Michael. *The Islamic State in Britain: Radicalization and Resilience in an Activist Network*. Cambridge: Cambridge UP, 2018.

Lee, Benjamin. "*Spectre*: The Villains, The Women, The Ending—Discuss the Film (with Spoilers!)." *The Guardian*, Oct. 27, 2015. https://www.theguardian.com/film/filmblog/2015/oct/27/spectre-james-bond-villains-women-ending-sam-mendes.

London Spy. Created by Tom Rob Smith. Starring Ben Whishaw, Jim Broadbent, and Edward Holcroft. Aired in 2015 on BBC2.

Lyons, Margaret. "*London Spy* and the Problem with Contemporary 'Good' TV Shows." *Vulture*, Jan. 20, 2016. https://www.vulture.com/2016/01/london-spy-and-the-problem-with-good-tv.html.

MacGyver. Created by Lee David Zlotoff. Starring Richard Dean Anderson. Aired from 1985 to 1992 on ABC.

The Man from U.N.C.L.E. Created by Sam Rolfe. Starring Robert Vaughn, David McCallum, and Leo G. Carroll. Aired from 1964 to 1968 on NBC.

Marian, Cate Lecuyer. "AMC Taps into Today's Politics to Promote 'Turn: Washington's Spies'." *Promax*, July 4, 2016. http://brief.promaxbda.org/article/amc-taps-into-todays-politics-to-promote-turn-washingtons-spies.

Marshall, Alan. *Intelligence and Espionage in the Reign of Charles II, 1660–1685*. Cambridge: Cambridge UP, 2003.

Martin, Alexander J. "How the Edward Snowden Leaks Revealed Unlawful Spying." *Sky News*, June 6, 2018. https://news.sky.com/story/how-the-edward-snowden-leaks-revealed-unlawful-spying-11395290.

Mataconis, Doug. "Did '24' Help Make Torture Acceptable?" *The Christian Science Monitor*, Dec. 19, 2014. https://www.csmonitor.com/USA/Politics/Politics-Voices/2014/1219/Did-24-help-make-torture-acceptable.

McDaniel, Daniel. *The Dagger Affair*. New York: Ace Books, 1965.

Miller, Nathan. *Spying for America: The Hidden History of U.S. Intelligence*. St. Paul, MN: Paragon House, 1989.

Mission: Impossible. Created by Bruce Geller. Starring Peter Graves, Barbara Bain, and Greg Morris. Aired from 1966–1973 on CBS.

Modern Spies. Directed by Mike Rudin. Aired on Apr. 2, 2012, by BBC2.

Morris, Nigel. "Edward Snowden: GCHQ Collected Information from Every Visible User on the Internet." *The Independent*, Sep. 25, 2015. https://www.independent.co.uk/news/uk/home-news/edward-snowden-gchq-collected-information-from-every-visible-user-on-the-internet-10517356.html.

Mullins, Sam. *'Home-grown' Jihad: Understanding Islamist Terrorism in The U.S. and U.K.* Singapore: World Scientific, 2015.

Newton, Verne W. *The Cambridge Spies: The Untold Story of Maclean, Philby, and Burgess in America*. Lanham, MD: Madison Books, 1993.

The Night Manager. Series 1, episode 5. Screenplay by David Farr. Based on the novel *The Night Manager* by John le Carré. Directed by Susanne Bier. Aired on March 20, 2015, by BBC1.

O'Brien, Michael. "Obama Task Force Calls for Overhauls to Surveillance Tactics." *NBC News*, Dec. 18, 2013. http://nbcpolitics.nbcnews.com/_news/2013/12/18/21955636-obama-task-force-calls-for-overhauls-to-surveillance-tactics?lite.

Patten, Dominic. "'The Night Manager' Ratings Score Best Ever Debut Live + 3 Rises For AMC." *Deadline*, Apr. 25, 2016. https://deadline.com/2016/04/the-night-manager-ratings-live3-surge-amc-hugh-laurie-tom-hiddleston-1201743872/.

Patterson, Thom. "The Russian Spies Living Next Door." *CNN*, July 19, 2017. https://www.cnn.com/2017/07/19/us/russian-spies-united-states-declassified/index.html.

Person of Interest. "The Cold War." Season 4, episode 10. Written by Amanda Segal. Directed by Michael Offer. Aired on Dec. 16, 2014, by CBS.

———. "Deus Ex Machina." Season 3, episode 23. Written by Greg Plageman and David Slack. Directed by Chris Fisher. Aired on May 13, 2014, by CBS.

———. "The Devil's Share." Season 3, episode 10. Written by Amanda Segal and Jonathan Nolan. Directed by Chris Fisher. Aired on Nov. 26, 2013, by CBS.

———. "Lethe." Season 3, episode 11. Written by Erik Mountain. Directed by Richard J. Lewis. Aired on Dec. 17, 2013, by CBS.

———. "Panopticon." Season 4, episode 1. Written by Erik Mountain and Greg Plageman. Directed by Richard J. Lewis. Aired on Sep. 23, 2014, by CBS.

Porter, Bernard. *Plots and Paranoia: A History of Political Espionage in Britain, 1790–1988*. London: Routledge, 2016.

The Prisoner. Created by Patrick McGoohan and George Markstein. Starring Patrick McGoohan. Aired from 1967 to 1968 on CBS.

Rose, Alexander. *Washington's Spies: The Story of America's First Spy Ring.* New York: Bantam, 2006.

R/turn. *Reddit.* https://www.reddit.com/r/turn/.

The Saint. Created by Leslie Charteris. Starring Roger Moore. Aired from 1962 to 1969 on ITV and NBC.

Scarecrow and Mrs. King. Created by Brad Buckner and Eugenie Ross-Leming. Starring Kate Jackson and Bruce Boxleitner. Aired from 1983 to 1987 on CBS.

Schou, Nicholas. "How the CIA Hoodwinked Hollywood." *The Atlantic*, July 14, 2016. https://www.theatlantic.com/entertainment/archive/2016/07/operation-tinseltown-how-the-cia-manipulates-hollywood/491138/.

Sherlock. Created by Steven Moffat and Mark Gatiss. Starring Benedict Cumberbatch and Martin Freeman. Aired from 2010 to 2017 on BBC1 and PBS.

Spooks (Mi-5). Created by David Wollstencroft. Starring Peter Firth, Hugh Simon, and Nicola Walker. Aired from 2002 to 2011 on BBC1.

"*Spooks*: Five Shocking Moments." *The Telegraph*, Aug. 11, 2011. https://www.telegraph.co.uk/culture/tvandradio/8695492/Spooks-five-shocking-moments.html.

Spymasters: CIA in the Crosshairs. Written by Chris Whipple. Directed by Gédéon Naudet and Jules Naudet. Aired on Nov. 28, 2015 by Showtime.

Sulick, Michael J. *Spying in America: Espionage from the Revolutionary War to the Dawn of the Cold War.* Washington, DC: Georgetown UP, 2012.

Thomas, Gordon. *Secret Wars: One Hundred Years of British Intelligence Inside Mi-5 and Mi-6.* New York: Palgrave Macmillan, 2010.

Thomas, June. "A Conversation with *The Americans* Showrunners Joe Weisberg and Joel Fields." *Slate*, Jan. 1, 2013. https://slate.com/culture/2013/01/the-americans-fx-spy-series-creators-joe-weisberg-and-joel-fields.html.

Turn: Washington's Spies. Created by Craig Silverstein. Starring Jamie Bell, Heather Lind, and Samuel Roukin. Aired from 2014 to 2017 on AMC.

TV Series Finale: Cancelled and Renewed Television Shows. Mar. 26, 2019. https://tvseriesfinale.com/tv-show/amc-network-tv-show-ratings-33643/.

U.S. Department of Justice. "The USA PATRIOT Act: Preserving Life and Liberty." https://www.justice.gov/archive/ll/highlights.htm.

U.S. Senate Select Committee on Intelligence. "Report of the U.S. Senate Select Committee on Intelligence Committee Study of the Central Intelligence Agency's Detention and Interrogation Program." S. Report 113–288. 113th Congress, 2nd Session, Dec. 9, 2014. https://www.intelligence.senate.gov/publications/committee-study-central-intelligence-agencys-detention-and-interrogation-program.

Volkman, Ernest. *The History of Espionage: The Clandestine World of Surveillance, Spying, and Intelligence from Ancient Times to the Post-9/11 World.* London: Carlton Books, 2007.

Walker, Shaun. "The Day We Discovered Our Parents were Russian Spies." *The Guardian*, May 7, 2016. https://www.theguardian.com/world/2016/may/07/discovered-our-parents-were-russian-spies-tim-alex-foley.

Warner, Michael. *The Rise and Fall of Intelligence: An International Security History*. Washington, DC: Georgetown UP, 2014.

Waxman, Olivia B. "The Real CIA behind 'The Americans'." *Time*, Jan. 30, 2013. http://entertainment.time.com/2013/01/30/qa-the-cia-officer-behind-the-new-spy-drama-the-americans/.

West, Nigel and Oleg Tsarev, eds. *Triplex: Secrets from the Cambridge Spies*. New Haven: Yale UP, 2009.

Wilson, Derek. *Sir Francis Walsingham: Courtier in an Age of Terror*. Boston: Little, Brown, 2013.

Winters, Bradford. Interviewed by Darcie Rives-East. Nov. 2, 2017, Dordt College, Sioux Center, Iowa.

CHAPTER 5

Conclusion: Double-Conditioning, Surveillance, and the Future of Television

In this volume, I have endeavored to show how surveillance, terror, and the U.S. and U.K. state responses to those concerns have fundamentally structured, penetrated, and informed our television discourse since the attack on the Twin Towers nearly two decades ago. These British and American programs about the prison, police, and national intelligence apparatuses—those tasked with state surveillance in the name of public safety and national security—are more than simply expensive dramas or low-budget docuseries that entertain. Rather, these series both reflect and inform the manner in which we as British and Americans currently construct our national identities through the prism of this era of surveillance and terror. How we as two interconnected nations have responded to terrorism, how we define terrorism, and the ways we understand surveillance on the state and cultural levels are at the heart of much of what we as viewers consume and networks and writers produce. In his article, "The global order of Muslim surveillance and its thought architecture," James Renton convincingly argues that the current surveillance order of the global West arose out of Islamophobia and the desire to target, contain, and "fix" the figure of the Muslim, as that idea or image is defined by the West—in other words, the West's "thoughts" of what constitutes Islam and Muslims post-9/11 is what in turn created and continues to sustain the "architecture" of the West's state surveillance apparatus.[1] I would like to borrow Renton's idea of "thought architecture" here as a means of

© The Author(s) 2019
D. Rives-East, *Surveillance and Terror in Post-9/11 British and American Television*,
https://doi.org/10.1007/978-3-030-16900-8_5

summarizing my own argument regarding representations of surveillance and terror in British and American television.

The "thought architecture" within these programs is one in which the desire to imagine and believe in a democratic U.S. and U.K., which subscribe to and uphold liberal values, the dignity of the individual, and the rule of law, is haunted by the specter of two powerful nation states which have abandoned and tarnished that image in the wake of 9/11, or, even more disturbingly, have never inhabited nor enabled such an image in the first place. In this way, the "thought" which structures the "architecture" of the television series is one that is fraught and unsteady in its construction. The perceived overreach of U.S. and U.K. state surveillance apparatuses like the prisons, the police, and the spy agencies in real life becomes a central focus of narratives which often try desperately to square Guantanamo Bay, police brutality, massive CCTV systems, and NSA (National Security Agency) and GCHQ (Government Communications Headquarters) monitoring of citizens' communications with two nations who have often depicted themselves, at various times and ways, as John Winthrop's "citty [sic] on a hill" or William Blake's "The New Jerusalem," the shining beacons of liberal democracy and examples and models for other nations to follow.

In so doing, to attempt to stabilize and ground their "architecture," the dramas and docuseries, both consciously and unconsciously, draw on long-standing and deep-rooted narratives about surveillance and terror within British and American literature, journalism, and popular culture, only to find that even these historical narratives are equally uncertain about what either "America" or "Britain" stands for as nation states. From the early modern period onward, these older narratives anticipate Michel Foucault by recognizing that the state panoptic gaze informed and structured the modern American and British nation states from their beginnings; even if, as Renton contends, the current surveillance order centers on Islamophobia, such narratives allow us to see that earlier versions of that order—such as slavery or colonial government—were structured around fears of other Others, whether African, African American, or Asian. Indeed, these older narratives demonstrate how this gaze was presented as necessary for U.S. and U.K. public safety and national security but was often abused and utilized to deem some groups as Other and as terrorist threats to be contained or eradicated and for whom the privileges of liberty, privacy, and full participation in government and society were disallowed.

This book, then, asks the reader to consider our television landscape since 9/11 at a deeper level and to understand it as intimately bound up with the use of surveillance and terror to use the panoptic gaze not only to monitor and gauge British and American national identities, but also to continue to construct and reconstruct them. I have argued in this volume that television viewers, producers, and writers are, to borrow from Elvis Costello, "watching the detectives," so to speak. However, in so doing, we are also watching ourselves and turning the panoptic gaze inward to imagine for ourselves what exactly it means to be "British" or "American." That the issue of surveillance and terror comes back to our own individual selves is not surprising, given that we are as much a part of the surveillance order that we view with ambivalence in the dramas and docuseries that occupy our screens. Therefore, to conclude, I would like to consider, for a moment, our own individual participation in the British and American surveillance culture that we inhabit post-9/11. I want to acknowledge other ways than television viewing that the individual, as much as the U.S. or U.K. state, operates the social panoptic apparatus. To connect this conversation to television, this conclusion will touch on what I have described in the previous chapters: the role of the viewer in monitoring and influencing the creation and development of television series, and how we might extrapolate where this participation might lead in the future regarding narratives of surveillance and state control.

As I have observed in the previous chapters, the power and influence of the television audience has grown considerably with the advent of social media as well as alternative platforms for watching and even creating or funding series. By the latter, I mean that technology now permits individuals to produce their own series or films that can be distributed online (such as through YouTube) and which can be funded through crowdsourcing sites such as GoFundMe or Kickstarter. In these ways, individuals can create webisodes or films without the need for traditional networks or production companies, and they can still reach an audience through social media word of mouth. One such example would be the fan-produced *Star Trek Continues*, perhaps the most well known of various unofficial *Star Trek* films and series, in which the characters and the Enterprise of the original *Star Trek* have been revived for new adventures.[2] The series is completely fan funded through Indiegogo and Kickstarter campaigns, and, as a result, the production values are much higher than what once was expected of amateur television: "While most 'Star Trek' tribute videos make it hard to suspend disbelief—see: poor lighting, forgettable acting, low production value—'Star Trek Continues' looks and feels so much like the original series that it's easy to forget it's filmed nearly 50 years later."[3] Indeed, according to Vic Mignogna, the series's creator, "One thing that I wanted to accomplish from the very beginning, before we ever rolled one frame of film, was to bring together a team of people that could really take the idea of a fan production to the next level."[4] This audience-directed method of creating and distributing content has important implications in terms of what series are produced and how, and it certainly empowers the public to produce the kind of television texts they want, rather than rely on professional writers and producers to do it for them.

It will be interesting to see what other kinds of programs are created via this pipeline and if any might highlight or focus on the state surveillance apparatuses discussed in this book or if they might examine more generally the notion of panoptic power, whether on the part of the individual or the state. For example, one self-produced YouTube series, "lonelygirl15," purported to be an authentic video diary, or vlog, illuminated the complexities of social media and surveillance when it was revealed in 2006 that the vlog was scripted and the "lonelygirl" portrayed by an actress.[5] The confusion between authentic and fake in terms of surveillance culture even inspired the NBC series *Law and Order: Criminal Intent* to center an episode, "Weeping Willow," around the concept of a video vlogger who had supposedly been kidnapped, and the detectives are unsure what is real and what is simulacrum in the online world.[6]

Moreover, many now use camera phone technology, YouTube, and other social media sites (Twitter, Facebook) to record and distribute footage of various state surveillance apparatuses, in effect turning the panoptic eye back on these institutions of social control. Most often, these videos illustrate ways in which these apparatuses exceed the law or violate moral and ethical codes. Particularly, this public countersurveillance has centered on the police apparatus; footage of police brutality directed at African Americans has been distributed through social media platforms to expose racism within the U.S. and U.K. police apparatus. Indeed, within some reality programs about law enforcement, the police themselves comment on how they are now always being filmed by the public, and how this panoptic eye feels oppressive because the video might not contain complete information regarding what is going on and why the police might need to use force.[7] While these countersurveillance videos do not constitute television series per se, they are viewed by the public on their televisions or other screen devices. In this way, as with the television dramas discussed in the previous chapters, the audience can feel as if they maintain an eye on the state apparatuses of social control.

Further, such panopticism on the part of the public makes its way back into programs about the police apparatus. For example, many current programs about the police, whether fictional or documentary, have had to address narratively police brutality and racism brought to light by citizens recording their own footage of the surveillance apparatus. However, such as in the *CSI: Cyber* (CBS) episode "Brown Eyes, Blue Eyes,"[8] these programs can often "both sides" the issue of racism and police power to attempt to recuperate the police apparatus (i.e., the video does not show the complexity of the situation, or, in this case of *CSI: Cyber*, a policeman's body cam has been hacked and the video distributed online). In addition, rather than understanding this public countersurveillance as a balance to state power, the programs can view social media as social chaos. As claimed by one *CSI: Cyber* character: "Social media is out of control!"[9] In so doing, these series can narratively undermine public countersurveillance and encourage viewers to reject the need to check the state apparatuses and embrace the need for social control on the part of the state.

Through such television production and distribution capabilities, we are witnessing what Foucault refers to in his chapter "Method," from *The History of Sexuality, Vol. 1*, as "double conditioning."[10] Here, he famously discusses power as something that is not predicated on a top-down, ruler-ruled model: "The analysis, made in terms of power, must not assume that the sovereignty of the state, the form of the law, or the overall unity of a domination are given at the outset; rather, these are only the terminal forms power takes."[11] Instead, power can arise from many points in society. Further, in any relationship of power, there is always a resistance to that power (albeit this resistance is not always continual or the same). And so, even if the state pervades the individual, the individual also pervades the state or, in an economic sense, the corporation, in terms of panoptic power; hence, double-conditioning: "One must suppose rather that the manifold relationships of force that take shape and come into play in the machinery of production, in families, limited groups, and institutions, are the basis for wide-ranging effects of cleavage that run through the social body as a whole."[12] Thus, individual resistance, in the case of television, can influence how series are produced and how they are shown.

The usefulness of Foucault's concept of double-conditioning in thinking about current television series can be seen with the docuseries discussed in Chapter 3, *Making a Murderer*, which premiered on Netflix in

2015. This docuseries chronicled what its writers and producers, Laura Ricciardi and Moira Demos, argued were gross violations of conduct on the part of the Manitowoc County, Wisconsin, sheriff's office, which worked with the prosecutor's office to convict two men, Steven Avery and Brendan Dassey, who might be innocent. The film contends that Dassey, who was 16, was interviewed in violation of procedure for a juvenile suspect with cognitive impairment. Dassey was shown on the police's own video recording as being coaxed into giving a confession, even though he did not have the full capacity to understand his rights or what was occurring in the interview. The series reflects Foucault's ideas about the multivalence of power in television in that it was written and produced by not by mainstream sources but by small-time filmmakers who wanted to see justice done. Netflix, as an independent distributor, was in turn able to screen it for a mass audience. Viewers, horrified by what they saw, then used social media to put public pressure on the Wisconsin jurisdiction in question. Such pressure resulted in a review by a judge who threw out Dassey's conviction, stating that his confession was gained in violation of ethics and his constitutional rights[13] (although, in 2017, the Seventh Circuit court upheld his original conviction[14]). In addition, due to the notoriety of the series, Avery gained a new lawyer, Kathleen Zellner, who is determined to get a retrial for her client.[15] In this case, a television documentary series about the abuse of power by a state surveillance apparatus resulted in at least some change and drew attention to a potential miscarriage of justice. Like *Making a Murderer*, the podcast *Serial*, which in its first season covered the trial and conviction of Ahmed Syad for the murder of his ex-girlfriend, also resulted in a new trial from public pressure. The podcast alerted listeners to potential failings on the part of the Baltimore police and legal apparatus. Although it is not a television series, *Serial* nevertheless demonstrates the power of a media text to direct public attention toward state surveillance apparatuses and how they might be corrupt or negligent in their duties. And, as the result of social media, viewers and listeners can then participate in the panoptic eye that looks back at the surveillance apparatus.

I argue that texts like *Making a Murderer* suggest the future for television will be one which involves the increasing presence of double-conditioning, as series are made and distributed through more diffuse and diverse channels that do not require the funding and pipelines that mainstream programs currently do. In addition, these series would have the freedom to critique apparatuses such as the police, the intelligence agency, and the prison without concern for ratings, as is true for traditional television programming. Further, social media could disseminate and popularize these series in ways current networks and studios cannot manufacture. Word of mouth is now word of Twitter or Facebook, given that programs like *Making a Murderer* gained momentum through social media forums, rather than through conventional advertising methods. Social media, as I have noted in the previous chapters, also enables audience input; writers, producers, and studios cannot avoid what fans say on social media, and these enthusiasts now expect a response, such as bringing back a character, extending a program another season, or adding and ending certain storylines.

In this post-9/11 world concerned with terror and the actions of state apparatuses of surveillance and social control, it remains to be seen how the landscape of television and its narratives regarding these topics will alter over the next decades as the ways in which we produce, access, and watch television series constantly change. As this book has shown, many television programs have, until this point, echoed older surveillance narratives to make sense of an uncertain Anglo-American future. One wonders if series will interrogate state apparatuses even further to create new narratives about the place and purpose of surveillance and social control in our lives. Further, we are only beginning to witness dramas, such as *Black Mirror* (Netflix) in which surveillance within the everyday lives of people is explored and visualized narratively. In other words, programs are emerging in which the series' narrative considers the ramifications of not only the state apparatuses, but also of the social media all of us use daily to watch each other and make public our own lives.

Foucault and Louis Althusser both argue, in different ways, that the state and the personal are intertwined. In terms of apparatuses, Althusser theorized that much of our lives are governed by the Ideological State Apparatuses, such as the school, the church, the workplace, which, while not directly controlled by the state were and are nevertheless ideologically extensions of it.[16] To extend Althusser's ideas, I argue that social media is another apparatus that broadens the interests of the state into the lives of individuals. However, as Foucault contends, private power can work in opposition to the panoptic power of the state. Therefore, social media can reinforce as well as work against state apparatuses of surveillance and social control. For instance, I have noted how state apparatuses can be watched and policed by the public using social media, but we, in turn, also police each other ideologically, controlling and monitoring one another for information that can be used in personal situations. Like Bradley Headstone in Dickens' *Our Mutual Friend*, we can stalk and follow one another to learn where we are and what we do. Sometimes, this ability results in serious and violent outcomes; but, in a more mundane sense, it means we know we are judging and being judged for what we do. Reality television programs like *Big Brother* and *Survivor* are simply extensions of the everyday surveillance that goes on in our lives, in which we watch to judge and critique—and it is this ability that can make us feel powerful.

In other words, our own lives are becoming a kind of television drama that we watch and which we produce for the entertainment of others—to judge and be judged. This begs the question if everyday life can be molded and shaped into visual stories that we tell. Indeed, Instagram and Facebook have recently developed functions that allow just for this: participants can craft "stories" using pictures of their own life. Further, social media creates a leveling effect, since writers, producers, and celebrities from film and television mingle, speak with, and create pages, stories, and texts alongside and with their fans. Is this the future of television? When will the line blur between watcher and watched, and between television and real life? As I write this, there is much media buzz regarding the film *Black Mirror: Bandersnatch*, which premiered on Netflix in 2018. As a series, *Black Mirror* tells Twilight Zone-like horror stories about social media and surveillance, given that the "black mirror" of the title signifies smart phone or computer screens. *Bandersnatch*, named after the fantastical, monstrous creature from Lewis Carroll's *Through the Looking Glass* and "The Hunting of the Snark," is nominally about a video game programmer who struggles to tell real from imaginary as he adapts a dark fantasy novel to a gaming format; in this sense, he goes "through the looking glass" or, more aptly, "through the black mirror."

But *Bandersnatch* is unique in that it unfolds in a visual "choose your own adventure" format; as viewers watch, they must make choices that take the story in various directions. On the one hand, this format speaks to the current reciprocal, double-conditioning power of television and the viewer: the viewer is an interactive participant in crafting the story, to some extent (although there are only a limited number of permutations available). On the other, it might reflect a new surveillance opportunity for networks, production companies, and streaming platforms: some have speculated that Netflix could gather viewer information and build a profile based on one's choices when watching *Bandersnatch* (which, tellingly, is set in 1984, thus suggesting an Orwellian scenario). This speculation arises from Netflix's current algorithms which attempt to tailor programming suggestions to suit each individual taste. While this might seem innocuous compared to data gathering by state surveillance apparatuses, the concern is what might happen with that data: "And are we really comfortable with corporations gathering data not only about what we watch, but how we watch it and how to manipulate the choices we make? It's almost fitting that *Black Mirror* should be the show to raise these questions."[17] Perhaps we will see a future in which the lines between state, corporate, private, fictional, real, television, and social media conflate such that we will not be able to speak about these as separate entities in any sense. We will live inside and operate the panopticon continually, watching us watching one another.

NOTES

1. James Renton, "The Global Order of Muslim Surveillance and Its Thought Architecture," *Ethnic and Racial Studies*, 41.12 (2018): 2187.
2. Sam Sloan, "*Star Trek Continues*—A *Slice of SciFi* Review," *Slice of SciFi*, May 26, 2013, https://www.sliceofscifi.com/2013/05/26/star-trek-continues-a-slice-of-scifi-review/.
3. Court Mann, "Expert Nostalgia: 'Star Trek' Fan Tribute Sets a New Standard," *Daily Herald*, Apr. 3, 2014, https://www.heraldextra.com/entertainment/television/expert-nostalgia-star-trek-fan-tribute-sets-a-new-standard/article_8e00665c-83eb-5b23-8be5-fc7eeeaf6c68.html.
4. Ibid.
5. Elena Cresci, "Lonelygirl15: How One Mysterious Vlogger Changed the Internet," *The Guardian*, June 16, 2016, https://www.theguardian.com/technology/2016/jun/16/lonelygirl15-bree-video-blog-youtube.
6. *Law and Order: Criminal Intent*, "Weeping Willow," season 6, episode 10, teleplay by Stephanie Sengupta, story by Warren Leight and Stephanie Sengupta, directed by Tom DiCillo, aired on Nov. 28, 2006, on NBC.
7. In the *Traffic Cops* episode "Selling a Line," police are filmed and accused of assaulting a drunk driver. Meanwhile, in the *Coppers* episode "Saturday Night," the police are filmed while they contend with drunk and violent citizens outside of pubs. *Traffic Cops*, "Selling a Line," series 4, episode 3, aired June 6, 2006, on BBC1; and *Coppers*, "Saturday Night," series 1, episode 4, aired Nov. 22, 2010, on Channel 4.
8. *CSI: Cyber*, "Brown Eyes, Blue Eyes," season 2, episode 3, written by Devon Greggory, directed by Alec Smight, aired Oct. 18, 2015, on CBS.
9. Ibid.

10. Michel Foucault, *The History of Sexuality, Vol. 1: An Introduction* (New York: Vintage, 1990), chap. 2, "Method," Kindle.
11. Ibid.
12. Ibid.
13. "Netflix's *Making a Murderer* Subject Brendan Dassey has Conviction Overturned," *ABC News* (Australia), Aug. 13, 2016, https://www.abc.net.au/news/2016-08-13/netflix-making-a-murderer-brendan-dassey-conviction-overturned/7731450.
14. Michael Tarm, "Conviction of Brendan Dassey in 'Making a Murderer' Case Narrowly Upheld by Appeals Court," *Chicago Tribune*, Dec. 8, 2017, https://www.chicagotribune.com/news/nationworld/ct-brendan-dassey-case-making-a-murder-20171208-story.html.
15. "Steven Avery's Attorney Requests New Trial, New Judge," *WBAY News*, Mar. 12, 2019, https://www.wbay.com/content/news/Steven-Averys-attorney-requests-new-trial-new-judge-507032821.html.
16. See Louis Althusser, *On the Reproduction of Capitalism: Ideology and Ideological State Apparatuses* (New York: Verso, 2014).
17. Kieran Mielek, "Is *Black Mirror: Bandersnatch* the Start of an Interactive TV Takeover?," *Epigram*, Dec. 31, 2018, https://epigram.org.uk/2018/12/31/bandersnatch/.

Bibliography

Althusser, Louis. *On the Reproduction of Capitalism: Ideology and Ideological State Apparatuses*. New York: Verso, 2014.
Black Mirror: Bandersnatch. Written by Charlie Brooker. Directed by David Slade. Released on Dec. 28, 2018 by Netflix.
Coppers. "Saturday Night." Series 1, episode 4. Aired Nov. 22, 2010, on Channel 4.
Cresci, Elena. "Lonelygirl15: How One Mysterious Vlogger Changed the Internet." *The Guardian*, June 16, 2016. https://www.theguardian.com/technology/2016/jun/16/lonelygirl15-bree-video-blog-youtube.
CSI: Cyber. "Brown Eyes, Blue Eyes." Season 2, episode 3. Written by Devon Greggory. Directed by Alec Smight. Aired Oct. 18, 2015, on CBS.
Foucault, Michel. *The History of Sexuality, Vol. 1: An Introduction*. Vintage, 1990. Kindle.
Law and Order: Criminal Intent. "Weeping Willow." Season 6, episode 10. Teleplay by Stephanie Sengupta. Story by Warren Leight and Stephanie Sengupta. Directed by Tom DiCillo. Aired on Nov. 28, 2006, on NBC.
Making a Murderer. Written and directed by Laura Ricciardi and Moira Demos. Released on Dec. 15, 2015 by Netflix.
Mann, Court. "Expert Nostalgia: 'Star Trek' Fan Tribute Sets a New Standard." *Daily Herald*, Apr. 3, 2014. https://www.heraldextra.com/entertainment/

television/expert-nostalgia-star-trek-fan-tribute-sets-a-new-standard/ article_8e00665c-83eb-5b23-8be5-fc7eeeaf6c68.html.

Mielek, Kieran. "Is *Black Mirror: Bandersnatch* the Start of an Interactive TV Takeover?" *Epigram*, Dec. 31, 2018. https://epigram.org.uk/2018/12/31/bandersnatch/.

"Netflix's *Making a Murderer* Subject Brendan Dassey has Conviction Overturned." *ABC News* (Australia), Aug. 13, 2016. https://www.abc.net.au/news/2016-08-13/netflix-making-a-murderer-brendan-dassey-conviction-overturned/7731450.

Renton, James. "The Global Order of Muslim Surveillance and Its Thought Architecture." *Ethnic and Racial Studies*, 41.12 (2018): 2125–2143.

Serial. Season 1. Executive produced and hosted by Sarah Koenig. Produced by WEBZ Chicago. Released on Oct. 3, 2014 by WEBZ Chicago.

Sloan, Sam. "Star Trek Continues—A Slice of SciFi Review." *Slice of SciFi*, May 26, 2013. https://www.sliceofscifi.com/2013/05/26/star-trek-continues-a-slice-of-scifi-review/.

"Steven Avery's Attorney Requests New Trial, New Judge." *WBAY News*, Mar. 12, 2019. https://www.wbay.com/content/news/Steven-Averys-attorney-requests-new-trial-new-judge-507032821.html.

Tarm, Michael. "Conviction of Brendan Dassey in 'Making a Murderer' Case Narrowly Upheld by Appeals Court." *Chicago Tribune*, Dec. 8, 2017. https://www.chicagotribune.com/news/nationworld/ct-brendan-dassey-case-making-a-murder-20171208-story.html.

Traffic Cops. "Selling a Line." Series 4, episode 3. Aired June 6, 2006, on BBC1.

Index[1]

NUMBERS & SYMBOLS

7/7 (London transport network
   attack), 15, 123, 127, 154, 156,
   160, 206, 212
9/11 (inc. post-9/11)
   and Abu Ghraib, 24, 73
   and Afghanistan, 31, 215
   and American (America/U.S.),
      1–33, 55, 59–61, 65, 66, 73,
      79–81, 84, 85, 94n16, 94n18,
      109, 110, 119, 121, 144, 157,
      159, 163, 191–193, 197, 199,
      201–205, 210, 212, 215, 238
   and British/Anglo (Britain/U.K.),
      1–33, 55, 57, 60, 61, 65, 70,
      73, 79, 80, 85, 88, 94n16,
      94n18, 107–110, 121, 133,
      146, 154, 157, 160, 162, 163,
      191–193, 195, 201–206,
      211–213, 238, 239
   and captivity, 3, 25, 27, 55, 59–63,
      66, 70–80
   and culture, 5, 25, 27, 30, 32, 204
   and exceptionalism, 20, 21, 27,
      59–61, 63, 68, 70, 73, 79, 80,
      199
   and fiction(al), 3, 14, 26, 30, 55,
      61, 79, 84, 85, 88, 206
   and Guantanamo Bay, 59–61, 73,
      94n18
   and identity, 93, 202
   and Iraq, 2, 31, 80
   and Muslim (Islam), 60, 66, 68, 80,
      146, 157
   narratives of, 1, 3–6, 11, 13, 14, 17,
      20, 23–25, 27, 30, 60–62, 66,
      68, 73, 79, 127, 144, 157,
      162, 202, 204, 205, 216, 220,
      243
   and NYPD, 157
   and police, 2, 8, 23, 26–33, 111,
      112, 119, 121, 123, 144, 146,
      157, 163
   and post-9/11 era, 112

[1] Note: Page numbers followed by 'n' refer to notes.

9/11 (inc. post-9/11) (*cont.*)
  prisons, 2, 4, 7, 21, 23, 24, 26–33,
    55–62, 70–93, 133, 163
  and rhetoric of, 14, 66, 68, 157
  and Sherlock Holmes, 31, 107, 210
  and society, 14, 22
  and spy (espionage), 3, 8, 23, 30,
    31, 56, 192–195, 199–205,
    210, 211, 213–216, 238
  and surveillance (state), 1–33,
    55–59, 66, 68, 70–80,
    110–112, 128, 130, 132, 134,
    146, 156, 157, 160, 191, 195,
    196, 199, 200, 202, 203, 207,
    213–216, 221
  and television, 1–33, 55, 61, 63, 70,
    79–93, 107–109, 114–128,
    163, 191, 192, 196, 238, 239,
    243
  terror(ism), 1–33, 60, 68, 94n16,
    108, 110, 157, 159, 160, 163,
    191, 196, 211, 215

A
Abu Ghraib scandal, 24, 73, 91
A&E Network, 77, 97n66
Afghanistan, 31, 66, 141, 178n188,
  215
African American (Black)
  and Draft Riots, 121, 129
  and incarceration, 87, 92, 148
  and police apparatus, 121, 145, 149
  and police brutality, 144, 240
  and racism, 87, 129, 240
  and sentencing, 88
  and slavery, 65, 129
Age of Terror, 107, 108, 111, 196
Alaska State Troopers, 132
Albers, Jan, 81, 85, 90, 92
Alcatraz, 88
The Alienist, 29
al-Qaeda, 24, 60, 66, 156, 161, 193,
  206, 220

Amazon, 8, 9, 16, 28, 83, 110, 127,
  132, 200, 209
America, *see* United States of America
American Broadcasting Company
  (ABC), 29, 88, 110, 192, 221
American Civil Liberties Union
  (ACLU), 194, 195, 223n11,
  223n16
The Americans, 8, 29, 31, 192,
  216–219, 227n66
Ang, Ien, 8, 12
*Anti-Oedipus: Capitalism and
  Schizophrenia*, 218, 228n69
Apparatus, *see* and national intelligence
  apparatus; Police apparatus ;
  Prison apparatus; State apparatus
Appointment viewing, 8
Ashes to Ashes, 29, 110
Assange, Julian, 213
Assemblage, 22, 196
AT&T, 194
The Avengers, 7, 192, 210

B
Babylon Berlin, 29
Baepler, Paul, 65, 67, 68, 94n25
*Banged Up Abroad, see Locked Up
  Abroad*
Barbary
  Barbary states, 27, 62, 64, 66, 67,
    74, 94n24
  and captivity narratives, 17, 62, 63,
    65, 66, 71
  and Muslim (Berbers), 62
  and Native American, 27, 62, 64,
    66, 75
  and slavery, 65
Battle of Alcatraz (1946), 88
Baudrillard, Jean, 86, 99n126
Bauer, Jack, 210, 211
BDSM, *see* Sado-masochism
Bell, Detective Marcus, 143, 147
Bentham, Jeremy, 28, 81, 84

Berlin Station, 8, 31, 213–215
Berman, Jacob Rama, 59, 60, 63, 64, 67, 68, 94n17
Big Brother, 10, 22, 93, 244
Big Other, the, 77
Bin Laden, Osama, 66, 158, 159, 215
Binge-watching, 8
Biopower, 21
Birch, Harvey, 201
Black British (citizens), 147
Black Mirror (inc. *Black Mirror: Bandersnatch*), 243–245
Blair, Tony, 2, 15, 163, 178n188, 201
Bleak House, 117, 134, 142
Bloomberg, Michael, 110
Bodycams, *see* Camera
Bond, James, 197, 199, 205–208, 210, 211, 222
Breaking Bad, 85, 210
Brexit, 18, 19, 157, 162
British Broadcasting Corporation (BBC)
  and Ashes to Ashes, 29, 110
  and City of Vice, 29, 110
  and Doctor Who, 141, 158
  and Life on Mars, 29, 110
  and London Spy, 31, 207, 209, 210
  and Modern Spies, 228n75
  and *The Night Manager*, 31, 207, 209, 210, 226n48
  and Panorama, 57, 138
  and Porridge, 55, 57
  and Ripper Street, 8, 28, 110
  and Sherlock, 16, 28, 107, 141, 143, 148, 152, 154, 158, 171n120, 172n124, 174n126, 174n132, 174n133, 174n134, 175n155
  and Spooks, 31, 205, 209, 221
  and the U.S., 29, 85, 110, 205, 209, 210
British Empire, 17, 108, 205

See also Commonwealth nations
Broadcast era, 8, 9
See also Network era
Broadcasting, 6, 15, 16
Brody, Nicholas, 206, 220
Brown, Michael, 111, 241
Bucket, Inspector, 117, 134, 135, 142
Bush, George W., 15, 60, 66–68, 162, 193, 194, 201

C
Cable, 6, 7, 9, 200, 209
The Cambridge Five, 202
Camera, 24, 75, 83, 88, 89, 112, 126, 133, 134, 139, 141, 142, 150, 164, 202, 213, 240
  bodycam, 139, 141
Capitalism, 25, 30
Capital punishment (death sentence, death row), 65, 88, 90, 91
Captivity narratives
  and Barbary, 17, 27, 62–68, 70, 71, 75, 77
  and exceptionalism, 27, 61–65, 68, 72, 79
  and Iranian hostage crisis, 61
  an *Locked Up Abroad*, 27, 71–73, 75, 78, 79
  and Lynch, Jessica, 63, 76
  and Muslim (Islam) (Arab and Berber), 64, 67
  and Native American, 62–64, 66, 75
  and prison, 27, 55, 61, 71, 76
  and Puritan, 11, 17, 27, 62–64, 66–68, 71, 75–77
  and Rowlandson, Mary, 63, 67, 76, 78, 79
  and slavery, 62–65
  and surveillance, 55, 62, 65, 70, 71, 76, 77

CBS Network
  and *CSI: Cyber*, 241
  and *Elementary*, 28, 107, 108, 141,
    151, 152, 158, 165n4,
    172n127, 172n135, 172n136,
    172n137, 172n138, 174n150,
    175n162, 176n165, 176n168,
    176n169, 178n185, 178n187
  and *The Equalizer*, 192
  and *Mission Impossible*, 192
  and *Person of Interest*, 1, 31, 152,
    202
  and *The Prisoner*, 56, 192
  and *Scarecrow and Mrs. King*, 192
CCTV network, 139
Cell phones (phone, mobile phone), 6,
    10, 111, 112, 128, 133, 143,
    160, 164, 195, 240, 244
Central Intelligence Agency (CIA),
    30, 110, 131, 163, 191, 193,
    195, 202, 206, 208, 210, 211,
    213–215, 220, 221
Channel 4, 26, 29, 131
Christianity, 67, 68
CIA, *see* Central Intelligence Agency
City of Vice, 29, 110
Civil liberties
  and erosion of, 212
  and espionage, 30, 199, 204
  and exceptionalism, 19–21
  and police, 21, 29, 112, 131, 133,
    135, 160
  and prison, 21, 27, 28
  and privacy, 3, 8, 112, 160, 203
  and rights, 4, 133
  and safety (security), 25, 60,
    112–114, 160, 210
  and surveillance, 2, 15, 23, 30, 160,
    199, 203
  and terror(ism), 8, 29, 203
Cold War, 7, 8, 30, 31, 108, 157, 191,
    192, 195, 197, 199, 202, 207,
    211, 216, 217

Collins, Wilkie, 29, 58, 112, 117
Commonwealth nations, 18
Communism, 30, 203
Conrad, Joseph, 219, 220
Constitutional law, 85
Convergence, 9
Cooper, James Fenimore, 30, 201
Copper, 8, 29, 110, 114, 128–134,
    152, 164, 178n190, 245n7
Cops, 132, 134
Corcoran, Corky, 129–131
Correctional officers (COs), 81, 90
Corruption, 82, 127–129, 152,
    176n166
Counternarrative, 30, 127, 137
Covert Affairs, 31
Crowdfunding (Kickstarter,
    Indiegogo, GoFundMe), 239
CSI (and *CSI: Cyber*), 126, 136, 241,
    245n8
Cuff, Sergeant, 112, 117
Culper Spy Ring, 30
Cult (status/following), 58, 70, 71
Cultural forum, 6, 7

D
Danny *(London Spy)*, 207, 219
Data, 21–23, 191, 194, 198, 202,
    221, 245
Deleuze, Gilles, 22, 218, 219
Demos, Moira, 114, 242
Department of Homeland Security,
    110
Detective Jack Wicher, 117
Devices, 6, 91, 112, 156, 206, 221,
    240
Dickens, Charles, 13, 28, 29, 33, 81,
    86, 117, 134, 135, 142, 145,
    163, 164, 244
  and *Bleak House*, 117, 134, 142
  and Charles Frederick Field, 134
  and detective fiction, 11, 137

Inspector Bucket, 117, 134, 135,
142
and *Little Dorrit*, 81, 86
and *Our Mutual Friend*, 163, 164,
244
and police, 29, 117, 134, 135, 163,
164, 243
and police docuseries, 134, 135
and prisons, 22, 27, 28, 81, 86
and readers, 13, 134, 164
and serialization, 13
and surveillance, 13, 85, 134, 135,
163, 164, 244
Doctor Who, 9, 18, 158
Docuseries
and authenticity, 91
and *Coppers*, 133
and *Cops*, 132
and espionage, 56
and *First and Last*, 83, 84
and *The Force: Manchester*, 146
and *Forensic Files*, 126, 136
Frontline, 90, 138, 146
and *Fugitive Chronicles*, 77
and *The Joy*, 84
and *Las Vegas: Jail*, 91
and *Locked Up Abroad*, 84
and *Lock Up*, 89, 91
and *Making a Murderer*, 113,
241
and *Motorway Cops*, 133
and *Panorama*, 57, 138
and police, 222, 237, 242
and *Police Interceptors*, 133
prison, 7, 61, 70–79, 82–84, 87–93,
132, 133
and Prison: First and Last 24 Hours,
84
and Strangeways, 92
surveillance, 56, 70–79, 82, 84, 89,
93, 114, 133, 134, 136, 138,
239
and *Traffic Cops*, 8, 133 (*see also*
Reality Television/Programs)

Doherty, Robert, 203n127, 203n136,
204n138, 205n150, 207n162,
207n165
Double-Conditioning, 237–245
Downton Abbey, 209
Doyle, Sir Arthur Conan, 11, 13, 28,
29, 33, 107–109, 113, 114, 122,
131, 136, 137, 140–145,
148–151, 154–156, 158–161,
163, 208
and detective fiction, 11, 137
and *Elementary*, 107, 109, 140,
141, 143, 144, 159, 208
and John Watson, 141
and Moriarty, 158, 159, 161
and portrayal of Americans, 88
and portrayal of women, 155
and race, 148
and readers, 11, 140, 149, 150, 154
and *Sherlock*, 33, 109, 142, 143,
145, 148, 154, 162, 163, 208
Sherlock Holmes, 13, 28, 140, 143
and *The Strand*, 33
and terror(ism), 11, 108, 154, 155,
161
and the Whitechapel murders, 29,
122, 156
Draft Riots, New York City, 29, 118,
129
Drakovitch, Rasha, 89
Drugs, 71, 72, 86
Duggan, Mark, 111, 123

E
Elementary
and 9/11, 28, 107, 108, 114–128,
144, 153, 157, 160
and CBS, 28, 107, 108, 141, 158
and espionage, 150, 156
and Joan Watson, 32, 147, 162
New York Police Department
(NYPD), 108, 141, 143–145,
148, 152, 153, 157

Elementary (*cont.*)
  and race, 144–149
  and *Sherlock*, 28, 31, 109, 110, 131,
      139–150, 152–164, 208, 218
  and Sir Arthur Conan Doyle, 28
Ellis, John, 2, 3, 6, 8, 10, 12, 87, 135
England, *see* United Kingdom
Enhanced interrogation techniques,
    20, 193, 195, 211
Episodic, 7, 12, 32, 33, 214
Epix Network, 235
Erotic (sexuality), 65
Espionage
  and 9/11, 213, 215
  and *24*, 156
  and the American Revolutionary
      War, 209
  and *The Americans*, 8
  and attitudes towards, 128
  and *Berlin Station*, 8, 213
  and the Cold War, 8, 30, 202
  and *Elementary*, 205
  and history and historical narratives
      of, 238
  and *Homeland*, 156
  and intelligence, 8, 31, 192, 199,
      202, 205, 207
  and James Bond, 197, 199,
      205–208
  and James Fenimore Cooper (*The
      Spy*), 30
  and Joseph Conrad's *The Secret
      Agent*, 219
  London Spy, 31
  and the Middle East, 215
  and the national intelligence
      apparatus, 156, 237
  and *Person of Interest*, 1, 2, 210
  and *The Prisoner*, 56
  and psychological effects of, 215
  and *Sherlock*, 150
  Sherlock Holmes, 192
  and *Spooks (Mi-5)*, 31, 156

  and surveillance, 3, 8, 30, 31, 56,
      192, 196, 198, 199, 201, 202,
      210, 212, 215, 221
  and *Turn*, 8
  and U.S. and U.K. tensions
      regarding, 113
Ethics, 7, 8, 30, 31, 85, 112, 191,
    193, 198, 202, 213–215, 242
European Union, 18, 92
Exceptionalism
  and 9/11, 7, 20, 21, 63, 73, 79, 80
  and American, 18, 19, 27, 61, 68,
      195, 199
  and Anglo-American, 18–21,
      59–61, 63–66, 68, 72, 73, 75,
      79, 80, 87
  and British, 18–20, 60, 67

F
Facebook, 11, 33, 216, 240, 243, 244
Fans, 6, 9, 12, 13, 139, 140, 155,
    243, 244
Federal Bureau of Investigation (FBI),
    110, 111, 138, 191, 206
Feminism, 58
Ferguson police shooting, 111
Field, Inspector Charles Frederick,
    134
Financing (inc. production costs,
    funding (parsed)), 16
Finch, Harold, 1, 202, 210
First and Last, 83, 84, 89
Five Points borough (NYC), 129
Fontana, Tom, 80, 81
The Force: Manchester, 146
Foreign Intelligence Surveillance Act
    (1978), 194
Foreign Intelligence Surveillance
    Court (FISA), 194
Forensic Files, 126
Forensic science, 8, 28, 122, 125,
    136–138, 221

Foucault, Michel, 10, 21, 22, 25, 32, 33, 55, 59, 70, 76, 77, 86, 135, 164, 203, 238, 241–243
Fox Broadcasting Company (FOX), 26, 31, 88, 210
France, 116, 162, 196, 212
The Frankenstein Chronicles, 29
Freud, Sigmund, 218, 220
Frontline (US & Scotland), 89
Fugitive Chronicles, 77
Fugitive Slave Act (1850), 145

G
Garner, Eric, 148
Gatiss, Mark, 140
Gender, 57, 65, 76, 85, 148, 149, 157, 195
Germany, 29, 213
Google, 21
Government Communications Headquarters (GCHQ), 30, 191, 238
Greater Manchester Police, 128
Greenwald, Glenn, 193
Greer, John, 202, 203
Guantanamo Bay (aka Gitmo)
   and 9/11, 24, 59–61
   and captivity (narratives), 60–62
   and exceptionalism, 20, 59–61
   and *Locked Up Abroad*, 27
   and prison (programs), 21, 23, 59–61
   and terror(ism), 21, 60
   and the U.K., 20, 60, 238
The Guardian, 132, 139, 193, 194, 211
Guattari, Felix, 218–220
Gunpowder Plot (1605), 153, 156

H
Hard Time, 27, 89

Hartley, John, 8, 9
HBO Network, 56
Heart of Darkness, 220
Her Majesty's Prison Service (H.M.), 92
Holmes, Mycroft, 31, 148, 150, 151, 155, 162, 204, 208
Holmes, Sherlock
   and 9/11, 107, 108, 144, 153, 156, 157
   and *Elementary*, 28, 31, 109, 114, 131, 141–144, 148, 152, 159, 161, 163
   and espionage, 192, 208
   and Moriarty (James/Jamie), 144, 151, 158, 159, 161
   and physicality of, 122
   and race, 144, 148
   and *Sherlock*, 31, 107, 131, 140, 142, 143, 148, 150, 151, 153–156, 158, 161
   and Sir Arthur Conan Doyle, 28
   and Watson (John/Joan), 32, 131, 137, 141, 147–154, 156, 158, 204, 205
   and the Whitechapel murders, 118, 122, 145, 156
Homeland, 156, 206, 220
Homophobia, 148
Hostage, 61, 62, 76, 88
Household Words, 134
Hulu, 16, 125, 209

I
The Illustrated London News, 117, 122
Internet (inc. online), 7, 12, 128, 140
Interrogation, 20, 32, 76, 113, 193, 195, 215, 218, 220, 222
Iran, 60, 66, 67, 215
Iraq, 15, 20, 31, 60, 63, 67, 79, 80, 162

Islamic State of Iraq and Syria (ISIS), 156, 158, 161, 213, 217
ITV Encore, 29

J
Jack the Ripper, 108, 117, 119, 127
Jefferson, Thomas, 196
Jenkins, Henry, 9
The Joy, 83, 89

K
Kelly, Ray, 110
Knight, Stephen, 107
Kray brothers (London criminals), 123, 127

L
Lacan, Jacques, 77
Lacey, Steven, 1, 2, 15
Lang, Amy Schrager, 68
Las Vegas Jailhouse, 89, 91
Latinx, 87
Law and Order, 240
Lay, Julia Anna Hartness, 119, 120
Layton, Bart, 70, 77, 97n66
Le Carré, John, 207
Lesbian, 58, 85
    See also Sexuality
Life on Mars, 29, 110, 128–131, 134
Literary analysis, 3, 5
Little Dorrit, 81, 86
Locked Up Abroad
    and 9/11, 73, 79, 80
    and Abu Ghraib, 73
    and captivity narratives, 71–73, 75, 78, 79
    and docuseries, 26, 71, 79, 84, 90
    and Guantanamo Bay, 73
Lock Up, 89–91

London Spy, 31, 207, 209–211, 213, 219
Lonelygirl15, 240
Lotz, Amanda D., 6, 7
Lyon, David, 22

M
MacGyver, 192
The Machine, 202–204, 207, 210
Mad Men, 210
Magna Carta, 19
Making a Murderer, 113, 114, 241–243
The Man from U.N.C.L.E., 192
Massachusetts Bay Colony, 19, 68
Matheson, Carrie, 220
McGrath, John E., 11, 32
Meme, 1, 2
Metropolitan Police (aka the Met), 111, 115, 116, 122–124
Mi-5, 30, 31, 110, 191, 205, 206, 209, 221
Mi-6, 30–32, 150, 162, 163, 191, 202, 204–208, 210
Mignogna, Vic, 240
Miller, Daniel, 213
Miller, Toby, 5, 10
Mission: Impossible, 7, 192
Moriarty, 144, 151, 153, 158–161, 192
Modern Spies, 228n75
Moffat, Steven, 155, 156, 158
The Moonstone, 112, 117
Morris, Norval, 91, 92
Motorway Cops, 133
MSNBC, 27, 81, 91
Multi-platform, 9, 27
Murdoch Mysteries, 29, 110, 125
Muslim & Islamic
    and Barbary (states), 62, 67
    and captivity narratives, 67

and depiction of after 9/11, 146
and Islamophobia, 147
and portrayal as terrorists, 68, 157,
    211

N
Narragansett, 63, 64, 68, 74, 75,
    78–80
Narrowcasting, 6
National Geographic, 26, 27, 70, 73,
    89, 91, 133
National intelligence apparatus, 156,
    237
National Security Agency (NSA), 23,
    30, 31, 110, 150, 191, 193–195,
    198, 202, 204, 208, 212, 221,
    238
Native American, 27, 62–64, 66, 75
Neame, Gareth, 209
Netflix, 7, 16, 26, 83, 85, 99n107,
    110, 113, 125, 132, 200, 210,
    214, 241–245
Network era, 6
    See also Broadcast era
Network Ten, 56
New York Police Department (NYPD)
    and 9/11, 23, 108, 110, 153, 157
    and Copper, 130, 152
    and the Draft Riots, 145
    and Elementary, 141, 144, 148,
        152, 153, 157
    Eric Garner, 148
    and Life on Mars (U.S. version), 128
    and race, 144–146
    and stop-and-frisk, 148
    and surveillance, 141, 151, 153,
        157
The New York Times, 81, 118, 145,
    194
The New York Tribune, 119
The Night Manager, 31, 207,
    209–211, 215, 218, 226n48

The Night Of..., 26, 83
1980s, 29, 31, 58, 92, 96n52, 121,
    127, 202, 216
1990s, 16, 33, 92, 148, 192
1970s, 29, 92, 121, 128, 202
NSA, see National Security Agency

O
Obama, Barack, 18, 111
OITNB, see Orange Is the New Black
Orange Is the New Black (OITNB), 26,
    83, 85–88
Orientalism, 63, 162
Our Mutual Friend, 163, 164, 244
Oz, 7, 26, 56, 58, 76, 80–88

P
Paget, Derek, 1, 2, 14, 15
The Pall Mall Gazette, 115
Panopticon, 10, 32, 69, 152, 164,
    203, 204, 215, 217, 221, 245
Panorama, 57, 138
Paramilitarization, 111
Participatory model, 9
Passivity, 10, 11, 87, 114, 135
PATRIOT Act, 23, 193, 194
PBS, see Public Broadcasting Service
Penny dreadfuls, 135, 136, 145,
    170n105
Person of Interest, 1, 2, 31, 33, 152,
    203–207, 209, 210, 226n40,
    226n41, 226n42, 226n45
Podcast, 27, 242
Poe, Edgar Allen, 29
Police and Criminal Evidence Act
    (1984), 131
Police apparatus
    and African Americans, 129, 144,
        145, 240
    and corruption and abuse, 28, 128,
        129, 152

Police apparatus (*cont.*)
  and failure(s) of, 118, 123, 157
  and the Metropolitan Police, 123,
    125
  and militarization of, 111
  and NYPD, 151, 152
  and public opinion or perception of,
    113, 114, 121
  and Sherlock Holmes, 28, 109, 142,
    144, 149–152, 161, 218
  and slavery, 145
  and surveillance (of), 28, 29,
    109–114, 117, 118, 135,
    137–139, 142, 145, 149, 151,
    154, 160, 163, 164
  and television, 28, 29, 110, 123,
    152, 163
  and terror(ism), 29, 112, 120, 123,
    154, 157
Police brutality, 12, 29, 33, 133, 144,
    238, 240, 241
Police Interceptors, 132, 133, 139
Porridge, 55–57, 59
Post-network era, 6
Press ("news sources"), 29, 110, 114,
    115, 117, 122–124, 127, 128,
    145, 197
Prevent policy (UK), 146
Prison apparatus
  and Anglo-American exceptionalism,
    59–61, 73, 80, 87
  and Guantanamo Bay, 59–61
  and riots, 82, 88, 92
  surveillance (of), 28, 57, 59, 70–80,
    82–85, 87, 89, 93
  and television, 70, 73, 79–93
  and treatment of inmates, 85
  and women, 72, 76, 85, 88
Prison Break, 26, 88
Prisoner (aka Prisoner: Cell Block H),
    56–59, 75, 85
Prison industrial complex, 82

Privacy, 3, 8, 10, 24, 26, 30, 111–113,
    133, 160, 195, 196, 198, 203,
    222, 238
Productive model, 9
Public Broadcasting service (PBS), 16,
    17, 89, 138, 139, 171n111,
    171n118, 209
Puritan
  and captivity narrative, 11, 17, 27,
    62–64, 66–68, 71, 75–77
  and "citty on a hill," 19
  and exceptionalism, 19, 63, 68, 75
  and John Williams, 76
  and John Winthrop, 19, 68, 69
  and Mary Rowlandson, 64, 67, 75,
    76
  and Native American
    (Narragansetts), 64, 68

Q
Queer (sexuality), 58

R
The Radio Times, 209
Raidió Teilifís Éireann (RTÉ), 83
Ratings, 9, 121, 200, 214, 243
Reality television/programs, 10, 32,
    92, 93, 132–140, 240, 244
Rear Window, 33
Reddit, 12, 200
Reese, John, 202, 210
Reform (prison, penal), 28, 65, 93
Reid, Edmund (Inspector), 123–125
Renton, James, 147, 154, 157, 237,
    238
Revolutionary War, 8, 17, 29, 31,
    196–201, 209
Reynolds's Newspaper, 115
Ricciardi, Laura, 114, 242
Riots

and Attica prison, 82
and the Draft Riots, 29, 118, 119,
    121, 129, 145
and 1887 Bloody Sunday, 114
and 1830s New York, 116
and the 1946 Battle of Alcatraz
    prison, 88
and Oz, 82
and Strangeways prison, 82
Ripper Street, 8, 28, 29, 110, 114,
    123, 125, 127, 128
Rixon, Paul, 15, 16, 209
Rose, Alexander, 196, 197
Rowlandson, Mary
    and criticisms of British army, 78,
        79
    and faith, 69, 70
    and portrayal of Native Americans,
        64, 78–80
    and prison, 69
    and sexuality of, 75, 76
    and surveillance, 66, 70
    and treatment of in captivity, 63
Russia (Soviet), 19, 84, 192, 203,
    206, 216–219

S
Sado-masochism, 75
The Saint, 192, 210
St. James's Gazette, 115
Samaritan, 202–204
San Bernardino attack (2015), 160
Satellite, 6
Screen Education, 5
The Secret Agent, 219
Security
    and 9/11, 7, 30, 65, 110, 154, 160
    and airports, 21, 40n92, 71
    and borders, 71
    and the Central Intelligence Agency
        (CIA), 30, 110, 191

and Homeland Security, 65, 111,
    155
and national security, 118, 154,
    158–161, 191, 195, 205, 210,
    213, 221, 237, 238
and the National Security Agency
    (NSA), 23, 30, 110, 191, 238
and police, 2, 17, 21, 26, 160
and prison, 2, 4, 17, 21, 25, 26,
    55–93
and security state, 147
and social security numbers, 164
and terror(ism), 1–33, 107–164,
    237–239
Sentencing, 88, 90–92
September 11, *see* 9/11
Serial, 242
Sexism, 148
Sexuality, 57–59, 75, 76, 85, 195
The Shawshank Redemption, 86
Sherlock
    and 9/11, 16, 31, 108, 153, 156,
        159
    and the BBC, 16, 28, 107, 108,
        140, 141, 143, 148, 152, 154,
        171n120
    and *Elementary*, 28, 31, 109, 110,
        114, 131–140, 144–151,
        153–164, 218
    and espionage, 192
    and portrayal of Sherlock Holmes,
        144
    and portrayal of women, 155
    and race, 144–149
    and Sir Arthur Conan Doyle, 28,
        107
    and terror(ism), 107–164
Sherlock Holmes (2009 film), 107, 131
Showtime, 31, 206, 220, 221
Silverstein, Craig, 196, 197
60 Minutes, 110
Sky News, 195

Sky 1 UK/Deutschland, 29
Slavery, 62–65, 121, 129, 145, 238
Snowden, Edward, 23, 42n109,
    193–195, 213
Social amnesia & cultural amnesia, 25,
    130
Social control, *see* Surveillance
Social media
    and fans/fandom, 6, 9, 139, 155
    and influence on programs, 9, 12,
        241
    and surveillance, 240, 244
    and television, 32, 140, 217, 239,
        245
    and television ratings, 9, 200, 214
Societies of control, 22
Solitary confinement, 90
"Special relationship" (between U.S.
    and U.K.), 18, 19, 30, 31, 163,
    201
Spectacle, 31, 128–134, 136–138,
    221
Spiegel, Lynn, 5–7
Spooks (Mi-5), 8, 31, 156, 205, 206,
    208, 209, 219, 221
The Spy: A Tale of the Neutral Ground,
    30, 201
Spymasters: CIA in the Crosshairs, 221
Spy, *see* Espionage
Star Trek (Star Trek Continues), 239
State apparatus, 4, 7, 14, 17, 21–26,
    28, 33, 59, 140, 160, 164, 191,
    196, 211, 218, 241, 243
Stop-and-frisk (frisk, "stop and search"
    U.K.), 112, 139, 148
The Strand Magazine, 33
Strangeways, 27, 89, 92
Strangeways riot (1990), 82, 92
Streaming, 6–9, 16, 89, 200, 209,
    214, 244
Sturtevant, John J., 116, 117
Surveillance
    and 9/11, 1–33, 55–59, 70–79,
        134, 144, 157, 202, 203,
        213–215, 221
    and control, 3, 4, 21, 22, 26, 149,
        203
    and espionage, 30, 192, 198, 199,
        207
    and fear, 3
    and imprisonment, 55, 56, 65, 66,
        70, 71
    and intelligence, 108, 214
    and Islamic fundamentalist
        terrorism, 157, 207, 211, 212,
        220
    and literature (narratives), 11
    and Muslim, 147
    police, 2, 4, 17, 21, 25, 26, 56, 84,
        109–114, 132–140, 142–149,
        151, 156, 164, 238, 240
    and state apparatus, 4, 7, 14, 17,
        21–26, 28, 33, 243
    studies, 3, 21, 40n93
    and surveillance culture, 11, 22, 32,
        33, 59, 87, 93, 140, 164, 203,
        216, 239, 240
    and surveillance state, 13, 154, 219
    and techniques of, 1
    and terror(ism), 1–33, 107–164,
        237–239
    and the viewer, 216–222 (*see also*
        Panopticon)
Survivor, 10, 93, 244
Synopticon, 10, 32

T
Tablets, 6, 10
Takacs, Stacey, 63, 66, 76, 79
Tammany Hall scandal, 152
Television studies, 3, 5, 6, 8
Terrorism
    and 7/7, 15, 123, 156, 206

and 9/11, 1–3, 5, 21, 23, 129, 146,
    156, 206, 211
and civil liberties, 8, 29
and domestic terrorism, 154, 160,
    203
and Draft Riots, 129
and espionage series, 156
and Guantanamo Bay, 60, 215, 238
and the police apparatus, 154
and portrayal of Muslim (Islam) as,
    157, 211
and security, 7, 154, 159
and Sherlock Holmes, 108,
    153–164
and Sir Arthur Conan Doyle, 107
and surveillance, 1–3, 7, 10,
    153–164, 220, 237
and television, 17
Textual studies, 4
Thomas, Ronald R., 141, 142
TNT Network, 29
Torture, 20, 193, 195, 211, 213
Totalitarian regimes, 60, 111
Traffic Cops, 8, 132–134, 139, 164,
    178n190, 245n7
*A True History of the Captivity and
    Restoration of Mrs. Mary
    Rowlandson*, 38n72, 95n29,
    96n44
Turn: Washington's Spies, 29, 196, 198
24 (and 24: Live Another Day), 31,
    211
Twitter, 11, 33, 214, 216, 240, 243
Tyler, Gene, 131
Tyler, Sam, 128, 130, 131

U
United Kingdom (U.K., Britain)
    and 7/7, 123, 127, 154, 156, 160,
        206, 212
    and 9/11, 1–3, 7, 14, 15, 17, 20,
        21, 23, 29, 30, 55, 60, 70, 73,
        107, 108, 110, 146, 154, 157,
        160, 193, 212
    and exceptionalism (Anglo-
        American), 18–20, 60, 61, 67
    and the intelligence agency, 30, 193,
        195, 219
    and Muslim citizens of, 23, 146
    and the nation state, 25, 238
    and police, 111, 118, 123, 131,
        132, 134, 146, 148, 149, 212,
        240
    and prisons, 2, 7, 24, 27, 28, 55,
        57, 61, 80, 84, 89, 90, 92
    and relationship with U.S.
        (America), 17–19, 30, 31
    and surveillance, 1, 19, 21, 30, 109,
        110, 113, 147, 160, 195
    and television, 1, 2, 4, 18, 20, 192,
        239
    and terrorism, 17, 23, 24, 27, 154,
        160, 195
United States of America (U.S.,
    America), 210
    and 9/11, 1, 2, 4, 7, 14, 15, 17, 20,
        21, 23, 26–33, 55, 57, 60, 65,
        66, 70, 73, 79, 85, 88, 107,
        108, 110, 121, 157, 160, 163,
        191, 194, 195, 199, 201–205,
        213, 239
    and African Americans, 87, 92, 120,
        121, 129, 144–149, 238, 240
    and Anglo-American exceptionalism,
        18–21, 59–61, 63–66, 68, 72,
        73, 75, 79, 80, 87
    and captivity, 27, 55, 59–61, 63–65,
        68, 71, 79, 220
    and Guantanamo Bay, 59–61
    and the intelligence agency
        (espionage), 4, 21, 26–33, 160,
        191–196, 205, 206, 215
    and Islam (Muslim), 60, 64, 66, 67,
        157, 215, 220
    and the Middle East, 66

United States of America (U.S., America) (*cont.*)
the nation state, 25, 199, 238
and Native Americans, 27, 62–64, 66, 75
and police, 4, 21, 23, 26–33, 109–111, 121, 125, 128, 132–134, 144–147, 162, 208, 240
and prisons, 27, 78, 81, 84, 88, 90, 91, 163
and relationship with the U.K., 17–19, 30, 31, 220
and the Revolutionary War, 8, 29, 209
and Sherlock Holmes, 17, 31, 109, 110, 137, 148, 163
and surveillance, 1–33, 65, 89, 194–200, 213, 220, 238, 239
and television, 1–33, 55, 191, 192, 199, 238
and terror(ism), 1–33, 60, 68, 108, 111, 162, 163, 195, 203, 238
and torture, 193

V
Victorian era, 28, 155
Viewer, *see* Audience
Viewer society, 10
Voyeurism, 33, 57, 59

W
Walsingham, Sir Francis, 199

War on terror, 2, 3, 11, 15, 20, 23, 24, 67, 68, 96n52, 110, 132, 163, 197, 198, 212
Warrant, 88, 112, 194, 200
Washington, George, 196, 197
Watson, Joan and John, 32, 131, 137, 141, 143, 147–154, 156, 158, 162, 204, 205, 208
Webisodes, 239
Weisberg, Joe, 216, 217, 227n66
Weissman, Elke, 17
Weissman, Joe, 209
Wentworth, 26, 83, 85–88, 94n11
Whitechapel, 29, 110, 114, 123, 127, 128, 154
Whitechapel murders, 29, 37n57, 118, 121–123, 145, 156
Williams, Raymond, 5
Winters, Brad, 56, 87, 89, 214
Winthrop, John, 19, 68, 69, 96n53, 238
The Wire, 112
Within These Walls, 56
Witnessing, 2, 3, 75, 241
Woodhull, Abraham, 29, 197, 198
Working through, 2, 3, 5, 6, 158

X
The X-Files, 33

Z
Žižek, Slavoj, 77